INCUNABULA AND THEIR READERS

INCUNABULA
AND THEIR READERS
Printing, Selling and Using Books in the Fifteenth Century

Edited by
KRISTIAN JENSEN

THE BRITISH LIBRARY
2003

First published 2003 by
The British Library
96 Euston Road
St Pancras
London NW1 2DB

© The Contributors, 2003

British Library Cataloguing in Publication Data
A CIP record for this volume is available from The British Library

ISBN 0-7123-4769-0

Designed by John Trevitt
Typeset in England by Norman Tilley Graphics, Northampton
Printed in England by St Edmundsbury Press, Bury St Edmunds

CONTENTS

PREFACE

As part of our contribution to the celebration of the Gutenberg Year 2000, The British Library organized a conference entitled 'Incunabula and their readers' which took place at the University of London's Senate House. A selection of the papers given at the conference is published in this volume, some in a revised form; in addition my paper 'Printing the Bible in the fifteenth century' is included although it was taken out of the final conference programme to make room for other contributions.

The articles all address important aspects of a wide range of topics relating to books and their users in the fifteenth century. A unifying concern of most of the papers is the complex relationships between producers, be they authors, printers or decorators, the economic conditions of book distribution, and the requirements of readers or other users of books. Two contributions focus on technical aspects of the production of books, which the history of bibliography in the twentieth century showed to be an essential prerequisite for understanding how texts reached their readers. All the articles incorporate knowledge and methods from a wide range of disciplines, not as inter-disciplinary exercises but as the result of an understanding of the distinct concerns of various disciplines. Art history, liturgical studies, textual criticism, the history of literacy, economic history, typographical analysis, and clustering models all contribute towards this end.

This openness on the part of students of books and printing towards other disciplines, and the openness of other disciplines towards the importance of printing, must be integral to the development of our understanding of why the European invention of printing was successful – of why books became the first successful mechanically mass-produced marketable product. Associated questions relating to the nature of the invention itself are also profoundly reassessed. Chronologically, the articles range from the invention of printing to an analysis of the intellectual background to the first catalogue of books printed in the fifteenth century.

The conference was organized by The British Library in association with the Society for Renaissance Studies, and the University of London's School of Advanced Study through the Institute of Classical Studies, and the Institute of English Studies. We are grateful for financial and practical support for the event from the British Academy, the Gale Group, the Foundation for Intellectual History, the Society for Renaissance Studies, and the Institute of Classical Studies.

KRISTIAN JENSEN
The British Library

ABBREVIATIONS

BL   London, The British Library

BMC   *Catalogue of Books Printed in the XVth century now in the British Museum [British] Library. Parts I-X, XII. (Parts I-IX reproduced from the Working Copies of the Original Edition (London, 1908-62) Annotated at the Museum)* (London, 1963-85 [in progress])

BNF   Paris, Bibliothèque nationale de France

BSB-Ink   *Bayerische Staatsbibliothek: Inkunabelkatalog*, Bd I [etc.] (Wiesbaden, 1988- [in progress])

CIBN   *Bibliothèque Nationale, Catalogue des incunables* (Paris, 1981- [in progress])

Claudin   A. Claudin, *Histoire de l'imprimerie en France au XVe et au XVIe siècle*, 4 vols (Paris, 1900-14), *Tables alphabétiques*, ed. by Paul Lacombe (Paris, 1915); reprint (Nendeln, 1971)

DBI   *Dizionario biografico degli Italiani* (Rome, 1960-)

Duff   E. Gordon Duff, *Fifteenth Century English Books* (Oxford, 1917)

Einbl.   *Einblattdrucke des XV. Jahrhunderts: Ein bibliographisches Verzeichnis*, ed. by the Kommission für den Gesamtkatalog der Wiegendrucke, Sammlung bibliothekswissenschaftlicher Arbeiten, 35/36 (Halle an der Saale, 1914)

Goff   Frederick Richmond Goff, *Incunabula in American Libraries: A Third Census of Fifteenth-century Books Recorded in North American Collections* (New York, 1964)

GW   *Gesamtkatalog der Wiegendrucke*, ed. by the Kommission für den Gesamtkatalog der Wiegendrucke, vols 1-7 (Leipzig, 1925-40), ed. by the Deutsche Staatsbibliothek zu Berlin, vols 8- (Stuttgart, Berlin, New York, 1972-)

H   Ludwig Hain, *Repertorium bibliographicum, in quo libri omnes ab arte typographica inventa usque ad annum MD. Typis expressi ordine alphabetico vel simpliciter enumerantur vel adcuratius recensentur*, 2 vols (Stuttgart and Paris, 1826-38)

HC   Ludwig Hain with W. A. Copinger, *Supplement to Hain's Repertorium Bibliographicum*, Part I (London, 1895); and W. A. Copinger, *Supplement to Hain's Repertorium Bibliographicum*, Part II, 2 vols and *Addenda* (London, 1898 and 1902)

HR   Ludwig Hain with D. Reichling, *Appendices ad Hainii ... Repertorium Bibliographicum. ... Emendationes*, 6 vols and index (Munich, 1905-11) and *Supplement* (Münster, 1914)

Hodnett   Edward Hodnett, *English Woodcuts 1480-1535* (Oxford, 1973)

IBP   *Incunabula quae in bibliothecis Poloniae asservantur*, ed. Maria Bohonos and Elisa Szandorowska, 2 vols (Wrocław, 1970)

ISTC   *Incunable Short-Title Catalogue,* online data base (British Library, London)

LB   H. Bohatta, *Liturgische Bibliographie des XV Jahrhunderts* (Vienna, 1911)

MBK   *Mittelalterliche Bibliothekskataloge Deutschlands und der Schweiz*, ed. by Christine Elisabeth Ineichen-Eder (Munich, 1977)

PBSA   *The Papers of the Bibliographical Society of America*

PML   New York, Pierpont Morgan Library

STC   A. W. Pollard and G. R. Redgrave, *A Short-title Catalogue of Books Printed in England, Scotland, and Ireland and of English Books Printed Abroad*, 2nd rev. edn by W. A. Jackson, F. S. Ferguson, & K. F. Pantzer, 3 vols (London, 1986-91)

VD16   *Verzeichnis der im deutschen Sprachbereich erschienenen Drucke des XVI. Jahrhunderts: VD 16* (Stuttgart: 1983-95)

VL   *Die deutsche Literatur des Mittelalters. Verfasserlexikon*, 2nd edn, ed. by Kurt Ruh, Burghart Wachinger et al., 10 vols (Berlin and New York, 1978-99, Supplement, 2000sq. [in progress])

LIST OF CONTRIBUTORS

BLAISE AGÜERA Y ARCAS graduated in Physics from Princeton University in 1998, and began the research presented here during the following summer, in collaboration with Paul Needham. He is continuing this work through Princeton's graduate programme in Applied Mathematics. His other projects include research in neuroscience, graphics, and software engineering.

LILIAN ARMSTRONG is Mildred Lane Kemper Professor of Art at Wellesley College in Massachusetts where she teaches Italian Renaissance Art. Her publications focus on Venetian Renaissance manuscript illumination and on the decoration of early printed books.

CRISTINA DONDI is Assistant Librarian, Special Collections, at the Bodleian Library, Oxford, where she has been working at the Bodleian incunable cataloguing project since 1996. She has recently been appointed Lyell Research Fellow in the History of the Early Modern Printed Book, Lincoln College, Oxford.

MARY KAY DUGGAN, Professor in the School of Information Management and Systems and in the Department of Music, University of California, Berkeley; from 2002 to 2004 Director of the University of California's Education Abroad Program, California House, London. Research interests include incunabula, music, and the history of information especially with the introduction of print technology.

FALK EISERMANN worked as a researcher on fifteenth-century broadsides at the University of Münster 1994-9 and at Rijksuniversiteit Groningen 2000-2. He is currently at the University Library of Leipzig, cataloguing medieval German manuscripts of the Forschungsbibliothek Gotha. He has published on medieval magic, epigraphy, devotional literature, manuscripts, and incunables.

JOHN FLOOD is Emeritus Professor of German in the University of London and Senior Research Fellow at the Institute of Germanic Studies, School of Advanced Study, University of London. He currently holds a Leverhulme Emeritus Research Fellowship. He has published extensively on the History of the Book, Medieval and Early Modern German literature, the History of Medicine, and the History of Linguistics. His books include *The German Book 1450-1750* (edited with W. A. Kelly, 1995).

LOTTE HELLINGA is a former Deputy Keeper of The British Library. Her publications include *The Fifteenth-century Printing Types of the Low Countries* and numerous articles on the history of the book and textual transmission in the early modern period.

KRISTIAN JENSEN is Head of British and Early Printed Collections at The British Library. His publications on fifteenth- and sixteenth-century book history mainly concentrate on the distribution and the use of books in schools and universities.

ix

List of Contributors

HOLGER NICKEL has worked since 1970 at the *Gesamtkatolog der Wiegendrucke*, and has been editor-in-chief since 1989. He has researched and published widely in the field of fifteenth-century book history.

BETTINA WAGNER is head of incunable cataloguing at the Bayerische Staatsbibliothek, Munich.

MARY BETH WINN is Professor of French and Director of the Doctor of Arts programme in Humanistic Studies at the State University of New York at Albany. Author of *Anthoine Vérard, Parisian Publisher, 1485-1512: Prologues, Poems, and Presentations* (Geneva: Droz, 1997), her research and publications focus on French literature, the arts, and printing in the fifteenth and sixteenth centuries. She is currently collaborating on the critical edition of the chansons of Thomas Crecquillon (died *c.*1557) for the American Institute of Musicology.

TEMPORARY MATRICES AND ELEMENTAL PUNCHES IN GUTENBERG'S DK TYPE[1]

BLAISE AGÜERA Y ARCAS

INTRODUCTION

THE 'STANDARD MODEL' for Western typographic printing comprises two different processes, one for making movable types, and another for printing from them. Type-making begins with the carving of a steel punch for each sort, which is then punched into a copper matrix; the matrices are then used to cast a large supply, or fount, of interchangeable pieces of lead-alloy type in an adjustable mould. To produce a printed page, types are composed in lines, locked into a forme, inked, and pressed against paper or vellum. Inking and pressing are repeated. After the desired number of copies has been printed, the type is cleaned and re-distributed into the typecase, ready to be composed into another page.

Gutenberg's position as the first European typographic printer is difficult to contest on the basis of the surviving evidence. Yet historians of printing, from the eighteenth century through the first half of the twentieth century, have consistently encountered difficulty in defining Gutenberg's intellectual contribution to the history of technology. This entails knowing precisely *what* Gutenberg invented. It has often been assumed that he invented the 'standard model', as first described in detail by Joseph Moxon in 1683 – a technology that would persist with only incremental improvements until the late nineteenth century. Perhaps in an attempt to isolate the elements of the standard model which distinguish it from earlier Chinese and Korean printing, the punch, matrix, and adjustable mould have been singled out as the essence of Gutenberg's invention, and indeed as the foundation of the typographic arts. The adjustable mould allows the creation of characters with non-uniform widths; and the casting method, because it uses a durable matrix struck from a unique punch, enables the mass-production of any number of virtually identical types of each sort.

But is there any evidence that Gutenberg in fact used these tools and methods to manufacture his type? Harry Carter, in his 1969 survey *A View of Early Typography up to about 1600*,[2] wrote only, 'I can find nothing in the documents on early printing or in the printing itself to negative the use from the first of punches, matrices, and moulds' (pp. 13-14). This surprisingly noncommittal statement summed up the state of the field in 1969, and indeed in 1999. There has never been any direct evidence that Gutenberg used the type-making and printing processes described by the standard model.

Documentation of the workings of printshops in the incunabula period is extremely scarce. Our first direct view inside the shop is not until the famous *Danse macabre*[3] woodcut of 1499, printed by Mathias Huss in Lyons. Yet the essential first step, type-making, is not addressed in this image, nor is it discussed technically in any surviving fifteenth century source. We are afforded a certain amount of indirect documentation about typemaking in lawsuits, inventories, and wills that mention punches and matrices, but the earliest of these references, to our knowledge, date to the late 1470s.[4] In sum, for the first quarter-century of printing, the only evidence that can give us insight into the underlying technological process comes from the printed survivals themselves. We can never prove that any particular technology was used to create these; but we can *disprove* the use of particular technologies by showing that their use is inconsistent with the printed result, which we can see, touch, and analyse at first hand.

In our research, we have used digital imaging and computational methods to study several early incunabula, focusing on survivals from Gutenberg's press, and we have found that the earliest printing exhibits irregularities inconsistent with the usual punch/matrix system for type manufacture. In the sections that follow, we will first discuss our methods, and then present our findings. Finally, we will advance a hypothetical type-making method consistent with our observations.

METHODS

The main subject of our analysis is the unique Scheide Library copy of the 1456 *Bulla Thurcorum*, a 20-page papal Bull of Calixtus III printed in Gutenberg's DK (*Donatus-Kalender*) fount (Fig. 1). Sample quires of the 42-line Bible, printed in the smaller B42 fount, had been completed as early as 1454. However, the earliest known European printing – the *Sibyllenbuch* and the 27-line *Donatus* fragments of circa 1450 – are all in DK, so to the best of our knowledge DK is Gutenberg's first fount. These earliest works are highly irregular in appearance and lack kerned sorts. The *Bulla* is more regular, and the fount is in a later state, though the overall effect is still less polished than the 42-line Bible.

To digitize the *Bulla* we have used a high-resolution scanning camera.[5] After scanning each page, we convert the resulting data from colour into an estimate of ink density at every point, or, to a good approximation, 'blackness'. In areas where the blackness falls below a threshold, it is assumed to be zero. The threshold is set to filter out most of the image features that are irrelevant to our analysis, including paper grain, stains, marginalia in brown ink, and rubrication in red ink. The result is similar to a high-contrast photocopy (Fig. 2). There are occasional imperfections – for example, the red stripes through the title and through the capitals that mark the beginnings of sentences may partially obliterate the ink underneath – but on the whole, the 'ink image' is an accurate reflection of the printing surface, though slightly thickened by ink spread.

The original printing surface would have consisted of many movable types locked into a forme; hence the next step in a complete typographic analysis would be to identify the boundaries between these types. Though trivial for a modern fount, this presents special challenges in Gutenberg's typography, due to the complexity of the textura character set and its profusion of contractions and ligatures. It is often unclear, for example, whether pairs of ligatured letters constitute a single type (as is likely for

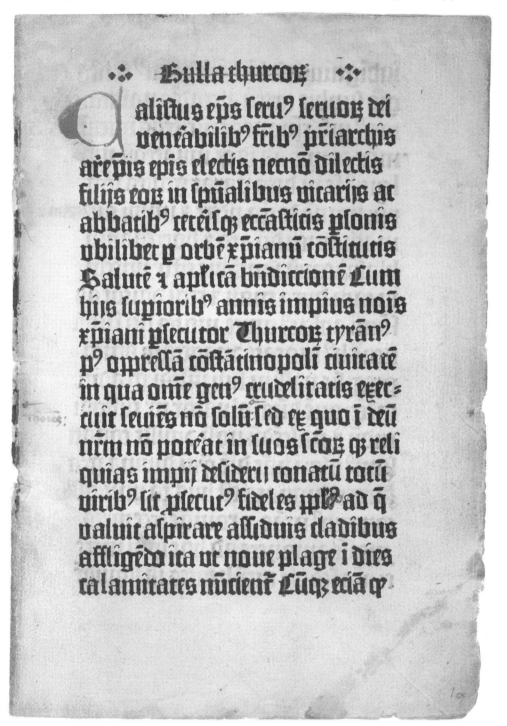

Fig. 1. The Scheide Library *Bulla Thurcorum*, Mainz 1456.

3

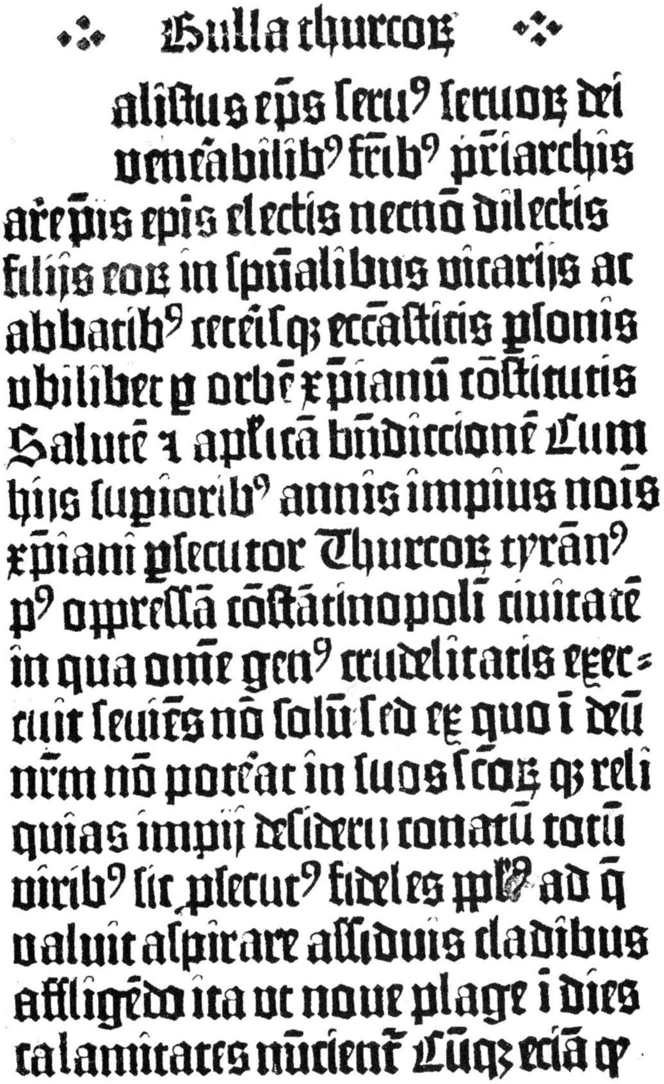
Bulla thurcorum
alistus eps servus servorum dei
venerabilibus fratribus patriarchis
archiepis epis electis necnon dilectis
filiis eorum in spiritualibus vicariis ac
abbatibus ceterisque ecclesiasticis personis
ubilibet per orbem christianum constitutis
Salutem et apostolicam benedictionem Cum
hiis superioribus annis impius nominis
christiani persecutor Thurcorum tyrannus
post oppressam constantinopolim civitatem
in qua omne genus crudelitatis exer-
cuit seviens non solum sed ex quo in deum
nostrum non poterat in suos sanctorum que reli
quias impii desiderii conatum totis
viribus sic persecutus fideles populos ad quos
valuit aspirare assiduis cladibus
affligendo ita ut nove plage in dies
calamitates nuncient Cumque etiam quod

Fig. 2. 'Ink image' corresponding to fig. 1.

st) or two specially designed and closely set types (as is the case for *de*). Rather than addressing the complete problem here, we will restrict our analysis to a single representative letter: the lower-case *i*.

Collation of *i*s alone would be of limited interest for a modern fount, because there is normally only one *i* sort – though such a collation could identify individual damaged *i*s, in the spirit of Charlton Hinman's typographic analysis of Shakespeare's *First Folio*.[6] In DK, however, an *i* may be abutting or non-abutting, it may be decorated with a bow, an overbar, or a tilde, or it may take the '*j*-form' if it is the second *i* in a pair. An *i* following an overhanging letter, like *f*, will be undotted, to allow tighter kerning. Hence all three *i*s in the word *filii* would be typeset with different sorts in the DK fount (Fig. 3a). Because each sort presumably corresponds to a different punch, making a synopsis of *i*s alone presents, in miniature, all the challenges of making a complete DK synopsis.

The *i* is especially well suited to computational collation for several reasons: first, because it is the narrowest letter, it is usually well separated from the adjacent letters. The *i* body, or minim stroke, thus tends to form an isolated 'ink island'. The bows, tildes or overbars form a second 'ink island'. It is easily verified that these accents, as we will call them, are on the same piece of type as their corresponding *i* bodies; as, for example, when an *i* is mistakenly set upside-down (Fig. 3b). We can therefore test the accuracy of our computational collation methods by verifying that independent collations of the *i* bodies and accents match up. In principle, this test could fail also if the matrices for types like the *i* are struck using a separate accent punch; then, for example, identical bows might occur above a variety of *i* body forms.

The principal technique we have used for collation is *pairwise clustering*. This method assumes that pairs of objects – ink islands, in this case – can be compared to yield a quantitative measure of difference, or dissimilarity. Schematically, we calculate dissimilarity between a pair of ink islands by overlaying them in the position and orientation such that their shapes overlap as much as possible, and summing their area of non-overlap. Identical ink islands would overlap precisely, yielding a dissimilarity of zero. Any alteration in one (but not both) of the ink islands will then necessarily increase the non-overlapping area.

The clustering algorithm itself breaks a large set of heterogeneous objects into smaller, homogenous groups, or clusters.[7] Similar objects will be classified as belonging to the same cluster, while dissimilar objects will be separated into different clusters. The number of desired clusters must be set externally; the algorithm may then produce either a few clusters containing many objects each, or many clusters with only a few objects each. One of the limitations of most clustering techniques is that they are unable to determine the 'correct' number of clusters automatically. For example, if there are only 20 meaningful categories for a set of objects, then attempting to cluster them into 21 clusters will usually split one of the meaningful clusters in half arbitrarily. Conversely, requesting only 19 clusters will usually yield one cluster containing two categories. It is often difficult to determine the best choice of cluster count.

It must also be kept in mind that, in our data, two ink islands never have precisely zero dissimilarity, even if they were printed from the same piece of type. Random variations, generically called *noise*, inevitably arise from slight differences in paper and printing conditions. Sometimes these random variations are large enough that they confound the clustering, and the algorithm fails to assign a particularly irregular or smeared impression to the appropriate cluster. This uncertainty in the collation process contrasts with most bibliographic analyses. For example, in analysing paper stock, there is seldom any doubt about whether the shape of a watermark is a bull's head or a bunch of grapes: no intermediate states exist. The same cannot be said of the analysis of single types. As Janet Ing Freeman writes in *Johann Gutenberg and His Bible* when discussing a synopsis of the 42-line Bible, 'Because one bibliographer's "alternate sort" may be another's "defective type", not even the exact number of sorts in the B42 fount can be stated with confidence'.[8] In the language of clustering, one might say that a

Fig. 3. filii and upside-down *i*. (a) Three variants of *i* used to print *filii* (Scheide *Bulla Thurcorum*, fol. 1ʳ line 5).

Fig. 3. (b) *singulis* with upside-down *i* (*Bulla Thurcorum*, fol. 7ᵛ line 10).

systematically deviant type may belong in its own cluster, or it may be merely an outlier in a larger cluster.

EVIDENCE

In their unpublished 1988 synopsis of DK type as represented in the *Bulla Thurcorum*, Janet Ing Freeman and Paul Needham identified twelve differently-shaped *i* variants, shown in Fig. 4. Several of these variants are typographically identical, that is, both used interchangeably and lacking salient differences in design. These 'supererogatory types', as they were termed, are nonetheless distinctive enough in shape that they could not have been manufactured from a common punch. Forty-eight of the 204 sorts identified in the 1988 synopsis were similarly supererogatory, including examples of almost every lower-case letter. In general only rare characters, such as the upper-case initials, were *not* found to have supererogatory forms; because in most of these cases there were only one or two occurrences of the character in the *Bulla*, it is likely that a larger text would have revealed many more variants in a similar analysis.

Our automated clustering of *i* bodies and accents not only confirms this surprising variability, but also shows that the 1988 synopsis identifies only a fraction of the redundant *i* forms in the *Bulla*. Fig. 5a shows a sample of the several hundred *i* accent clusters discovered. Each line, consisting of a black accent followed by between two and eight grey accents, represents a cluster. The grey accents are individual cluster members, as extracted from the *Bulla* ink images. The black accent is the cluster average, constructed by superimposing all cluster members, as if they were transparencies. Fig. 5b shows an independent clustering of *i* bodies, which yielded very similar results. Fewer clusters are shown, due to space constraints.

We do not claim that our cluster count is definitive, or even accurate; it is in fact likely that the true number is higher, as we have attempted to be conservative and we have been limited by the size of the document. Neither can cluster assignment ever be error-free, due to the unavoidable random variations arising from the printing process itself. We can assert, however, that the clustering is meaningful, based upon several lines of evidence. First, we note that certain of the *i* bodies have nicks, or other obvious distinctive features. In each such case, the clustering algorithm successfully identifies the damage, and groups together all *i* body impressions with the same damage in the document. In an independent visual search for damaged *i* bodies, we could find no errors of misclassification or omission in the automated clustering of these 'easy' cases. At a minimum, this suggests that our methods can perform damaged type collation in the spirit of Hinman's *First folio* analysis. It also suggests that the clusters of figure 5 can be interpreted as identified single type pieces, with each cluster member representing a re-use of the type piece. Type pieces typically recur approximately every four pages; this gives some impression of the printing and composing environment, as well as the size of the type-case.

A majority of the clusters lack any obvious damage, and would be extremely difficult to collate by hand; yet most of the accent clusters correspond well to a single body cluster, and vice versa. This observation holds for both damaged and undamaged examples. Because accent and body clustering are carried out independently and without any contextual knowledge, this is strong statistical proof that both accent and body

Fig. 4. Twelve *i* variants identified by Janet Ing Freeman and Paul Needham in their 1988 synopsis of the DK type as represented in the *Bulla Thurcorum* (unpublished).

clusterings are meaningful. Put differently, if *i*s were clustered solely on the basis of their accents, the resulting cluster assignment would be very similar to that of a clustering based solely on their bodies.

Thus our visual impression of Fig. 5 is confirmed: namely, that both accents and bodies differ sufficiently to clearly distinguish one cluster from another – hence, one piece of type from another. The high variability observed in the type impressions therefore does not arise primarily from the printing process itself, for within a cluster impressions are quite similar. The variability is in the printing surfaces of the type pieces. Although most letterpress printing is sprinkled with damaged type impressions, this degree of variability in undamaged types is not found in later printing. We have verified this using a variety of control cases, including the Aldine *Saint Catherine of Siena* of 1500,[9] Plantin's *Biblia polyglotta* of 1568-72,[10] and even the Ashendene Press *Inferno* of Dante, printed in 1902.[11]

Other aspects of DK typography exhibit a similar lack of repeatability. For example, it has been suggested that the suspension stroke might have been struck with a separate punch; this would certainly have improved efficiency, as strokes occur above *a, c, e, g, i, m, n, o, p, q, r, s, t,* and *u*. Tildes and other accents are used above many letters as well. Such situations could even have been addressed by making an entirely separate piece of type for the accent, though this would have complicated typesetting and made it harder to lock up the types in the forme. The near-perfect correspondence between a sub-population of *i* body clusters and their matching suspension stroke clusters, however, rules out this possibility in DK. Not only do particular *i* bodies always co-occur with particular suspension strokes, but if these *i*s with strokes are overlaid, there is no discernible jitter between the body and the stroke within a particular cluster. As with bows, suspension strokes are clearly on the same piece of type as their companion letters.

More surprisingly, however, suspension strokes are unique: particular versions of the stroke correspond to particular versions of the *i* body. Moving between clusters instead of within a cluster, we find both substantial jitter between the body and the stroke, and widely varying stroke lengths and shapes. *i8* and *i9* in the 1988 synopsis (Fig. 4) illustrate this effect; the clustering algorithm finds more than twelve different versions of this character (non-abutting *i* with overbar) in the *Bulla*. All the suspension strokes in the *Bulla* have also been clustered out of context, with similar results. There are again many distinct and well-defined clusters, although only a small fraction of these show

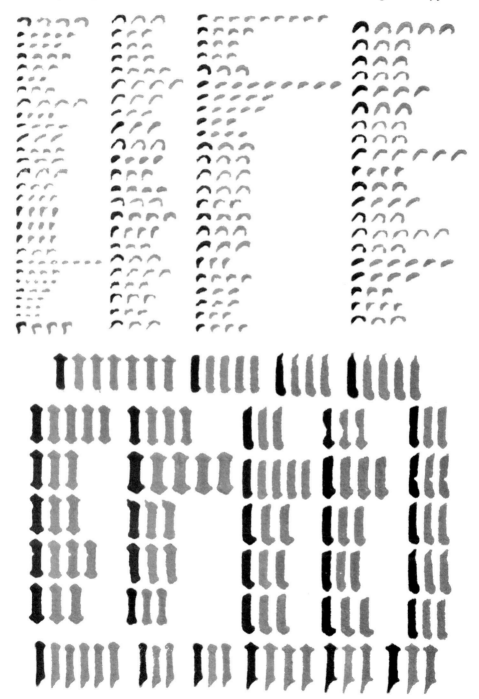

Fig. 5. A selection of *i* accent (*top*) and body (*lower*) clusters from independent clusterings of accents and bodies. Black images are cluster centroids, and the grey images to their right are the individual cluster members (lightened ink images from the document).

Fig. 6. B36 hyphens: 14 hyphens, chosen at random, from a 10-page sample of the 36-line Bible.

any discernible damage. Most of the clusters correspond to strokes that occur above only one of the fourteen possible companion letters. At least for the *is*, we know that this correspondence goes much further, with most particular stroke clusters matching particular letter body clusters.

Careful study of the suspension strokes confirms, then, that not only are they on the same piece of type as their companion letters, but that there is no common, separate suspension stroke punch. Suspension strokes appear to have been manufactured along with the rest of the type piece, and their shapes show the same distinctiveness as the shapes of the type bodies.

The nature of this variability between types cannot in general be explained by differential wear or damage, beginning with a common original shape. Many of the type impressions appear perfectly sharp and well-formed, but have overbars of different lengths, or with different shapes. Movement of the entire overbar up or down relative to the letter is particularly difficult to explain as an effect of damage, given that the overbar is clearly on the same piece of type as the letter.

The irregularity of DK printing can be demonstrated in yet another way using the 36-line Bible (B36). This final appearance of the much-used DK fount does not come from Gutenberg's shop, but was printed in Bamberg in 1461. Hyphens, which hardly appear in the *Bulla*, are used liberally in the two-column B36. Fig. 6 reproduces a random selection of these hyphens, based on digital photography of ten leaves. Great variability between hyphens is evident: the lengths of the two strokes vary substantially, as do their angles, and the spacing between them. While differing stroke lengths might be explained by partial obliteration of some of the types or imperfect casting, such defects cannot account for variable spacing between the strokes.

CONCLUSIONS

The high degree of variability between pieces of DK type presents problems for the standard hypothesis of type manufacture, involving the use of steel punches, copper matrices, and a hand mould to produce a fount of lead-alloy types. Even the one or two duplicate forms per character evident in the 1988 synopsis posed a minor mystery in light of this standard model. A steel punch is time-consuming and difficult to carve, even today requiring a full day of work by a skilled craftsman. Why would Gutenberg have chosen to repeat this exercise several times per sort? An examination of the type variants across DK states does not consistently suggest an aesthetic evolution to explain this effort.

With new evidence not only confirming duplicate type forms, but raising their number from one or two per sort to – conservatively – dozens, the hypothesis that DK type was manufactured using the standard method becomes untenable. The most obvious conclusion consistent with our evidence is that each physical piece of type was manufactured individually, and was not the outcome of a mass-reproduction process at all.

While a discussion of the historical precedent for the argument is beyond the scope of this paper, we note that this position has been taken before. It is possible to print from wooden type, and such types must be individually carved. The suggestion that Gutenberg's DK type was wooden is problematic, however. The effort involved in carving an entire such fount by hand would have been immense. Ensuring square, proportional wooden type bodies would have presented further challenges. Finally, wood is not particularly durable, and would have suffered much from high turnover and heavy use. It is one thing to use wood for a large, infrequently used decorative initial, and quite another to use it for a minuscule *i*, which is re-used every few words for every kind of publication, ranging from bibles to grammar books to indulgences, the latter of which might have been printed in very large runs. While wooden DK type cannot be absolutely ruled out on the strength of the evidence presented here, this possibility seems unlikely from a practical point of view.

If the DK types were made of metal, then it is a near-certainty that they were made by casting. The only alternative is individual engraving from blanks – a process that Gerard Meerman proposed in the eighteenth century as part of his 'rational' schema for the invention of printing in small steps.[12] Although this would also produce the variability we observe, the amount of work involved in engraving an entire fount would have been still greater than the effort of carving it in wood. Once again, individually engraved blanks are unlikely, especially as we know that Gutenberg was familiar with casting. Aside from his father's oft-cited connection with a mint, he may have used sandcasting to mass-produce pilgrim mirrors during his Strasbourg period. He certainly used casting of some sort to make the two-line slugs with which he printed the Mainz *Catholicon* and several smaller works.[13]

If types were cast, yet differ greatly in their final shape, then they could not have been cast from a common matrix. Either many matrices were used in parallel, or equivalently, the matrix was temporary and needed to be re-formed between castings – or both. Lead and sand matrices are temporary, but there are other possibilities as well, such as clay, plaster, and papier mâché. All of these have been used, at one time or another, to make secondary castings during the era of hand printing.

Whether many matrices existed in parallel or were re-formed sequentially, it is also clear that the matrices for a single sort could not have been formed by a common whole-letter punch or pattern. If they had been, then while we might observe higher variability between types than expected due to imperfectly formed matrices, the nature of this variability would be different. In particular, overbars would not move relative to their companion letters, and the strokes of the hyphen would not move relative to each other. A handful of patterns per sort still do not suffice to explain our observation; if whole-letter patterns were used, it would appear that the number of such patterns would need to be of the same order as the number of single types.

It is possible to reconcile a casting process with the apparent absence of reused whole-letter patterns by considering systems in which temporary matrices are made by striking or impressing not a single punch, but a series of smaller, 'elemental' punches. A matrix would then be the product not only of the shapes of the constituent elements, but of their overall configuration, which would inevitably vary every time the matrix is re-formed.

This suggestion, too, is not entirely unprecedented. Separate accent punches, as discussed in *Evidence*, present a simple case of matrices formed by combinations of two punches. More interestingly, typefounders have occasionally produced ligatured types, such as Œ, from a combination of the O and E punches, struck in an overlapping configuration, which saves the work of making a separate Œ punch. Eighteenth century matrices struck in this fashion by Rosart survive in the Enschedé collection.[14] Were this technique used in combination with temporary matrices, the effect would be a set of Œ types with variable overlap between the letters, resulting in a variety of shapes.

Preliminary observations suggest that DK types may have been constructed in a similar way, though from more elemental components corresponding roughly to single scribal strokes rather than entire letters such as O and E. Hence the hyphen would have been made from two such elements, but even simple letters might have been formed from between four and seven elements. If we take overbars to be representative of single elements, then the non-uniformity of overbar lengths across multiple sorts – or even across different variants of the same sort – suggests that, if these 'elemental punches' existed, they did not have the permanence or uniqueness of true whole-letter punches. This is unsurprising, as their shapes are very simple, and if temporary matrices were used, they could easily have been carved from wood.

In summary, our observations appear to be inconsistent with the assumption that permanent matrices were used in casting DK type. They are also inconsistent with the idea of static whole-letter punches for each sort. A consistent picture emerges if we hypothesize the use of temporary matrices, in combination with 'elemental punches' which would have allowed the typemaker to form these matrices from multiple overlapping strokes. Preliminary results suggest that this rather counter-intuitive type-making method was not merely an early experiment of Gutenberg's, but may have been common to a number of early typefoundries.

TRADITION AND RENEWAL
ESTABLISHING THE CHRONOLOGY OF WYNKYN DE WORDE'S EARLY WORK

LOTTE HELLINGA

DOCUMENTATION ON CAXTON'S estate is very incomplete and difficult to interpret, merely suggesting that the settlement was protracted and complicated. There is nothing to reveal to posterity the nature of the transaction that resulted in Wynkyn de Worde taking over Caxton's printer's workshop after his former master's death in the early months of 1492.[1] Caxton's heirs, his daughter Elizabeth and her husband, Gerard Crop, who may not have been interested in or capable of taking an active part in the continuation of the printing business, presumably decided that it was preferable to rely on the skills of someone who knew the workshop inside out. Besides, the going concern must have represented substantial value. Initially, some of Wynkyn de Worde's work after Caxton's death may even have been commissioned by the heirs, thus continuing de Worde's former working relationship with Caxton himself. There is no indication whatever that de Worde also took over from Caxton as stationarius, while several documents indicate that his heirs were still disposing of books in stock as late as 1498.

Some significance should probably be attached to de Worde's continued use of Caxton's device, and to his address given as 'in Caxton's house', occurring as late as 1499,[2] perhaps suggesting that he may not have become the outright owner of the printing office until at least seven years had passed. Alternatively, he may occasionally have used the designation as an address until his move to Fleet Street, in 1501. We are on firmer ground, however, when we consider what decisions Wynkyn de Worde had to face at the beginning of his at least partially independent activity. Among the formal transactions in 1492 an inventory must have been drawn up of the assets of the business: unsold stock, supplies of paper, typographical materials and of the 'hardware', presses, compositors' tools, and, inevitably, various odds and ends. Very occasionally such inventories survive,[3] but to form any idea of the inventory of 'Caxton's house' after the Master's death we have to rely on silent witnesses, the books printed by Caxton in his later years. As to unsold stock, the titles in the documents offer puzzles rather than clarification, but we can take note of the Caxton texts which Wynkyn de Worde reprinted soon after he took over: the *Golden Legend*, the pseudo-Bonaventura *Meditations on the Life of Christ*, the brief Lydgate texts, Higden's *Polychronicon* and the *Description of Britain*, and a little later the *Chronicles of England*, the *Canterbury Tales*, and Malory's *Morte Darthur*. Any remnant supply of copies of these titles must have been much smaller than expected demand.

I recently revisited the description and analysis of the typographical material used by de Worde in the fifteenth century (a *terminus* coinciding with his move from Caxton's

13

House in Westminster to premises in Fleet Street) in the concluding phase of preparations for the section 'Wynkyn de Worde' in the volume 'England' of the *Catalogue of Books printed in the XVth Century now in the British Museum (Library)*, hereafter referred to as *BMC* vol. xi. Not unlike Wynkyn de Worde, I am aware of dealing with a metaphorical 'inheritance', continuing a well-established and respected tradition while also feeling obliged, indeed wishing, not to miss the opportunity to respond to the requirements of a changing world. Moreover, also like Wynkyn de Worde, I am following in the footsteps of distinguished predecessors who have handled this material before me. My recent analysis of de Worde's type breaks with the *BMC* tradition in that it is more directed towards understanding the production of type and its functions in the representation of text than the purely descriptive format of previous *BMC* volumes. While sparing with their illustrations these had as primary purpose the identification of distinctive features of the type in support of the incunabulists' classification system. The present analysis (which in *BMC* will be combined with illustration of details) led to changes in the hitherto accepted dating of undated editions. It also brought a better understanding of de Worde's decisions as to how to make best use of the existing materials, while introducing some modernization and contributing his own experience and his own connections in the world of printers. As it happens, at this particular time, when early typefounding methods are revealed (as shown elsewhere in this volume), the analysis of Caxton's and de Worde's supply of type highlights the rapid development in the production of and trade in printing types. After the first decades of printing a stable method had evolved, a production sequence of cutting punches, striking matrices (the work of specialists), and casting characters from the matrices. In the following centuries this allowed printers to make choices about the level of investment they wished to make in typographical materials. They could plan either for long-term or short-term use, that is, by buying either matrices (if not acquiring a monopoly on a typeface by buying punches) or cast type. Caxton, and after him de Worde, faced these choices.

Wynkyn de Worde found in Caxton's workshop four or perhaps five complete and usable founts of text type, as well as a complete fount of a large type used especially for liturgical works and for headings in combination with smaller types. This last fount (Caxton Type 3:135G) had been in Caxton's possession since 1476.[4] Three of the text founts (Caxton Types 6, 7, and 8) were found cast and in good shape. Type 8, a fine Parisian type, was in fact almost brand new. Type 7: 84 G, a small typeface, had been used for indulgences since 1489. Caxton Type 5, a text type used by Caxton from *c.*1485-6 was last used by him *c.*1489-90, and we cannot know whether it was still in the shop.[5] In any case, it was never used by Wynkyn de Worde. There was also a fourth text type, a fount in the bastarda style first favoured by Caxton. It is Caxton Type 4, by now an old war-horse that had served Caxton for many of his books from 1480 and continued to be used by him after it was recast on a larger body in 1483, in spite of looking very worn, irregular and badly aligned in the recast version. In this state it was last used in 1489.[6] Caxton himself had this fount recast, but that is not the only evidence that he owned the matrices for it. Wynkyn de Worde must also have decided that this was still an economical typeface for setting a very large book and had it recast for reprinting the *Golden Legend*, by far the largest of the early books to come off his press, and the first to bear a date (20 May 1493).[7] The *Golden Legend* was probably preceded by the undated *Life of St Catharine*, Duff 403, set in the same type. De

Worde's recast was technically well executed, resulting in a much better appearance than it had in Caxton's second version. Nevertheless, after printing the one very large book in this typeface, de Worde abandoned it, merely plundering its upper case to supplement a French type he acquired not much later. There is another feature in the two books printed in the old Caxton type which may be a clue to the identity of the very competent typefounder who recast the type. They contain a set of woodcut initials and two very large initials surely cut by the same hand. The set was first seen in use in Gouda in 1486, in a book produced by 'the Gouda typecutter' whose actual name remains an enigma to bibliographers.[8] The presence of these initials in de Worde's early works suggests that he lost no time in calling on his connections in his (native) Holland. A few years later, in 1496, the one typeface firmly connected with the Gouda typographer appeared just once in de Worde's *oeuvre*, in *The Book of St Albans*, there adapted to show characteristics for English use.[9] Some of de Worde's woodcut illustrations were first used by printers in Holland and thus confirm his Dutch connections.

In Caxton's inventory there were therefore matrices for Caxton's Type 4, and in all likelihood also for his Type 3 which continued to be used by Wynkyn de Worde (de Worde type 6:135G) as a spectacular display type. It is a type that was also in use by printers in Louvain and Antwerp, and poor casts of it make appearances in the work of two other printers in England, the Schoolmaster printer in St Albans, and the shop of John Lettou and William de Machlinia in London. The printers in England may well have obtained these casts from Caxton.[10]

The other three founts demonstrate effectively that Caxton decided after 1483 no longer to invest in matrices but to buy cast founts. The poor effect of the recasting of his Type 4 may have persuaded him to buy cast type, and from then on he no longer procured type from Johan Veldener, who had in all likelihood provided his Types 2, 3, and 4, but from foundries in Paris which by now worked for an extensive market. There is no sign, in any case, that either he or Wynkyn de Worde recast the other types that were in the shop in 1492, Types 6, 7, and 8. Caxton's Type 6 (Wynkyn de Worde Type 3:120B) was used by de Worde for only two or three books, two of them usually found combined, both undated and possibly the first books produced by him since the type did not need any adjustment, unlike Caxton's Type 4.[11] Caxton's Type 8, the fine French type, was used only twice by de Worde as main text type (de Worde Type 2:114G), in two books printed in 1494,[12] but it continued to be used for a long time in a subsidiary role, to set off de Worde's new main text type.

Apart from the founts of text type, there was other typographical material in the shop: a fine set of 21 large woodcut initials, from 1485 onwards an instantly recognizable feature of most of Caxton's books, and six sets of lombard initials of various sizes. Wynkyn de Worde continued to use these almost indiscriminately, partly in recasts with slight variations, as Caxton had also done before him. There were also extensive sets of woodcuts, some of them never to be used again because the texts for which they were designed were not reprinted by de Worde (e.g. *The Game of Chesse*, *The Mirrour of the World*, *Aesop*); others were destined for a productive prolongation of their shelf-life, e.g. some 70 blocks used for the *Golden Legend*, 22 for the *Canterbury Tales*, 24 for the *Mirrour of the Life of Christ* (a set of fine cuts that was particularly heavily used), and some 50 other religious cuts for *Horae* and other devotional publications.[13] And then, among the blocks, there was also Caxton's large printer's device, that remained intermittently in use until 1500, often, but not invariably, in further editions of texts associated with Caxton.[14]

Although Wynkyn de Worde had a rich supply of material almost immediately to hand, he must have decided very soon to extend this with a high-quality fount of recent design that he designated as his main text type, for English as well as for Latin, for large as well as for small books. Two of Caxton's types (Types 3 and 8) were successfully called into service to contrast with it in titles, chapter headings and headlines. The acquisition of this text-type (Wynkyn de Worde Type 4: 96G), which is closely related to founts used in Paris by major printers, Antoine Vérard and Antoine Caillaut among them, was therefore a significant policy decision. It was recast at least once, and we can therefore infer that de Worde reversed Caxton's recent strategy of buying cast type. He decided to invest in matrices, perhaps encouraged by the high-quality work of the typefounder who recast Caxton's Type 4 for him. By choosing a fount of French origin and with a number of characteristics adopted by printers in Paris and Rouen, he consolidated a process that had begun in Caxton's last years. Perhaps we may also assume some influence of Richard Pynson, his direct competitor, whose origins in Normandy are apparent in the presentation of many of his books. From then on the typographical style known as 'black letter', which was an adaptation of Parisian typographical style to English use, became dominant and remained so for a very long time for printing in English.

When we compare his work with that of his predecessor, there can be little doubt that de Worde intended to improve and update the typography of Caxton's workshop. Another factor was probably the decision to compete with the Paris printers who produced Books of Hours for the use of Sarum in ever increasing quantities, to be sent straight to England.[15] The fount which de Worde bought was fully equipped for printing Latin and in particular Books of Hours. From the gradual extension of the fount we can deduce that the kalendars in two undated Books of Hours represent its earliest state.[16] Throughout its use, a type-case including the sorts for Latin was kept separate from the English cases.

The intense use of this type for some nine years, use that was prolonged by recasting, is convincing evidence that Wynkyn de Worde purchased matrices. By all accounts it must be considered a rewarding investment. No fewer that 84 titles survive printed in this type by de Worde in the fifteenth century alone. From the rarity of many of them we may assume that he produced more such small books than can now be recorded. The 84 surviving titles also include some very substantial works, among them Higden's *Polycronicon*, Bartholomaeus Anglicus, the *Golden Legend*, the *Morte Darthur*, and the *Canterbury Tales*. The fount continued to be used by de Worde after his move to Fleet Street, until finally its remnants were passed on to Hugo Goes. Altogether a creditable record, sustained by due vigilance and care for correct use.

Taking a French type to England requires adaptation. The continuous process of expansion of its use into areas for which it was not designed (printing in English, legal printing) and subsequently the improvements to the adaptations, allow us to establish sets of features with chronological implications. It is therefore worth setting these out in some detail.

Even printed in Latin, the calendar of a book of hours for Sarum use requires a capital W for saints like Winifred and Willibrord. A lower-case w was present in the fount from its first use by de Worde, and each of the two saints got a lower-case w in the surviving calendars of three Books of Hours; for this reason they are given a early position in the chronological sequence. However, as soon as English texts were to be printed, expansion was required, and we see the gradual introduction of contractions of y with integrated superscript e, t, and u, for 'the', 'that', and 'you', and w with superscript t for 'with'. The y- contractions were obviously the first priority, followed by the introduction of terminal lower-case m and n, with extended final flourish, to be set at the end of a word. It is remarkable how strictly this convention was observed by Wynkyn de Worde's compositors when they set texts in English. Not until 1499 did this discipline appear to be somewhat relaxed.

How and by whom these additional characters were produced we do not know. Apparently, someone was capable of producing them on the spot, for they were introduced very gradually, one after the other. Although it is not difficult to notice these additions, they harmonize reasonably well with the type. Other elements are required to make a book with an English text look English. The letter I occurs very frequently in English texts, and the distinction between a slender form and a flourished form is a very marked feature of English script and printing of the period. For the flourished form de Worde resorted to raiding Caxton's type supply, and he took the I from the bastarda-style Caxton Type 4. This second and rather ornamental capital I was successfully used for the whole period during which he used the type, that is until 1502.

Meanwhile, de Worde still did not have a capital W nor capitals K and Y, which were all of course lacking in the French fount. In the first of his books printed entirely in English, a set of one-line lombards did service, probably obtained at the same time in Paris, but a more permanent solution was obviously necessary. This was again found in Caxton's Type 4, that provided a W and Y, two frequently used characters, and a K that is used only rarely. Finally a capital L from this type, looped and therefore also more 'English' was introduced after a few years. W and Y stand out on the page and are certainly not in harmony with the style of the type, even when yet another introduction modified its aspect considerably. This was a looped ampersand, rather exuberant and used with abandon, whereas the Parisian type had a very restrained, straight small one (Fig. 1). The last major addition to this cast of the type was a set of characters required for setting Norman-French, the language of the set of *Statutes* printed early in 1496, shortly after the end of the parliamentary session 11 Henry VII. These particular graphic forms were a stylistic element traditional in the chancery hand, and had been adopted by the London printers who first printed legal texts (Fig. 2). Richard Pynson had already largely captured this market, and de Worde clearly took some pains to outdo his competitor.

These gradual developments took place before 1497. At about that time the decision must have been taken to recast the type on a slightly smaller body, probably in antici-pation of the production of some very large books that were to be printed in 1497-8, the *Canterbury Tales*, with Lydgate's *Assembly of gods*, Malory's *Morte Darthur*, the *Chronicles of England* with the *Description of Britain*,[17] and, above all, another edition of the *Golden Legend*. The new cast is characterized in the first place by the difference in size, but we also see that the struggle with the English characters continues. The terminal m and n were replaced by more pronounced forms, and the contractions for y

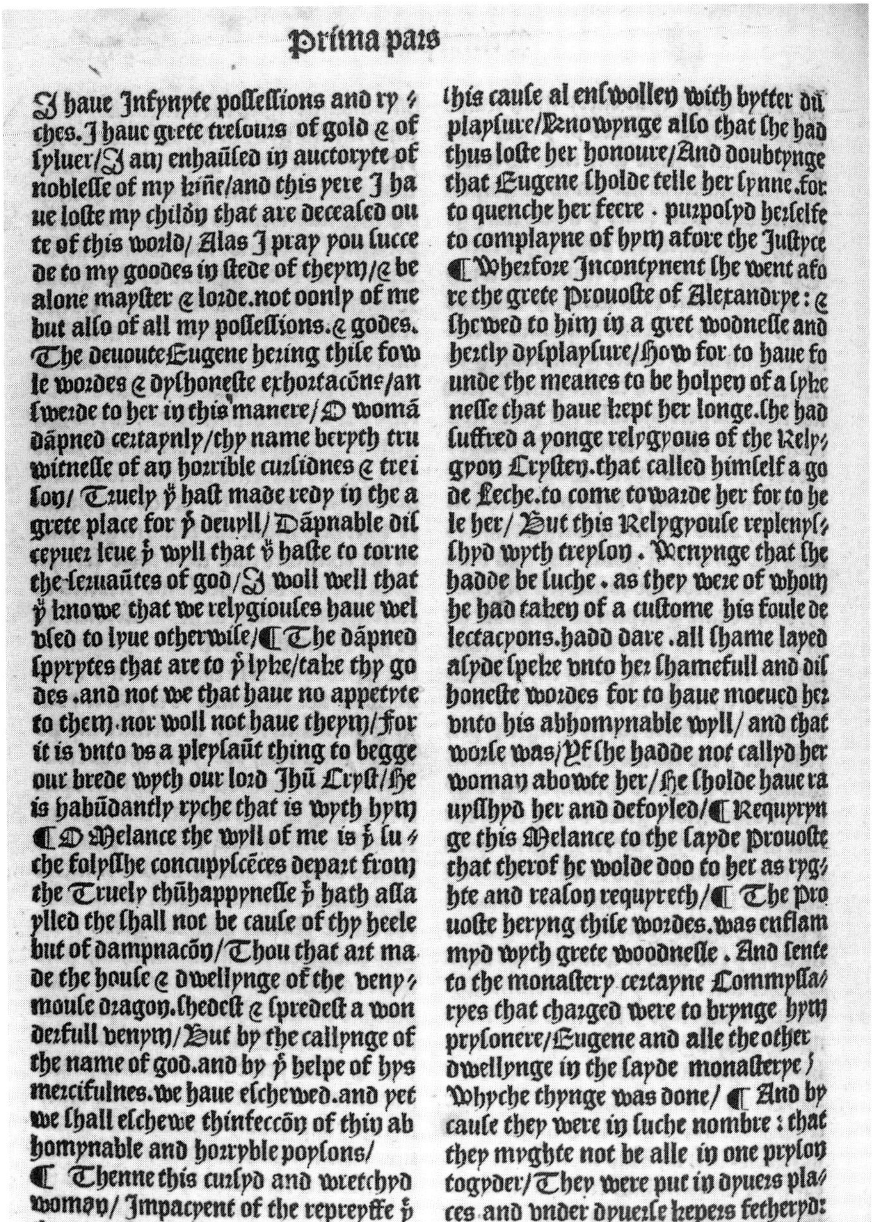

Prima pars

I haue Infynyte possessions and ry-
ches. I haue grete tresours of gold & of
syluer/I am enhaunsed in auctoryte of
noblesse of my kyñe/and this yere I ha
ue loste my chyldn that are deceased ou
te of this world/ Alas I pray you succe
de to my goodes in stede of theym/& be
alone mayster & lorde.not oonly of me
but also of all my possessions.& godes.
The deuoute Eugene hering thise fow
le wordes & dyshoneste exhortacõns/an
swerde to her in this manere/O womã
dãpned certaynly/thy name beryth tru
witnesse of an horrible cursidnes & trei
son/ Truely yͧ hast made redy in the a
grete place for yͤ deuyll/ Dãpnable dis
ceyuer leue yͭ wyll that yͧ haste to torne
the seruauntes of god/I woll well that
yͧ knowe that we relygiouses haue wel
vsed to lyue otherwise/¶ The dãpned
spyrytes that are to yͤ lyke/take thy go
des .and not we that haue no appetyte
to them.nor woll not haue theym/For
it is vnto vs a pleysaũt thing to begge
our brede wyth our lord Jhũ Cryst/He
is habũdantly ryche that is wyth hym
¶ O Melance the wyll of me is yͭ suche folysshe concupyscẽces depart from
the Truely thũhappynesse yͭ hath assa
ylled the shall not be cause of thy heele
but of dampnacõn/Thou that art ma
de the house & dwellynge of the veny-
mouse dragon.shedest & spredest a won
derfull venym/But by the callynge of
the name of god.and by yͤ helpe of hys
mercifulnes.we haue eschewed.and yet
we shall eschewe thinfeccõn of thin ab
homynable and horryble poysons/
¶ Thenne this cursyd and wretchyd
woman/ Impacyent of the repreffe yͭ
the good Eugene had sayd to her / & at
this cause al enswollen with bytter dis
playsure/Knowynge also that she had
thus loste her honoure/And doubtynge
that Eugene sholde telle her synne.for
to quenche her fere . purposyd herselfe
to complayne of hym afore the Justyce
¶ Wherfore Incontynent she went afo
re the grete Prouoste of Alexandrye : &
shewed to him in a gret wodnesse and
hertly dysplaysure/How for to haue fo
unde the meanes to be holpen of a syke
nesse that haue kept her longe.she had
suffred a yonge relygyous of the Rely-
gyon Crysten.that called himself a go
de Leche.to come towarde her for to he
le her/ But this Relygyouse replenys-
shyd wyth treyson . Wenynge that she
hadde be suche . as they were of whom
he had taken of a custome his foule de
lectacyons.hadd dare .all shame layed
asyde speke vnto her shamefull and dis
honeste wordes for to haue moeued her
vnto his abhomynable wyll/ and that
worse was/Yf she hadde not callyd her
woman abowte her/He sholde haue ra
uysshyd her and defoyled/¶ Requyryn
ge this Melance to the sayde Prouoste
that therof he wolde doo to her as ryg-
hte and reason requyreth/¶ The Pro
uoste heryng thise wordes.was enflam
myd wyth grete woodnesse . And sente
to the monastery certayne Commyssa-
ryes that charged were to brynge hym
prysonere/Eugene and alle the other
dwellynge in the sayde monasterye /
Whyche thynge was done/ ¶ And by
cause they were in suche nombre : that
they myghte not be alle in one pryson
togyder/They were put in dyuers places and vnder dyuerse kepers fetherydr:
well harde & faste/The sayd Prouoste

Fig. 1. Hieronymus, *Vitas patrum* [English]. Westminster, 1495. Actual size: 236 × 180 mm
Duff 235. British Library, C.11.b.3, leaf x7 verso.
Type 4: 96G, first cast with y^e (l. 16), y^t (l. 17), y^u (l. 15).
terminal m^1 (l. 3), terminal n^1 (l. 5).
I^1 and I^2 (l. 1).
ampersand^2 (l. 2).
K (col. b, l. 2) W^1 (col. b, l. 7).

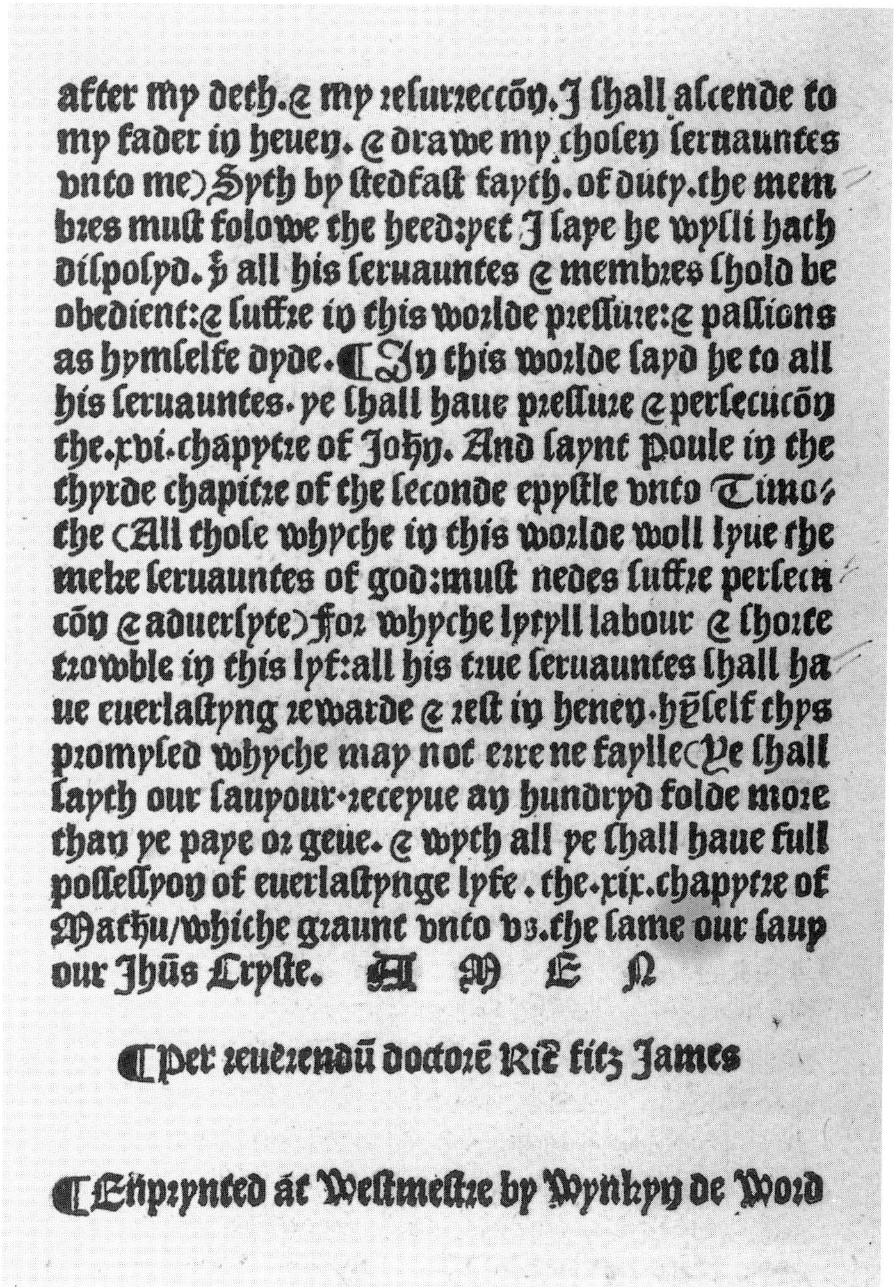

after my deth.& my resurreccōn.J shall ascende to
my fader iŋ heueŋ. & drawe my choseŋ seruauntes
vnto me)Syth by stedfast fayth. of duty.the mem
bres must folowe the heed:yet J saye he wylli hath
dispolyd. ẏ all his seruauntes & membres shold be
obedient:& suffre iŋ this worlde pressure:& passions
as hymselfe dyde.¶Jŋ this worlde sayd he to all
his seruauntes. ye shall haue pressure & persecucōn
the.xvi.chapptre of Johŋ. And saynt poule iŋ the
thyrde chapitre of the seconde epystle vnto Timo/
the (All those whyche iŋ this worlde woll lyue the
meke seruauntes of god:must nedes suffre persecu
cōŋ & aduersyte)for whyche lytyll labour & shorte
trowble iŋ this lyf:all his true seruauntes shall ha
ue euerlastyng rewarde & rest iŋ heueŋ.hȳself thys
promysed whyche may not erre ne faylle(ye shall
sayth our sauyour.recepue aŋ hundryd folde more
thaŋ ye paye or geue. & wyth all ye shall haue full
possessyoŋ of euerlastynge lyfe . the.xix.chapptre of
Mathu/whiche graunt vnto vs.the same our sauy
our Jhūs Cryste.   A M E N

¶Per reuerendū doctorē Riē fitz James

¶Enprynted at Westmestre by Wynkyn de Word

Fig. 2. Richard Fitzjames, *Sermon*. Westminster [*c*. 1496].   Actual size: 152 × 96 mm
Duff 151, British Library IA.55253, leaf g6 recto.
Type 4:96G, first cast with 'legal' sorts added.
h with stroke (l. 9), c with suspension (l. 22).   1-line lombard (l. 21).
Note also W¹ (l. 23) and Y (l. 16).

with superscript e, t, and u and the w with superscript t were also gradually replaced. Another capital W was introduced which stands out even more than its predecessor (Fig. 3). A third form of capital I identifies the last phase of the use of the type by de Worde. This third form was probably introduced as being in better harmony with the type when printing Latin than the flourished I^2. The sorts for Latin were also recast in this body-size. The use of I^3 as an emphatic capital, in contrast with the inconspicuous I^1, is strikingly obvious in the edition of Maydestone's *Directorium*, Duff 296. However, it soon found its way into the English texts, as it can be seen in the *Golden Legend*, Duff 411, dated 8 January 1498/9.[18] The capital I of Type 8, which resembles the I^3, makes occasional appearances as a wrong-fount type at a very late stage, for example in the *Ortus vocabulorum* of 1500, and in the undated *Eglamour* (Fig. 4). Conversely, some capitals of Type 4 were mixed in with Type 8, as in the *Statutes 11 Henry VII*, Duff 383 (Fig. 5).

The introduction of new sorts from 1497/8 has been observed by Dr O. D. Macrae Gibson who concentrated on Wynkyn de Worde's edition of *Merlin*, and by Margaret Lane Ford in a publication on her re-dating of the *Proprytees of Hors*.[19] Extending their observations over the full range of material available in the British Library, and (as far as was feasible) beyond, confirms their findings and lends them some more precision.

The gradual introduction of these replacements helps in establishing the chronology of the production of these books. There is, however, more to be gained, in the first place an insight into the organization of production. In large books, where copy was divided over two or more compositors who worked in parallel, we can distinguish their type-cases when replacements or extensions were not introduced simultaneously. That gives us the opportunity either to surmise the division of printers' copy between compositors, or to confirm it. For example, in the *Chronicles of England* and in the *Malory* there is clearly parallel use of distinct type-cases, and there is an even clearer division in the *Golden Legend*, where the distinct type-cases coincide with the use of different type in the headlines.

The most satisfactory observation is, however, in Wynkyn de Worde's edition of the *Canterbury Tales*. The different speed of introducing the new English sorts into two type-cases was observed by Ford. In addition, her observation of the distinction between two type-cases, and by inference of two compositors, coincides with the break in copy I had observed by collating Wynkyn de Worde's edition with Caxton's second edition, traditionally reputed to be de Worde's *exemplar*. That relationship became fairly obvious for the first part of the book after it had been established by the work of Sir Walter Greg and of W. F. Hutmacher in collating the Knight's Tale in both versions.[20] The change-over of type-cases occurs much later in the book, between the Tale of the Prioress and the Parson's Tale.[21] From this place on there are many variations from Caxton's text, there are changes of layout in the Tale of Sir Thopas, and there are omissions and changes in the order of the strophes in the Monk's Tale; it must be assumed that from then on a different version, not transmitted in print but a manuscript *exemplar*, was used. I had also noticed that from this point on a new set of one-line lombard initials was used, confirming the change-over of type-case and compositor. Recently, Satoko Tokunaga has demonstrated that the manuscript source here used for the Monk's Tale, now lost, is close to the Hengwrt manuscript. This is a confirmation of my more general approach; her specific conclusion is based on research well beyond

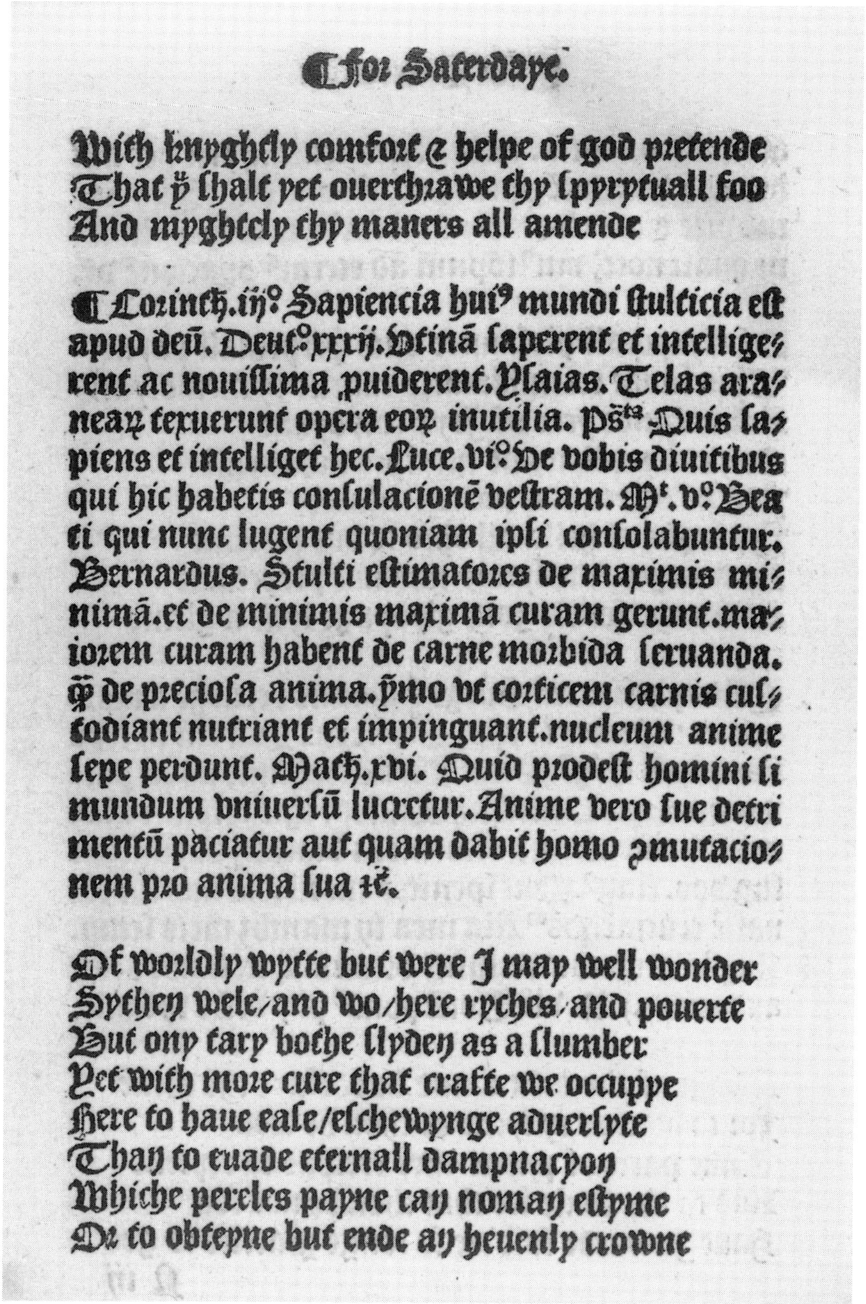

¶ for Saterdaye.

With knyghtely comfort & helpe of god pretende
That þ shalt yet ouerthrawe thy spyrytuall foo
And myghtely thy maners all amende

¶ Corinth.iij? Sapiencia huj⁹ mundi stulticia est
apud deū. Deutº.xxxij.Vtinā saperent et intelige=
rent ac nouissima puiderent.Ysaias.Telas ara=
neaꝶ texuerunt opera eoꝶ inutilia. p̄s̄ᵗᵃ.Quis sa=
piens et intelliget hec.Luce.vjº De vobis diuitibus
qui hic habetis consulacionē vestram. M̄ᵗ. vº Bea
ti qui nunc lugent quoniam ipsi consolabuntur.
Bernardus. Stulti estimatores de maximis mi=
nimā.et de minimis maximā curam gerunt.ma=
iorem curam habent de carne morbida seruanda.
ꝗ de preciosa anima.ymo vt corticem carnis cus=
todiant nutriant et impinguant.nucleum anime
sepe perdunt. Math.xvi. Quid prodest homini si
mundum vniuersū lucretur.Anime vero sue detri
mentū paciatur aut quam dabit homo ꝯmutacio=
nem pro anima sua ꝛc.

Of worldly wytte but were J may well wonder
Sythen wele/and wo/here ryches/and pouerte
But ony tary bothe slyden as a slumber
Yet with more cure that crafte we occuppe
Here to haue ease/eschewynge aduersyte
Than to euade eternall dampnacyon
Whiche perles payne can noman estyme
Or to obteyne but ende an heuenly crowne

Fig. 3. *William Touris, The Contemplation of Sinners.* Westminster, 10 July 1499. Duff 106. British Library IA.55215, leaf N3 verso. Actual size: 160 × 110 mm
Type 4C: 94G, recast, with replacements.

terminal n² (ll. 21, 22).
y^{u2} (l. 2).

W² (ll. 1, 26). L2 (l. 8).
Latin case (ll. 4-19) with ampersand¹ (l. 19).

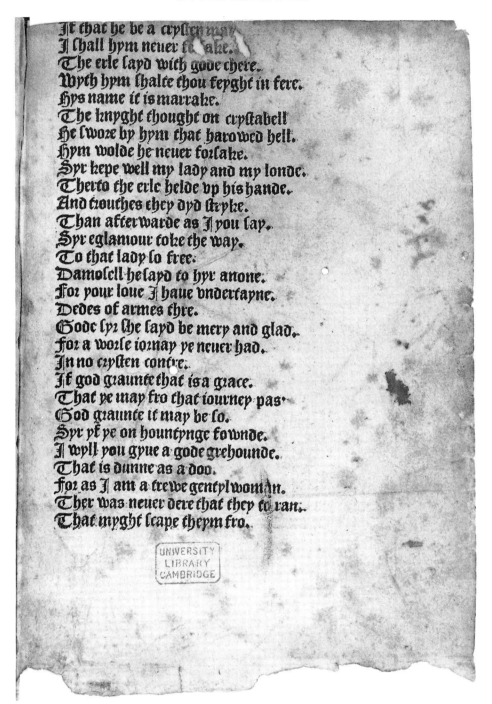

If that he be a cryſten may
I ſhall hym neuer forſake.
The erle ſayd with gode chere.
Wyth hym ſhalte thou feyght in fere.
Hys name it is marrake.
The knyght thought on cryſtabell
He ſwore by hym that harowed hell.
Hym wolde he neuer forſake.
Syr kepe well my lady and my londe.
Therto the erle helde vp his hande.
And trouthes they dyd ſtryke.
Than afterwarde as I you ſay.
Syr eglamour toke the way.
To that lady ſo free.
Damoſell he ſayd to hyr anone.
For your loue I haue vnderſayne.
Dedes of armes thre.
Gode ſyr ſhe ſayd be mery and glad.
For a worſe iornay ye neuer had.
In no cryſten contre.
If god graunte that is a grace.
That ye may fro that iourney pas·
God graunte it may be ſo.
Syr yf ye on hountynge fownde.
I wyll you gyue a gode grehounde.
That is dunne as a doo.
For as I am a trewe gentyl womȧn.
Ther was neuer dere that they to ran.
That myght ſcape theym fro.

Fig. 4. *Sir Eglamour.* [Westminster, 1499-1500].   Actual size: 174 × 125 mm
Duff 135. Cambridge University Library, Oates 4156 (fragment).
Type 4C: 94G, with I³ (ll. 1, 2, 12), W² (l. 4).

22

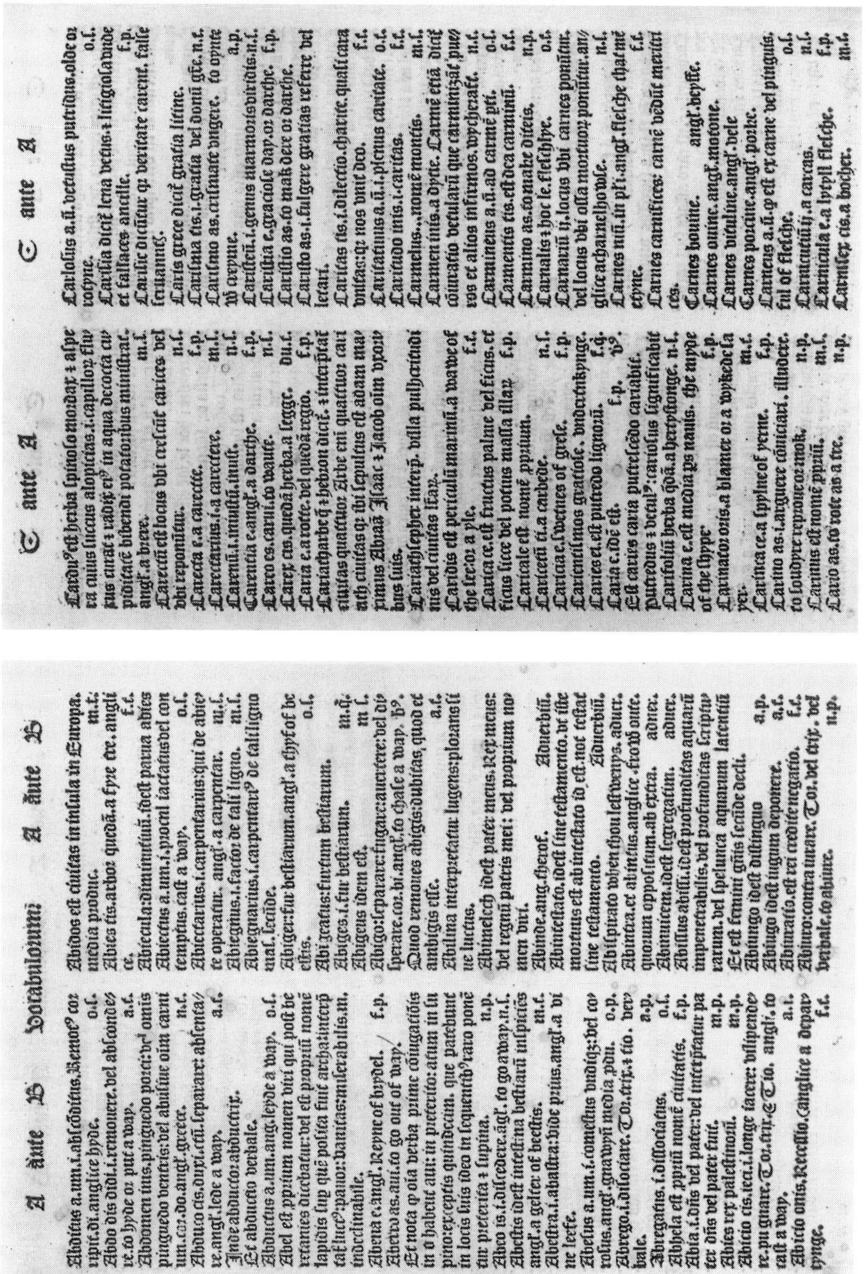

Actual size (each page): 240 × 167 mm

Fig. 5. *Ortus vocabulorum*. Westminster, 1500.
Duff 202. British Library G.7620.
Type 4C: 94G, with wrong-fount capitals from type 8.
(*left*) leaf A2verso, with wrong-fount A (l. 34) and I (l. 10). (*right*) leaf E8 verso, l. 17, with I³ (Iacob) and wrong-fount I (Isaac).

what I would have been capable of doing in the context of *BMC*.[22] Generally, however, I may point out that there is a risk in concentrating on single tales, as successively Sir Walter Greg for the Knight's Tale, W. F. Hutmacher for the General Prologue and the Knight's Tale, and T. Garbáty for the Tale of Sir Topas, have done, leading from the particular instance to generalizations in, for example, the textual note in the River-side Chaucer, that are plainly wrong, namely that Wynkyn de Worde simply reprinted Caxton's second edition.[23] A book as textual source has to be examined as an integral production, as well as in its constituent textual parts.

The main impact of the analysis of Type 4 is, indubitably, on the chronology and overall survey of Wynkyn de Worde's production, sometimes suggesting that the texts produced by him should be viewed in a somewhat different context. Whereas the other sets of type that Wynkyn de Worde acquired between 1492 and 1500 or took over from Caxton's shop are stable, showing no development, the almost constant internal development of his Type 4 permits the establishing of a new chronological arrangement of the books printed in this type, in so far as they are represented in the British Library or examined in copies elsewhere. The result is presented in the Appendix, with indications where significant changes with the dating of undated editions in Duff and *STC* are found. The dating by Duff in particular relied heavily on the state of devices and woodcuts, taking progressive deterioration as evidence. In the case of the cracks appearing in the much-used crucifixion woodcut (Hodnett 374) this is undoubtedly correct; the cracks appearing in device C, also a woodcut, play an important part in dating books printed in state 4C of the type and therefore assigned to 1499 or 1500. However, the impressions of device B, the smaller printer's device that de Worde used as an alternative to Caxton's large device, seem to vary with the quality of the press-work; where dating based on the state of the device suggested by its impression and the state of the type appear to be in conflict, I have taken the state of the type as decisive evidence.

In the Appendix the 48 items in The British Library are marked with an asterisk. Obviously, it was possible for me to examine (and re-examine) them more extensively than any of the items in other collections. I got acquainted with most of these on visits, later supplemented by photographs or microfilms, each of these methods being subject to limitations. As it stands, the Appendix is a vivid demonstration of the problems encountered when the descriptive work on a collection, even if it is a very large one, is expected to produce statements with more general application, as the previous volumes of *BMC* came to be relied on. Less than half of the surviving titles of Wynkyn de Worde's output before 1501 are represented in The British Library. The proposed chronological listing has therefore to be considered as provisional; also, the linear presentation may be somewhat misleading, because distinct type-cases may have been used in parallel, for instance the Latin type-case as distinct from the type-cases used for printing English. Analysis of the paper stocks used may provide further refinement in the present groupings of undated editions.

Returning to detail, one change in particular may be pointed out. The pseudo-Eusebius, *Vita et Transitus Sancti Hieronymi*, shows all the characteristics of a very early phase of Type 4, thus placing the book early in de Worde's productions, instead of *c*. 1499 as was thought until now.[24] The book ends with an impression of device B (Fig. 6). This impression, however, is slightly different from any of the other im-

⁋ Alia Oracio: Antifona

Aue amator quam famose Ieronime gloriose Mag
nus amator xpi: Doce nos bene viuere Deum vere
diligere vt in libris scripsisti/O amator castitatis.
Tenens vitam puritatis Cordis per mūdiciā fac
nos corpus castigare p pecatis qz ploiare diuinam
per graciā:Emuli te laniabāt Sed nequaqz super
abāt per inpaciēciā Ob amoie ihesu xpi fac iplere
quod fecisti Nos per diligēciam/ v. Oia pio nobis
gloiose ieronime Rz vt deū diligam⁹ coide oie ꝫ ope
Eus qui gloriosū cōfessoie tuū ieronimū mul
tis diuersaz nacionū linguis peritū.sacre bibli
e trāslatoie esse magna ex parte voluisti et ecclesie
tue doctoie luminosū fecisti presta qs nobis xpianis
et oībz iu mūdo creaturis racionis capacibus vt ei⁹
Doctrinā ꝫ exēpla bone vite sequētes in te fideliter
credam⁹ mētis mūdiciā teneam⁹ te toto coide dili
gam⁹ pro inimicis ex coide vero preces fundam⁹:et
in hiis perseuerātes:te doctore:te duce/ad te in celū
peiueniamus Per xpz;dominū nostroū amen .

10 MR 70

Printed by Caxton.

Fig. 6. Pseudo-Eusebius, *Vita et Transitus Sancti Hieronymi*. [Westminster, 1493].
Duff 236. British Library IA.55267, leaf D5 verso.   Actual size: 155 × 102 mm
Type 4:96G, early state.
with addition of E from type 2 (l. 7).   Device B, with double frame lines at top and bottom.
ampersand[1] (l. 10).

25

Fig. 7. John Mirk, *Liber festivalis*. Westminster, 1493.　　　Actual size: 172 × 114 mm
Duff 307. British Library, IA.55162, leaf ꝥ 5 verso.
Type 4: 96G, early state.
ampersand[2] first introduced (l. 22).　　Device B, with single frame-lines at top and bottom.
1-line lombards (ll. 5, 26).

pressions; the earliest of those is found in a dated edition of John Mirk's *Liber festialis*, of 1493, where Type 4 is found one stage more advanced in its development than in the Eusebius. In the Eusebius the device has a double line at the top and bottom of the border, whereas in all other impressions this is a single line (Fig. 7). In large-scale projection at the presentation of this lecture at the conference, some other small differences were obvious to the sharp-eyed typographers in the audience. The differences are, however, very small, and it seems therefore likely that the marks (the unique version of the mark in the Eusebius, and the mark designated as device B) were cast from the same metal mould. Wynkyn de Worde may not only have ordered a set of matrices from Paris, and a set of matching small lombard initials, but may perhaps be seen here to have decided to confirm the identity of his workshop in so far as it was an independent printing enterprise by ordering an elegant printer's device cast in metal. We can only speculate to what extent the various use of the two devices, Caxton's old device and de Worde's new one, should be taken as deliberately distinct, partly as tribute to Wynkyn de Worde's former master, and possibly also as indicators of dependence and independence as arranged in intricate financial arrangements with Caxton's estate.

The groupings of editions, provisional as the present result may be, begin to give rise to a picture of a more coherent publishing policy than Wynkyn de Worde has usually been given credit for. The small Lydgate quartos, included in his programme early on, could be marketed together to form collective volumes according to the taste and purse of the buyers; the devotional texts and the grammatical works were assembled in the same way. From the present record it would appear that buyers were offered increasingly ample choices. Even when allowing for the vagaries of survival it may still be instructive to compare the range of titles on offer in 1494, 1496, and 1498. The wider variety of books that were produced suggests that Wynkyn de Worde was in the course of pursuing a successful publishing strategy.

APPENDIX

Chronology of books printed by Wynkyn de Worde before 1501

The 48 items marked with an asterisk are in the collection of the British Library. Dates appearing in imprints are printed in bold type.

proposed date	Duff		type	Duff dated	STC	STC dated
*(1492-3)	85	Chastising	2+3	[1493]	5065	[1493]
(1492-3)	399	Treatise	2+3	[1493]	24234	[1493]
*(1492-3)	403	St Catherine	1+2	[1491-3]	24766	[1492?]
*20.5.93	410	Golden Legend	1+2		24875	
(1493)	54	Courtesy	3	[1491-3]	3304	[1492]
*(1493)	182	Horae	4+2	[1494]	15875	[1494]

Type 4:96G, *with lower case w and additional E from type 2 (Caxton type 8)*

*(1493)	183	Horae	4+2	[1494]	15876	[1494]
*(1493)	236	Hier. Trans.	4	[1499]	14508	[1499?]

proposed date	Duff		type	Duff dated	STC	STC dated
Type 4 *without additional* E						
(1493?)	182	(Lambeth) Horae	4+2	(not recorded as a distinct edition)		
(1493?)	185	Horae	2	[1494]	15878	[1494]
Type 4 *with* yᵉ, yᵗ, yᵘ. I² *added. A few* I *from type 1 (Caxton type 4) only in this edn*						
*(1493)	271	Lydg. Temple	4	[1500]	17032a	[1495?]
Type 4 *with* wᵗ, *terminal* m *and terminal* n *added.* &² *replaces* &¹						
*1493	307	Mirk	4+2		17962 pt.1	
*1494	308	IV Serm.	4+2		17962 pt.2	
*1494	203	Hylton	2		14042	
*1494	50	Bonaventura	2+5		3261	
Type 4 *with* W¹ *added*						
(1494)	110	Cordiale	4+2	[1499]	5759	[1496]
(c.1494)	364	Rote	4	[1496]	21334	[1496]
*(c.1494)	255	Lydg. Assemb.	4+6	[1500]	17007	[1500?]
Type 4 *with* Y *added*						
*(c.1494)	259	Lydg. Churl	4+6	[1500]	17011	[1497?]
*(c.1494)	268	Lydg. Siege	4	[1500]	17031	[1497?]
(c.1494)	263	Lydg. Horse	4	[1500]	17020	[c.1495]
(1495)	231	Introductor.	4+6	[1495]	13809	[1495]
Type 4 *with gradual introduction of* looped L² *and* K *from type 1*						
*13.4.95	173	Polycronicon	4+2		13439	
Type 4 *with reintroduction of* &¹, *in addition to* &²						
*1495	235	Hieronymus	4+2		14507	
(1495)	134	Accedence	4	[1499]	23153.5	[1499]
(*Latin type-case of type 4*)						
*1495	293	Maydestone	4+6		17723	
(1495-6)	131	Donatus	4+6	[1496]	7016	[1496?]
(1495-6)	133	Stanbridge	4+6	[1495]	23153.4	[1495]
(1495-6)	343	Parvula	4+6	[1496]	231633.6	[1496?]
Type 4 *with* terminal d *and* h *added and characters for printing law French*						
(early 1496)	381	Statutes 1Hvii	4	[1496]	9349	[1496?]
(early 1496)	382	Statutes 7Hvii	4	[1496]	9351a.7	[1496?]
(early? 1496}	384	Statutes 11Hvii	4+6	[1496]	9353	[1496?]
*(early? 1496)	385	Statutes 11Hvii	4+6	[1496]	9354	[1496]
(before 9.3.96)	397	Three Kings	4	(1496)	5572	[1496?]
9.3.96	41	Bernardus	4+6		1916	
*1496	57	Bk of Hawking	7		3309	

proposed date	Duff		type	Duff dated	*STC*	*STC dated*
(Latin type-case of type 4)						
*31.5.96	279	Lyndewode	4+2		17103	
Type 4 *including 'legal' characters*						
*(1496)	40	Barth. Anglicus	4+6	[1495]	1536	[1495]
22.9.96	12	Alcock, Mons	4		278	
(c.1496)		Abb. Holy Ghost	4		13608.7	[1496]
*(c.1496)	15	Alcock, Serm.	4	[1499]	282	[1499?]
(c.1496)	17	Alcock, Serm.	4+6	[1497]	284	[1497?]
*(c.1496)	151	Fitzjames, Serm.	4+6	[1495]	11024	[1495?]
*(c.1496)	342	Parvula	4+6	[1496]	23163.7	[1497?]
(c.1496)	225	Inf. Pilgrims	4+6	[1498]	14081	[1500]
*1496	312	Mirk	4+2		17965 pt.1	
*1496	313	IV Serm.	4+2		17965 pt.2	
Type 4 *without the* looped L^2						
*3.12.96	340	Dives & Pauper	4+6		19213	
*23.5.97	13	Alcock, Mons	4+2		279	
*(c.5.97)	1	Abb. H. Ghost	4+6	[1496]	13609	[1497?]

Type 4 RECAST *on smaller body with* L^2 *only,*
     type 4A: *94G, terminal* m1, n1, y, y, w^r *gradually replaced by* m^2, n^2, y^2, y^2 *and* w^2.
     type 4B: *94G, with* W^2 *replacing* W^1. m^2, n^2, y^2, y^2 *and* w^2 *the dominant forms.*
In the setting of Latin it is usually not possible to distinguish between sub-states 4A, 4B, and 4C

*1497	102	Chronicles	4A+4B+6		9996	
*1498	114	Descr.Brit.	4B+6		13440b	
*(c.1497-8)	264	Lydg. Horse	4A	[1500]	170021	[1499?]
(c.1497-8)	353	Propr. Horse	4A+6	[n.d.]	20439.5	[1525]
(1497-8)	19	Alcock, Spons.	4B+6	[1496]	286	[c.1497]
(1497-8)	18	Alcock, Serm.	4B+6	[1497]	285	[c.1497]
(1497-8)	16	Alcock, Serm.	4B+6	[1498]	283	[1498?]
(1497-8)	20	Alcock, Exh.	4B	[1497]	287	[c.1497]
(1497-8)	34	Ars moriendi	4B	[1497]	787	[1497]
(1497-8)	126	Doctrinal	4B	[1498]	6931	[1498]
(1497-8)	350	Prognost.	4B	[1497]	385.3	[1498]
(1497-8)	221	Indulgence	4B[Lat]	[1499]	14077b.148	[c.1499]
*1498	90	Canterb. Tales	4A+6		5085	
*(1498)	253	Lydg. Assembly	A+6	[1498]	7005	[1498]
(not bf.1498)	228	Bull	4A-C+6[Lat]	[1494]	14097	[1494]
25.3.98	284	Malory	4A+4B+6		802	
*(1498)	213	Indulgence	2+5	[1498]	14077c.86	[1498]
(1497-8)	286	Mandeville	4 B	[1499, after 10.7]	17247	[1499]
(1497-8)	171	Guy	4AorB(?)	[1500]	12541	[1497?]
*(1497-8)	251	Legrand	4B	[1498]	15397	[1498]
(1498-9)	232	Introduct.	4B+6	[1499]	13810	[1499]

proposed date	Duff		type	Duff dated	STC	STC dated
Type 4C: 94G, *with* I³ *added in Latin type-case of type 4*						
*(1499)	229	Bull	4A-C[Lat]+2	[1495]	14098	[1495]
(1499)	296	Maydestone	4C+2	[1499]	17726	[1499]
15.4.99	280	Lyndewode	4C		17104	
Type 4C: *with* I³ *and with* W² *only*						
*8.1.1498/9(?)	411	Golden Leg.	4B+4C+2+6		24876	
*19.4.99	157	Joh. de Garl.	8+9		11602	
20.5.99	355	Psalterium	8		16254	
*10.7.99	106	Contemplation	4C+6		5643	
Type 4C *with* W¹ *and* W²						
*(c.July 1499]	407	Treatise	4C+2	[1497]	24866	[1497]
*(1499, after 10.7)	398	Three kings	4C+2	[1499]	5573	[after 10.7.99]
(1499, after 10.7)	365	Rote	4C	[1499]	21335	[c.1499?]
(1499, after 10.7)	400	Profits	4C+2	[1499]	20412	[1499]
(1499)	372	Skelton, Bowge	4C	[1499]	22597	[1499?]
*4.12.99	390	Sulpitius	8+9		23427	
(after 4.12.99)	43	Betson	4C	[1500]	1978	[1500]
*(1499)	42	Bern. Medit.	4C+2	[1499]	1917	[1499?]
*1499	317	Mirk	4C+2		17967 (I)	
*(1499)	318	IV Sermones	4C		17967 (II)	
(1499-1500)		Merlin	4C		17840	[1510]
(1499-1500)	135	Eglamoure	4C	[1500]	7541	[1500]
(1499-1500)	254	Lydg. Assembly	6+8	[1500}	17006	[c.1500]
(1499-1500)	272	Lydg. Temple	2+8	[1500]	17033	[1500?]
(1500?)	44	Bevis	4C	[1500]	1987	[1500]
(1500)		Bevis	4C		1987.5	[c.1500]
(1500)	107	Contempl.	4C		14546	[1500?]
*1500	202	Ortus vocab.	4C		13829	
6.2-17.3.99/00	142	Hym. & Sequ.	6+8+9	1499	16114	[1500]
*12.3.1500	162	Garlandia	8+9		17006	
Capitals of type 4 mixed in with type 8						
(1500 or later)	383	Statutes 11Hvii	8+6	[1496]	9352	[1500?]
after 1500?	356	Remigius	4C	[1500]	20878	[1500?]

Not included are:
Duff 361 (*STC* 13689.3: York, H. Goes, 1506?)
Duff 344 (*STC* 23163.11: [1501?])

Not seen:
Duff 2, 185, 265, 297, 413

ILLUSTRATIONS IN PARISIAN BOOKS OF HOURS

BORDERS AND REPERTOIRES

MARY BETH WINN

PARIS HAS LONG BEEN recognized as the centre of production for Books of Hours, from the earliest editions of the 1480s well into the sixteenth century. Because of their abundance as well as their beauty, Parisian Books of Hours have been prized by collectors but greeted with perhaps somewhat less enthusiasm by bibliographers facing the daunting task of describing them. Typical bibliographical records – of titles and colophons, format and collation, text incipits and illustrations – do not always adequately describe the Hours' rather complex combinations of texts, both Latin and vernacular, and images, both sacred and secular, in layouts that vary incessantly even when certain patterns have become conventional. Perhaps more than other volumes, moreover, Books of Hours require attention to copy-specific details – manuscript annotations, miniatures, coats of arms, etc. because these books served so often as family registers.

My consideration of the illustrations in Parisian Books of Hours begins with an element of text: namely, a repertoire which appears in some of the earliest Parisian editions produced by Jean Du Pré and Anthoine Vérard. The repertoire is in fact a table of images used in the book, and the very presence of a repertoire underscores the importance that publishers attributed to their illustrations. But the repertoried illustrations are not always, indeed not often, the large pictures which set off the major divisions of the text, those which announce, for example, the beginning of Matins or Lauds, the Penitential Psalms or the Office of the Dead. They are not those typically cited in catalogues and used to discriminate among printers' editions. Most of the known repertoires refer to small images, located not in centre page, but in the borders.

The centre page of the Book of Hours was reserved for the core texts, the prayers and devotions to be recited at each of the canonical hours of the day, and for their illustrations, the subjects of which had already become standardized. The margin of the page, however, as printers soon recognized, offered space for innovations which could distinguish their editions from those of their competitors. Newly created border pieces began therefore to 'frame' the Hours, surrounding the standard liturgical texts in centre page with new and varied words and pictures.

A century ago, in his landmark studies of early illustrated Books of Hours, A. W. Pollard noted that many borders formed a 'continuous series' which 'reinforced the teaching of the main illustrations'.[1] For the earliest of these series, a typological life of Christ based on the analogy between Old and New Testament figures, Pollard rightly noted that the printer himself (Jean Du Pré) underscored the importance of the borders in an elaborate five-page repertoire included at the beginning of the book. For Pollard as well as for the great French bibliographer Anatole Claudin,[2] this repertoire was significant not so much for its contents as for its revelation that the illustrations were printed with metal rather than wood: 'imprimees en cuyvre'. I would like, in contrast, to examine this, and other, repertoires for what they say, and then to investigate the repertoried elements themselves – the images, and their placement within the book.

REPERTOIRES

Repertoires are quite uncommon in Books of Hours, and for that reason alone they attract our interest, but they also demand careful attention, for not all repertoires are the same. Jean Du Pré used two different repertoires, a fact which seems to have been largely overlooked. Both Pollard and Claudin cite Du Pré's repertoire of 4 February 1488/89 with its important reference to printing on copper, but this repertoire is in fact the second one used by Du Pré. The first appeared nearly a year earlier, in an edition of 28 March 1487/88; it makes no mention of the materials used, and it lists images found within the text. Its very presence suggests that Du Pré wanted not just to identify the subject of the illustrations but also to call them to readers' attention, presumably because they were new and different. Du Pré printed only three dated editions prior to this one, of which two were for Anthoine Vérard. All three used a set of just ten woodcuts for the major sections of the book.[3] Du Pré's repertoire rightly emphasizes, therefore, his innovation: this edition of 28 March 1487/88 employs 42 images to illustrate not merely the major divisions of the Hours, but individual lessons and psalms within those divisions.

Repertoire I is known from three editions, all for the use of Rome: 28 March 1487/88,[4] 10 May 1488,[5] and an undated edition presumably post-dating the other two.[6] Although the content of the repertoire is largely the same, a few differences are noteworthy. The first example from March 1487/88 is printed on the first three pages of a separate gathering, signed with four dots in triangle formation and thus independent of the alphabetical signatures for the rest of the book. It is bound as the first gathering in the Berlin copy of the edition, but as the last in the Wrocław copy.[7] The introductory rubric specifies that the images of the repertoire are 'spread through-out the Hours': 'S'ensuit la table des hystoires semees parmy les heures, pseaulmes et leçons'[8] (Fig. 1). The wording is as significant as the number of images listed: 42 in all. Besides providing illustrations for the beginning of the main sections of the Hours, as expected, Du Pré has added images for each of the psalms recited within those sections. His repertoire therefore begins with the Annunciation, typically used to announce Matins, but ends with the mother of Tobias, to illustrate the third lesson of the Office of Advent. Moreover, while the Annunciation is a large woodcut (113 × 81 mm),[9] all the others – those for the beginning of Lauds, Prime, and the other Hours, as well as those for the individual psalms and lessons – are small (36-40 × 28 mm).[10] Du Pré's innovation, as the repertoire emphasizes, is not one of size but of quantity: there are numerous pictures throughout the Hours.

The repertoire lists the images in the order in which they appear in the Hours and articulates the list by indenting the first line of each item. In the Berlin copy, painted paragraph markers further highlight this articulation. For each image, the table provides a brief description, usually introduced by the word 'Comme', then the Biblical source, and finally the Latin incipit of the lesson or psalm which it illustrates: 'Comme Nostre Seigneur est au buysson parlant a Moyse au .iii. chapitre de Exode. secunda lectio. Et sic in Syon' (Fig. 1). Since this Latin incipit is printed next to the image in the book, it serves both to locate the image and to verify its subject. For the images used at the beginning of each Hour, the table cites the name of that Hour in its description. Thus the Visitation, used to begin the section of Lauds (Fig. 2), is listed in the repertoire as follows: 'Hystoire de la visitacion Nostre Dame a Elizabeth au premier chapitre saint Luc. Laudes. Deus in adiutorium' (Fig. 1).

The table is not comprehensive: some pictures in the book are absent from the repertoire. Among those not included are the smaller woodcuts illustrating the Hours of the Cross and of the Holy Spirit, even though in this edition of 'mixed' Hours they are interspersed with those of the Hours of the Virgin. These and other exclusions are noted in a statement printed below the last item in the table:

Et tout le residu des hystoires tant des sept Pseaulmes, des Heures de la Croix et du saint Esperit que aussi des Vigilles des mors et de plusieurs suffraiges de saintz et sainctes mis a devocion en la fin de cesdictes heures n'en faisons en ceste presente table aucune mencion pour ce qu'ilz sont assés communes et en usaige. Et aussi pour eviter prolixité de langaige. [Fig. 3.]

This text is worth analysing on several fronts. First of all, it indicates that the printer classified the images according to the texts which they illustrate. The 'hystoires' constitute sets, determined by their use within the book. Du Pré has summarized the subjects for the core text, the Hours of the Virgin, but has gone no further, he says, for two reasons: first, the remaining pictures are 'assés communes' – rather ordinary or familiar, and 'en usaige', in common use. It would seem that Du Pré wanted to distinguish his own, unique, illustrations from the more common ones used by other printers. Second, a longer table would run the risk of excessive prolixity. This dual argument, founded on both iconographic and verbal elements, suggests that the printer anticipated a certain level of visual literacy on the part of his readers and, perhaps, some impatience with too much explanation.[11]

The statement on the omission of certain subjects is nonetheless accurate. The repertoire excludes the small images of the evangelists, the Passion of Christ, and the saints as well as two large woodcuts, of David and of the Feast of Dives, used respectively to begin the Penitential Psalms and the Office of the Dead. In addition to these large pictures, a single, smaller illustration is used for each of these sections: David kneeling in prayer, for the Psalms, and the skeletal figure of Death seizing the Pope, for the Office of the Dead. All these images were perhaps, as the repertoire states, so familiar to readers as to need no explanation. The saints, even if not immediately recognizable by their emblems, were identified by name in the text accompanying the corresponding picture. One wonders, nonetheless, whether size or prior use had any bearing on the exclusion of the two larger images from the repertoire. Finding conclusive answers to these questions is hindered by difficulties of comparing extant editions now located in geographically distant collections, of ascertaining how many editions Du Pré actually produced, and of dating those that are known. These impediments notwithstanding, if Du Pré used the repertoire to announce only the new images, then his exclusion of

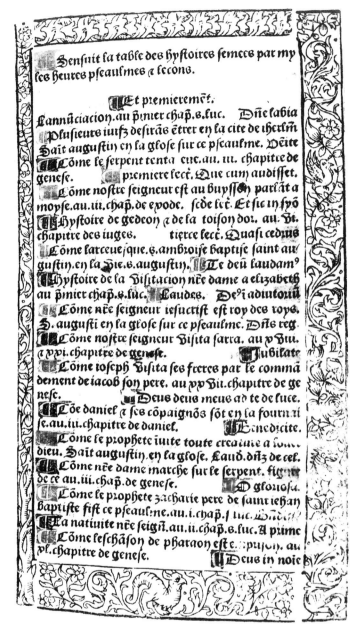

Fig. 1. Du Pré, Hours for the use of Rome, 28 March 1487/88, fol. ∴1ʳ (Berlin SB, Inc. 4735): beginning of the repertoire.

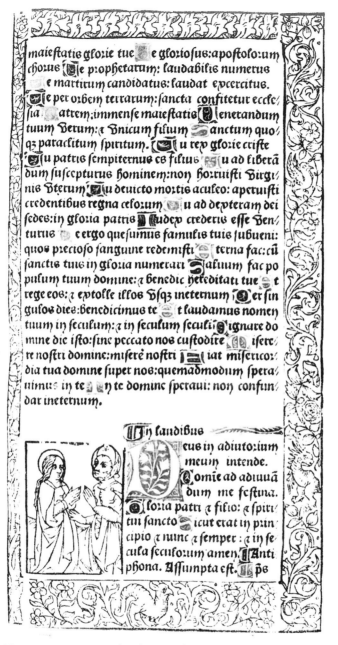

maieftatis gloꞛie tue e gloꞛiofus:apoftoloꞛum
choꞛus e pꞛophetarum: laudabilis numerus
e martirum candidatus: faudat epcercitus.
e per oꞛbem terrarum:fancta confitetur eccle/
fia atrem:immenfe maieftatis enerandum
tuum Verum:ꞇ Vnicum filium anctum quo/
qꝫ paraclitum fpiritum. u reꞅ gloꞛie crifte
u patris fempiternus es filius u ad liberã
dum fufceptutus hominem:non hoꞛruifti Virgi/
nis Vterum u deuicto moꞛtis aculeo: aperuifti
credentibus regna celoꞛum u ad depteram dei
fedes:in gloꞛia patris udep crederis effe Ven/
turus e ergo quefumus famulis tuis fubueni:
quos pꞛeciofo fanguine redemifti terna fac:cũ
fanctis tuis in gloꞛia numerari aluum fac po
pufum tuum domine:ꞇ benedic hereditati tue t
rege eos:ꞇ eptolle illos Vfqꝫ ineternum er fin
gufos dies:benedicimus te t laudamus nomen
tuum in feculum:ꞇ in feculum feculi ignare do
mine die ifto:fine peccato nos cuftodite ifere/
re noftri domine:mifere noftri iat mifericoꞛ
dia tua domine fuper nos:quemadmodum fpera/
uimus in te n te domine fpetaui: non confun
dar ineternum.

In laudiBus
eus in adiutoꞛium
meum intende.
omie ad adiuuã
dum me feftina.
foꞛia patri ꞇ filio: ꞇ fpiri
tui fancto icut erat in pꞛin
cipio ꞇ nunc ꞇ femper : ꞇ in fe
cula feculoꞛum amen. Anti
phona. Affumpta eft. ꝑs

Fig. 2. Du Pré, Hours for the use of Rome, 28 March 1487/88,
fol. b4ʳ (Berlin SB, Inc. 4735): woodcut of the Visitation to begin
Lauds.

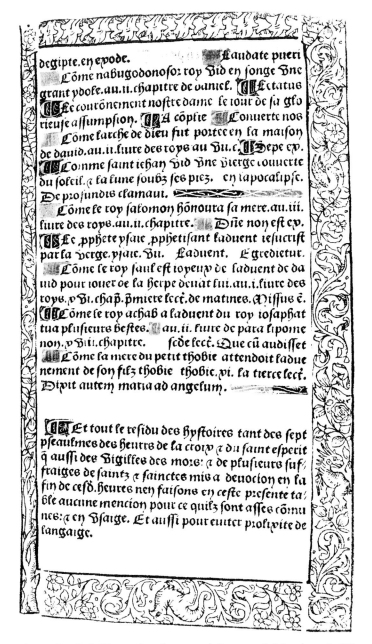

Fig. 3. Du Pré, Hours for the use of Rome, 28 March 1487/88, fol. ∴2ʳ (Berlin SB, Inc. 4735): end of the repertoire.

certain ones offers an invaluable guide to the chronology of his editions and indeed to the dating of his illustrations.[12]

The second use of Repertoire I occurred two months after the first, in an edition dated 10 May 1488. This edition is printed in two columns of 28 lines each, a detail whose relevance will shortly be seen. The presence of the repertoire is obscured somewhat by its placement in a separate gathering of four leaves, signed on the first two leaves by four dots in triangle formation, again unrelated to the alphabetical signatures in the rest of the volume. The repertoire begins, moreover, only at line 15 of column 2 of fol. 3^r, after the Office of the Conception of the Virgin (Fig. 4). That this was confusing is suggested by the placement of the gathering at the beginning of the Chantilly copy, but at the end of the Paris copy. More significant still, while fol. 3^r is printed in two columns, as for the rest of the book, fol. 3^v and all of fol. 4 are printed in a single column of 28 lines (Fig. 5) – so that, apart from the first three items, the repertoire is printed in the long lines used for the earlier edition of March 1487/88. As in that edition, the repertoire describes images printed within the text, running from the Annunciation to the mother of Tobias. However, the list is shorter than before, with 37 rather than 42 items.[13] This is because the May edition makes use of a new set of larger woodcuts for the main sections of the Hours, and only the first two of these (for Matins and Lauds) are cited in the repertoire. The woodcut for Lauds, for example (Fig. 6), is substantially larger (80 × 46 mm) than that used in the previous edition (Fig. 2), and it is further enlarged on three sides by the addition of rectangular pieces so as to occupy a space of 103 × 70 mm.[14] The space allotted has been dictated by the use of three even larger woodcuts (103 × 70 mm): Adam and Eve driven from the garden of Eden, the Death of Uriah, and the Last Judgement. The May edition in fact presents two sets of large-format woodcuts, and only the first two, the Annunciation and the Visitation, are cited in the May repertoire, as they had been in March.

The rubric introducing the repertoire in the May edition is shorter than in the previous example and less insistent on the placement of images. It uses the word 'repertoire' rather than 'table': 'C'est le repertoire des histoires contenues en ces presentes Heures.' At the end of the list of images for the Hours of the Virgin, there is a summary statement about the illustrations for the Penitential Psalms and for the Office of the Dead:

Pour les sept Pseaulmes y a vii. histoires de David extraictes de plusieurs chapitres de la Bible.
    Item aux Vigilles des mors sont dix histoires contenantes la vie de Job extraictes de la Bible comme dessus. [Fig. 5.]

A concluding statement follows: 'Cy fine la table des histoires contenues en ces presentes Heures.'

Although no details are given about the individual subjects for the Psalms and Vigils, Du Pré does not dismiss the images as too common to cite, but emphasizes instead their Biblical source. His count, however, needs clarification. The Psalms are illustrated by two large and six small woodcuts. The large illustrations are both new to this edition: the Death of Uriah (103 × 70 mm) and David and Bathsheba (80 × 46 mm). The small woodcuts have the same dimensions as those repertoried for the Hours of the Virgin, and it seems likely that Du Pré mentions them here because they are new. The March edition had used only one small and one large woodcut of David, both different from

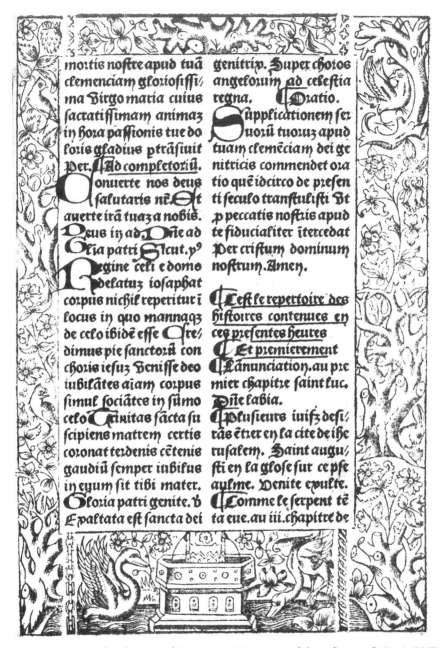

Fig. 4. Du Pré, Hours for the use of Rome, 10 May 1488, fol. .:.3ᵛ = 101ᵛ (Paris BNF, Rés. B. 27672): beginning of the repertoire. (cliché Bibliothèque nationale de France – Paris)

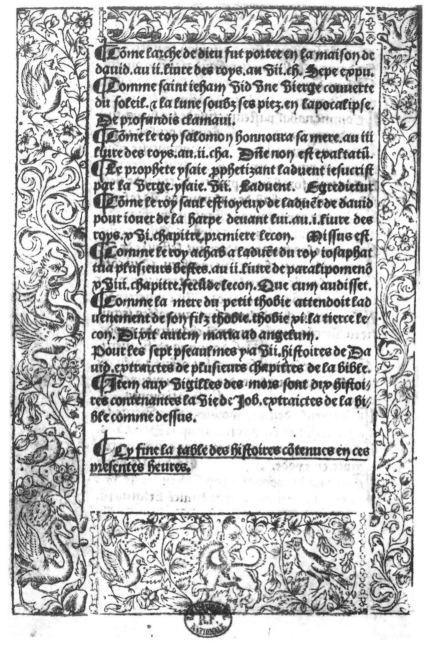

Fig. 5. Du Pré, Hours for the use of Rome, 10 May 1488, fol. .:.4^v = 102^v (Paris BNF, Rés. B. 27672): end of the repertoire. (cliché Bibliothèque nationale de France – Paris)

Fig. 6. Du Pré, Hours for the use of Rome, 10 May 1488, fol. b5ᵛ (Paris BNF, Rés. B. 27672): woodcut of the Visitation, for the beginning of Lauds. (cliché Bibliothèque nationale de France – Paris)

those used in May, and both omitted from the repertoire. Du Pré's tally of 'vii histoires' must include one of the large woodcuts, in addition to the six small ones, or else reflect an error in counting. It seems plausible that the woodcut of Uriah, more 'uncommon' in both size and subject than those of David, warranted mention in the repertoire.

The Office of the Dead is likewise illustrated by two large and nine small images. The latter, again of the same format as those repertoried in the Hours of the Virgin, depict episodes in the life of Job. Since they seem to be new to this edition, the repertoire calls them to the readers' attention. The first of the large woodcuts portrays the Last Judgement (103 × 70 mm), and it seems likely that Du Pré referred to this one in his total of ten since the second large woodcut, the Feast of Dives (113 × 77 mm), was used in the prior edition of March and not cited in the repertoire at that time. Du Pré's count of ten illustrations for the Vigils seems, as for the Psalms, to highlight the new work.

It should be noted that in addition to being cited in the repertoire, most of the small woodcuts in this edition are identified within the text itself by a caption in French, printed vertically to the side of the image. Thus, the image of Moses and the Burning Bush is identified: 'Figure de Moyse ou iii. chapitre d'Exode' (Fig. 7).[15] The repertoire would seem redundant, but in fact its descriptions are usually longer than the captions, and it includes the Latin incipit of the psalm or lesson illustrated by each image. The repertoire helps, moreover, to locate the images within the book by citing them in the order of their appearance.

The small woodcuts *not* cited in the repertoire are similarly identified by captions next to them in the text. The nine images of the cycle of Job, for example, are explained by corresponding phrases: 'Job parlant a sa femme et a ses enfans' (fol. g4^r), 'le dyable voulant batre Job' (fol. g6^v), and so forth. In this edition, some of the large woodcuts also bear texts in French. Thus, the picture of Adam and Eve driven from the garden of Eden by an Angel (103 × 70 mm) is identified by two lines of verse printed below: 'Par le pechié de desobeissance / se mist Adam et nous tous en souffrance.' Since this scene was surely recognized by readers, the text probably reflects Du Pré's experimentation with captions in verse more than his concern with readers' comprehension of the subject.

In the third and final example of its use, Repertoire I is altered once again for an undated edition printed by Du Pré for Antoine Caillaut. It appears in long lines, 21 lines to the page, as the first gathering of the book (fols 1^v-4^r), beginning on the verso of the title-page, which contains only Caillaut's device. Both the title ('C'est le repertoire …') and the conclusion ('Cy fine la table …') are identical to the May 1488 edition, and 37 images are described. At the end, however, no mention is made of the illustrations for the Office of the Dead, which consist of only two images, both of them large: one of the Three Living and the Three Dead (116 × 82 mm, fol. k7^r), and the other of the Feast of Dives (113 × 77 mm, fol. l2^v). The latter had been used in the March 1487/88 edition. The former, whose design and dimensions relate it to the earlier series,[16] seemingly makes its first appearance here. Because it is not cited in the repertoire, however, it seems likely to have been used prior to this edition, even though its dated use elsewhere is not yet attested.

For the Penitential Psalms, the Caillaut edition uses the same large woodcut of David and Goliath as in the March edition as well as the set of six small woodcuts of David found in the May edition. Despite their re-use here, the repertoire includes these

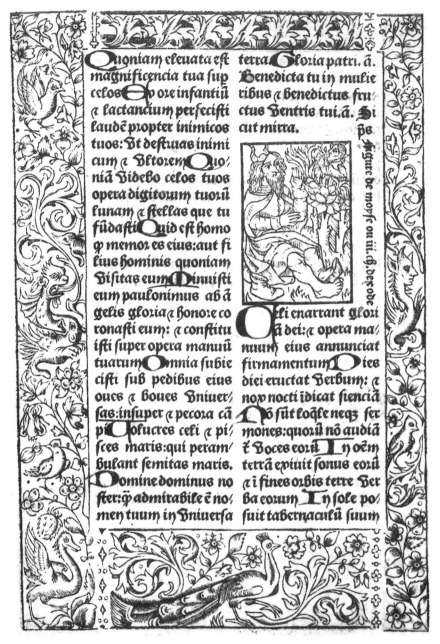

Fig. 7. Du Pré, Hours for the use of Rome, 10 May 1488, fol. b2ᵛ (Paris BNF, Rés. B. 27672): woodcut of Moses and the Burning Bush. (cliché Bibliothèque nationale de France – Paris)

'hystoires' in the repertoire, introducing them with the same statement as in the May edition: 'Pour les sept pseaulmes y a vii histoires de David. extraictes de plusieurs chapitres de la Bible.'

To summarize, it appears from the three examples of its use that Repertoire I served to announce and identify the new illustrations which Du Pré had developed for his Hours, in particular for the most important section of the book, the Office of the Virgin. It focuses primarily on the small woodcuts placed within the text to illustrate not just the beginning of each Hour, but rather all the lessons and psalms of the Office. The set is unusual therefore in quantity as well as in iconography. While the eight subjects for the beginning of each canonical Hour were quite standardized by the time Du Pré issued his edition of 1487/88, the 32 additional images for the individual lessons and psalms had few precedents. Du Pré drew partly upon the *Speculum Humanae Salvationis*, partly upon the *Biblia Pauperum*, whose relevance for the second type of repertoire is essential, as we shall now see.[17]

The second type of repertoire displays an immediate difference in wording that bears not only upon the subject of the images but on their placement. According to Du Pré's edition of 4 February 1488/89:

C'est le repertoire des hystoires et figures de la Bible tant du Vieilz Testament que du Nouveau contenues dedens les vignettes de ces presentes heures, imprimees en cuyvre. En chascune desquelles vignettes sont contenues deux figures du Vieilz Testament signifians une vraye histoire du Nouveau. Comme il appert par les chapitres cottez et alleguez au propos, tant en latin que en françoys, en chascune desdites figures et histoires. [Fig. 8.]

This repertoire (henceforth called Repertoire II) contains a description of the pictures ('hystoires') and 'figures de la Bible' which are not spread throughout the Hours, as for Repertoire I, but contained in the 'vignettes' of the Hours. This distinction is important: Du Pré refers to the borders as 'vignettes', retaining the etymological derivation of the word.[18] This is evident from his statement that each vignette contains two Old Testament 'figures' which 'signify' or foretell one true New Testament 'hystoire'. The visual relationship, he further notes, is manifest in the written texts which accompany the images, the 'chapitres cottez et alleguez au propos'. Because each item consists of three pictures plus two Old Testament citations for each of the 49 items enumerated, the table occupies five full pages of text, 30 lines to the page. A simple concluding statement ('La fin de la table') marks the end of the repertoire on the last line of fol. 4ᵛ (Fig. 9). In this table, the first example is not the Annunciation, which is the first of the pictures cited in Repertoire I, but the Birth of Mary, which appears, as the table records, on the page after the Annunciation.[19] Each item in the table is again articulated by indentation of the first line and further highlighted in the London copy by manuscript paragraph markers. At the beginning of the table, the word 'Item' is used to distinguish seven items, but this practice was quickly abandoned. Since the repertoire does not include any Latin text from the page on which the pictures appear, one must determine their placement within the book by their order within the table.

This repertoire includes none of the main cuts used for the major sections of the book, but focuses solely on the border illustrations. The borders are a new typological set of 49 lateral pieces with a corresponding footpiece. The set is based upon the *Biblia Pauperum*, which summarizes the life of Christ in 40-50 major episodes, each of which

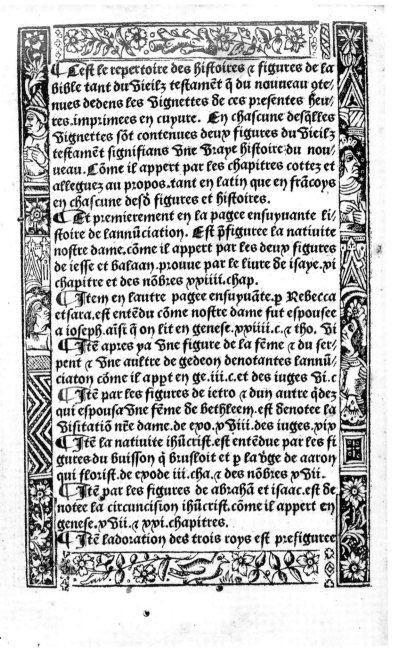

Fig. 8. Du Pré, Hours for the use of Rome, 4 February 1488/89, fol. 2ᵛ (London BL, IA. 39821): beginning of the repertoire.

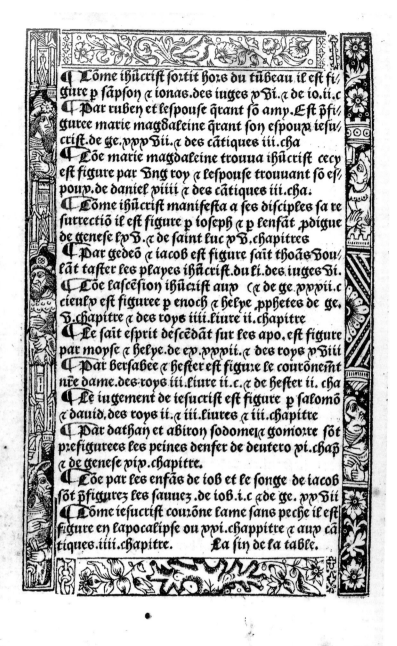

Fig. 9. Du Pré, Hours for the use of Rome, 4 February 1488/89, fol. 4ᵛ (London BL, IA. 39821): end of the repertoire.

is prefigured by two Old Testament events. The three related scenes are placed in the lateral piece, with the New Testament event in the centre, flanked above and below by its Old Testament prefigurations. This tripartite design is used by Du Pré, Vérard, and at least six other Parisian printers, albeit with some differences.

Du Pré's lengthy repertoire is repeated almost verbatim in several editions issued by Anthoine Vérard of which the earliest seems to be that of 8 February 1489/90.[20] However, according to one French source,[21] this same repertoire appeared in an edition of 8 October 1488, preceding by four months the earliest edition by Du Pré.[22] Vérard in fact championed the repertoire and the borders which it described, in editions from 1488 to 1490. Whoever initiated the series, the medium used for the borders apparently differed since Vérard omits the key words 'imprimees en cuyvre', suggesting that his border cuts were made of wood, not copper. Du Pré and Vérard each had a set of typological borders, similar to each other, but not identical.

Repertoire II also appeared in other editions by Vérard, but with variations. In an unsigned, undated, and uncatalogued edition in a private Dutch collection,[23] the introductory statement ('Cy commence le repertoire …') is followed by a new element: 'Et premierement, incontinent apres ceste presente table aux premiers fueilletz est pourtraite la creacion des anges, du ciel, et de la terre, avec la creacion de l'omme ainsi qu'il est escript en Genese au premier livre de la Bible &.1: chapitre' (Fig. 10). This is the first time the table refers to images that precede the typological series. The creation story is recounted in two large woodcuts and four borders.[24] Assuming that the publisher is using the repertoire to announce a new set of woodcuts, this edition would be the first to use the Creation series, in which case the edition must date from before 8 February 1489/90 when these woodcuts are also used but not listed in the repertoire to the edition.

In Vérard's Hours of 10 April 1489/90,[25] the introductory statement and the repertoire are the same as those cited above for Du Pré's edition of 4 February 1488/89, except for the reference to copper printing.[26] For the editions of 20 February 1489/90 and 20 July 1490, the repertoire is preceded by a lengthy prologue in French which explains the value of figural interpretation. A slightly earlier edition, dated 8 February 1489/90, provides the same repertoire and prologue, but both in Latin.[27] In these three editions with prologues, the typological borders themselves have been identified with guide letters and accorded lengthier descriptions in the table.[28]

If we compare the typological sets used by Du Pré and Vérard, the latter's distinctive corner design is striking, and it resulted in two important features (Fig. 11). First, each lateral border was joined to its own pair of prophets in the footpiece. More importantly, because of its L-shape, each border was restricted in placement to either the recto or verso of a page. The opening of the page was clearly framed by a pair of borders. Du Pré's set avoided the corner design, except for the first border, and his prophets could have been interchanged, but in fact, no two are identical.[29]

Du Pré cites the Biblical sources of the images within the borders themselves. In his edition, moreover, as the repertoire indicates, the 'figures' appear with explanatory inscriptions in two languages. The whole series of metal cuts is used twice, first with Latin, then with French texts. For example, the fifth typological border (Fig. 12) presents the Nativity between the two Old Testament types of Moses and the Burning Bush and Aaron's Flowering Rod. Above the former, a prophet holds a scroll with the

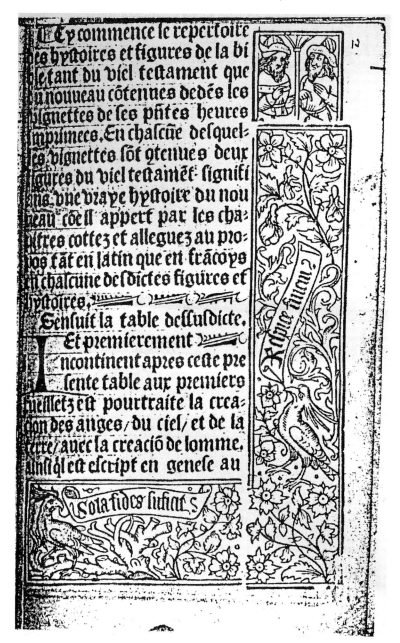

Fig. 10. [Vérard], Hours for the use of Rome, *c*.1488, fol. 12^r (priv. coll.): beginning of the repertoire.

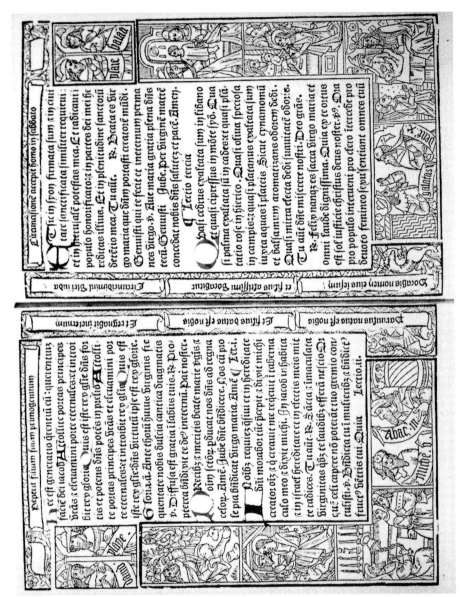

Fig. 11. Vérard, Hours for the use of Rome, 8 February 1489/90, fols a6ᵛ-a7ʳ (Typ Inc 8414.5, Department of Printing and Graphic Arts, Houghton Library of the Harvard College Library): typological borders no. 5, the Nativity, and no. 6, the Circumcision.

48

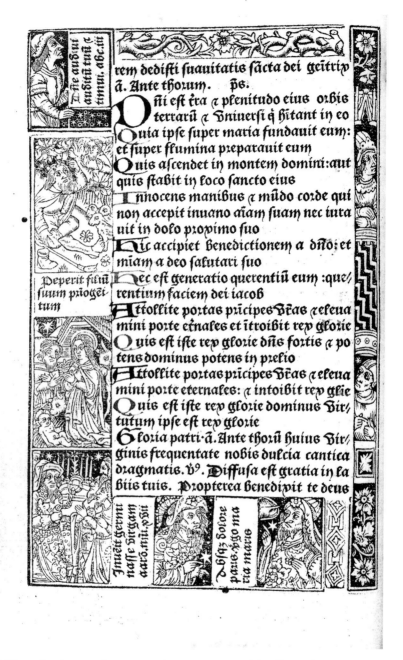

Fig. 12. Du Pré, Hours for the use of Rome, 4 February 1488/89, fol. c3ᵛ (London BL, IA. 39821): typological border no. 5, the Nativity.

text 'Domine audivi auditum tuum et timui. abc. iii' (Habakkuk 3). Below the figure of Moses is printed the text 'Peperit filium suum primogenitum'. In the footpiece, two other prophets point to the texts beside them, 'Invenit germinasse virgam Aaron. num. xvii' and 'Absque dolore paris Virgo Maria maris'. The borders themselves identify thereby two Biblical sources for the texts; the repertoire provides one other (Exodus) and explains the subject of the pictures: 'Item la nativité Jhesucrist est entendue par les figures du buisson qui brusloit et par la verge de Aaron qui florist. de Exode iii. chapitre et des Nombres xvii' (Fig. 8). By consulting both the repertoire and the border texts, readers can ascertain the Biblical sources for each of the images in the *Biblia Pauperum*. Moreover, for those who favour the vernacular, the border images reappear a second time with the text in French.[30] In Vérard's edition of 8 February 1489/90, Latin inscriptions appear on the pages with borders, but they are printed in scrolls along the upper and inner borders (Fig. 11), not in the outer margin with the Biblical scenes, as in the Du Pré edition. The texts are derived from the Old Testament sources, but they are not identical to those used by Du Pré,[31] nor are chapter and book indicated. However, two prophets are depicted above the Biblical border, and two more in the footpiece, each identified by a scroll bearing his name. The typological set is used only once, in consecutive order, and the texts are in Latin.[32]

Did Du Pré and Vérard think it necessary to explain all the border images to their readers? Their use of repertoires indicates in any event that they sought to identify their subjects. Judging from extant editions, no other contemporary printer employed a repertoire, yet many developed their own set of typological borders, attesting thereby to the popularity of the subject and design. Philippe Pigouchet launched a first set in 1491 which he soon discarded, since it appeared in 1492 in an edition by Morand and Marnef; he employed a second set in 1497 and a third *c.* 1502.[33] Thielman Kerver used a set of 47 pieces which are characterized by text written horizontally in the footpiece as well as in the lateral piece. He updated this set during his career, using a more Renaissance style of arch and image, but retaining the fundamental tripartite design. Jean Jehannot printed several editions of Hours using a set where each image is framed by two columns and an arch, but only 26 lateral pieces are known from the extant examples, and by 1510 only eleven pieces are used, repeatedly and with no apparent order. Similarly, only one piece is known from what seems to have been a set by Denis Meslier, and four pieces are repeated in editions by Jean de Coulonces.[34] It seems likely that Le Rouge had a set since two related images from one border appear in an edition cited by Claudin. Paris may have been the centre of production for such borders, but at least one example comes from Kirchheim: that of Marcus Reinhart who in 1490 printed an edition of Hours for the use of Rome.[35]

The fact that so many printers had similar sets allowed for exchanges as needed. For example, in one copy of Hours for the use of Sarum, printed by Jehannot for Nicolas Lecomte in 1498, one gathering contains two bifolia (K2/7 and K3/6) of an edition by Thielman Kerver using his typological set.[36]

BORDER SETS

I would like to emphasize that such borders represent narrative sets, and that while the term 'historiated border' is useful to distinguish them from purely decorative, non-figural, or grotesque borders, the term does not adequately indicate either the subject or the length of the series. Not all Parisian printers used typological borders, but many employed other narrative sets of substantial length. One of the most celebrated is the life of Christ printed in numerous editions by Philippe Pigouchet for Simon Vostre. Like the typological sets, it features a tripartite design for the lateral border, but its footpiece contains, instead of prophets, a single image depicting another episode in the story. The three scenes in each lateral border are separated by captions of Latin text printed on separate blocks, or by architectural motifs without text. The complete set consists of 27 lateral pieces and an equal number of footpieces, for a total of 108 subjects.[37]

The tripartite system of borders characterizes another famous set by Pigouchet and Vostre: the Dance of Death, consisting in its most developed form of 30 male and 36 female figures, arranged in groups of three for a total of ten borders in the male series and twelve in the female.[38] Pigouchet and Vostre developed numerous sets of narrative borders, and their quantity is indicative of their importance for the publishers. The most complete lists of border subjects are those compiled by Hugh William Davies for the Fairfax-Murray catalogue.[39] Davies focuses on Pigouchet for whom he defines 24 different sets, but certain subjects were adopted by other printers so that they can be considered 'standard' for the time: life of Christ, Sibyls, Dance of Death, Virtues and Vices, stories of Joseph, Judith, Susannah, etc.

Most catalogues pay little attention to the borders, equating their place in the margins with their significance within the book or indeed within the printers' corpus of work. Their importance is viewed as 'marginal' rather than 'central'. Yet early printers obviously considered them worthy of attention, in part because they offered the greatest opportunities for invention and innovation. Du Pré and Vérard both provided repertoires of border subjects, calling them to the attention of their public. By the sixteenth century, printers publicized them on title-pages and in colophons as distinctive features of the book. Simon Vostre, for example, issued an edition *c.*1507 with this introduction: 'Ces presentes heures a l'usaige de Cambray ... avec les hystoires de l'apocalipse et les miracles Nostre Dame et plusieurs aultres hystoires faictes a l'antique ont esté imprimees pour Symon Vostre, libraire.'[40] The pictures he mentions are all found in the borders. Similarly, *c.*1501, the printers Gillet and Germain Hardouyn cite the 'figures de la vie de l'homme et la destruction de Hierusalem' as notable features of their edition, and these subjects, again, appear in the borders.[41] The colophon to Kerver's edition of 1506 likewise highlights borders that contain 'plusieurs belles hystoires de la Bible, avec les figures de l'Apocalipse et plusieurs aultres'.[42]

Significant, too, is the fact that printers sought to correlate border designs with the core texts. The Dance of Death series, for example, was designed for the Office of the Dead; the various renditions of the life of the Virgin and Christ frame the principal text, the Hours of the Virgin. Other sets were destined for the kalendar and the suffrages. Although respect for this correlation must have waned as border pieces wore out, the principle of relating border to central text remained constant and seems to have governed the vast majority of editions. The borders reinforced not only the teaching of the main illustrations, as Pollard noted,[43] but also that of the texts themselves.

Du Pré and Vérard both used repertoires to call attention to their illustrations, not those in centre page but those that were 'spread throughout the Hours' or placed in 'vignettes' framing the text. Their initiative compels us to consider more than just the major components of the Book of Hours. It alerts us to the presence of narrative sets within the illustrations, small as well as large, in borders rather than centre page. Emulating their example, modern 'repertoires' would do well to document these narrative sets, particularly in the borders: their dimensions, design, and number of pieces; their use of guide letters or other indications of sequence; their placement (random or intentional), repetitions, apparent order or disorder; the presence of text, its form (verse or prose) and language. To ignore the borders is to disregard an element which printers themselves both prized and promoted. Attention to the borders sheds light not only on the printers' development of materials, innovations in design, and transmission of texts and illustrations, but also on the use of the book by readers. In all probability, the borders – for both their texts and their illustrations – contributed almost as much as the core components to the popularity of the Book of Hours, in Paris and abroad.

BOOKS OF HOURS
THE DEVELOPMENT OF THE
TEXTS IN PRINTED FORM[1]

CRISTINA DONDI

THE POPULARITY ACHIEVED by Books of Hours from the later Middle Ages is reflected by the vast number of surviving manuscripts,[2] and by the continued success of the genre after the invention of printing. The Book of Hours was one of the most frequently printed works in the fifteenth century, with 422 editions registered by *ISTC*, a number which is bound to rise when the *GW* has completed its survey.[3]

Despite their popularity[4] we know relatively little about the textual content of Books of Hours, or the intellectual and economic background for their production. While cataloguing the Books of Hours for the Bodleian Incunable Project[5] I became aware of the great diversity of the content of these books, which are usually regarded as being very uniform. Books of Hours present considerable variation not only among editions of different uses, but also, within the same use, among editions printed by different printers, or by the same printers in different years, or in different formats.

The present paper summarizes the first results of a comprehensive survey of the printed Hours which aims to determine the transmission of this body of texts by providing a systematic analysis of each edition. In this paper I will concentrate on Hours of the Roman use, and in particular on those printed in Italy and France.[6] This group, with 226 editions, is by far the largest, but also the most neglected because its content is usually assumed to be comparatively uniform.

The printed Hours were not initially best-sellers. Their production began in a fairly small way in Italy. A pioneering edition was produced by Theobaldus Schencbecher *c.*1473 (no. 1 in the appendix) and, judging by his other printing activities, was probably stimulated by the environment of the Curia. Nicolaus Jenson then produced two editions in 1474 (nos 2-3) and three in 1475 (nos 4-6),[7] Jenson's first liturgical enterprise.[8] Again in 1475, Andreas Belfortis (no. 7) in Ferrara experimented with the production of a Book of Hours, his only liturgical book out of some 56 editions, as did Antonius Zarotus in Milan (no. 8), whose work was probably the result of a commission from one of the local religious houses, considering the strong local bias of the sanctoral contained in the calendar.[9] In 1476 Mathias Moravus's first Roman Hours appeared in Naples (no. 9). Like Zarotus, Moravus was to produce other liturgical material, as well as eight further Books of Hours.[10] No Hours were printed in 1477, but in 1478 appeared the only Hours printed by the Venetian Andreas de Paltasichis (no. 10; Needham 171 no. 47, 175 no. 97), whose output of 38 editions also includes a Bible, a Roman missal, and, interestingly, the privileges of the Dominican order. In the same year we also find the second and third of Moravus's editions (nos 11-12), and we have an unassigned Venetian edition from 1480 (no. 13). In 1481 Georgius Herolt in Rome produced a Roman Hours (no. 14), his only liturgical production, as did Boninus de Boninis in Verona (no. 15; Needham 192), although the latter's 41 editions produced in Brescia include a Benedictine breviary and a Carmelite missal.[11] Also in 1481 Nicolaus Girardengus (no. 16; Needham 172 no. 68) put on the market an edition of Roman Hours, one of only three liturgical productions from his press, the other two being an Augustinian breviary printed in the previous year and a Roman breviary in the following. Finally, a fourth 1481 edition of the Hours was printed in Venice by Andreas Torresanus (no. 17; Needham 174 no. 86) for Johannes de Colonia, Nicolaus Jenson, and other associates.[12] By this date Torresanus had already printed two Roman breviaries for Franciscan use, and one each for the Carmelite and Dominican uses and for the diocese of Bourges. He was to become a specialist printer of liturgical texts, with an output that included breviaries, diurnals, and missals for the Franciscans, Carmelites, Dominicans, Carthusians, and Cistercians, and for foreign dioceses including Bourges, Nantes, and Urgell. He also printed the *Breviarium glagoliticum* for the Slavonic Church. 1482 saw only one edition, by Nicolaus de Frankfordia in Venice (no. 18; Needham 174 no. 92). This was his only Book of Hours, although between 1475 and 1500 he printed a substantial number of other religious texts, including bibles, breviaries, diurnals, and missals, mostly of Roman, Franciscan, or Dominican use.

The only Book of Hours to appear in Italy in 1483 was the Florentine edition by Nicolo di Lorenzo (no. 19), his only liturgical imprint out of 15 editions of Italian texts. The strong local bias of the calendar in this edition of supposedly Roman Hours suggests that the work was commissioned. In 1484 we find only Georgius Arrivabenus's Venetian edition (no. 20; Needham 175 no. 103).[13] To the following year may be assigned the Venetian edition of Johannes Leoviler (no. 21; Needham 177 no. 127), dated to between 1485 and 1488.[14] In the years 1486-7 the printing of the Hours was concentrated in Naples, with three more editions by Moravus (nos 22-4) and one by Cristannus Preller (no. 25). Among Preller's 21 editions, we find five further Roman Hours.[15] In 1488 Johannes Hamman printed his first Roman Hours in Venice (no. 26; Needham 178 no. 138). Hamman's output of 91 editions includes not only a further seven editions of the Hours, but also a substantial number of other liturgical texts commissioned from abroad. 1488 also saw another of Moravus's editions (no. 27).

In 1489 only one edition appeared, printed by Torresanus in Venice (no. 28); in 1490 one edition by Moravus (no. 29), one by Preller (no. 30), and three by Hamman (nos 31-3); in 1491 one edition by Hamman (no. 34); in 1492 one edition by Moravus (no. 35), and Theodorus de Ragazonibus's only Roman Hours (no. 36; Needham 179 no. 149). De Ragazonibus, whose 31 editions also include a Roman psalter and a Roman missal, otherwise concentrated on classical, theological, devotional, and grammatical texts. In 1493 we have two more of Hamman's editions (nos 37-8) and the first of Johannes Emericus de Spira's nine editions of the Roman Hours (no. 39; Needham 182 190), seven of which were printed for Lucantonio Giunta (Needham 188 no. 31). De Spira was evidently among the printers who specialized in liturgical texts: more than half of his output consists of breviaries and diurnals for Roman, Franciscan, Dominican, and Benedictine uses, missals for Roman, Dominican, and Carmelite uses, and for the dioceses of Paris, Esztergom, Messina, Pécs, and Segovia, some nine psalters, of Roman, Dominican, or monastic uses, and even a Roman gradual and a

Roman antiphonary. In 1494 appeared another of de Spira's editions (no. 41) and Hieronymus de Sanctis's only Book of Hours (no. 40; Needham 179 no. 144), part of a small output of nine editions, most of them devotional texts in Latin and in Italian. 1495 saw the only Hours to be printed in Turin, the edition by Nicolaus de Benedictis and Jacobinus Suigus (no. 42), whose only other liturgical enterprise is a breviary for the diocese of Fréjus. In the same year a de Spira edition appeared in Venice (no. 43), for Lucantonio Giunta, and a Preller edition in Naples (no. 44). 1496 saw the Hours of the Neapolitan Ayolfus de Cantono (no. 45), his only liturgical undertaking. In the same year followed one edition by Preller (no. 46) and two by de Spira (nos 47-8), the second printed for Giunta. In 1497 two Roman Hours were printed by de Spira (nos 49-50), the second again for Giunta, and one by Hamman for Octavianus Scotus (no. 51; Needham 190 no. 57). In 1498 one edition was printed by Preller (no. 52) and one by de Spira (no. 53) for Giunta, and the fifteenth-century Italian production of the Roman Hours came to an end in 1499 with another edition printed by de Spira for Giunta (no. 54).

Meanwhile Parisian printers, in particular Du Pré and Pigouchet, had begun to produce Roman Hours in 1485, and this activity increased from 1487. The arrival on the market of the Parisian Roman Hours was not only a turning point in the production of this genre, but also occasioned an evident increase in the quantity and quality of Italian Hours. With the exception of de Cantono's and de Sanctis's editions, from the early 1490s Italian printed Hours gradually ceased to be the occasional enterprise of relatively small printers, and production was increasingly concentrated in the hands of more specialist printers, familiar with liturgical texts. Under the influence of the Parisian Hours the contents of the Italian Hours also grew. Compared with the simple collection of offices of the 1470s and 1480s, the increasing number of prayers, offices, and illustrations of later editions must be the result of careful examination by Italian printers of the books offered to the market by their Parisian rivals.

On this occasion I will not be more specific about the great variety of content and its different arrangement, but it should be pointed out that, as far as the structure of the texts is concerned, a first general distinction can be made between Hours printed in Italy and those printed in France. The Italian Hours are much simpler, their content generally consisting of a calendar, Offices of the Virgin and of the dead, the seven penitential psalms, litanies, Offices of the Cross and of the Holy Spirit, and occasionally a few prayers, such as the prayer of St Anselm,[16] the Athanasian Creed, the prayer of St Gregory,[17] suffrages, and the Passion of Christ according to St John.[18] Interestingly, in the early Hours printed in Italy the very frequent prayers to the Virgin, O *intemerata*[19] and *Obsecro te*,[20] classics in the French tradition, do not appear. French Hours, on the other hand, have a highly complex structure that often includes a large number of prayers in French[21] as well as in Latin. This reflects the existing highly-developed French manuscript tradition, as well as the demand from a new market for innovative texts. If we look at the arrangement of the texts in Pigouchet's huge and varied output of Roman Hours, for example, we find that only rarely is a new edition a simple reprint of a previous one. Instead, different prayers have usually been introduced, and their overall arrangement has changed.

The relatively small number of textual innovations identified by Albert Labarre as the Hours pass from manuscript into print[22] can be attributed, I believe, to Parisian printers. Most noticeably, the title-page, which did not exist in manuscripts, shows the mark of the printer or of the bookseller.[23] This is followed by another new element, the Almanac. Covering a period of 10, 15, or 20 years, it gives the golden numbers (the position of the year within the Greek lunar cycle), the dominical letters, indication of leap years, and dates of principal movable feasts.[24] Within the actual text of the Hours some new offices appear, such as the Hours of the Conception of the Virgin, the Hours of Our Lady of Pity, the Hours of the Trinity, and, later, the Hours of the Holy Sacrament. We may add to these changes noted by Labarre the development of picture cycles with accompanying text in the borders, a space that in the manuscript Hours was decorated, but did not contain a parallel narrative.[25]

Eventually the overwhelming Parisian production of Hours must have inhibited Italian production. By the end of the fifteenth century Parisian hours were already circulating in Italy, as the substantial number which survive in Italian provincial libraries seems to indicate.[26]

It is difficult to establish the early distribution of a book like the Hours. In the first place, many editions now survive in very few copies, a significant indication of how these books were used. This is particularly true of the Hours produced in Italy. The poor survival rate of these Hours may be in part due to the early disposal of old-fashioned Italian books in favour of more sophisticated Parisian ones. It is my opinion, however, that a number of Italian editions also had smaller print-runs, especially those which were commissioned by particular religious institutions.

Furthermore, Books of Hours became highly collectable at an early stage. Only by establishing the provenance of each copy will it be possible to identify a partially accurate pattern of original distribution. For the present, a tentative evaluation can be based on editions of the Hours which survive in provincial libraries since books in these institutions are more likely to have come from local religious foundations or local owners. Surviving copies of Books of Hours printed in Italy can still be found close to where they were originally printed: the Veneto and northern Italy for Venetian editions, Florence for the Florentine edition, Rome and central Italy for the Roman editions, and Naples for Neapolitan editions. French editions, on the other hand, survive in greater numbers, not only in French provincial libraries, but also in Italy, particularly in the northern and central regions, showing that by the 1490s Parisian printers were catering for the Italian market as well. It would be interesting to investigate whether special provisions were made in Hours printed for sale in Italy. While there were Parisian Hours printed in Spanish (*CIBN* H-250), such vernacular printing was not provided for the Italian market.[27] In fact some editions found in Italian provincial libraries are in Latin and French.

Before examining how printers worked with their manuscript exemplars, and more generally the variety of texts that a Book of Hours might contain, I would like to address the issue of the contribution made by early printed Hours to the spread of the Roman liturgy.

The liturgical use of a Book of Hours may be stated on the title-page or in the colophon, or it may be identifiable from the Offices of the Virgin and of the dead. The same liturgical use should also be reflected in the selection of saints listed in the calendar, the litanies, and the suffrages. However, it is not uncommon to find, in the calendar in particular, a hagiographical selection that does not relate to the use as given in the title-page, but is instead representative of a different liturgical tradition. This is particularly frequent in liturgical books according to the use of Rome and reflects the spread of the Roman custom in the fifteenth century and its different reception by various ecclesiastical institutions.

In fact the production of about 226 editions of Hours according to the use of Rome demonstrates the diffusion of the Roman use nearly a century before the appearance of the official publications issued by Pius V (1566-72).

The period from the invention of printing to the Council of Trent is crucial for the history of the process of romanizing the western liturgy. As pointed out by Pierre-Marie Gy, the liturgical unification of the West was achieved in two phases, the first from the Carolingian period to the time of Gregory VII (1073-85), and the second after the Council of Trent.[28]

The first step towards unification depended on the adoption of liturgical books of a Roman type practically everywhere except Milan. This first romanization of the liturgy was the product of three factors: the attraction and devotion of local churches to the liturgy of Rome, the unifying ideology of the Carolingians, and the Gregorian ecclesiology, the theological idea of the relationship between the unity of faith and the unity of liturgy combined with the concept of papal authority in liturgical matters.

The spread of the Roman liturgy had been a continuous process during the period from the papacy of Innocent III (1198-1216) to the Council of Trent. By the end of the thirteenth century the liturgy of the papal chapel had been adopted by the Franciscans as well as by all the churches of Rome,[29] and in the fourteenth century the Roman liturgy was adopted by the churches of central Italy.[30] No local diocesan breviaries or missals were produced in Italy using the new technology of printing, with a few exceptions in the north and the south of the peninsula, such as the dioceses of Milan and Aquileia, or Messina, where a Norman liturgy was still in use. In France, as a consequence of the Avignon papacy, the Roman liturgy was adopted by the church of Avignon and by those churches headed by a cleric of the Curia. However, such churches were the exception; the large number of diocesan-printed breviaries and missals in France and, to a lesser extent, in Germany suggest that local liturgical traditions were still strong,[31] even if it is not uncommon at this stage to find that their diocesan calendars are in fact a Roman calendar adapted to local use.

The second step towards liturgical unification in the West was the work of the Roman Curia: it consisted in the uniform adoption (i.e. imposition) of the Curia's liturgy, that is, that of the papal chapel. As a result of the Council of Trent, in 1568 the new Roman breviary and missal were published. The first approved Book of Hours, the *Officium Beate Marie Virginis nuper reformatum*, was printed in Rome in 1571,[32] then in Antwerp by Plantin in 1573,[33] and in editions from 1575 onwards.

The move towards the adoption of the Roman use in the fifteenth century therefore presents a split situation, as the printed liturgical books show. Whereas the strictly liturgical use, as given by the offices, was adopted ever more frequently, the Roman sanctoral, and the calendar in particular,[34] were not as firmly canonized and continued to be supplemented with saints venerated locally. As I shall show, in the Hours in particular this phenomenon was determined by a number of factors: by printers selecting local manuscripts as exemplars for publication, by institutions or individuals commissioning specific liturgical material, but also by the working practice of some printers who, for purely technical reasons, relied on the productions of their colleagues, and in so doing arbitrarily disseminated in one community the hagiographical uses of another.

The Franciscans played an important role in the spread of Roman breviaries and missals from the earliest days of printing. In this they were faithful to the tradition of their order, which had done so much to fix the liturgy of the Roman Curia in the previous two centuries. A.-G. Martimort has showed how closely they worked with printers, particularly in Venice, in their attempts to revise the texts.[35]

The work of the Franciscan Redemptus Menth for the GW in 1932[36] constituted a systematic effort to distinguish Roman breviaries from Franciscan and Augustinian ones.[37] The analysis of the rubrics, used by Menth as a means to classify the transmission of the printed Roman breviary, had been suggested by the research conducted by Giovanni Mercati in 1903.[38]

The presence of local (i.e. non-Roman) saints in their calendars has not, however, been sufficiently examined in the Roman breviaries and missals. For example, the breviary printed by Jenson in 1478 (GW 5101) has been rightly recognized as the earliest 'pure' edition of the Roman breviary;[39] its calendar, however, still contains Venetian feasts.[40] This type of information is of as much value for the bibliographer as for the student of liturgy, since it sheds further light on the printer's methods of production and his relationships with the surrounding environment.

This is precisely the kind of analysis with which my work on the printed Roman Hours is concerned. Moreover, while breviaries and missals, which are strictly ecclesiastical books, reflect the attitude of a strictly ecclesiastical environment, the fact that Books of Hours were produced for the laity as well as for religious communities provides even more valuable evidence of popular cults. In fact the greater variety found in their sanctorals reflects the fact that, unlike breviaries and missals, the Hours did not generally come under the editorial supervision of the higher ecclesiastical authorities.

As I have already mentioned, the first Book of Hours for the use of Rome, printed in Rome c. 1473 (no. 1), does not contain a calendar, although one is included in the second edition of the Roman Hours, printed by Jenson in 1474 (no. 2). The adoption of the Roman rite was granted in perpetuum by Pope Callixtus III (1455-8) to the diocese and patriarchate of Venice in 1456, at the request of the patriarch Maffeo Giovanni Contarini (1456-60).[41]

A first survey of a number of editions of the Roman Hours prepared by Venetian printers has brought to light two interesting points. First, Venetian saints can be detected in their calendars, due, unsurprisingly, to the manuscript exemplars that were used by the printers. Secondly, these Venetian entries vary from edition to edition. This peculiarity reflects the highly diversified Venetian hagiographical distribution, where cathedral (San Pietro di Castello), ducal chapel (St Mark), parishes, and monasteries venerated different groups of saints. The cause of such variety lies primarily in the relatively late creation of the Venetian diocese and development of its sanctoral. Unlike most cities of northern Italy, which could claim a collection of local martyr saints from antiquity, the foundation of Venice dated to a period which was already Christian. As the importance of the Venetian Church grew, a number of relics from the patriarchate of Aquileia and Grado, which came to form the patriarchate of Venice, were transferred to the city.[42] However, it was in the east that the Venetians were to find the means to enrich their hagiographical tradition, and with the arrival of the relics of St Mark in 828 a substantial and continuous flow began.[43]

Giulio Cattin has analysed the liturgical tradition of the ducal chapel of St Mark on the basis of the extant manuscript and printed sources. However, the study of the Venetian sanctoral is complicated by two factors: first, even for St Mark itself, the sources are relatively late.[44] Secondly, there is not, at present, a comparable study of the liturgical tradition of the diocese itself, San Pietro di Castello,[45] nor of the many churches of Venice which, as we shall see, developed independent cults.

According to Cattin, the liturgy of St Mark can be traced back not to the legendary Oriental influence but to a north Italian tradition: even the impact of Aquileia has to be reassessed.[46] However, it is undeniable that a substantial number of oriental saints appear in the sanctoral of St Mark itself, as well as in those of the many parish churches of Venice.[47] Whether this phenomenon extends to, or originates from, the cathedral church of San Pietro di Castello, is impossible to say at this stage.

From the end of the eleventh century, and with particular intensity during the time of the Crusades, relics arriving in Venice were not merely treasured, as would normally be the case elsewhere,[48] but generated new cults. A new literary activity, the writing of *Vitae*, *Passiones*, and *Translationes*, developed as a means of promoting such acquisitions.[49] The translations of the bodies of Mark, Nicholas, or Stephen Proto-martyr required little explanation to achieve public recognition, but those of secondary oriental saints into the churches of local ecclesiastical institutions, whether individual monasteries or parishes, needed to be made known. As their cults never reached an official patriarchal level,[50] it was up to the institutions themselves to promote the veneration of newly-arrived saints by producing hagiographical texts to inform the public about them, and by inserting them into the liturgy. Unfortunately, very little survives today of what must once have been a rich hagiographical tradition.[51] Two hagiographical collections of the later Middle Ages, compiled by two Venetians, are therefore of great importance: the *Legendarium* of the Dominican Pietro Calò of Chioggia and the *Catalogus sanctorum et gestorum eorum* of the Bishop of Jesolo Pietro Natali o Nadal (Petrus de Natalibus).[52] As Chiesa notes, the two authors most probably used hagiographical material which they found in Venetian libraries and ecclesiastical archives in the fourteenth century, and of which very little survives today.[53]

By identifying calendars, based on manuscripts belonging to local Venetian insti-tutions, used as exemplars by the Venetian printers and now lost, we gain an insight into the working methods of these printers. In most cases these printed Hours also constitute our sole evidence for the liturgical tradition of these institutions in fifteenth-century Venice.

A number of entries from the calendars of the Hours do appear in the sanctoral of St Mark. When such an occurrence is substantiated by a proper office in books of St Mark's we may safely believe that an entry is derived from its hagiographical tradition or shared with it. On the other hand, where an entry from the Hours finds only a generic match (no proper office) in the St Mark tradition, this common appearance cannot be taken to be derived from St Mark; it could in fact provide evidence to the contrary, implying a superficial acknowledgement by the ducal chapel of an important relic kept in a parish church or monastery of the city.

The calendar of the first Hours printed in Venice by Jenson in 1474 is indeed based on the Roman version.[54] In addition it presents a number of Venetian feasts,[55] for instance:

*Fusca v[56] (13 Feb.); *Faustinus m[57] (15 Feb.); *Iuliana v[58] (16 Feb.); Bassus[59] (4 Mar.); Donatus[60] (13 Mar.); *Sigismundus rex[61] (2 May); *Marina[62] (17 July), *Ludovicus[63] (19 Aug.), bishop of Toulouse; *Moyses[64] (4 Sept.) the prophet; *Iustina v[65] (7 Oct.), of Padua; *Gallus ab[66] (16 Oct.); *Prosdocimus[67] (7 Nov.), bishop of Padua; Johannes ep [Traguriensis][68] (14 Nov.); and *Maurus m[69] (21 Nov.).

As well as these Venetian entries we encounter in this 1474 Jenson edition another group of saints, few of whom can be identified in the tradition of St Mark. This group requires further investigation, but it appears to belong to the proper of a specific Venetian institution. It includes a large number of Byzantine and Southern Italian saints:

Felicianus ep[70] (24 Jan.); Sabinus (8 Feb.), bishop of Canosa in southern Italy; Bonitius ep (11 Feb.), unidentified; Germanicus[71] (17 Feb.); Ugo ep (18 Feb.), unidentified on this date; Severianus[72] (19 Feb.); Constantia v (25 Feb.), unidentified; Metranus of Alexandria[73] (26 Feb.); Poliotus[74] (28 Feb.); Cirionis presb[75] (5 Mar.); Simon ep (14 Mar.), unidentified; Iulianus (19 Mar.), unidentified; Romanus ab (20 Mar.), possibly the little-known Byzantine saint Rodianus (*BSS* XI 275); Albinus ep (24 Mar.), unidentified; Marianus ep (27 Mar.), unidentified; Petrus m (29 Mar.), possibly a misplaced entry for the Dominican saint venerated on 29 Apr., whose relics were venerated in San Giovanni e Paolo, Venice, and who was the titular saint of a parish church in Murano;[76] Cyriacus (2 Apr.), unidentified; Maximianus (5 Apr.), unidentified; Alexander m (7 Apr.), unidentified; Sixtus pp (15 Apr.), unidentified on this date; *Gothardus (5 May) bishop of Hildesheim; Theodora (13 May), unidentified; Iuvenalis ep (21 May) unidentified, although it should be remembered that on this day is venerated in Venice the blessed John, whose body is buried in San Lorenzo;[77] Iustinus m (1 June), the second-century philosopher venerated on this date by the Byzantine Church; *Ludovicus [IX] rex [Francie] (25 Aug. canon. 1297); Gratianus (18 Nov.), probably the bishop of Tours venerated on 18 Dec.

The entry for *Monica, mother of St Augustine (4 May), indicates the influence of the Augustinian Hermits. She is also co-titular of the church of Sant'Agostino in sestiere di San Polo. Anselmus (18 Mar.), bishop of Lucca; *Herculianus (1 Mar.), bishop of Perugia, and the Dedicatio Salvatoris[78] (9 Nov.) are Roman feasts descending from the sanctoral of the Canons of the Lateran which, unlike the calendar of the Papal Chapel, contains a number of feasts with an origin in Lucca.[79]

A group of saints from the coast of Latium and Campania have also been identified by Chiesa in a fifteenth-century hagiographical collection of definite Venetian origin, now in the Biblioteca Braidense of Milan.[80] He suggests as a possible link the Venetian Franciscan Paolino Minorita (died 1344) who, in the first half of the fourteenth century, was often in Naples on diplomatic business and later became Bishop of Pozzuoli (1324-44).[81] Hagiographical material from southern Italy would thus have been incorporated into Nadal's collection and thence into the fifteenth-century Hours. It is clear that a large number of as yet unidentified entries from the printed Venetian Hours can be found in Nadal's collection, which, at least with that date, do not even appear in the *Bibliotheca Sanctorum*.

In the 1475 Jenson edition (no. 6), on the other hand, not all of these saints are present and the calendar shows a familiar Roman aspect with more marked Franciscan connotations,[82] and with a few Venetian saints,[83] while a number of new prayers are introduced into the text.

The editions of the Roman Hours printed in Venice by Girardengus, Hamman, Theodorus de Ragazonibus, and Johannes Emericus de Spira, not only have a detectable common Venetian base, but also present other characteristics which suggest that Venetian calendars from different sources had been used. The calendar of Girardengus's 1481 edition of the Roman Hours (no. 16) is a copy of Jenson's 1474, with the omission of a few oriental saints and of some of those entries which are still unidentified:

Bonitius (11 Feb.), Metranus (26 Feb.), Poliotus (28 Feb.), Bassus (4 Mar.), Cirionis (5 Mar.), Albinus (24 Mar.), Marianus (27 Mar.), Cyriacus (2 Apr.), Maximianus (5 Apr.), and Iustinus (1 June). In addition we find Vincentius (5 Apr. OP canon. 1458), the Venetian saints *Secundus[84] (1 June) and *Magnus[85] (6 Oct.), Dedicatio Petri et Pauli (18 Nov.), and the Lucca entry Dedicatio s Martini ep (8 Oct.).[86]

In comparison with Jenson's 1474 edition, the contents of Girardengus's hours are further augmented with a set of prayers (fols x_7^v-y_7^v) which has been added after the colophon (fol. x_7^r).

Hamman's editions (nos 31-4) appear to be very close to that of Girardengus.[87] An exception, however, is his edition of 1 Oct. 1497 for Octavianus Scotus (no. 51). For this edition Hamman's exemplar can be identified as the Hours printed by Hieronymus de Sanctis on 26 Apr. 1494 (no. 40): not only is the calendar identical, but also the articulation of the various offices and the many prayers are the same, with the addition of some further texts in the Hamman's edition for Scotus.

In addition to the saints found in Hamman's previous editions, the calendar contains additional entries not previously noted in Venetian calendars. To list only a few:

Sabinus presb (19 Feb.), unidentified; Gallus presb (20 Feb.), unidentified; Romanus (28 Feb.), Abbot of Condat; Maximus (3 Mar.), unidentified, although on this date Marinus et Asterius are venerated in St Mark; Zacharia (14 Mar.), the eighth-century pope generally venerated on the following day (*BSS* XII 1446-8); Johannes heremita[88] (27 Mar.); *Secundus[89] (30 Mar.); *Trodora (i.e. Theodora, 1 Apr.), a Roman martyr (*BSS* XII 225-6); Pancratius (3 Apr.), bishop of Taormina; *Ermenegildus rex (13 Apr.), the Visigothic king (*BSS* V 33-47); Ubaldus (16 May), bishop of Gubbio; *Iulia[90] (22 May); *Bonifacius (5 June), the apostle of Germany; Diogenes (16 June), unidentified; Paternianus (10 July), bishop of Fano; *Zacharia[91] (6 Sept.); Philippus (13 Sept.), a doubtful martyr of Alexandria (*BSS* V 725-6); *Victor[92] (18 Sept.); Candidus m (3 Oct.), unidentified; Eustachius presb (12 Oct.), a priest of Syria or Egypt (*BSS* V 280); Valerianus (15 Dec.), venerated in Ravenna on 16 Dec. according to the Martyrology of Jerome (*BSS* XII 901); Antonilla v (18 Dec.), unidentified; *Theodosia[93] (22 Dec.); *Servulus (23 Dec.), who gave his name to the Venetian island of San Servolo with its Benedictine monastery.

This same calendar is reproduced exactly in the Hours for the use of Rome printed in Lyons by Jacobinus Suigus and Nicolaus de Benedictis for Boninus de Boninis, 20 Mar. 1499/1500.[94]

The calendar of Emericus de Spira's edition of 1493 (no. 39) presents a different group of Venetian feasts, among them the *apparition of St Mark (25 June), *Magnus (6 Oct.), and *Fantinus (31 July), the Italo-Byzantine saint of this name who was venerated on 24 July. The commemoration of St Fantinus on 31 July is typically

Venetian. Fantinus the Elder of Tauriana was a Calabrian Greek saint who probably lived between the second half of the third and the beginning of the fourth century, and is venerated on 24 July. Fantinus the Younger was another tenth-century Calabrian saint buried in Thessalonika, and venerated on 14 November in Byzantine Calabria and by the Byzantine Church.[95] Erica Follieri suggests that the date of 31 July is probably connected with the construction of the church dedicated to Fantinus in Venice at the beginning of the twelfth century by families involved in trade with a number of cities of the Greek peninsula, in particular with Thessalonika, where the cult of Fantinus the Younger originated around the saint's burial place. During the fourteenth century the Venetian hagiographers Calò and Nadal would have attached to the titular saint of the Venetian church the legend of Fantinus of Tauriana, filtered through a Sicilian tradition.[96] St Fantinus is not present in the Hours printed by Jenson in 1474 (no. 2), and [c.1475] (no. 6), in the Hours printed by de Paltasichis in 1478 (no. 10), in the unassigned edition of c.1480 (no. 13), nor in those printed by Girardengus in 1481 (no. 16). He appears, however, in the Roman breviary printed by Jenson in 1478,[97] in the Hours printed by Boninus de Boninis in 1481 (no. 15), in that printed by Torresanus in 1489 (no. 28), in those printed by Hamman in c.1490 (no. 32), 1490 (no. 33), 14[93] (no. 38), and 1497 (no. 51), in the Hours printed by de Ragazonibus in 1492 (no. 36), by de Sanctis in 1494 (no. 40), and in those printed by Johannes Emericus de Spira in 1493 (no. 39), 1494 (no. 41), 1495 (no. 43), and 1497 (no. 50). He is also present in the Neapolitan Hours printed by Moravus in 1492 (no. 35), and in the Parisian Hours printed by Pigouchet c.1493-6 (Pr 8182).

Johannes Emericus de Spira's 1494 (no. 41), 1495 (no. 43), and 1497 (no. 50) editions, the last two for Lucantonio Giunta, share the same calendar, but it is very different from that of 1493: indeed their exemplar is found in the Roman Hours printed by de Ragazonibus in 1492 (no. 36). Moreover only the two editions for Lucantonio Giunta also share the same text, an arrangement which differs from either de Ragazonibus's or de Spira's previous editions. De Ragazonibus's calendar appears to have taken as its base the 1474 Jenson edition, to which entries from the Roman Lateran tradition and the new Franciscan feasts were added:

Regulus[98] (30 Mar.), martyr in Populonia; Torpes m[99] (17 May); Stigmata Francisci (17 Sept); Translatio Clare (2 Oct.); Dedicatio s Martini (8 Oct.); Hilarius ep[100] (3 Nov); Dedicatio Petri et Pauli (18 Nov.).

Among the Venetian saints we find:

Poliotus (28 Feb.); Bassus (4 Mar.); *Eleutherus ep[101] (18 Apr.); Maxima v [of Fréjus][102] (16 May); Maximianus ep[103] (29 May); *Quirinus ep[104] (4 June); *Apparitio s Marci (25 June); Osea et Aggeus (4 July); *Foca ep[105] (14 July); *Fantinus (31 July); *Victor m (18 Sept.), also found in de Sanctis's edition (no. 40); *Magnus (6 Oct.); *Iustina [of Padua] (7 Oct.); *Theodorus[106] (8 Nov.); *Sirus ep[107] (9 Dec.).

The calendar, however, contains a large number of saints who are not found in other Venetian editions, namely:

Satirus (12 Jan.), martyr in Acaia(?); *Policarpus (26 Jan.), bishop of Smyrna; Hypolitus (30 Jan.), of Antioch; *Eufrosine v[108] (11 Feb.); Alexander (26 Feb.), patriarch of Alexandria; Maximus m (3 Mar.), also found in de Sanctis's edition (no. 40); *Longinus (15 Mar.), martyr in

Cappadocia; *Patritius [of Ireland] (16 Mar.; really 17 Mar.); Montanus et Maxima [of Sirmio][109] (26 Mar.); Iohannes heremita (27 Mar.); Gondranus rex[110] (28 Mar.); Isidorus (4 Apr.), archbishop of Seville; Dyonisius[111] (8 Apr.) bishop of Corinth; Symeon ep[112] (21 Apr.); Martianus m (30 Apr.), unidentified, on this date Massentia is venerated in St Mark; 310 martyrs (9 May), unidentified; Petrus et Andrea (15 May), martyrs in Lampsacus, Hellespont; Iulia v (22 May), also found in de Sanctis's edition (no. 40); Desiderius (23 May), bishop of Vienne; Vincentius[113] (24 May), martyr of Lérins; Emilius[114] (28 May); *Bonifacius (5 June), the apostle of Germany; Philippus (6 June), deacon of Jerusalem; Leufridus[115] (21 June); Zostus m[116] (27 June); Eularius cf (3 July), unidentified, Eliodorus in St Mark; Zoe m (5 July), a little known Roman martyr (*BSS* XII 1484-5); Pentem[i?]us cf (7 July; i.e. Pantenus see *BSS* X 119-20); *Procopius m (8 July), of Caesarea (*BSS* X 1159-66); Eustachius (16 July; i.e. Eustatius bishop of Antioch?); *Margarita v (19 July), venerated on 20 July in St Mark; *Rochus[117] (16 Aug.), red in de Ragazonibus's edition; Anastasius m (21 Aug.), unidentified; *Ruffus[118] (27 Aug.); Serapia v (3 Sept.), according to Adon the date of her invention (*BSS* XI 540-2); Victorinus (5 Sept.), martyr of Amiterno, now San Vittorino, according to Adon he was buried in Naples (*BSS* XII 1300-01); Sirus ep (12 Sept.), unidentified; Philippus ep (13 Sept.), also found in de Sanctis's edition (no. 40); Marianus cf (19 Sept.), unidentified; Germanus ab (24 Sept., i.e. Geremarus, abbot of Flay, Oise, *BSS* VI 203-4); Lupus (25 Sept.), bishop of Lyon, venerated on 24 Sept. in the Martyrology of Jerome (*BSS* VIII 387-8); Apolinaris (5 Oct.), the bishop and patron saint of Valence who is generally venerated on 6 Oct. (*BSS* II 249-50); Eustachius presb (12 Oct.), also found in de Sanctis's edition (no. 40); Feriatus ab (13 Oct.), unidentified, Siriacus in de Spira's editions; Florentius (17 Oct.), bishop of Orange; Tholomeus m (19 Oct.), unidentified; *Severinus (23 Oct.), bishop of Cologne (*BSS* XI 963-5); Felix ep[119] (24 Oct.); *Quirinus ep (31 Oct.), i.e. Quintinus martyr of Vermand, now St-Quentin near Amiens (*BSS* X 1313-16); Felix (15 Nov.), bishop of Nola; *Pontianus pp (20 Nov.), venerated on 19 Nov. in St Mark; Marcialis m (27 Nov.), unidentified; Sostenis cf (28 Nov.), disciple of St Paul, venerated on this date in the Martyrology of Adon (*BSS* XI 1323-4); Albinus m (1 Dec.), i.e. Albanus of Mainz, the basilica dedicated to him in Mainz having been consecrates on 1 Dec. 805 (*BSS* I 659-61); Cassianus (3 Dec.), martyr of Tangiers and confused by Nadal with the homonymous martyr of Imola (*BSS* III 914-15); Paulus (12 Dec.), bishop of Narbonne, venerated on this date according to Usuardus (*BSS* X 261-2); Valerianus (15 Dec.), Valentinus ep in de Spira's editions, also found in de Sanctis's edition (no. 40); Gratianus (18 Dec), bishop of Tours.

Some of the evident confusion in the spelling of saints' names and feast days may be attributed either to the printer's difficulty in copying from a manuscript exemplar, or to the corruption of the manuscript itself. A careful collation should result in the identification of some of these saints with the martyrology of Pietro Nadal, highlighting a Venetian tradition in an otherwise apparently confusing selection. About half of the entries listed above can be found in the calendar of the Hours printed by Andreas Torresanus in 1489 (no. 28).[120] Again, a number of these entries[121] appear in the calendar of the 1562 edition of the Roman breviary printed in Venice by Giovanni Varisco & Socii,[122] which is also the last example of the pre-Tridentine trend to inflate calendars. The presence of these 'Venetian' saints in Torresanus's, de Ragazonibus's and later in de Spira's 1494, 1495, and 1497 editions, as well as in the 1562 Roman breviary, confirms that they are all part of an established Venetian tradition; it is hoped that, with further work, it will be possible to identify this as belonging to a specific Venetian institution.

In the following section we shall see that the early Hours of Roman use printed in Venice were used as exemplars by other European printers.

The first edition of the Roman Hours printed in Milan has been assigned to Zarotus *c.*1475 (no. 8).[123] Its calendar, in martyrological form, based on the Roman model, contains many saints who can be found in Zarotus's 1474 edition of the first Roman missal:[124]

Savina (30 Jan.); Policrimius ep (17 Feb.); Simeon ep (18 Feb.); Gabianus ep (19 Feb.); Fugarius ep (20 Feb.); Vialantus m (25 Feb.); Fortunatus ep (26 Feb.); Fridolinus m (5 Mar.); Macedonius presb (13 Mar.); Gerundius m (17 Mar.); Gutibertus ep (20 Mar.); Pigmerius ep (24 Mar.); Castulus m (26 Mar.); Successus m (10 Apr.); Carpus ep (13 Apr.); Vasius ep (16 Apr.); Torquatus cf (15 May); Aquilinus et Victorianus (16 May); Trofinus m (18 Sept.); Theophilus ep (13 Oct.); Antiochus ep (15 Oct.); Iacobus intercisus[125] (28 Nov.); Usuiane v (1 Dec.); Ceremonis ep (22 Dec.).

Among the entries not found in the missal there are:

Babilla ep (24 Jan.); Calocerus m (19 Mar.); Ambrosii archiep depositio (4 Apr.); and Dominus ep (7 May). Torpes m (17 May), and Mammas (17 Aug.) are also found in Jenson's [*c.*1475] edition.

However, the Venetian Fusca and Prosdocimus, and the southern Italian Sabinus ep (8 Feb.) appear, suggesting that for the production of his first Book of Hours Zarotus looked at Jenson's products.

The persistence of the Venetian sanctoral can be observed in most of the editions of Roman Books of Hours printed in Naples. Among the Neapolitan editions that I have been able to examine so far (nos 12, 22, 27, 30, 35, 44), only the third of Moravus's editions, of 10 Nov. 1478 (no. 12), shows no Venetian influence. Its calendar is a rather old-fashioned Roman one, without even the new Franciscan entries, to which have been added a number of French and German saints:

Gertrudis (17 Mar.), patron saint of Nivelles; Ivo (20 May), bishop of Chartres; Udalricus (4 July), Bishop of Augsburg; Kilianus (8 July), patron saint of Würzburg; Leodegarius (3 Oct.), Bishop of Autun; Hedvigis (15 Oct.), Duchess of Silesia and Poland and founder of the Cistercian monastery of Trzebnica; 11,000 martyrs (21 Oct.); Conradus (26 Nov.), bishop of Constance.

The calendar of Moravus's edition of 30 June 1486 (no. 22) is a copy of the one that is found in Jenson's 1474 edition, with only a few exceptions:

the omission of Costantia (25 Feb.); Metranus (26 Feb.); Poliotus (28 Feb.); Albinus (24 Mar.); Petrus (29 Mar.); Sigismundus (2 May); Johannes pp (27 June); Marina (17 July); Martha (29 July); Moyses (4 Sept.); and Iustina (7 Oct.); and the addition of Leo I (11 Apr.); 10,000 martyrs (22 June); Transfiguratio domini (6 Aug.); Lambertus (17 Sept.); Victor et Gereon (10 Oct.); Crispinus et Crispinianus (25 Oct.); Quintinus (31 Oct.); and Dedicatio Petri et Pauli (18 Nov.).

Moravus's edition of 15 Oct. 1488 (no. 27) appears instead to rely on the edition printed by Girardengus in 1481 (no. 16). Of course Moravus also included Neapolitan feasts.[126] In addition, some entries relate to the calendar of Lucca, for example Anellus ab[127] (14 Dec.). Evidence of this Lucca dimension in Moravus's edition shows that he must have used a Roman exemplar of the Lateran kind as well as Girardengus's edition.

A brief look at Moravus's Books of Hours shows that each new edition contained some new text. Moreover, while the text of his 1492 edition (no. 35) relies on that of 1488, their calendars are completely different. The former is based on Girardengus's edition, while the latter has many unusual entries in common with the edition printed by de Sanctis in 1494 (no. 40). This suggests the existence of a common Venetian source, which I hope will be found among Venetian calendars that I have not yet analysed.

The Book of Hours printed by Preller in 1490 (no. 30) contains a calendar based on that printed by Jenson in 1474,[128] but with the addition of a large number of French and German saints, some of them in common with Moravus's 1478 calendar. These northern European saints belong to a Neapolitan hagiographical tradition and probably have their background in religious houses founded by the Angevins in the period 1268-1442, or perhaps even in the earlier Norman tradition. It is likely that at least some of these editions, like those printed in Venice, were commissioned by members of the religious establishment. It cannot be doubted, however, that both Moravus and Preller looked very closely at the products of their Venetian counterparts.

Less surprisingly, Venetian saints are also found in the calendar of the only Book of Hours printed in Verona, by Boninus de Boninis on 24 Oct. 1481 (no. 15). While its content is very simple, of the kind encountered in the Books of Hours printed in Italy in the 1470s, its calendar is highly local and includes many Venetian entries, but also other north-Italian saints, some of which can be found in the Milanese Hours. Again we seem to be confronted with the hagiographical selection of a specific institution, from the Veneto, which may be identified after careful analysis.

The influence of the early Venetian products also extended beyond Italy and can be detected in French editions and possibly in Spanish ones. The first Hours ever printed by Pigouchet on 21 Nov. [1487?][129] and those printed some time between 1493 and 1496[130] are of the use of Rome. Their calendar, however, is based on a Venetian edition.[131] Moreover, as in the Neapolitan editions, we find entries pertaining to the Lateran tradition of the Roman calendar that are generally not found in the so called 'Roman' calendars printed in France.[132] Their litanies and suffrages, on the other hand, present the common series found in most Parisian editions, and especially in Pigouchet's own, while the variety of texts included is also typical of the French Hours. The arrangement of the text is the same in the two editions, the latter containing some further prayers in French, which can be found in Pigouchet's 1489 edition[133] although this has a different calendar.

The Venetian Felicianus ep (24 Jan.), Geminianus (29 Jan.), Constantia (25 Feb.), Theodora (13 May), and Magnus (6 Oct.) are all listed in the 1486 edition of the Roman Hours printed in Valencia by an unidentified printer.[134] The content of this Book of Hours, the first printed in Spain, is also Italian in style, with only the Offices of the Virgin, of the Dead, of the Cross and of the Holy Spirit, the seven penitential psalms and the litanies present. The litanies correspond to those found in the 1474 Jenson edition, with the sole addition of Saturninus in prominent third position among the martyrs.

The presence of Venetian saints in calendars printed elsewhere allows us to track the spread of the Roman Hours as printed in Venice. More generally, the detection of similarities within calendars provides a valuable method alongside typography in determining the relation between liturgical editions.

Roman calendars can be found not only in the editions of Hours of Roman use, but also in Hours of local uses. A large number of Hours printed in Paris for local uses present what we may call the French variant of the Roman calendar: this is indicated by the addition of three French saints to the regular calendar of the Roman Curia.[135] The Hours of Bayeux printed in Paris in 1497,[136] the Hours of Le Mans printed in Paris in 1498/99,[137] the Hours of Paris printed in Paris in 1498,[138] and the Hours of Rouen printed in Paris in c. 1497,[139] all have this type of calendar. Here we can see the Roman calendar adapted to the French use. All these editions contain local litanies and suffrages in the French style, but the printer, Etienne Jehannot, who rivaled Pigouchet in producing Books of Hours for the entire French market, provided the same basically Roman calendar in each, a clear indication of his methods.[140]

I would like to conclude with two examples where a more detailed analysis of the text has highlighted a link between printer and patron, which, in the absence of any record such as is found in the mandate for publication, would otherwise remain unknown.

A systematic survey of the 148 Roman Hours printed in Paris will surely confirm a highly standardized and commercial process of production. It will be of great interest to establish how exactly this production was organized. An initial survey of some exemplars reveals, however, that, alongside the 'mass production' of Books of Hours, some editions were published on demand or aimed at for more specific markets.

BMC noted that the Roman Hours printed in Paris by Vérard and dated 10 Apr. 1489[141] contains a sanctoral from Rennes, detectable only in the calendar and litanies, since the Offices of the Virgin and of the dead are Roman, as stated in the heading that opens the office of the Virgin on fol. a$_3$,^{v} (this has been deleted in the British Library copy, but can be seen in the copy kept in the Bibliothèque Municipale in Millau).[142] The Hours printed by Bocard about 1500[143] present a similar case, with the same calendar from Rennes.

Again, in the Roman Hours printed by Jehannot c. 1499,[144] each gathering except for the first has the catchword 'ro' for Rome. The first gathering contains a calendar of Roman use, but adapted to the use of Langres, with on 26 Aug. the dedication of the church of St Mammas and its octave, and on 10 Oct. the translation of the saint. No missals were printed for the church of Langres in the fifteenth century, and only three early-sixteenth-century editions of the breviary of Langres are recorded in *ISTC*.[145] Each of these three editions survives in only one copy; all are in the Bibliothèque Nationale de France, and two are in a fragmentary condition. It is therefore useful to have rescued from the anonymity of the Roman Hours a book actually commissioned by someone from a specific French town, reflecting a local liturgical tradition for which very few texts survive.[146]

My second example is not actually a Book of Hours but a *Psalterium latinum cum hymnis et precibus*, printed in Venice in 1495.[147] The evaluation of its calendar and litanies reveals that it could have been made only for the Benedictine nuns of San Lorenzo in Venice. Founded in the first half of the ninth century in the sestiere di Castello, this convent became one of the richest in Venice, because it received the daughters of the nobility and of the richest families of the city; indeed, it became famous for its luxury and worldliness. It also housed a great collection of the relics of saints, all of whom can be found in the calendar and litanies of this psalter.[148] In the calendar we find:

Themisencius et Securus (12 Jan.), unidentified; *Translatio s Marci[149] (31 Jan., red); *Depositio s Symeonis[150] (4 Feb.); Gastrensis[151] (11 Feb.); *Fusca (13 Feb.); *Symeon proph (19 Feb), venerated on 18 Feb. in St Mark; Hermolaus presb[152] (27 Feb.); Transitus s Leonis[153] (19 Apr.); Tharasis[154] (8 May); Barbarus m et Felix (13 May), relics of the former in San Lorenzo; Dedicatio ecclesie s Laurentii (3 July, red); Inventio corporis s Ligoris[155] (8 July); *Hermacora et Fortunatus[156] (12 July, red); *Ligorius (13 Sept.); Dedicatio ecclesie s Marci [i.e. Michaelis] (29 Sept. red); *Plato[157] (18 Nov.); *Liberalis cf[158] (30 Dec).

In the litanies Mary appears first in every order of saints. Then we find Ligorius, Barbarus, Plato, Thoma, Tabra Tabrata et Theonistus[159] among the martyrs; Severus, Athanasius,[160] Vincentius, Florentius et Vindemiale[161] among the confessors; Pater Benedictus and Paulus among the monks; and finally Barbara,[162] Scolastica, Apolonia, Cristina, Candida,[163] Ursula, Undecim milia virgines among the virgins.

Both the specificity of the psalter's sanctoral and the wealth of the nuns of San Lorenzo suggest that the psalter was commissioned by the convent, or by one of its wealthy members, either for use in the convent's own services, or perhaps to be given or sold as a souvenir to visitors and friends of the institution.

This psalter in 1495 has been assigned to Bernardinus Stagninus, de Tridino by *IGI*, *CIBN*, tentatively to Baptista de Tortis by Goff, to Antonius de Zanchis by Proctor, and left unassigned by *BMC*. Considering that in 1497 Antonius de Zanchis printed a Benedictine breviary for the nuns of San Lorenzo,[164] but that the psalter appears to be printed, according to Sheppard, in Stagninus' types 95 G and 82 G, we may follow Rhodes's[165] suggestion that Antonius de Zanchis was more a publisher than a printer in Venice and consider this psalter to have been printed for him by Stagninus.[166]

This and the previous example testify to the value of a detailed investigation of the structure, but most importantly of the local characteristics of Books of Hours. Still mostly hidden behind the generic definition of Roman Hours is substantial historical data relating to the history of religious institutions, their liturgy, their libraries, and their attitude towards the new invention of printing.

A number of breviaries and missals contain, in the mandate for publication or in a preface, information about the person who commissioned the edition, generally the abbot of a religious order's mother-house, or an archbishop or bishop of a diocese. This kind of patron was not concerned with more private devotional works such as Books of Hours. The only known mediator is the bookseller, whose name or device appears in the colophon or on the title-page. However, it is now clear that a detailed analysis of the contents of the calendars and litanies can reveal how the printing trade used diverse liturgical sources, sometimes reflecting the accident of what was available, but sometimes precise local requirements. This is interesting for a further reason. Given the less formally ecclesiastical nature of a Book of Hours or a psalter, the persons or institutions who commissioned the edition will turn out to be not the head of a religious order or a bishop, but, as in the Venetian case, a single church or a local branch of an order, possibly even an individual member of it. This means that we can bring into the history of printing minor institutions, whose relationship with the press would otherwise be unknown, in the absence of explicit evidence such as prefaces or mandates for publication.

At the same time we can gather more evidence of the practices of individual printers. Antonius de Zanchis (Needham 184 no. 211) printed very little, producing eleven editions in Venice between 1496 and 1506, of which eight were liturgical, and three editions in Mantua, where he was active between 1512 and 1519.[167] The more we investigate his output, the more evident it becomes that he worked mostly on commission, printing the breviary and the psalter for the nuns of San Lorenzo, the *Diurnale Benedictinum Monialium Monasterii Sancti Zachariae Venetiarum*,[168] the *Legenda del Beato Zanebono*[169] (i.e. the blessed Augustinian Hermit from Mantua Giovanni Bono, *BSS* VI 629-31) for Federico Mantuano, an Augustinan Hermit of Mantua, to be used by the local community. More evidence can be found of work produced on commission. The *Martyrium S. Theodosiae virginis*,[170] for example, relates to a Venetian feast, and so should probably be connected with the parish church of San Tomà, in sestiere di San Polo, where there was a relic of St Theodosia. Again the colophon of the *Missale monasticum secundum ordinem Camaldulensem*[171] reveals that it was printed for the Camaldulese communities of San Michele and of San Mattia, both in Murano.[172] While the breviary of the order was commissioned by the General Petrus Delphinus[173] from Bartholomaeus Miscomini in Florence and printed in 1484,[174] no missal was printed for the order in the fifteenth century. Examining fifteenth-century book production and use in the monastery of San Mattia in Murano, Edoardo Barbieri notes that a manuscript missal was written by the Dominican scribe Filippo da Strada for the Camaldulese community of San Mattia while Nicolò da Tolmezzo was prior (1462-79);[175] it seems however that this manuscript was never used and therefore the production of de Zanchis's 1503 printed missal has to be seen within this Venetian context.

The copying of Venetian calendars by Parisian and other printers gave strictly local feasts an unexpectedly wide but largely accidental dissemination. One day we should be able to draw a family tree for the transmission of the printed Hours, which will enable us to distinguish between editions printed on commission and probably based on manuscript exemplars, and those based more clearly on previously printed exemplars. Once this first essential distinction has been made, we may consider further why an individual or institution commissioned a book from a specific printer: maybe because his printing shop was in the same parish or sestiere? Is it by chance that the female Benedictine convent of San Lorenzo as well as that of San Zaccaria, practically contiguous to each other in the sestiere di Castello, had their liturgical books printed by de Zanchis? I wish the Venetian printers had been as scrupulous as their Parisian colleagues in recording in their colophons their location in the city. The task of identifying Venetian institutions with specific calendars of the early printed Hours would have been easier.

It is worth noticing that for their Books of Hours Venetian printers used as exemplars material that reflects the liturgical practice of different local religious institutions, from the cathedral to parish churches and monasteries. Whether the selection of exemplar was the choice of the printer, or of a wealthy and pious lay person, or of a member of a religious institution (and the last two social groups might well overlap), the result remains the same: early printed Venetian Books of Hours were primarily created for a local community.

I have suggested ways in which more information may be gained on the relationships among printers, booksellers, and some of the ecclesiastical institutions that commissioned these texts, even in the absence of the explicit mention generally found in breviaries and missals. The few examples that I have provided show how much still remains to be done in identifying such relationships, but also how much can be done. As has become clear from this initial survey, a full understanding of the historical relevance of early printed Books of Hours can be achieved only by a detailed analysis of their contents. For the Venetian and Neapolitan editions this need can only be met by clarifying the cities' hagiographical traditions. Similarly, to give proper historical relevance to the many Parisian editions we have to untangle their calendars by making a distinction between what was produced on commission and what was offered by a printer to a larger market. It is a slow process, but one that will benefit scholars by illuminating a number of historical issues concerning printing and publishing, hagiography, liturgy, and ecclesiastical and social history.

APPENDIX

Horae ad usum Romanum printed in Italy in the Fifteenth Century[176]

1. *Horae.* [Rome: Printer of 'Mercuriales Quaestiones' (Theobaldus Schencbecher?), [*c.* 1473]. 32° (the only known copy, on paper, presents vertical chain-lines, it is not therefore a 16°). *ISTC* no: ih00357200.
2. *Horae.* Venice: N. Jenson, 1474. 16°. *ISTC* no: ih00357230.
3. *Horae.* [Venice: Nicolaus Jenson, not after 1474]. 16°. *ISTC* no: ih00357240.
4. *Horae.* Venice: Nicolaus Jenson, 1475. 32°. *ISTC* no: ih00357250.
5. *Horae.* [Venice: Nicolaus Jenson, *c.* 1475]. 16°. *ISTC* no: ih00357260.
6. *Horae.* [Venice:] Nicolaus Jenson, [*c.* 1475]. 32°/16° [*CIBN*]. *ISTC* no: ih00357270.
7. *Horae.* [Ferrara: Andreas Belfortis, Gallus, *c.* 1475]. 8°. *ISTC* no: ih00357290.
8. *Horae.* [Milan: Antonius Zarotus, *c.* 1475]. 8°. *ISTC* no: ih00257280.
9. *Horae.* Naples: Mathias Moravus, 11 June 1476. 16°. *ISTC* no: ih00357295.
10. *Horae.* Venice: Andreas de Paltasichis, 20 Apr. 1478. 16°. *ISTC* no: ih00357300.
11. *Horae.* [Naples: Mathias Moravus], 13 June 1478. 16°. *ISTC* no: ih00357340.
12. *Horae.* Naples: Mathias Moravus, 10 Nov. 1478. 8°. *ISTC* no: ih00357360.
13. *Horae.* [Venice: n.pr., about 1480]. 16°. *ISTC* no: ih00357450.
14. *Horae.* Rome: [Georgius Herolt,] 17 Mar. 1481. 16°. *ISTC* no: ih00357500.
15. *Horae.* Verona: Boninus de Boninis, de Ragusia, 24 Oct. 1481. 24°. *ISTC* no: ih00357600.
16. *Horae.* Venice: Nicolaus Girardengus, de Novis, 10 Nov. 1481. 16°. *ISTC* no: ih00357650.
17. *Horae.* [Venice: Andreas Torresanus, de Asula], for Johannes de Colonia, Nicolaus Jenson et Socii, 22 Dec. 1481. 32°. *ISTC* no: ih00357700.
18. *Horae.* Venice: Nicolaus de Frankfordia, 1482. 16°. *ISTC* no: ih00357740.
19. *Horae.* Florence: Nicolo di Lorenzo, 5 July 1483. 8°. *ISTC* no: ih00357750.
20. *Horae.* Venice: Georgius Arrivabenus, 1484. 12°. *ISTC* no: ih00357770.
21. *Horae.* Venice: Johannes Leoviler, de Hallis, [between 1485 and 1488]. 8°. *ISTC* no: ih00357780.
22. *Horae.* Naples: Mathias Moravus, 30 June 1486. 32°. *ISTC* no: ih00357800.
23. *Horae.* Naples: Mathias Moravus, 3 Oct. 1486. 8°. *ISTC* no: ih00357850.
24. *Horae.* [Naples:] Mathias Moravus, 3 Oct. 1487. 16°. *ISTC* no: ih00357930.
25. *Horae.* Naples: Cristannus Preller, 15 Nov. 1487. 8°. *ISTC* no: ih00357950.
26. *Horae.* Venice: Johannes Hamman, 1488, 32°. *ISTC* no: ih00359730.

27. *Horae. [Naples:] Mathias Moravus, 15 Oct. 1488. 16°. ISTC no: ih00359643.

28. *Horae. Venice: Andreas Torresanus, de Asula, 23 July 1489. 32°. ISTC no: ih00361500.

29. Horae. Naples: Mathias Moravus, 5 Mar. 1490. 16°. ISTC no: ih00364600.

30. *Horae. Naples: Cristannus Preller, 9 Apr. 1490. 8°. ISTC no: ih00364800.

31. *Horae. Venice: Johannes Hamman, 4 Dec. 1490. 32°. ISTC no: ih00365300.

32. *Horae. [Venice: Johannes Hamman, c.1490]. 16°. ISTC no: ih00366600.

33. *Horae. Venice, Johannes Hamman, 1490. 12°. ISTC no: ih00366400.

34. *Horae. Venice: Johannes Hamman, 3 Dec. 1491. 32°. ISTC no: ih00369350.

35. *Horae. Naples: Mathias Moravus, 10 Feb. 1492. 16°. ISTC no: ih00369700.

36. *Horae. Venice: Theodorus de Ragazonibus, 12 July 1492. 16°. ISTC no: ih00370300.

37. Horae. Venice: Johannes Hamman, 4 Feb. 1492/93. 16°. ISTC no: ih00370950.

38. *Horae. Venice: Johannes Hamman, 14[93]. 8°. ISTC no: ih00375500.

39. *Horae. Venice: Johannes Emericus de Spira, 6 May 1493. 32°. ISTC no: ih00373300.

40. *Horae. Venice: Hieronymus de Sanctis, 26 Apr. 1494. 8°. ISTC no: ih00374500.

41. *Horae. Venice: Johannes Emericus de Spira, 30 Nov. 1494. 16°. ISTC no: ih00377300.

42. Horae. Turin: Nicolaus de Benedictis and Jacobinus Suigus, 31 Jan. 1495. 8°. ISTC no: ih00377550.

43. *Horae. Venice: Johannes Emericus de Spira, for Lucantonio Giunta, 31 July 1495. 16°. ISTC no: ih00377900.

44. *Horae. Naples: Cristannus Preller, 13 Aug. 1495. 8°. ISTC no: ih00377800.

45. Horae. Naples: Ayolfus de Cantono, 22 Mar. 1496. 8°. ISTC no: ih00378300.

46. Horae. Naples: Cristannus Preller, 26 Mar. 1496. 16°. ISTC no: ih00378400.

47. *Horae. Venice: Johannes Emericus de Spira, for Lucantonio Giunta, 31 July 1496. 24°. ISTC no: ih00378700.

48. Horae. Venice: Johannes Emericus de Spira, for Lucantonio Giunta, 31 Aug. 1496. 32°. ISTC no: ih00379100.

49. Horae. Venice: Johannes Emericus de Spira, for Lucantonio Giunta, 9 May 1497. 32°. ISTC no: ih00383200.

50. *Horae. Venice: Johannes Emericus, de Spira, for Lucantonio Giunta, 31 Aug. 1497. 16°. ISTC no: ih00388800.

51. *Horae. Venice: Johannes Hamman for Octavianus Scotus, 1 Oct. 1497. 12°. ISTC no: ih00389500.

52. Horae. Naples: Cristannus Preller, 22 Jan. 1498. 8°. ISTC no: ih00393400.

53. *Horae. Venice: Johannes Emericus de Spira, for Lucantonio Giunta, 30 Sept. 1498. 16°. ISTC no: ih00395500.

54. Horae. Venice: Johannes Emericus, de Spira, for Lucantonio Giunta, 21 May 1499. 64°. ISTC no: ih00399800.

Pl. 1. Rogier van der Weyden. *The Seven Sacraments Altarpiece*, c. 1 4 4 0 - 5. Oil on oak panel, central panel 200 × 97 cm, side panels each 119 × 63 cm (Koninklijk Museum voor Schone Kunsten, Antwerp, Belgium).

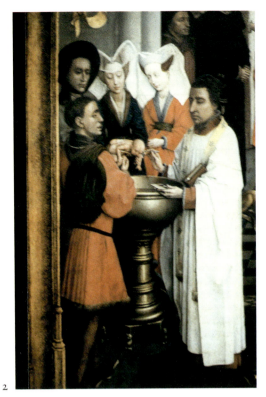

2

3

4

5

6

7

8

Pl. 2. Baptism.

Pl. 3. Children leaving Confirmation.

Pl. 4. Eucharist at main altar; choirbook on atril; missal open on rear altar.

Pl. 5. Couple attending Mass, rear altar.

Pl. 6. Plaque on column; book under grill.

Pl. 7. Holy Orders; Matrimony.

Pl. 8. Woman with book, Extreme Unction.

Pl. 9. Penance; Mass in rear chapel.

Pl. 10. Extreme Unction.

Pl. 11. Pico Master, Death of Eli, King Saul enthroned, and floral and gold-dot borders, in *Biblia italica*. Venice: Vindelinus de Spira, 1 August 1471, opening to I Kings (I Samuel) (Zürich, Zentralbibliothek, Sig. 2.6, fol. 119ʳ).

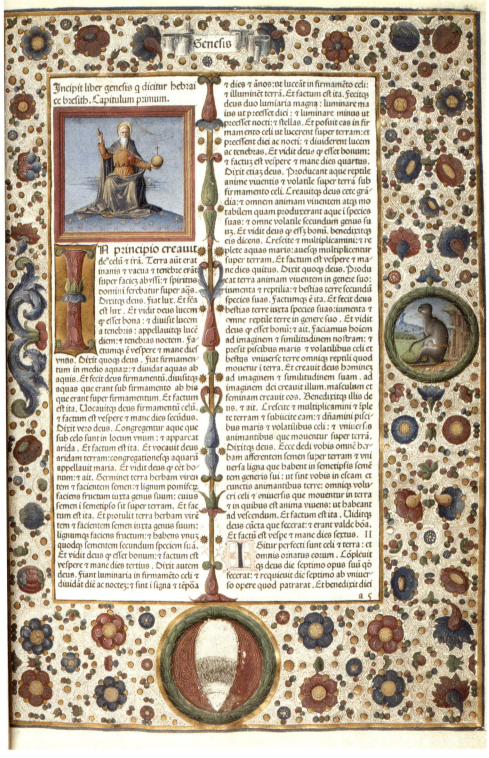

Pl. 12. Girolamo da Cremona, God the Creator, and floral and gold-dot borders with a monkey, in *Biblia latina*. Venice: Nicolaus Jenson, 1476, opening of Genesis (Manchester, John Rylands University Library, 9382, fol. a5ʳ, vellum).

Pl. 13. Pico Master, God the Creator, and Scenes of Creation, in *Biblia latina cum postillis Nicolai de Lyra*. Venice: Franciscus Renner, 1482-3, opening to *Commentary on Genesis* (Città del Vaticano, Biblioteca Apostolica Vaticana, Inc. Ross. 1157, fol. 17ʳ [c1ʳ], vellum).

Pl. 14. Ferrarese miniaturist, St Jerome, Isaiah, and Nicholas of Lyra (?) in a landscape, and borders with putti, cameos, and classical motifs, in *Biblia latina cum postillis Nicolai de Lyra*. Venice: [Johannes Herbort de Seligenstadt] for Johannes de Colonia, Nicolaus Jenson, et Socii, 31 July 1481, opening of Prologue to Isaiah (Paris, Bibliothèque nationale de France, Rés. Vél. 113, fol. AA1ʳ, vellum).

READING LITURGICAL BOOKS

MARY KAY DUGGAN

LITURGY IS A FIXED religious ritual, to be performed in a communal setting. While the act of ritual performance includes the reading of texts, it goes beyond reading to include physical actions, singing, and varying levels of speech by the major celebrant, the choir, the canons, and, rarely, the public. Therefore, users of liturgical books are not merely readers but also singers or even performers. A particular liturgical book can contain only part of any ritual; both texts and directions (called rubrics because written in red) are often highly abbreviated, and assume that substantial texts, melodies, and physical actions are either to be memorized by the participants, or to be sought by reference to liturgical books for other participants. For example, the liturgical psalter contains the entire corpus of psalms and often the hymns for the hours of the Divine Office, but contains only abbreviated references to the plainchant to be sung by the choir, the full text of which is in the antiphonal. In the era of scarce and costly manuscripts, few liturgical participants had access to books and texts had to be memorized. Gradually memorizing was integrated with the use of books as an *aide-mémoire* as well as for reading. The fixed nature of ritual itself, with repetition daily, weekly, or annually, evolved from the necessity of communal participation by many who had to rely on memory for words, music, or physical activities.

The proliferation of liturgical books in the fourteenth and fifteenth centuries changed the balance of memorisation and reading. The very nature of the reading of the majority of clerics and religious underwent a fundamental change from a communal setting to a private chamber, from oral performance to the silent meditative process that can affects one's identity.[1] This change was accelerated by the proliferation of liturgical incunabula, and the location of liturgical books evolved in the social system from large, scarce, expensive objects whose permanent home was on a lectern in the church to hundreds of thousands of cheap portable objects that were designed to be read in choir stalls but could be carried elsewhere for perusal. Liturgical incunabula themselves supply clues to the change that occurred, through their format, design, texts, and records of provenance. Artists' representations of the use of liturgical books in fifteenth-century illuminations, paintings, and woodcuts provide more clues. By 1550 liturgy had taken two divergent paths, one of a synthesis of Catholic liturgy into a single authorized set of books in Latin printed under monopoly in Rome and another of very different vernacular liturgies in reformed churches; those processes of centralization and standardization along with a move to the vernacular are trends that emerged in the fifteenth century. In particular, the liturgical psalter, with its collection of the complete psalms and hymns, had been transformed from a tool of monks, clerics, and aristocracy into the reading or singing of everyman, or at least every literate man and woman. A key to that transformation is an understanding of how liturgical books were read.

Liturgical incunabula can be defined as those books which support the two main rituals of the Catholic Church, the Mass and the Hours of the Divine Office, as well as other rituals for the sacraments, processions, and local services. The books for the Mass are the missal, with its collection of texts and plainchant for the celebrant or priest, and the gradual, with plainchant for the choir. The books for the Office include the antiphonal for the choir, the liturgical psalter for the cantor and participating religious or clerics, and various books of textual readings for the celebrant. In order to be ordained, a priest was required to own a missal. Secular clerics and religious might supplement communal celebrations of the Office with private reading, and by the fifteenth century it was not unusual for them to own personal breviaries, which contained the daily required reading. The major categories of liturgical incunables – breviarium, missale, psalterium, and a few choirbooks (graduale and antiphonarium) – account for 1087 editions between 1457 and 1500, or about five per cent of the total production (see Table 1).[2] Since most of those editions were large folios of hundreds of pages, liturgical incunabula probably account for about a fifth of the total number of pages produced for fifteenth-century readers. If an average edition size were 500 copies, about half a million liturgical books were printed by 1501.

In 1500 the population of Europe was about 65.8 million and an estimated five per cent, or 3.3 million, were secular clerics or religious men and women in monasteries and convents.[3] In cities priests and religious made up about one-tenth of the population.[4] Sufficient liturgical incunabula were printed for each of the 3.3 million to own on average 1.5 new liturgical books. There was a major textual reform effort by the pope, cardinals, and bishops to replace manuscript missals with the approved texts of the Roman rite, or reformed diocesan and monastic texts.[5] Printing had less impact on choirbooks, of which only sixteen editions were printed by 1501. The largest number of liturgical incunabula were breviaries whose 453 editions, or about a quarter of a million copies, placed the complete biblical texts, prayers, and songs of the Office in the hands of clergy and religious, male and female, certainly for many the first book they owned.[6] Second in number of editions were the missals, 80 per cent in folio format for use upon the altar. Included in the genre of liturgical psalter are those books containing the complete psalms as well as rubrics for their performance within the hours of the Office; such rubrics could be printed but most often had to be written by hand by the owner in blank space provided in printed editions, thus allowing regional variation.[7]

The conservative nature of the choirbook is apparent in its folio format, including the largest book printed in the fifteenth century (*Graduale Romanum*. Venice: Johannes Emericus, de Spira, for Lucantonio Giunta, 28 Sept. 1499; 14 Jan. 1499/1500; 1 Mar. 1500. *ISTC* ig00332000). Such enormous tomes were intended to remain in church, placed on a lectern to be used by many singers for controlled reading during supervised rehearsals and performances. The twenty per cent of missals that were printed in the last decade of the century in quarto and octavo format are a significant indication of the movement of the missal from the altar into other environments for different kinds of reading. Small breviaries were already in private ownership in the manuscript era, and the large number of incunables bears testament to the triumph of private reading and meditation among clerics and religious in the fifteenth century who no longer had to rely solely on a communal celebration of the Office for their daily ritual. Incunable liturgical psalters were read by the intended audience of clerics and religious and a few

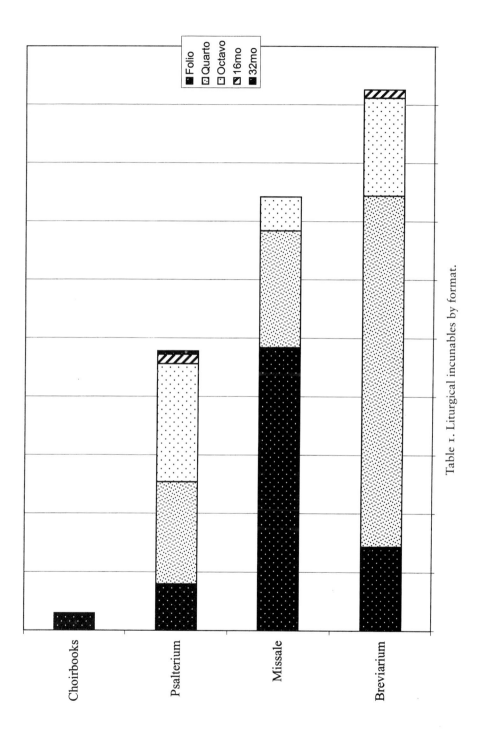

Table 1. Liturgical incunables by format.

men and women of Europe's cities. Editions of the psalter were published not only in Latin but also in bilingual and in vernacular editions. In 1460 most liturgical psalters were folio books, meant to remain in church on a lectern before the choir stalls. By 1500 most liturgical psalters were in octavo and smaller formats and belonged to individuals.

Readers of liturgical books fall into several categories. That they are primarily clerical and religious is no surprise, since what little is conjectured about literacy before 1500 suggests a rate of about five per cent, equalling the proportion of the population thought to have made up the clerical and religious sector.[8] Ideally monastic communities were educated in Latin grammar and were required to memorize the 150 psalms that they would sing weekly for the rest of their lives. That printed incunable psalters served an educational function is known from the inscription in extant monastic copies of such phrases as 'des junges Buch'. In the fifteenth century many orders established houses at the great universities of Europe so that their novices could continue their education. Female religious were not regularly literate in Latin, but numbers of incunable Latin psalters printed in Germany and the Netherlands belonged to nuns.[9] Cathedral and collegiate canons in the cities had usually been well educated in associated schools, often going on to universities. Some cathedrals still retain multiple copies of incunable liturgical books whose entire editions must have been directed at their canons.[10] On the other hand the village priest was often completely unschooled, relying on private tutoring from the incumbent priest he had followed.[11] Requirements for ordination were few, and those lightly enforced (own a missal, and pass an oral examination before the bishop on the ability to read a page of that book). There were no seminaries, a lack which had been addressed by Jean Gerson at the Council of Constance and brought up again at the Council of Basel. Fifteenth-century textual reformers directed their efforts at the most literate members of the population, who were generally found in monastic institutions. Prefaces to editions by sponsoring bishops prescribed their purchase, at a subsidized price, by all 'prelates, those belonging to churches as well as those holding benefices', within a jurisdiction.

When he [Reyser] has finished this work he is required to sell it to anyone demanding to have the book from him, bound, for four Rhenish guilder. Therefore we admonish and exhort, piously and paternally in our Lord, the prelates, ecclesiastics, holders of benefices, and others under our jurisdiction to prepare themselves for the purchase of said missal ...[12]

In the late fifteenth century visitations by bishops to each place of worship in the diocese were begun and a part of their protocol was an inventory of liturgical books to enforce the purchase of reformed texts. As a result of such visitations through the end of the sixteenth century, most incunable liturgical books were destroyed, to be replaced by the new editions prescribed by the Council of Trent. But the intended purchasers of liturgical books were not only the most literate.[13] Less literate users of a folio liturgical book in a communal setting would be reading less for discovery than for recognition.[14] For instance, the large initial 'B' that began the liturgical psalter was sufficient for recall of the first verse of the first psalm, whose musical melody was so well known that it was never printed.

Some changes in presentation by editors and printers that increased legibility and accessibility to less fluent readers were common to all incunables, such as replacement of abbreviations by full spelling. Features particular to liturgical books were added for a number of reasons: to provide assistance for less literate readers such as the isolated parish priest, to aid the scholar, to control reading in a manner that fulfilled the reform goal of uniform performance of the liturgy, and, not least, to sell books. A combination of these aims explains the addition of greatly extended rubrics, as well as preliminary gatherings in missals of instructions for the use of the perpetual calendar, prayers to be said while preparing for Mass, and *cauteles* or warnings on how to deal with accidents involving the consecrated bread and wine. 'New' or 'added' features of a printed text were touted on the emerging title-page, even when those features ran counter to hierarchical reforms ('cum certis officiis annexis' *Missale strigoniense*, Venice: Emericus de Spira, 26 II 1498/99; 'cum multi benedictionibus' *Liber baptismalis*, [Pavia: Girardengus & Bireta, 1480-90]; 'additis certis actibus et benedictionibus' *Agenda brevis*, Venice: Hamman, 1 X 1495). Tables of feasts and votive masses in missals, tables of hymns and antiphons, with foliation, would have assisted all levels of readers. More for the scholarly audience were such ancillary publications as translations, explanations (often called *Auslegung* in incunable bibliographies), dictionaries of liturgical Latin, and commentaries on the psalms, canon, gospels, and epistles. Almost a textbook was the preliminary gathering of the first volume of the choirbook *Graduale Romanum* (Venice, 1499); seeking a wide European market, it contained an introduction to plainchant and defended the flats and sharps inserted in melodic lines at a time when the use of such accidentals varied on either side of the Alps.[15] Such changes in the presentation of liturgical books suggest that both the intended audience and the intended use of liturgical books had moved beyond the most proficient Latin readers and outside the church services themselves.

For many of this group of required readers, the Latin language was a sacred language in which they were somewhat illiterate, and texts were ritually sung or read aloud as textual units without reference to their content, much as the Hebrew liturgical texts described by Robert Bonfil in his discussion of reading in Jewish communities.[16] Some readers of liturgical books sought assistance in understanding the Latin texts through printed incunables that provided translations or bilingual editions of the prayers of the missal, the gospels and epistles, or the psalter, perhaps along with dictionaries of church Latin and learned commentaries that would assist clerics in preparing sermons for their congregations, and encourage educated lay to understand their religion.[17] Well into the sixteenth century the argument was being made by Catholic clerics that at least the rubrics and gospels and epistles of the Roman missal should be printed in the vernacular for the celebrant.[18] While the breviary might be translated for nuns, the author of *The Myroure of oure Ladye* cautioned that the English text is only 'to be vnderstonde of them that haue sayde theyre mattyns or redde theyr legende [in Latin] before'.[19] Several owners of Latin liturgical psalters entered a vernacular title of each psalm in the margin of the printed text. Alternatively, owners of vernacular psalters entered rubrics for Latin antiphons and hymns. For example, one copy of the German psalter printed at Ulm by Conrad Dinckmut in 1492 begins with two manuscript leaves in German which contain directions for matching psalms to the services of the hours on each day of the week, followed by a printed table of contents of the psalms in Latin and German, and with manuscript rubrics added in German in the margins of psalms throughout, for nocturns, lauds, matins, and complines.[20] In this transitional period the spoken liturgy might be in Latin, but the silent prayer of the mind appears to be in the vernacular for many, clergy and lay.

The most intensive level of reading of liturgical incunabula was done by editors involved in the preparation of reformed texts, calendars of feasts, and plainchant; occasional annotations in incunable missals prove that they were used well into the sixteenth century by individuals and committees to compile revisions.[21] The work of translation of the psalms that is visible in incunable vernacular liturgical psalters, plenaria, and bibles encouraged scholars like Erasmus (d. 1536) and Lefèvre d'Étaples (d. 1536) to produce scholarly editions such as the multilingual *Quincuplex psalterium* (Paris: Henri Estienne, 1509) and the gospels and epistles for the Sundays of the year in French (1536) that explored differences between traditions of Roman and Gallican rites and Hebrew codices. Luther used the Parisian psalter of Lefèvre d'Étaples to teach his course on the psalms in Wittenberg, and he used German incunable liturgical translations in his own liturgical and biblical research. The drive for a uniform liturgy required the reform of the calendar proclaimed by Pope Gregory XIII in 1582, necessitating the elimination of nine days in that year. Germany did not adopt the Gregorian system until 1700, and the British Parliament debated the reform until 1752.[22] Because of widespread interest in the calendar sparked by the drive toward uniformity in reformed texts of liturgical incunables, one might point to liturgical reading by textual editors as the cause of this major scientific advance, one that stimulated the publication of such incunables as Regiomontanus's *Calendarium* ([Venice]: Bernhard Maler, Erhard Ratdolt, & Peter Löslein, 1476).

An indication of a more independent kind of liturgical reader comes from extant copies of a genre entitled *Missale itinerantium* or *Vade mecum*. A compilation of manuscript material, woodcuts, and printed gatherings, the *Missale itinerantium* commonly lacked a liturgical calendar and replaced the prescribed yearly ritual with a few offices for major feasts like the Resurrection, a few saints of regional importance and votive masses (against temptation, for farmers, for the ill or the dead, etc.).[23] One such collected volume would presumably satisfy the complete liturgical needs of a celebrant. An example at Cologne contained a printed quarto *Missale itinerantium* of 22 leaves along with manuscript gatherings containing a psalter, a collection of votive masses, votive orations, and finally a Mass and vespers for the dead.[24] The owner of the printed leaves was promised an indulgence of 500 days if he would insert the new prayers into Sunday masses; would such an attraction have helped to persuade him to purchase the printed canon and ordinary of the mass? It would be a mistake to consider the owner of a *Missale itinerantium* to be a less qualified reader; the manuscript leaves of the Cologne example are written in a fine gothic hand in red and black, with two sizes of script. After the woodcut Crucifixion of fol. A1^v is inserted a vellum leaf with manuscript prefaces (28 lines to a page) plus a repetition of the printed words of the Consecration (12 lines to a page) and an initial decorated in gold, apparently to satisfy a need for a more distinctive setting than the printed version. Another example of a collective volume that includes the *Missale itinerantium* ([Cologne: Quentell, c. 1500]) appears to be a compilation for home study. It is bound with (1) Nicolaus de Byard, *Dictionarius pauperum omnibus predicatoribus verbi divini pernecessarius de tempore et de sanctis* (Cologne: July 6, 1504); (2) Augustinus de Leonissa, *Sermones pulcherrimi super orationem dominicam ...* (Cologne: Apud Predicatores, 1503); (3) *Abbreviatura exercitij spiritualis patrum et fratrum de obseruantia Bursfeldensis ex libro de tribus regionibus claustralium incipit* (Cologne: Martinus de Werdena, 1505).[25] The studious owner has taken a decisive step away from oral repetitive prayer to religious thought and meditation that fully involves the mind. This *Missale itinerantium* bound with three other printed books belongs not on the altar but in the scholar's study.

A challenge to the monastic practice of communal repetition of oral prayer had been building for centuries. The fourteenth-century Carthusian Robert de St Martin described the highest form of prayer as adoration and contemplation, though he placed the Mass and Office as the first responsibility of a religious. He encouraged monks to add the daily Office of Our Lady in addition to the communal celebration of the Hours.[26] Jean Gerson, Chancellor of the University of Paris who died in 1429, urged the avoidance of mechanical repetition of oral prayer without thought or mental prayer.[27] Regulations about private prayer were being inserted in the statutes of many orders, including the Franciscans in 1451; a study of language used to describe the level of reading from singing to saying at full voice to low voice reveals a deep concern about what was happening to the meaning of such private monastic prayer and about the change in the rhythms of monastic life.[28] In 1452 Juan de Capistrano (1386-1456), writing to Albert Puchelbach, the guardian of the Observant friary at Nuremberg, referred at some length to the matter. The saint had accepted a number of novices and was sending them to Nuremberg for their training. He was anxious that they be brought up in the right way, and that included instruction in the art of mental prayer. While it was important that they should learn to sing the Divine Office, 'it would be very much better if they were taught to be sorry for their sins and to pray. Far too much time could be spent on singing the offices. Let Mass and Vespers be sung and the rest said [read aloud]. The novices can then spend an hour a day on their meditations'.[29] Religious were supposed to memorize the psalms in their early years as novices. To a novice who wished to have a psalter, St Francis is said to have replied: 'When you have a breviary you will sit in a chair like a great prelate, and will say to your brother, "Brother, fetch me my breviary".'[30] An illumination of bookless Franciscan friars in choir stalls for the Divine Office is included in the psalter of Richard II of England, used by him as a boy about 1400; a repertoire of illuminations of members of various religious orders, most with psalter in hand or shared, indicate that the prince was to learn to distinguish monastic garb and customs along with the psalms of the text.[31]

Not just reading but writing was required of the owners of many liturgical editions. Owners often had to provide a liturgical calendar, music notation in blank space provided, and in the liturgical psalter rubrics and incipits for any texts or songs beyond the psalms required for the Hours of the Office. The ability to write Latin and plainchant may have been common in the monastery, where liturgical manuscripts existed from which to copy the needed information, but the persistence of blank space in extant printed liturgical books is a clue to missing writing skills in the monastery or to a lay owner who lacked both the writing skills and the needed information to complete the book, and who may have acquired the book solely for silent reading, though the psalms may well have been sung even at home.[32]

Manuscript material was also added to presumably complete printed books. The replacement of tens of thousands of manuscript liturgical books that contained decades or centuries of local accretions by centrally authorized texts that conformed to diocesan and papal standards amounted to a revolution in the celebration of liturgy from monastery to village. Resistance to the change enabled by the technology of printing can be seen in lengthy manuscript additions which were made to liturgical incunabula before they were bound by their owners. For example, the late medieval sequences of northern Europe were often added in manuscript to Italian editions of the *Missale Romanum*, offices of regional saints were inserted in added gatherings and in calendars, and votive Masses excised by reformers were restored to satisfy local demand.[33] In one quarto incunable psalter of 1480 the eight psalm tones that would have aided sung performance in the absence of a cantor have been inserted in manuscript.[34]

A final category of reader of liturgical incunables is the lay reader. While provenance records of extant incunables tell us that all choirbooks, almost all missals and breviaries, and most liturgical psalters belonged to clerics or religious, a few of the survivors did find their way into the hands of lay owners, male and female. For example, a 16° Dutch psalter in which the printer left as many as twelve lines a page blank for the owner to fill in rubrics for the Hours of the Office was owned by one Jan van Veerse (fifteenth-sixteenth centuries).[35] A quarto Latin *Missale Romanum* (Venice: Andreas Torresanus, de Asula, Bartholomaeus de Blavis, de Alexandria, & Mapheus de Paterbonis, 2 July 1482) (*ISTC* im00692500; Weale-Bohatta 874) was owned in 1505 by one Rutgerus Haenrath. One copy of a Latin liturgical psalter left blank the ample space for rubrics and filled the margins and space for initials with decoration typical of a Book of Hours, suggesting to me that it had a lay owner, from England judging by the language of the rubrics of thirteen leaves of manuscript Latin prayers at the end.[36] Inventories of private libraries in France show that men were as likely to own a Latin psalter as a Book of Hours, while female owners of psalters were greatly outnumbered by owners of Books of Hours.[37] Some of the finest manuscript breviaries seem to have been used by royalty and aristocracy, but that kind of owner did not favour printed versions of the genre.[38] By the fifteenth century, chapels in private houses were increasingly common and the offices and Mass were a daily ritual.[39]

New vernacular rituals had emerged for the spiritual brotherhoods of urban laity, such as the Stations of the Cross, the Passion, and the rosary. For example, several incunable pamphlets of the Brotherhood of St Ursula's Ship were printed in German in Strasbourg with prayers and the text and music of the first printed German song.[40] Hymns in Latin or German were for sale in broadsheet form to take home and tack up on the wall.[41] While the printed Latin rituals of the Mass and Office were not intended by authorities for lay readers, printed vernacular psalters began the rise in popularity that would make them the bestsellers of the sixteenth century.[42] It is likely that such books were sung to many more than were sufficiently literate to read the texts. If it is true that 'printing altered and adapted the process of national identity formation', one might look to the vernacular psalter for an example of that process.[43] The great majority of psalters of the sixteenth century were printed with music notation, or letter notation for the lay unskilled in reading music, so that the psalms could continue to retain a sung performance. Indeed, reformers in Lyon used sung psalms as their marching music ('Blessed be the Lord my strength who teaches my hands to war and my fingers to fight,' Psalm 143), provoking King Henry II to ban the public singing of psalms in 1558.[44] The king specifically allowed Protestants to sing psalms privately, though not in assemblies or communal gatherings, even at home. Thus as psalters moved out of the church in portable formats, owners continued to sing aloud the verses in their monastic cells or at home. Perhaps the verses were also sung silently in the mind, in the way in which we silently 'sing' to ourselves familiar songs and hymns. Not until the end of the seventeenth century were bilingual Latin and French missals finally distributed widely by the Catholic Church, in the hope that they could be used to convert Protestants. In 1685, the year of the Revocation of the Edict of Nantes, a hundred thousand copies of Catholic Books of Hours in French, preceded by the ordinary of the mass in French, were printed by the Archbishop of Paris on the order of Louis XIV. There was vigorous opposition to such translations, which were characterized as Jansenist. Detractors still feared that lay Catholics would imagine that 'they are priests in the same sense as the priest'.[45] How much power lay in the small incunable vernacular psalters! Reading has been described by Michel de Certeau with a metaphor of poaching. Every reader invents in texts something different from what was intended.[46] That demonstrators would use a psalm as a marching song would not have occurred to the monastic trainer of novices, some of whom were to lead those marches in the sixteenth century.

A secondary source of evidence about fifteenth-century readers of liturgical books comes from representations by artists. A carving of a fifteenth-century young novice immersed in silent reading of her breviary was carved on the end of the choir stalls in Bamberg.[47] The psalter read or sung by clergy or religious is ever-present in representations of services for the dead both in church and in the home.[48] Readers form the contents of the psalter's standard historiated initial 'C' that begins the service for Saturday with the psalm 'Cantate domino canticum novum': groups of singers crowd around the antiphonal that holds the antiphons and hymns that surrounded the psalms in services.[49] Illuminations and engravings of aristocratic services show similar large groups of singers around giant choirbooks, as well as reading of other books by illuminaries and their courtiers.[50] Nearly every fifteenth-century Annunciation shows Mary reading a psalter, an encouragement to women viewers to emulate her.[51] A manuscript illumination of a procession in Bruges, 1463, shows two monks sharing a large book, whereas a procession in Italy in the second half of the fifteenth century shows both clerics and lay people with small books, and the woodcut in the incunable *Processionarium fratrum predicatorum* (Venice, 1494) shows each monk with a book.[52]

An entire array of books, liturgical and other, is portrayed in the *Seven Sacraments Altarpiece* completed about 1440-5 by Rogier van der Weyden as a commission by Jean Chevrot (*c.* 1400-60), an important political figure who became the head of the duke of Burgundy's Great Council in 1433 and, after a struggle over the right of appointment between the king of France and the duke, bishop of Tournai in 1438. The altarpiece is thought to have been painted for the so-called Chapel of Tournai he had had constructed in the collegial Church of St Hippolytus at Poligny, France, his place of birth.[53] The chapel, completed on 15 November 1453, was particularly devoted to the Holy Sacrament to which its confraternity was dedicated. Chevrot's will of 1458 provided well for the chapel, including a tapestry of the sacraments and a chained library of his books.[54] While Chevrot is best known for his financial acumen and diplomatic skill, it is true that like many other northern bishops of his time he did hold a synod (14 April 1445) to reform the statutes of his diocese. In his vision of the ideal *ecclesia* portrayed in the altarpiece, books figure prominently in most of the sacraments as well as in the hands of many lay persons in the church. The sacraments form a circuit of life and death from Baptism in the left foreground, to the Eucharist in the middle, to Extreme Unction on the right (col. pl. 1). In the left foreground the priest holds a small baptismal or *rituale* under his arm before the font (col. pl. 2). A newly-confirmed boy carries a small book of many leaves (catechism? psalter?) as he leaves the bishop, a portrait of Chevrot himself (col. pl. 3).[55] There is no book visible for the sacrament of Penance, but there is a plaque hanging on one of the pillars to the right of the altar in front of which stands a man reading what is likely a vernacular Our Father, Creed, and Ten Commandments, a good preparation for and conclusion to confession (col. pl. 6).[56] At a side chapel at the left rear, several laymen kneel at Mass with books open in their hands (liturgical psalters, books of hours, prayerbooks?) (col. pl. 9). One assumes a clear dichotomy between oral performance by the priest from the folio Latin missal and silent reading by the congregation.

A banner for the Eucharist is above the main altar where a priest reads from a folio missal (col. pl. 4). Behind the main altar a robed priest sings from a choirbook (gradual) on a lectern and another missal is just visible on a rear altar. At the right rear two well-dressed citizens attend the service in progress at the rear altar, she reading from a small cloth-bound book (Book of Hours?) and he with a closed book at his side (psalter?) (col. pl. 5). For the sacrament of Holy Orders on the right a pontifical is held by an assistant for the bishop who is ordaining a priest (col. pl. 7). No books appear among the group at the marriage ceremony; the couple's hands are bound by a stole as specified by the Ghent-Tournai rite. There is a book (psalter?) in the hands of the woman reading quietly on the floor beside the bed of the dying man; two clerics administer the sacrament of Extreme Unction, the only sacrament represented in a venue outside the church (col. pl. 8, 10). One more book remains to be identified: some distance behind the reader of the plaque is a layman reading a large folio book secured behind an iron grille (col. pl. 6). Secure niches are extant in French churches where they are known to have been created to hold liturgical psalters or breviaries for poor clergy. Such books would then be available to literate laymen such as the one pictured by Weyden.[57]

Weyden's large altarpiece can only present an idealized version of liturgical practice as desired by Chevrot for his home town of Poligny. Sauerländer drew attention to the importance of fifteenth-century paintings of gothic churches in defining a reformed use of their space, a space which in the case of the *Seven Sacraments* was called 'a profound synthesis of Christian spirituality' by Jacques Toussaert.[58] An integral part of this vision of reform is the importance of liturgical and devotional reading by both cleric and lay, male and female. No doubt in Chevrot's ideal conception of the sacraments and devotional reading all books were in Latin, though the plaque was likely in the vernacular. The array of manuscripts in the altarpiece of 1445 could be seen as an agenda for the print shop of the next decades.

The cost and scarcity of the manuscript liturgical book had meant that it was usually provided only to the major celebrant, and then in a large ceremonial form whose physical weight meant that it remained in the church, the site of communal performance. Large folio books for the two main rituals of the Catholic Church, the Mass and the Hours of the Divine Office, remained on the altar or the lectern. Much of the performance of liturgical ritual depended on the memory of the participants, and it is likely that even the major celebrants used much of the repetitive text of liturgical books as an *aide-mémoire* rather than for actual reading. But by the middle of the fifteenth century smaller, more portable liturgical books had begun to proliferate: the breviary for the secular cleric or monastic religious to supplement services in a communal setting; the *rituale, agenda, vigilia, baptismale* for the priest who administered sacraments; the processional for the choir on the march, the quarto psalter for the residents of choir stalls whose memory was failing and who were unable to make out the letters of the large psalter. While the first printed liturgical books were designed to continue to function as large formal books to remain in the church for communal performance, the smaller books were carried to the chamber to be read. Early bilingual psalters (German/Latin) may have been intended for the monastic community, but such publications as the eighteen editions of the psalter in German, eight editions of the Dutch psalter (1473-98), a Bohemian psalter (Prague, 1487), a thousand copies of a Catalan *Psaltiri* (Venice, 1490), and a Serbian *Psaltir s postedovaniem* printed in Montenegro (Cetinje, 1495) surely were aimed at the general literate population as well.[59] Translations of the prayers of the missal had been available in German in manuscript since the fourteenth century, and began to be printed in the 1470s.[60] An edition of the prayers of the Mass in Dutch was printed in 1481.[61] Translations of the gospels and epistles appeared in the 1470s, and the baptismal appeared as *L'Ordinaire des chrestiens* in the 1490s. It was readers of liturgical incunables who would develop the new religions of the next century and who would write liturgies to serve them. If hierarchical reformers intended print to fix a monolithic Latin ritual in the West, the technology instead placed books in the hands of those who were empowered to continue the reform to vernacular congregational rituals outside of the monastery and canonical stalls.

THE HAND ILLUMINATION OF VENETIAN BIBLES IN THE INCUNABLE PERIOD[1]

LILIAN ARMSTRONG

IT IS WELL KNOWN that the first Venetian bible fully illustrated with narrative woodcuts was the Italian translation by Nicolò Malerbi (Malermi in the older literature), printed by Giovanni Ragazzo for LucAntonio Giunta in 1490. Its opening folio with six scenes of the Creation is a monument to early woodcut design and its 384 small narrative woodcuts form an unprecedented treasure-trove of illustrative material which was drawn upon by later artists as notable as Michelangelo.[2]

But many editions of the Bible both in Latin and in Italian were printed in Venice in the twenty years before 1490, and this paper seeks to characterize their illustration and decoration. Three periods of Venetian bible decoration before the advent of woodcuts can be categorized. Experiments in illustration and decoration occasioned by bibles printed in 1471 constitute the first category. Consolidation of the schemes used to decorate bibles between 1475 and 1484 are the second. Finally, the decoration and illustration of bibles printed with the Commentary of Nicholas of Lyra in 1481 and 1482-3 present new demands for diagrams and presage the arrival of the woodcut.[3]

From the beginning, Latin bibles printed in Italy distinguished themselves from their German counterparts not in their texts, but in their experimental design and in the sheer quantity of illumination and hand-work.[4] The first bible to be printed in Italy was issued in Rome by Sweynheym and Pannartz in 1471.[5] Although its text is closely modelled on the Gutenberg bible, its appearance is certainly not (Fig. 1). The unique layout of the Sweynheym and Pannartz edition with its single block of text in roman or *antica* typeface is almost shocking when compared to the two-column text in black-letter gothic type of the Gutenberg bible.[6] Sweynheym and Pannartz had been printing in Italy since 1465, and by 1471 had already printed some thirty editions primarily of classical and patristic authors, all using a roman font.[7] For their 1471 bible, Sweynheym and Pannartz used a layout to which they and their clients were accustomed, and for which they had an available font.

In addition, to provide decoration for individual copies of the 1471 bible, they called upon the same miniaturists who had been adding white vine-stem borders to printed copies of humanist texts. Their standard first-text-page decoration can be seen in a copy in the John Rylands University Library in Manchester (Fig. 1).[8] Precisely interlaced white vinestems form regular borders, controlled by narrow frames of gold. The gold capital 'F' is embedded in the vines and rises far above the seven lines of text indented for the letter; in the lower margin a green wreath surrounds a blank circle awaiting the buyer's coat of arms. Exuberant vines edged in intense blue burst out of the ends of the

Fig. 1. Roman miniaturist, White vine-stem borders in *Biblia latina*. Rome: Conradus Sweynheym & Arnoldus Pannartz, 1471, Letter of St Jerome to Paulinus (Manchester, John Rylands University Library, 14787, fol. 1^r).

borders and terminate in flowery finials and gold dots surrounded by delicate penwork. At first glance, the page is virtually indistinguishable from a Sweynheym and Pannartz edition of a classical or patristic author.[9]

VINDELINUS DE SPIRA'S *BIBLIA ITALICA* OF 1471

In 1471, the year of Sweynheym and Pannartz Latin bible, there were not one but two editions of the bible printed in Venice. Neither of these was the Latin Vulgate, but instead were Italian translations. The first to be issued was the newly completed translation by Nicolò Malerbi printed by Vindelinus de Spira on 1 August 1471 in a large royal folio format.[10] It is divided into two parts with the text of the second part beginning with Proverbs.

Unlike most subsequent Venetian bibles, the layout of the Vindelinus de Spira bible provides generous spaces for miniatures and hand-rubricated or illuminated initials. At least six copies printed on vellum survive, and copies both on vellum and on paper were more extensively illustrated than other fifteenth-century Venetian editions.[11] Similar to the Sweynheym and Pannartz Vulgate edition, the font is roman although the text is laid out in two columns (Figs 2-5, col. pl. 11). As can be observed in an undecorated copy in the John Rylands Library, almost half a page is left blank before the opening of Genesis (Fig. 2).[12] An eleven-line indentation in the first column of text reserves a space for the initial 'N' of *Nel principio* which has been rubricated by hand. The upper third of the pages at the beginning of I Kings and Proverbs were likewise reserved, and before these breaks in the text four lines were left blank for a title, and seven-line and five-line indentations for large initials. At the beginning of Psalms, there is an eleven-line indentation for an exceptionally large initial. Furthermore, at the ends of many books numerous lines have been left blank, so that the next Prologue or Book can start at the top of a recto. However, far fewer blank lines or spaces appear in the second volume, witness to a retreat in the extravagant use of paper or vellum found in the first part.

The most elaborately illuminated copies of the 1471 Vindelinus de Spira *Biblia italica* give some sense of the excitement with which clients greeted the edition and sought miniaturists to decorate and illustrate individual copies. Best known are two copies on vellum embellished by Franco de'Russi and the Master of the Putti. The miniaturist Franco de' Russi signed his name *Franchi* on the painted frontispiece of a vellum copy in Wolfenbüttel (Fig. 3), and illuminated other pages throughout the bible as well.[13] In the area left blank for the miniature, Franco painted multiple episodes of the Creation set in a verdant landscape: the Creation of Adam in the lower left; the Temptation on the right; and the Expulsion in the left background. God the Father holding a globe is depicted below where lines are indented for the initial 'N' of *Nel principio*, and a lush border with classicizing putti surrounds the whole. Unfortunately the coat of arms has been effaced from the lower margin. The dramatic difference between this hand-illuminated page and a page almost untouched after printing can be seen by comparing it with the undecorated Manchester copy (Fig. 2).

At the beginning of Part II of the Pierpont Morgan copy, a second distinguished miniaturist, the Master of the Putti, produced his most extravagant architectural frontispiece (Fig. 4).[14] In the margins are painted a monumental classical structure from

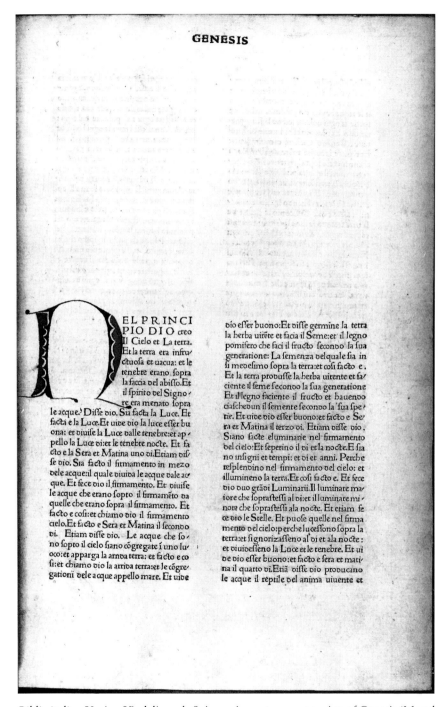

GENESIS

EL PRINCI
PIO DIO creo
Il Cielo et La terra.
Et la terra era infru
ctuofa et uacua: et le
tenebre erano fopra
la faccia del abiffo.Et
il fpirito del Signo
re era menato fopra
le acque. Diffe dio. Sia facta la Luce. Et
facta e la Luce.Et uide dio la luce effer bu
ona: et diuife la Luce dalle tenebre:et ap
pello la Luce di:et le tenebre nocte. Et fa
cto e la Sera et Matina uno di.Etiam dif
fe dio. Sia facto il firmamento in mezo
dele acque:il quale diuida le acque dale ac
que. Et fece dio il firmamento. Et diuife
le acque che erano fopto il firmameto da
quelle che erano fopra il firmamento. Et
facto e cofi:et chiamo dio il firmamento
cielo.Et facto e Sera et Matina il secondo
di. Etiam diffe dio. Le acque che fo
no fopto il cielo fiano cogregate i uno lu
oco:et apparga la arida terra: et facto e co
fi:et chiamo dio la arida terra:et le cogre
gationi dele acque appello mare. Et uide

dio effer buono:Et diffe germine la terra
la herba uirete et facia il Seme:et il legno
pomifero che faci il fructo fecondo la fua
generatione: La femenza delquale fia in
li medefimo fopra la terra:et cofi facto e .
Et la terra produffe la herba uirente et fa
ciente il feme fecondo la fua generatione
Et il legno faciente il fructo et hauendo
ciafchedun il femente fecondo la fua fpe
tie. Et uide dio effer buono:et facto e Se
ra et Matina il terzo di. Etiam diffe dio.
Siano facte eluminarie nel firmamento
del cielo:Et feperino il di et la nocte.E fia
no infigni et tempi: et di et anni. Perche
refplendino nel firmamento del cielo: et
illumineno la terra.Et cofi facto e. Et fece
dio duo gradi Luminarii.Il luminare ma
iore che fopraftaffi al di:et il luminare mi
nore che fopraftaffi ala nocte. Et etiam fe
ce dio le Stelle. Et puofe quelle nel firma
mento del cielo:perche luceffono fopra la
terra:et fignorizaffeno al di et ala nocte :
et diuideffeno la Luce et le tenebre. Et ui
de dio effer buono:et facto e fera et mati
na il quarto di.Etia diffe dio producano
le acque il reptile del anima uiuente et

Fig. 2. *Biblia italica*. Venice: Vindelinus dc Spira, 1 August 1471, opening of Genesis (Manchester, John Rylands University Library, 17102, fol. 11ʳ).

Fig. 3. Franco de'Russi, Creation Scenes, God the Creator, and putti in acanthus borders, in *Biblia italica*. Venice: Vindelinus de Spira, 1 August 1471, opening to Genesis (Wolfenbüttel, Herzog August Bibliothek, 2° 151, Vol. I, fol. 1ʳ, vellum).

Fig. 4. Master of the Putti, Shooting at Father's Corpse (a Judgement of Solomon), architectural monument, and Macigni arms, in *Biblia italica*. Venice: Vindelinus de Spira, 1 August 1471, opening to Proverbs (New York, Pierpont Morgan Library, 26984, fol. 3ᵛ, vellum).

which there appears to hang a torn piece of parchment containing the printed text. In the top third, putti support a *quadro riportato*, that is, an illusionistically framed painting depicting an apocryphal judgement of Solomon known as the Shooting at Father's Corpse.[15] The narrative scene reveals a row of brilliantly costumed figures whose robes are exquisitely highlighted with gold. A landscape with rustic buildings and a walled town spreads across the background, and distant hills are also touched with gold. Inscribed on banderoles hanging between the columns of text are the motto *Nosce te ipsum* in Latin and Greek, and in the lower margin music-making putti flank the coat of arms of the Macigni family of Venice. The Mantegnesque composition provides an innovative classicizing vocabulary that would appeal to a patron knowledgeable about the humanist movement.

Franco de'Russi and the Master of the Putti provided imagery in the other spaces reserved for illumination throughout these two bibles. In addition to the spectacular frontispiece of the second part of Morgan copy, the Master of the Putti painted the Creation of Eve for Genesis, a scene also framed by classical architectural motifs.[16] Franco depicted a Judgement of Solomon for Part II of the Wolfenbüttel copy,[17] and an associate painted the unusual episode of Hannah and the Priest Eli at the beginning of I Kings (I Samuel in contemporary bibles). He showed Hannah, mother of Samuel, praying outside the temple, observed by the priest Eli.

In 1471, no other miniaturist active in the Veneto would have had greater experience with bible illustration than Franco de'Russi. From 1451 until about 1460, Franco had been one of the two principal miniaturists of the *Bible of Borso d'Este*, the most extensively illustrated bible ever illuminated in Italy.[18] In the final reckoning, Franco is recorded as having been paid for miniatures and decoration on 17½ gatherings (each of 10 folios) and 11 *principi* or opening pages of individual books of the bible. These miniatures included illustrations for I Kings in which he depicted several episodes in the lives of Hannah, the High Priest Eli, and Samuel, so the iconography would not have been alien to his workshop.

Manuscript models for the unusual layout of the 1471 Vindelinus de Spira bible are not at all obvious, especially for the two-column wide reserved spaces at the beginnings of major divisions of the bible. However, one luxurious example of this format is the bible of Niccolò III d'Este, illuminated by Belbello da Pavia between 1430 and 1434 in Ferrara.[19] It has two major miniatures that occupy about one-half of a page: St Jerome and the Lion before the Prologue to Genesis (fol. 1^r), and the Adoration of the Magi at the beginning of Matthew (fol. 514^r). Throughout there are narrative miniatures interrupting the columns of text. Interestingly, the Este bible is also not a Latin Vulgate, but the French translation by Guiart de Moulins (the *Bible historiale*). The connection to Ferrara permits an intriguing speculation. When working on the bible of Borso d'Este, Franco de'Russi would have had access to the bible of Niccolò III, and later in Venice might have been consulted by Vindelinus de Spira on the layout of his innovative vernacular edition.

Like the Morgan and Wolfenbüttel copies of the De Spira *Biblia italica*, the vellum example in Berlin was provided with an elaborate miniature and borders for the first text-page of Part II (Fig. 5).[20] An anonymous North Italian miniaturist has depicted Solomon enthroned between his advisors on the left, and an executioner vigourously threatening to divide a baby on the right. Flat bands of gold leaf divide the margins into

Fig. 5. North Italian miniaturist, Judgement of Solomon, border with putti, Malipiero arms, initials 'I' and 'M', in *Biblia italica*. Venice: Vindelinus de Spira, 1 August 1471, opening to Proverbs (Berlin, Staatsbibliothek, 2 Inc. 3630 (perg.), fol. 3ᵛ, vellum).

segments: four scenes of mischievous putti playing on stony grounds fill the outer margin, while in the lower margin putti ride huge scaly fish on either side of the Malipiero of Venice arms. The initials 'I' and 'M' are painted on each side of the shield. Odd semi-human creatures with fish-tails and bat-wings line the inner margin. The overall effect verges on the bizarre because of the strange contrast of religious and pagan imagery.

Two copies of the 1471 Vindelinus de Spira *Biblia italica* printed on paper show the early activity of a miniaturist known as the Master of the Pico Pliny, or in shortened form, the Pico Master.[21] In copies now in Rovigo and Zürich the Pico Master painted elaborate borders and a miniature for the opening of Genesis. For the copy in Rovigo, the reserved space is divided into two scenes: the dove hovering over the waters to signify the division of the heavens and the waters of Day Two, and God creating Eve on the Sixth Day.[22]

The copy now in the Zentralbibliothek, Zürich, was splendidly illustrated by the Pico Master for a member of the Priuli family of Venice: miniatures fill the large reserved spaces at the beginnings of Genesis, I Kings, and Proverbs, and the painted initials for each book contain figures. For Genesis the Pico Master depicted God the Father dressed in brilliant red, holding a huge disk whose series of concentric circles represent the spheres surrounding the earth.[23]

As will be observed in later editions, printed bibles often accentuated Genesis, but the presence of the broad blank space before I Kings is exceptional. For this position in the Zürich copy of the De Spira *Biblia italica*, the Pico Master illustrates events drawn from chapters 4 and 11 of I Kings/Samuel, the Death of the Priest Eli and Saul Enthroned (col. pl. 11). Framed by red and green laurel wreath motifs, the scenes contrast Eli and Saul, the former collapsed before an empty throne, and the latter, dark-bearded and wearing a heavy crown, enthroned between two counsellors. An ancillary episode is provided in a roundel in the lower margin: Samuel anoints a younger beard-less man who may either be Saul, or more likely, David. Also embedded in the floral and gold dot border is a roundel with a half-length image of St Jerome. The Pico Master's gifts as a colourist are evident in the brilliant red of the costumes contrasted to the intense blues of the sky and green of the ground; these colours are taken up again in the floral motifs of the borders, harmonizing them with the narrative miniatures.

Like both the Master of the Putti and Franco de'Russi, the Pico Master illustrated Proverbs with a scene of King Solomon: in this case, not a judgement of Solomon but representations of Solomon reading and dreaming. Many years later these images were transformed into woodcut designs used in the frontispiece of Proverbs in the 1490 Giunta edition.[24] The Zürich illustration thus further supports the idea that the Pico Master was the principal designer of the 1490 *Biblia italica* woodcuts, and the Solomon images form a link between his earliest activities and the end of his career.

THE ADAM DE AMBERGAU EDITION OF 1471

From the point of view of design, the second Italian bible printed in Venice is distinctly the more peculiar. It was issued on 1 October 1471 and in all probability was printed by Adam de Ambergau.[25] Like the Sweynheym and Pannartz *Biblia latina*, the text is set in roman type in a single block, but at the opening of Genesis the text is interrupted by five reserved areas where ten or eleven lines have been indented either from the left or from the right (Figs 6-7). Opposite this verso, the second page of Genesis has two more large reserved areas, one on the right and one on the left. The first of these seven spaces was reserved for the capital 'N' of *Nel principio*, and the other six were presumably meant to be filled with scenes illustrating the Creation, such as those crowded into the Franco de' Russi bible in Wolfenbüttel (see Fig. 3).

The representation of multiple scenes of the Creation in bibles goes back to the Early Christian period, but since the twelfth century the most common mode of distributing such scenes was in a vertical sequence of images that formed the 'I' of *In principio*.[26] Usually included were the six Days of Creation, God resting on the Seventh Day, and often a Crucifixion or other Christian image at the bottom of the sequence. Many large Bolognese bibles of the late thirteenth and early fourteenth centuries typify this dominant tradition and were widely disseminated in northern Italy.[27]

A paper copy of the Adam de Ambergau bible in Vienna demonstrates how one anonymous north Italian miniaturist responded to the unusual format by filling the reserved spaces of the opening pages with a painted initial 'N' for *Nel principio* and four miniatures.[28] The scenes appropriately are: God hovering over the waters; God dividing the waters from the dome of the sky; God creating the land and vegetation on the land; and God creating the sun, moon, and stars. At the bas-de-page is the coat of arms of the noble Trevisani family of Venice. On the opposite recto, the lower reserved space is filled with the Creation of Man, but the upper left position of the other space led the miniaturist to fill it with a painted capital 'D', repeating the 'D' already printed: *Disse ancora idio*.

The curious layout of the Adam de Ambergau *Biblia italica* was probably intended not for illustration by hand but rather by woodcuts. A famous copy now in the John Rylands Library also has splendid images of the Creation filling the reserved spaces (Fig. 6).[29] As was recognized long ago by Essling, the outlines of the human figures and animals are established by woodcuts which were applied after the text had already been printed. Subsequently the figures and landscapes were coloured with water-based paints. The repetitious pose of God the Father facing to the right in Days 2, 3, 4, and 5 has clearly been made by applying the same inked woodblock four times. For Day 6, the design was reversed, occasioning God the Father to bless Adam and Eve with his left hand, rather than his right. Faint woodcut outlines are also visible for the figures of Adam and Eve, and for the animals clustered at their feet. The woodcuts were designed by the Master of the Putti, a miniaturist already noted for his illumination of the Morgan Vindelinus de Spira *Biblia italica*.[30]

Given the labour involved in cutting such woodblocks, it seems likely that the printer had originally envisaged using them to illustrate many copies of his edition. But like similar Venetian experiments with woodcut borders designed to be applied after a book had been printed, this trial of a semi-mechanical method of reproduction was soon abandoned.[31] No other copies are recorded that contain the woodcuts.

The reserved spaces in the Adam de Ambergau bible seem to have been inexplicable to some contemporary rubricators and miniaturists. In an undecorated paper copy in the Biblioteca Nazionale Marciana, Venice, the rubricator has appropriately added a large Lombard 'N' in blue ink for *Nel principio*.[32] He also thought that some capital letters were needed to fill the two lower spaces on the left, but neither letter is actually

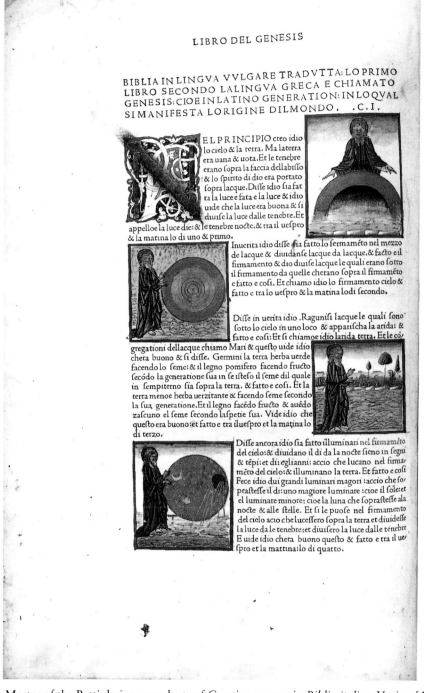

LIBRO DEL GENESIS

BIBLIA IN LINGVA VVLGARE TRADVTTA: LO PRIMO
LIBRO SECONDO LALINGVA GRECA E CHIAMATO
GENESIS: CIOE IN LATINO GENERATION: IN LO QVAL
SI MANIFESTA L ORIGINE DIL MONDO . .C.I.

EL PRINCIPIO creo idio
lo cielo & la terra. Ma la terra
era uana & uota. Et le tenebre
erano sopra la faccia dellabisso
& lo spirito di dio era portato
sopra lacque. Disse idio sia fat
ta la luce e fata e la luce & idio
uide che la luce era buona & si
diuise la luce dalle tenebre. Et
appelloe la luce die: & le tenebre nocte, & tra il uespro
& la matina lo di uno & primo.

In uerita idio disse sia fatto lo fermaméto nel mezzo
de lacque & diuidanse lacque da lacque, & facto e il
firmamento & dio diuise lacque le quali erano sotto
il firmamento da quelle cherano sopra il firmaméto
e fatto e cosi. Et chiamo idio lo firmamento cielo &
fatto e tra lo uespro & la matina lodi secondo.

Disse in uerita idio. Ragunisi lacque le quali sono
sotto lo cielo in uno loco & apparischa la arida: &
fatto e cosi: Et si chiamoe idio larida terra. Et le có
gregationi dellacque chiamo Mari & questo uide idio
chera buono & si disse. Germini la terra herba uerde
facendo lo seme: & il legno pomifero facendo fructo
secódo la generatione sua in se istesso il seme dil quale
in sempiterno sia sopra la terra. & fatto e cosi. Et la
terra menoe herba uerzitante & facendo seme secondo
la sua generatione. Et il legno facédo fructo & auédo
zascuno el seme secondo laspetie sua. Vide idio che
questo era buono: et fatto e tra il uespro et la matina lo
di terzo.

Disse ancora idio sia fatto illuminari nel firmaméto
del cielo: & diuidano il di da la nocte sieno in segni
& tépi: et di: eglianni: accio che lucano nel firma
méto del cielo: & illuminano la terra. Et fatto e cosi
Fece idio dui grandi luminari magori: accio che so
prastesse il di: uno magiore luminare: cioe il sole: et
el luminare minore: cioe la luna che soprastesse ala
nocte & alle stelle. Et si le puose nel firmamento
del cielo acio che lucessero sopra la terra et diuidesse
la luce da le tenebre: et diuisero la luce dalle tenebre
E uide idio chera buono questo & fatto e tra il ue
spro et la mattina: lo di quarto.

Fig. 6. Master of the Putti design, woodcuts of Creation scenes, in *Biblia italica*. Venice: [Adam de Ambergau], 1 October 1471, opening of Genesis (Manchester, John Rylands University Library, 3071, fol. 10^v).

required by the text. Puzzled by the spaces on the right side of the page, the rubricator left them blank. Similarly, the distinguished Paduan miniaturist Antonio Maria da Villafora presumed that the three reserved spaces on the left side of the page were intended for painted capital letters. In a copy of the Adam de Ambergau bible in the Bibliothèque nationale de France on vellum, Antonio Maria supplied the missing 'N' of *Nel principio*, an anthropomorphic 'D' repeating the 'D' of *Disse in verita iddeo*, and an 'E' preceding the *Disse ancora idio* in the third space on the left (Fig. 7).[33] He too left the reserved spaces on the right side of the page empty, not understanding what their function was.

Despite the ambitious illustrative program implied by the opening of Genesis, no further significant spaces were provided for miniatures elsewhere in the text of the 1471 Adam de Ambergau bible, except for an eight-line indentation at the beginning of the Proverbs of Solomon. In a copy of this 1471 bible in the Scheide Library at Princeton University, the second volume includes an image of King Solomon enthroned in this position, and in the lower margin are painted an unidentified coat of arms surrounded by dolphins, shells, cornucopias, and two standing winged angels.[34] The images and decorative motifs of both volumes are related to works by the Pico Master, but must have been done by an assistant less skilled in representing figures.

Close collaboration between printers and miniaturists for the two Venetian editions of 1471 seems likely. In both cases, the design of selected pages was planned for illustration in addition to the general phenomenon of spaces reserved for large capital letters. Franco de' Russi may have advised on the format of the Vindelinus de Spira edition, and the Master of the Putti must surely have been involved in the scheme to illustrate Genesis of the Adam de Ambergau edition with woodcuts. Indeed, the Master of the Putti also added a handsome image of King Solomon in the Vienna copy of the Adam de Ambergau bible, thus extending his involvement by decorating a copy of this edition.[35] The many links suggest that the printers sought assistance from miniaturists for page design as well as later enhancement of their editions.

CONSOLIDATION: 1475-1480

A gap of four years separates the Italian bibles of 1471 from the first Venetian Latin edition of 1475, printed by Franciscus Renner de Heilbronn and Nicolaus de Frankfordia.[36] At last a press in Italy had produced a bible whose text, type, and layout look the part. The Latin text derives from the Gutenberg bible, the type is black-letter gothic and the layout is two columns. The size is reduced from the royal folio of the bibles in Italian to chancery folio.[37] Modest provision was made for hand-illumination or rubrication. A 14-line blank area was reserved in column 1 of the Prologue to Genesis ([fol. a1r]), providing space for a capital 'F' of *Frater Ambrosius*, the opening words of St Jerome's Letter to Paulinus, the text normally functioning as this prologue. Two- and three-line indentations are made at the beginnings of books and chapters to be supplied with initials by rubricators. If a client were willing to pay for illumination, he or she might request an image of St Jerome, as in the copy in the Bridwell Library of Southern Methodist University in Dallas which can be attributed to the Pico Master (Fig. 8).[38] The miniaturist has depicted St Jerome in a bright red cloak, surrounded by a painted letter on a gold-leaf ground. Floral and gold-dot borders edged with gold fill

Fig. 7. Antonio Maria da Villafora, painted initials; French miniaturist, Beheading of St John the Baptist, and borders with acanthus, flowers, bird, and grotesque, in *Biblia italica*. Venice: [Adam de Ambergau], 1 October 1471, opening of Genesis (Paris, Bibliothèque nationale de France, Rés. Vél. 96, fol. 10ᵛ, vellum).

Fig. 8. Pico Master, St Jerome, and floral and gold-dot borders, in *Biblia latina*. Venice: Franciscus Renner & Nicolaus de Frankfordia, 1475, opening of St Jerome's Letter to Paulinus (Dallas, TX, Southern Methodist University, Bridwell Library, fol. 1ʳ).

the upper and inside margins, and a laurel wreath in the lower margin awaits the purchaser's coat of arms. Some copies of the 1475 Renner *Biblia latina* were printed on vellum and illuminated, for example, those in Chantilly and in Paris, but illuminations were also provided for copies on paper, as in the Bridwell Library example.[39] Indeed the empty space provided for a coat of arms suggests that copies were prepared speculatively, ready for a buyer to specify his blazoning. It is also clear from extant examples that undecorated copies were sent to Germany and the Lowlands where they were illuminated in local styles.[40]

The 1475 Renner Latin bible initiated a period of expansion in the printing of bibles in Venice. Between 1475 and the end of 1484, twelve editions of the Latin Vulgate were printed in Venice and four more editions of the Malerbi translation appeared as well.[41] Both the typographical format and formulae for decorating Latin bibles became codified. Large spaces were normally reserved at the beginning of the Prologue to Genesis and at the beginning of Genesis proper. Four- to six-line spaces were reserved for initials at the beginnings of each book; Psalms usually had even more lines indented for the 'B' of *Beatus Vir*. Although the beginning of the New Testament was not over-accentuated, there was usually the effort to have its Prologue begin at the top of a recto. Of each of these editions there were several hundred copies printed, and the totals for bibles printed in this period are in the thousands. Thus any of the generalizations about decoration can apply only to the artistic situation in Venice and other cities, rather than to the production and distribution of bibles more generally.

Franciscus Renner and Nicolaus de Frankfordia reissued their bible in 1476, but were met by their formidable rival, Nicolaus Jenson, who produced an edition in a very similar format, also in 1476.[42] Jenson, in turn, reissued his *Biblia latina* in 1479.[43] In Jenson's 1476 Latin bible, the design of the gothic type is more delicate than was Renner's. Jenson indented twelve lines for a capital 'F' for *Frater Ambrosius* at the beginning of the Prologue of St Jerome, but it is on the Genesis page that he provided a greater opportunity for illumination (col. pl. 12). There the printer reserved a fifteen-line space for a miniature at the top of the first column of text and below this an eleven-line indentation for the capital 'I' of *In principio*.

Of the surviving copies of Jenson's 1476 edition, at least eight were printed on vellum, more than any other contemporary Venetian edition.[44] The high number of vellum copies and their rich illumination by outstanding miniaturists show that Jenson continued to supply his clients with volumes of exceptional aesthetic value.[45] Two of the illuminated copies are attributable to Girolamo da Cremona, one of the finest miniaturists active in Venice in the 1470s. He illuminated a vellum copy now in the Biblioteca Classense, Ravenna for a member of the Agostini family whose coat of arms appear on the frontispiece.[46] The Agostini were bankers who supplied Jenson with the paper to print his famed edition of Pliny, translated by Cristoforo Landino and printed in 1476, the same year as the Latin bible.[47] Their arms appear at the bottom of the page and a classical bust in the right margin reveals the Agostini taste for the antique to which Jenson and Girolamo had many times catered. God the Creator stands triumphantly above the sphere of the heavens, his robe exquisitely modelled with gold highlights.

The beautiful copy of the 1476 Jenson bible on vellum in the Rylands Library, also illuminated by Girolamo, may have been destined for a more traditional client, since the borders are typical Venetian floral and gold-dot patterns (col. pl. 12).[48] In the reserved space at the beginning of Genesis, Girolamo has painted an extremely refined image of God the Creator seated above the curving sphere of the heavens. As in many of Girolamo's miniatures, the robes of God are modelled with minute strokes of gold, creating a shimmering effect. In the outer margin one of Girolamo's signature monkeys sits on a pebble-strewn ground, holding the cord of his own leash, attached to a jewelled belt around his torso. Unfortunately the coat of arms formerly in the lower margin has been effaced.

The problem for clients who may have wanted an illustrated bible, however, lay not with Genesis or its Prologue but in the layout of subsequent books. At the beginnings of the other Books and prologues in the Renner and Jenson bibles of 1475 and 1476, and in many subsequent editions, only three or four lines were indented for an initial to be added by hand. In Jenson's 1476 bible, the Psalms were provided with an exceptional five-line indentation and Proverbs with six. Girolamo da Cremona and a talented collaborator depicted tiny figures in the initials throughout the Rylands copy, but for the most part these are restricted to one or two heads, bearded prophets or crowned kings. For the Psalms opening, the miniaturist expanded the 'B' of *Beatus vir* into the interlinear space above the indentation, carving out a bit more space for his half-length image of David with a Psaltery. But the narratives of Judith or Esther are reduced to pairs of heads. Similarly in a vellum copy of the 1479 Jenson bible in Dresden, illuminated primarily by Antonio Maria da Villafora for Jenson's partner Petrus Ugelheimer, almost every book has an initial surrounding the tiny head of a prophet or saint.[49] But only the presence of a crown or part of a pilgrim's staff suggests that the head is King David or St James. In managing these very restricted spaces the Veneto artists are reminiscent of the French illuminators providing exceptionally small figures for the thirteenth-century Parisian small bibles.

Few patrons in this period seem even to have asked for narrative imagery. One of the only fully narrative sequences known to me is in a copy of Jenson's 1479 edition, illuminated for a member of the Bollani family of Venice and now in Vienna.[50] In scene after scene, tiny figures inhabit the initials and often expand into the margins to amplify the narrative. For example, Esther kneels before the seated Ahasuerus, both figures crowded into a painted four-line indentation that the artist has expanded upward and to the left (Fig. 9). Haman is depicted hanging on gallows in the margin above Esther, and decorative motifs of a shell, beads and a cornucopia further enliven the visual effect. Thus a few years after Heinrich Quentell had printed the famous Cologne bible with more than a hundred narrative woodcuts, Venetian printers apparently felt no demand to provide their bibles with illustrations.[51] It would be eleven more years before the first Venetian bible fully illustrated with narrative woodcuts would appear.

Despite this apparent lack of interest in illustration, many Venetian bibles in the late 1470s and early 1480s were handsomely decorated. The Master of the Pico Pliny, already noted for his illustration and decoration of the 1471 Vindelinus de Spira *Biblia italica* in Zurich (col. pl. 11), the 1475 Renner *Biblia latina* in Dallas (Fig. 8), and for copies of Jenson's 1476 and 1479 bibles in Paris and Vienna respectively (see note 44 and Fig. 9), dominated the luxury decoration of Venetian bibles in the late 1470s and early 1480s. A brilliant colourist, the Pico Master perfected the handsome formula initiated with the Dallas copy of the 1475 Renner *Biblia latina* (Fig. 8), as may be seen

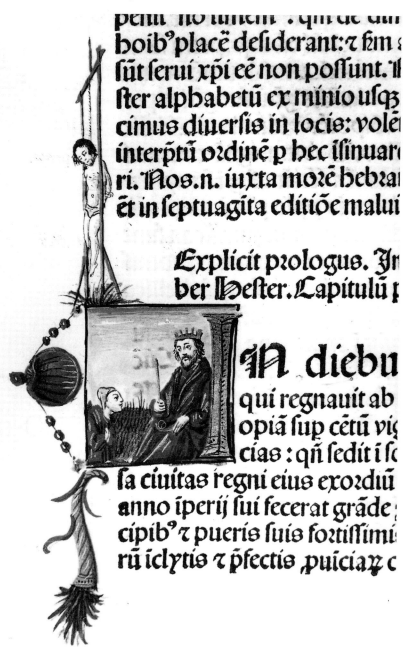

Fig. 9. Pico Master, Esther and Ahasuerus, and the Hanging of Haman, in *Biblia latina*. Venice: Nicolaus Jenson, 1479, opening of Esther (Vienna, Österreichische Nationalbibliothek, Inc. 8.E.10, fol. 171ᵛ, vellum).

in a copy of Franciscus Renner's *Biblia latina* of 1476 and in four copies of his 1480 *Biblia latina*.[52] Floral and gold-dot borders are edged in red and gold; a central baguette of gold and blue divides the two columns of text. In the sixteen-line space reserved at the beginning of the Prologue of St Jerome, the saint is usually portrayed in the initial 'F' dressed in red, reading or pointing to a book. In the lower margin is the obligatory roundel for a coat of arms, sometimes flanked by putti, as in the handsome British Library copy illuminated for a member of the De Soverin family of Venice (Fig. 10). If you had less money, you might obtain St Jerome without a full border, as in the examples in Dallas, Venice, and Vienna, or if you had more money, you might get a miniature in addition to St Jerome as in the Newberry Library copy.[53]

Genesis proper in the 1480 Renner *Biblia latina* begins at the top of a second column verso (fol. a3[v]), but does have an 18-line indentation for the capital 'I' of *In principio*. The Pico Master filled this space with a Creation of Eve in the Marciana copy; in the Newberry Library copy the 'I' is accompanied by a God the Creator and a miniature of the Creation of Eve is depicted in the lower margin.[54] In addition to a modest first text-page decoration, the Marciana copy includes four more initials with figures: a half-length King David for the Psalms and King Solomon for Proverbs; St John the Evangelist with his eagle for John, and a half-length St Paul for Romans. Also dazzling, but less well recognized, is the extraordinary amount of refined handwork in these Venetian bibles. Copy after copy received thousands of initials inscribed and flourished in red and blue inks; books and prologues were often also accentuated by painted initials on gold grounds. The productions of the Pico Master's workshop lack the extreme refinement of Girolamo da Cremona, but the overall effect was clearly satisfactory to a large number of owners around 1480.[55]

DECORATING BIBLES WITH THE COMMENTARY OF NICHOLAS OF LYRA: THE FIRST TEXT-PAGES

The third significant change in design of Venetian printed bibles came in 1481 with the first edition of the Latin bible with the Commentary of Nicholas of Lyra.[56] This huge edition, usually bound in four volumes, was printed by Johannes Herbort for Nicolaus Jenson's Company, that is Johannes de Colonia, Nicolaus Jenson et Socii, which was still using the name of Jenson despite his recent death. As if on cue, Franciscus Renner almost immediately brought out a second edition of the *Biblia latina cum postillis Nicolai de Lyra*, its three parts dated 1482 and 1483.[57] These two editions follow close on the heels of the *Biblia latina cum glossa ordinaria Walafridi Strabonis* printed in either Basel or Strasbourg by Adolf Rusch and Anton Koberger by 1480.[58] In all three editions, the need to combine the Bible text proper with an elaborate commentary led the printers to imitate contemporary printed books of canon and civil law.[59] The text proper is printed in two columns of gothic type and is surrounded by two columns of commentary printed in slightly smaller gothic font (Figs 11-14, col. pl. 13-14). Nicolaus Jenson had been printing in this format since his Gratian of 1474 initiated his impressive sequence of law editions.[60]

Copies of both the 1481 bible with the De Lyra commentary and the 1482-3 edition were splendidly illuminated and their elaborately decorated opening pages hark back

Fig. 10. Pico Master, St Jerome, and floral and gold-dot borders, De Soverin arms, in *Biblia latina*. Venice: Franciscus Renner, 1480, opening of St Jerome's Letter to Paulinus (London, British Library, C.9.b.12, fol. a1ʳ, vellum).

to the luxurious copies of the 1471 editions of the *Biblia italica*. Some copies were understandably destined for prominent churchmen. Jenson's debt to Pope Sixtus IV for having named him a Count Palatine in 1475 makes it not surprising that a vellum copy of the 1481 edition, now in the Vatican Library, was destined for that pope.[61] Each of the four volumes is initiated with a handsome first text-page incorporating the Della Rovere arms surmounted by the papal tiara (Fig. 11). The miniaturist appears not to be Venetian, but rather an artist working in Rome, suggesting that a style already familiar to the pope was preferred for this presentation copy. The bright primary colours and arrangement of motifs in the floral borders resemble a page in the Theophylact, *Commentary on the Letters of St Paul*, illuminated for Sixtus IV by Jacopo Ravaldi, a French miniaturist active in Rome in the 1470s and early 1480s.[62] The putti supporting coats of arms are not as long-limbed as Ravaldi's, but their yellow hair and heavy-lidded eyes are found in his works, and suggest that the 1481 bible was illuminated in his workshop.

The four volumes of the British Library vellum copy of the 1481 *Biblia latina cum postillis Nicolai de Lyra* are not uniformly decorated, but the arms of Jean Balue, Cardinal of Angers (1421?-91) have been painted in Volume IV. These were probably added somewhat later than the date of printing. Jean Balue had been arrested for treason in 1469 by Louis XI and kept imprisoned for many years, only returning to power in the 1480s.[63] Ownership of a copy of the 1481 *Biblia latina cum postillis Nicolai de Lyra* by another cardinal is testified by an unidentified coat of arms surmounted by a cardinal's hat in the example in the Annmary Brown Memorial of Brown University.[64] A copy of the 1482-3 edition was illuminated by Antonio Maria da Villafora for Pietro Barozzi, Bishop of Belluno (1471-87) and later Bishop of Padua (1487-1507).[65]

The Pico Master is again active in illuminating two copies of the 1481 *Biblia latina cum postillis Nicolai de Lyra*, and one of the 1482-3 edition. For the copy of the 1481 edition in the Biblioteca Medicea Laurenziana, the Pico Master executed figures and decorative motifs in pen and watercolour drawings in all four volumes.[66] The images appear near the beginning of each volume: Nicholas of Lyra, St Jerome, and the Creation of Eve for Volume I; St Jerome and an Enthroned King precede Kings in Volume II; a half-length King Solomon initiates Proverbs in Volume III; and a delicate Nativity opens the Commentary on Matthew. The images resemble the saints and abbreviated narrative episodes already seen in earlier Pico Master bible illustrations. The Laurenziana 1481 bible belonged to Girolamo Rossi (1454/55-1517), a member of a noble family of Pistoia who was a humanist and friend of Marsilio Ficino.[67] Rossi spent the period from about 1480 to 1495 in Venice where he acquired more than ten printed books illuminated primarily by the Pico Master. Late in life Rossi entered the Dominican Order and held the offices of Prior of San Marco in Florence and Vicar-General of the Order; his books were left to the Oratorio of Santa Maria di Lecceto (Siena).

The Pico Master also illuminated a copy of the 1481 edition for an unidentified owner whose emblem is a hand holding a green wreath.[68] Now in the Pierpont Morgan Library, Volume I of this set is handsomely provided with initials depicting some familiar figures: Nicholas of Lyra (a2[r]), Brother Ambrosius (?) (a3[v]); St Jerome (a4[r]), and a fully framed page with God the Creator at the beginning of the Commentary on

Fig. 11. Workshop of Jacopo Ravaldi, St Anthony of Padua, floral borders, arms of Pope Sixtus IV (della Rovere), in *Biblia latina cum postillis Nicolai de Lyra*. Venice: [Johannes Herbort de Seligenstadt] for Johannes de Colonia, Nicolaus Jenson, et socii, 31 July 1481, opening of Prologue to Chronicles (Città del Vaticano, Biblioteca Apostolica Vaticana, Memb. II, 7, fol. 1ʳ [p1ʳ], vellum).

Genesis (c1[r]). Beyond this, however, the patron's pocket was exhausted, and only one other initial in Volume II incorporates a half-length figure.

By far the most elaborate copy of a *Biblia latina cum postillis Nicolai de Lyra* illuminated by the Pico Master is the Vatican Library copy of the 1482-3 edition, printed on vellum and bound in three volumes.[69] In its three first text-page borders the Pico Master's gifts as a brilliant colourist come to the fore. In the lower margin of the Genesis page a verdant flower-filled landscape incorporates the Creation of Eve between pairs of deer. A stream filled with fish begins in the left margin and re-emerges in the right, and trees decked with dazzling birds reach up into the side margins (col. pl. 13). In the space reserved for the 'I' of *In principio*, an unusually monumental God the Creator appears, dressed in bright red and yellow and holding a large green sphere. The intensely blue heaven of the right margin is the setting for God creating the sun, moon and stars. The multiple scenes of the Creation, seen as fundamental to bible illustration both in manuscripts and in incunables, here receive a fully Renaissance treatment, united in a single Albertian space, illusionistically existing behind the suspended 'parchment page' of the text.

For the first text-page of Psalms, the Pico Master adopts the popular Venetian 'architectural frontispiece' with a turbaned David sitting in the lower margin bowing a stringed viol. The Pico Master here reveals the influence of two other gifted Venetian miniaturists: the Master of the London Pliny and Girolamo da Cremona. Around 1476 the former painted a similar David seated beneath an architectural structure in an exquisite breviary now in the Bodleian Library, Oxford; and the overall composition also echoes Girolamo da Cremona's first text-page for a Petrus de Abano, *Expositio problematum Aristotelis* of 1482.[70] Since the Pico Master painted a full-page miniature in the 1482 Petrus de Abano opposite the first text-page by Girolamo, the source of Vatican 1482-3 bible composition is not surprising. For the Matthew first text-page, the Pico Master employed a familiar grouping of the Virgin Mary and Joseph adoring the Christ Child in the lower margin, but elaborated the upper margins with jewels and cameos, again recalling borders by Girolamo. The compositions are witness to the lively interaction between Venetian illuminators around 1480.

The most unusual hand-illuminated copy of the 1481 *Biblia latina cum postillis Nicolai de Lyra* contains three sumptuous first text-pages and a number of diagrams drawn in pen and ink. This important copy exists in a mutilated state in the Bibliothèque nationale de France, lacking Genesis to Joshua.[71] The artistic significance of its first text-page borders requires discussion of their attribution; analysis of the innovative diagrams will be taken up in the last section of this paper. In contrast to most other illuminated bibles of the later 1470s and early 1480s, the borders of the Paris 1481 *Biblia latina cum postillis* are redolent with classicizing motifs: satyrs, cameos, vases, bucrania, and of course putti (Fig. 12, col. pl. 13). Their distinctive style reveals that they were painted by the same team of artists who illuminated incunables for Nicholas Jenson's business partner, the amazing bibliophile Petrus Ugelheimer. The most richly decorated Ugelheimer incunables are nine volumes printed between 1477 and 1483, thus painted exactly in the same period as the publication of the 1481 *Biblia latina cum postillis*.[72]

The identification of the miniaturists who illuminated Ugelheimer's books has been debated, although there is general agreement that Girolamo da Cremona was the dominant artist of the group.[73] Other miniaturists who joined Girolamo were Benedetto Bordon, the Pico Master, the Master of the Seven Virtues, and an anonymous Ferrarese artist. The Paris 1481 *Biblia latina cum postillis* borders show the closest affinities to two Ugelheimer volumes in the Hague, a Petrus de Abano, *Conciliator differentiarum philosophorum et medicorum* of 1483 whose opening text-page has variously been attributed to Bordon and to the Master of the Seven Virtues, and a Walter Burley, *In artem veterem Porphirii et Aristotelis* of 1481 earlier attributed to the Master of the Seven Virtues and more recently to an anonymous Ferrarese miniaturist.[74]

The relatively poor condition of the Paris borders complicates the attributions, but their overall sumptuous effects can still be appreciated. In the lower margin of the Prologue to Chronicles (Paralypomenon) bronze plaques with curving edges containing fictive reliefs in roundels appear on either side of a deep landscape in which a red-robed St Jerome meditates (Fig. 12). He sits before a rocky cliff in which rests a red-bound book; behind him is his companion lion. A dramatic shift in scale characterizes the classicizing motifs of the side margins. A satyr and satyress, monumentally sized and embracing each other, sit at the base of a large silver vase. Their yellow hair and large facial features resemble the satyrs of Benedetto Bordon's signed Justinian of 1477 and those of the 1483 Petrus de Abano *Conciliator* also recently attributed to Bordon.[75] Above the embracing satyrs and silver vase rise golden bronze foliage, other vases, and a wingless putto. Uppermost in this tier are disembodied human heads and a trio of bucrania. Similar disembodied heads rise out of a bowl in the Petrus de Abano border. The deep landscape prefigures Bordon later works and also supports an attribution to him of the *Chronicles* frontispiece.

The first text-page borders of Isaiah are even richer in their pile-up of jewels, dolphins, pairs of putti in grisaille and in flesh colours, cameos, and small figures seated in rocky landscapes (col. pl. 14). Two grey monochrome reliefs framed by golden dolphins interrupt the continuous landscape of the lower margin. In the landscape at the far left is St Jerome, in the centre Isaiah, and at the far right a seated Franciscan, probably Nicolaus de Lyra. The colours are lighter than those of the *Chronicles* border; the artist uses a clear yellow for Isaiah's robe and paler greys and flesh tones for the figures in the outer margin. The figures, rock forms, and draperies are crisper and more sharply detailed than Bordon's work of this time, and instead resemble features of the Hague Walter Burley borders, attributable to an anonymous Ferrarese miniaturist.[76]

Instead of the traditional Nativity, the Matthew first text-page in the 1481 Paris *Biblia latina cum postillis* shows the winged animals of the Evangelists in oval frames in the four corners. The jewels, cameos, putti, and vases filling the borders are set against a red-purple ground, and the overall colour range closely resembles that of the Chronicles border (Fig. 12). The Matthew border should likewise be attributed to Benedetto Bordon. Curiously, both the Chronicles and the Matthew borders have been excised from another folio and pasted around their respective first text-pages, further complicating the artistic history of these volumes.

No other hand-illuminated Venetian bible of this period exhibits the extensive classicizing vocabulary of the Paris 1481 *Biblia latina cum postillis Nicolai de Lyra*, departing so distinctly from strictly religious imagery. The unique programme of the Paris bible borders and the style of the illumination support the thesis that the volumes were originally destined for Petrus Ugelheimer, clearly known to prefer this kind of

Fig. 12. Benedetto Bordon, St Jerome in the Wilderness, and borders with satyrs and classical motifs, in *Biblia latina cum postillis Nicolai de Lyra*. Venice: [Johannes Herbort de Seligenstadt] for Johannes de Colonia, Nicolaus Jenson, et Socii, 31 July 1481, opening of Prologue to Chronicles (Paris, Bibliothèque nationale de France, Rés. Vél. 111, fol. p1ʳ, vellum).

imagery. The missing first volume of this set might have proved this hypothesis by the presence of Ugelheimer's coat of arms.

IMAGES FOR THE NICHOLAS OF LYRA COMMENTARY

The elaborate first text-page borders of the huge bibles with the commentary of Nicolaus de Lyra did not present essentially new compositional problems for the miniaturists commissioned to enhance them, despite the novelty of the Paris 1481 bible borders. But another aspect of these monumental publications did pose a new challenge. The De Lyra commentary describes certain objects and buildings, specifying that they should be illustrated with a '*figura*'. In the fourteenth-century manuscripts of the De Lyra text alone or combined with the Bible text proper, spaces were reserved by the scribes into which the figures or diagrams would be drawn. These include images of Noah's Ark, the Ark of the Covenant, the High Priest, ritual objects, plans and elevations of the Temple of Solomon, the Palace of Solomon, and the Visions of Isaiah and of Ezekiel.[77]

When the De Lyra text was printed, with or without the biblical text itself, printers likewise reserved spaces for diagrams (Figs 13-16). Woodcuts were obviously the ideal solution for illustrating the De Lyra figures, but the two Venetian editions of the *Biblia latina cum postillis Nicolaus de Lyra* of 1481 and 1482-3 were printed with blank spaces and no illustrations.[78] The Pico Master drew or painted sequences of diagrams for two of the illuminated copies already considered, that is for the Paris example of the 1481 bible and for the Vatican copy of the 1482-3 edition. In the Paris 1481 bible, the diagrams required in Isaiah and in Ezekiel are finely drawn in pen and brown ink, lightly touched with washes of pink, blue, and green. The inscriptions are written in a humanist hand in blue ink. In contrast, the diagrams throughout the entire 1482-3 Vatican bible are drawn in gold and labelled in blue, and some are even painted in full colours.

Many of the diagrams required by the Commentary of Nicolaus de Lyra are relatively simple plans of the Temple of Solomon, or parts of the Temple. More elaborate, however, are the Vision of Isaiah (Isaiah 6) and the Vision of Ezekiel (Ezekiel 1). In each case two versions of the image are mandated by the commentary, one according to the 'Latins' and one according to the 'Hebrews'. In the Pico Master's Vision of Ezekiel, God is represented enthroned and holding an orb (Fig. 13). In one version, the four creatures are bonded together as a Tetramorph, and in the other they appear as independent winged creatures. Both are carefully labelled *secundum latinos* and *secundum hebreos*. In the Vatican example, God wears red and blue robes, and hovers above wispy blue clouds. In the more expansive drawing in Paris, the heavens are extended to show rows of stars above the clouds and a complex double wheel below the winged beasts.

Drawn diagrams in the 1481 Paris bible are only provided in the third volume (Rés. Vélins 113, Isaiah-Maccabees). However, virtually all of the reserved spaces in the 1482-3 Vatican *Biblia latina cum postillis* have been filled with drawn or painted images. This sequence provides a richer program than is present in the only earlier edition with woodcuts, the Nicolaus de Lyra, *Postilla super totam Bibliam* printed by Anton Kobeger in Nuremberg in 1481.[79] Thus the miniaturist must have had a fully illustrated manuscript exemplar, rather than depending only on the woodcuts of the

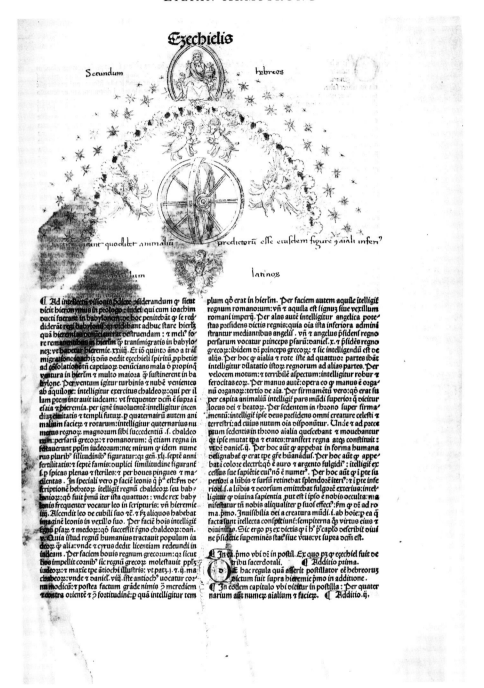

Fig. 13. Pico Master, Vision of Exekiel, in *Biblia latina cum postillis Nicolai de Lyra*. Venice: [Johannes Herbort de Seligenstadt] for Johannes de Colonia, Nicolaus Jenson et socii, 31 July 1481, in Commentary on Ezekiel 1 (Paris, Bibliothèque nationale de France, Rés. Vél. 113, fol. PP1ʳ, vellum).

recently printed Koberger edition. Another complete set of diagrams is provided for the copy of the 1482-3 *Biblia latina cum postillis* illuminated by Antonio Maria da Villafora for Bishop Pietro Barocci.[80] These diagrams parallel the Pico Master's images with minor variations, and further support the idea that a manuscript exemplar was available to these Veneto miniaturists.

A confusing aspect of the Paris 1481 *Biblia latina cum postillis* is that the miniaturist of the first volume seems not to have been following an authoritative manuscript model. Most of the spaces reserved in the books of Kings remain blank, but three have been filled with fully coloured miniatures rather than the traditional diagrams. In IIII Kings 20 (II Kings in modern bibles), the story is told that King Hezekiah, son of Ahaz, was dying, but as a result of his prayers, God sent Isaiah to tell him he was to have fifteen more years of life. Hezekiah asked for a sign, and the sign was to be the reversal of shadows on a sun-dial, the so-called 'Dial of Ahaz'. In the Vatican 1482-3 Bible the Pico Master filled the two spaces reserved for the 'Dial of Ahaz' with abstract two-dimensional diagrams of a sundial painted in gold. Similar diagrams are found in earlier manuscripts, and are repeated in the first Venetian edition of the *Biblia latina cum postillis* illustrated with woodcuts in 1489.[81] But in the Paris copy of the 1481 bible, Benedetto Bordon filled the two spaces with painted narrative miniatures (Fig. 14). The first depicts King Hezekiah in bed and Isaiah directing a servant how to cure him, and the second shows Isaiah and three others discussing the sundial. The colours are intense; the red tunic of the kneeling servant contrasts with the king's blue coverlet; and the king in the lower miniature wears a gold and black brocaded robe. The scene appropriately illustrates the biblical text, but departs from the De Lyra tradition of diagrams; this anomaly suggests that the exemplar available to Bordon was faulty for this section of the commentary.

In one other place in the Paris 1481 bible, Benedetto Bordon paints a miniature instead of the usual diagram. The building of the Temple of Solomon is related in III Kings 6 (I Kings in modern bibles). In the reserved space Bordon has depicted Solomon and two advisors supervising two workmen. Solomon wears a splendid gold and red brocaded robe, while the drooping and torn leggings of the workmen indicate their lower status (Fig. 15). The composition is reminiscent of Bordon's signed minia-ture for the Ugelheimer copy of a 1477 Justinian in which a splendidly garbed Justinian oversees a mason carving a stone capital.[82]

By the early 1480s German printers were successfully illustrating printed books with woodcuts, but Venetian printers largely resisted using the new means until the end of the decade. The availability of many highly competent miniaturists and rubricators in the Veneto may in part explain the delay in exploiting the new technology. But it was a bible, the *Biblia latina cum postillis Nicolai de Lyra* of 1489, which was one of the first Venetian editions to include numerous woodcuts.[83] The style of the figures in the 1489 woodcuts, such as those in the Creation of Eve, Noah and his family, the Vision of Isaiah, and the Vision of Ezekiel (Fig. 16), permits the attribution of their design to the Pico Master, the miniaturist most active in the illumination of bibles over the period from 1471 through the early 1480s. Lamberto Donati earlier noted visual analogies between the miniatures of the 1482-3 Vatican *Biblia latina cum postillis* and the 1489 woodcuts, and now even closer relationships can be seen between the woodcuts and the Pico Master's drawings in the Paris 1481 *Biblia latina cum postillis* (Figs 13, 16).[84] The

Regum

deinde rurſus oece hozis alijs ad occidéte currête ſole: ſ3 τ reſiduis oiei ouab' hozis τc.(| Seqtur figura ſm pmam opinioné in qua oue lineae faciút vnâ hozâ.

(| Vtrʒ aût iſta oies ſub eçechia fuerit maioz q̃ illa q̃ plõ gata fuerit tpe ioſue oictú fuit Joſue.x.(| Figura ſm ſcdaʒ opinionem in q̃ quelibet linea facit vnâ hoza.

Tlotãdũ q̃ iſte oue fi gure facte ſũt fʒ vnâ viâ quã poſui Joſue x.ſ.q̃ oies plõgata ſb eçechia fuerat i ſolſti tio hyemali: τ ſic bze uioz oie plõgata ſub ioſue.
r (| Jn illo tpe. Dic pſequenti rephmi iſur gês elatio: τ pmo ipa elatio oſcribit: τ ſcdo rephmi: ibi Uenit aut eſaias. Circa pmũ ſci endum: q̃ babyloniũ erât itêti circa curſus ſiderũ: vñ τ aſtrono mia pmo fuit iuenta in chaldea ſm aliq̃s:

vt reütatur totidéʒ g̃dib' τ Et ait eçechias: Facile eſt vmbzâ creſcere oecé lineis Tlec hoc volo vt fiat: ſʒ vt reütatur retrozſu oecé gra dib'. Jnuocauit itaqʒ eſai as ppheta oñm: τ reduxit vmbzã p lineas qbuſ iã oe ſcêdeât i horologio achaʒ retrozſu oecé g̃dib'. Jn tpe illo miſit mêrodach bala dã fili' baladã rex babylo nioz lfas: et mũera ad eçe chiã. Audierat eni q̃ egro

taſſʒ eçechias. Lêtat' ê aût in aduêtu eoz eçechias: et oñdit eis oomũ aromatuʒ τ auruʒ τ argêtũ: τ pigmê ta varia: vnguenta q̃3 τ oo mũ vaſoz ſuoz τ oia q̃ ha bere poterat i theſaul' ſuis Tlõ fuit qõ nõ oñderet eis eçechias in oomo ſua τ in poteſtate ſua. Uenit autez eſaias ppheta ad regeʒ eçechiam: oixitqʒ ei: Quid oixerunt viri iſti: aut vnde venerunt ad te? Cui ait eçechias. Dê terra longin qua venerunt ad me oe ba bylone. At ille reſpondit: Quid viderút i oomo tua? Ait eçechias: Oia q̃cunqʒ ſut in oomo mea viderût. Tlihil eni eſt qõ ñ mõſtra uerim eis i theſauris meis Dixit itaqʒ eſaias eçechie. Audi ſimoné oñi: Ecce oi es veniêt: τ auferétur oia q̃ ſut in oomo tua: τ q̃ pdide rút pres tui vſqʒ in oie hâc i babylone. Tlõ remãebit qcq̃ ait oñs. S3 et o filijs tuii q̃ egredieî ex te q̃s gna biſ tolletur: τ erût cunuchi i palatio regis babylonis Dixit eçechias ad eſaiam: Bon' ſmo oñi q̃é locut' eſt: Sit tñ pax τ veritas in oieb' meis. Reliq̃ aut ſimo nũ eçechie τ ois fortitudo ri': et q̃o fecit piſcinã τ a qducũ τ itroduxerit aq̃s i citatê nóne hec ſcpta ſut i libzo ſimonum oierum re gum iuda?

ſciendũ oe illa retroceſſione ſol' mirabſi: τ hoc ê qõ oi ñ.paralip.xxxi.q̃ nuncñ regis babylonie miſſi fuerãt ad eũ: vt interrogarêt oe pozteto qõ acciderat ſup terrâ v(| Letat' eſt aût i aduêtu eoz eçechias. leticia inepta pcedête ex elatôe: eo q̃ tant'rex τ oe tam longinq̃ terra miſiſſet ad eũ nũ cios τ munera.
x.(| Et oñdit eis τc.oiê ra ſa.q̃ nõ ſoluʒ oñdit eis ea q̃ erât i theſaurl ſuis τ i oomo ſua ſed etiã ea q̃ ſecre tiſſime τ reueren diſſime ſeruaban tur in têplo.ſ.vn ctôeʒ regũ τ pon tificuʒ: τ tabulas teſtimonij τ legeʒ q̃ nullo mõ erant gentilibus oſten denda: τ hoc no taſ cũ oi. Et in oi ptâte ſua. ſeqtur: v(| Uenit autez eſaias. Dic conſe quenter oeſcribiî pdicte elatônis τ trãſgreſſionis re prehenſio cum oi citur: 3 (| Quid oixerunt viri iſti τc. non q̃ſiuit b' ex ignozãtia quia totum erat ſibi a oeo reuelatum:ſʒ vt ex reſponſione eçechie conueniê ti' argueret eum.
a(| De terra lon guinqua venerunt ad me.q.o. h' fu it mihi ad ma gnâ gloziam: τ iõ oſtendi eis regnii mei magnificen tiam. b (| Ecce oies veniut τ au ferent oia τc. iſto fuit impletum quando nabuch. oia precioſa trã ſtulit oe hieruſa lem in babyloneʒ vt habetuꝛ infra xxv. c(| S3 τ oe filijs tuii τc. iſtud fuit impletum in oaniele: τ ſocijs ſuis qui fuerunt o ſemine regis iu

cuius metropol' eſt ciuitas babylon: τ ideo qñ pceperût re troceſſioné ſolis pdictã prra curſú nature: fuerút ſoliciti q̃ rere q̃liter hoc acciderat: τ cũ audiſſent q̃ hoc fuerat in ſa natôe eçechie oe conſilio ſapiêtũ rex babylonis s(| Mi ſit ad eçechiã lras.in ſignũ reuerêtie. t (| Et munera. ad

oe educti in babylone τ nutriti τ eruditi vt poſſet ſtare i palatio regi babylonis: vt hi oañ.j. o(| Dixit eçechi as ad eſaiã: bon' ê ſmo oñi. penituit eni τ ſic acceptauit oñi ſniaʒ: ſupza ſe τ regnũ ſuũ : ppter qõ τ pena iſta nõ fuit inducta tpib' ſuis: ſʒ fuit oilata vſqʒ ad tpe ioachi

Fig. 14. Benedetto Bordon, Isaiah and King Hezekiah; and The 'Dial of Ahaz', in *Biblia latina cum postillis Nicolai de Lyra*. Venice: [Johannes Herbort de Seligenstadt] for Johannes de Colonia, Nicolaus Jenson, et Socii, 31 July 1481, miniatures in Commentary on Kings IIII (Kings II) 20, in (Paris, Bibliothèque nationale de France, Rés. Vél. 111, fol. O6ᵛ, vellum).

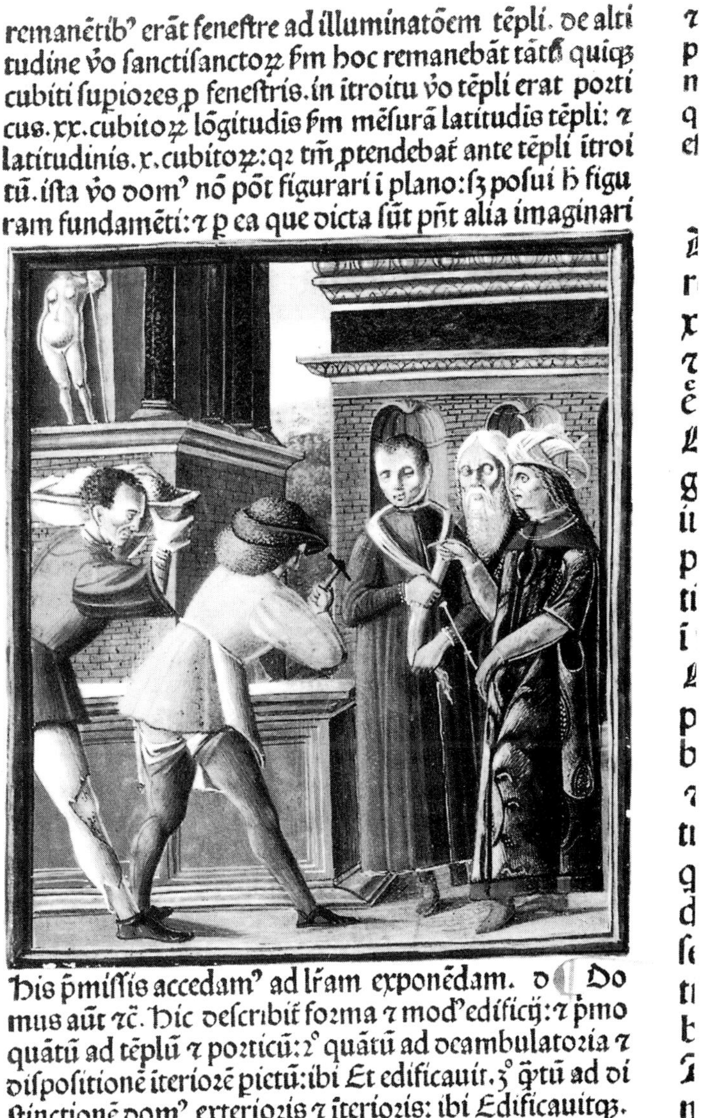

remanētib' erāt fenestre ad illuminatōem tēpli. de alti
tudine vo sanctisanctoꝝ ꝑm hoc remanebāt tātū quiqꝫ
cubiti supiores p fenestris. in itroitu vo tēpli erat porti
cus .xx. cubitoꝝ lōgitudis ꝑm mēsurā latitudis tēpli: ⁊
latitudinis .x. cubitoꝝ: qꝛ tm̄ ptendebat ante tēpli itroi
tū. ista vo dom' nō pōt figurari i plano: sꝫ posui h̄ figu
ram fundamēti: ⁊ p ea que dicta sūt pn̄t alia imaginari

His p̄missis accedam' ad lr̄am exponēdam. D Do
mus aūt ⁊c. Hic describit forma ⁊ mod' edificij: ⁊ p̄mo
quātū ad tēplū ⁊ porticū: 2° quātū ad dcambulatoria ⁊
dispositionē iteriorē pictū: ibi Et edificauit. 3° q̄tū ad di
stinctionē dom' exterioris ⁊ iterioris: ibi Edificauitqꝫ.
4° quātū ad itroitū ⁊ atriū: ibi Fecitqꝫ i itroitu. Circa
p̄mū describit mēsura tēpli ⁊ portic': ⁊ pꝫ lr̄a ex p̄dictis
vsqꝫ ibi: E Et .xxx. cubitos i altitudine. hoc vi' cōtra
dicere ei qđ dcm̄ ē q tēplū in altitudie hēbat .cxx. cubi

Fig. 15. Benedetto Bordon, King Solomon overseeing builders of the Temple, in *Biblia latina cum postillis Nicolai de Lyra*. Venice: [Johannes Herbort de Seligenstadt] for Johannes de Colonia, Nicolaus Jenson, et Socii, 31 July 1481, miniature in Commentary on Kings III (Kings I) 6, in (Paris, Bibliothèque nationale de France, Rés. Vél. 111, fol. K7r, vellum).

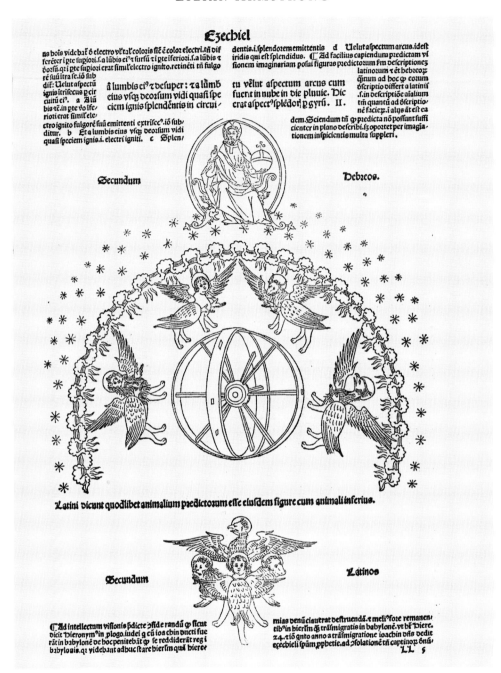

Fig. 16. Pico Master design, woodcut of Vision of Ezekiel, in *Biblia Latina cum postillis Nicolai de Lyra*. Venice: [Bonetus Locatellus] for Octavianus Scotus, 8 August 1489, Commentary on Exekiel I (Città del Vaticano, Biblioteca Apostolica Vaticana, Inc. Prop. II, 176, fol. LL5ʳ).

Pico Master's twenty-year involvement in hand-illuminating Venetian incunables had given him the skills to design the 1489 woodcuts, thus closing an era in the illustration of bibles printed in Venice.

CONCLUSION

By the early 1480s, the heyday of the hand-illuminated incunable was drawing to a close. The 1489 *Biblia latina cum postillis Nicolai de Lyra* was illustrated with woodcut diagrams and in 1490 LucAntonio Giunta published the Malermi Bible with 384 narrative woodcuts. Leading up to this achievement, however, were the three stages of decoration and illustration outlined in this paper. The initial presumption of Vindelinus de Spira and Adam de Ambergau was that a big bible should have some significant number of illustrations and they designed their printed Italian bibles to accommodate them. The more practical smaller bibles printed by Nicolaus Jenson, Franciscus Renner, and others in the 1470s generally ignored the traditions of bible illustration, but the printers and booksellers could and did still arrange for copies to be splendidly decorated for wealthy clients. The 1481 and 1482-3 Bibles with Nicholas of Lyra's Commentary in a sense precipitated a crisis, since the text actually requires diagrams and figures that were filled in only a few cases. Their glaring blank spaces may have been in part what finally led the reluctant Venetians to the printed book illustrated with woodcuts.

PRINTING THE BIBLE IN THE FIFTEENTH CENTURY

DEVOTION, PHILOLOGY AND COMMERCE

KRISTIAN JENSEN

DIVERSITY OR UNIFORMITY

'I AM A BIBLE THOROUGHLY corrected from Greek and Hebrew sources, and I am also beautiful. I call upon the gods and the stars as my witnesses: There is no printed Bible like me in the whole world. There are concordances to every passage and the lettering is neatly printed.'[1]

This invocation of the stars and the pagan gods first appeared in the colophon of Johann Amerbach's edition of the Latin Bible printed in Basel 1479. As a sales pitch the reference to the source languages must have had particular appeal in Basel in the late 1470s when Andronikos Kontoblakes was teaching Greek in the city, having among his pupils Johannes Reuchlin whose interest in Hebrew and Greek was to become so important.[2] But it must have appealed elsewhere too, for it was repeated by several other publishers. While Amerbach's linguistic claim may not be entirely substantiated, it reflects a set of cultural attitudes. The importance of the original languages for assessing the translation of the Bible ascribed to Jerome had long been understood. In the fourteenth century Nicolaus de Lyra argued for the importance of Hebrew for biblical studies, and it was a live issue in the late fifteenth century when polemical works were written about Lyra's use of Hebrew.[3] The Greek New Testament was also addressed with increased intensity by humanists like Ambrogio Traversari, Gianozzo Manetti, and, most famously, by Lorenzo Valla.[4] This was part of the environment out of which Erasmus's translation from the Greek was to grow.

Prominent among contemporary attitudes was the view that human endeavour should be kept separate from divine matters: for instance schoolboys were brought up on phrases like 'You must not desire to know exalted things'.[5] On the other hand, Amerbach's claim reflects an acceptance of the notion that even a sacred text had only potential uniformity, which in practice was approached through active human intervention. We are not confronted by the increasingly explicit challenge to the authoritative, divine nature of holy texts which later biblical scholarship was to pose, but we see an implicit tension within a hierarchical society in which diversity by its very nature seemed a challenge to authority.

Students of the fifteenth-century Bible have tended to emphasize textual stability, and there is indeed a significant element of stability, as one would expect of any text in early modern Europe. This has overshadowed the more surprising evidence indicating that diversity of a sacred text was expected and accepted. There were numerous attempts in the fifteenth century to create uniformity in liturgical matters, and the link between uniformity of faith and the uniformity of texts was often explicit.[6] These attempts were made at local, diocesan levels, or for particular religious orders, while the uniformity of the Bible was beyond the bounds of their authority. It is important for the study of the fifteenth-century Bible to bear in mind that the imposed, uniform biblical vulgate is a post-Tridentine phenomenon,[7] when the papacy had more power within the Roman church, while it was no longer an authority throughout the rest of western Europe.

My point of departure for this study was the cataloguing of the fifteenth-century printed Latin bibles in preparation for the Bodleian Library's incunable catalogue (*Bod-inc*),[8] which focuses on texts and on the evidence presented by the books themselves about how they were used. The entries identify all texts in each edition, the definition of what constitutes a text being very generous. Doing this for the Bible was an overwhelming task, but there was much help to be had. While many incunabula have been little studied from a textual point of view, this is not true of the Bible. In particular, the text of the Gutenberg Bible (B42) has been examined by distinguished scholars in several fields, and some later editions have also been subjected to a fair amount of scrutiny. The work of bibliographers has been crystallized for instance in the *GW*,[9] and in *CIBN*[10] where many new insights are to be found. Paul Needham has made contributions in several sale catalogues and has examined how the B42 was used by printers in the 1460s in an article to which I will refer frequently.[11] In a later wide-ranging article he indicated several possible avenues of exploration of the impact of the B42 and also suggested the importance of examining aspects of textual change.[12] Edoardo Barbieri's book on Italian printed translations of the Bible is important,[13] as is Denise Hillard's article on the bibles printed in France, in French and in Latin.[14]

Here I intend to explore the diversity of the biblical corpus, aiming in particular to understand the dynamic nature of the changes which it underwent. This requires drawing on methods and insights from a variety of disciplines. Using results from several disciplines necessitates an awareness of their aims in order to use them to their full extent and not to use them beyond the limits set by their methodology.

I will discuss methodological problems of using evidence from catalogues and individual books throughout, but initially I will address some issues arising from the use of evidence produced by various philological methods. Philologists have studied the transmission of the biblical text with aims and objective quite different from those of bibliographers and students of the history of texts and reading. Broadly speaking, they have aimed at establishing the original version of a text, not what text was available to be read in a particular period. In order to use their results properly it is important to know what they have set out to achieve, how they have gone about it, and how that has influenced their conclusions.

In 1922, Henri Quentin published a study intended as an introduction to the critical principles followed by the papal commission for the revision of the Vulgate, of which he was a member.[15] This contained the first detailed study of the text of the B42 and its *fortuna*. His overall aim was to establish a solid textual basis for the new edition. As far as incunable bibles were concerned his conclusion was stark: they were of no interest.[16]

Quentin was radical, in a sense, for the *textus receptus* of the Vulgate had rested largely on a tradition to which the B42 is related. It was the first time that the Roman Church accepted the principles of a modern critical approach to the Vulgate. In one important respect, however, the *textus receptus* was not abandoned: which texts were to constitute the canon was not a matter for discussion. Quentin was well aware that the texts included in fifteenth-century editions varied significantly, and his examination of them was the basis of his excellent classification of many printed bible editions. For Quentin himself it was a tool for the elimination of editions from his research, but it remains the best description of these texts, and his work was apparently the basis for the structure used by the *GW*.

While Quentin's study has been accepted, sometimes implicitly, by bibliographers, his edition has been examined more critically by philologists, for instance F. C. Burkitt who concluded that he had relied on inferior manuscripts.[17] On a theoretical level, Giorgio Pasquali and Sebastiano Timpanaro, two leading figures of twentieth-century philology, severely criticized Quentin's 'objective' method of textual criticism which rejected the use of subjective judgements of whether readings were correct or not, *recensio sine interpretatione*.[18] Instead of using his personal judgement, Quentin wished to rely on a quantitative approach to the classification of codices. Both Pasquali and Timpanaro acknowledged that the Bible presents a particularly complex textual transmission, often characterized by variants rather than by truly corrupt passages. While Timpanaro acknowledged that a quantitative method may provide some assistance, he and Pasquali pointed out that Quentin's method fails to take into account that it is only errors that allow us to group manuscripts together, that shared correct, or even possible, readings prove nothing, and that one must use one's judgement to identify errors. When dealing with a largely contaminated manuscript tradition factual and linguistic criteria, such as *lectio difficilior*, become more not less important.[19]

This criticism is of direct relevance for Quentin's approach to the text of incunable bibles. He listed five variants on which he based his conclusions about the relations between printed editions,[20] but none of them can be called an *error significativus*,[21] and each may have been present in any number of manuscripts, potential sources for later printed editions. They do not constitute philological evidence for a stemmatic relation between manuscripts nor are they sufficient when we examine printed bibles.[22] Quentin's use of these readings must therefore depend on the assumption that the text of the B42 was significantly at variance from the manuscript tradition, and this impression was promoted by his edition. Although he stated that the B42 was of no textual importance, it was included in the apparatus of his own edition, perhaps as a placating gesture towards traditionalists. In the apparatus the B42 is often quoted as the only evidence for the *textus receptus* of the pre-twentieth-century Vulgate, and the apparatus thus created an argument for seeing the later printed tradition of the texts as isolated from a manuscript tradition.

In an important study from 1954 Heinrich Schneider pointed out that Quentin's edition quoted only three manuscripts of the 'Paris Bible' tradition to which he related the B42, and that none of them is from the fourteenth or fifteenth centuries.[23] Schneider made significant steps towards placing the B42 in its chronological and geographical context, describing a number of later manuscripts, like the B42 from the Rhenish region.[24] In some sample passages Schneider found that these manuscripts had a high proportion of the variant readings for which the papal edition quoted the B42 as the earliest and only source.

Robert Weber examined further passages of the B42 and emphasized that later editions were critical of the *textus receptus* and sometimes used good sources for emendations.[25] Weber, however, only noted significant variants, and only variants which he, as an editor of the Vulgate, saw as progress towards a better text. This has again strengthened the perception that changes were minimal,[26] although that is not what Weber argued: his point was that, from the point of view of a modern editor of the Vulgate, few of the changes were good.[27] The level of variation is much greater if the text is examined without the end-result of the twentieth-century Vulgate in mind.

Quentin and Weber discarded early printed bibles as textual evidence, because they all represent traditions of which better texts survive in earlier manuscripts. Taken out of context, this has led to an emphasis on a static biblical tradition in the fifteenth century. It has also meant that expectations of fifteenth-century work on the biblical texts have been raised too high. In the modern sense of the word, there was no recension of any text in the fifteenth century, only emendation. Expecting the *textus receptus* of the Bible to have been radically challenged amounts to an anachronism, and leads us away from the more surprising fact that the biblical corpus was not static and unchallengeable, and that there was a continual desire to change and to improve.[28]

Some fifteen years after the B42 was printed we begin to see dramatic change and towards the end of the century diversity is remarkable.[29] In some ways this resembles the diversity among manuscript bibles, but, as we shall see, there are significant differences.

THE DYNAMIC DEVELOPMENT OF TEXTS

In the early decades of the thirteenth century a 'Paris Bible'[30] established itself, at least in northern Europe, as the most common bible type of the later middle ages supported by the emerging commercial book production in Paris. However, the subsequent history of the 'Paris Bible' is found to be one of a comprehensive contamination from manuscripts alien to the Paris tradition, some from traditions dating back to Latin translations predating Jerome, and some perhaps even from Hebrew sources.[31] However unsystematic in our eyes, to contemporaries this was a process of improvement.

It is normally said that the B42, being dependent on this process, is a 'Paris Bible'. This view however needs modification. Led by their focus on the texts which now constitute the Vulgate, textual critics have looked at the 'Paris Bible' as a tradition from which they selected those texts which were of interest to them. From its perspective the B42 may indeed be seen to be part of the 'Paris Bible' tradition. Students of the manuscript tradition of the Bible, however, see the 'Paris Bible' as a a textual corpus, consisting of the books of the Bible in a specific order, accompanied by 64 specific prologues and by Stephen Langton's *Interpretationes nominum hebraeorum*.[32] If understood like that, the B42 can barely be seen as a representative of the 'Paris Bible'. Twenty-three of the standard 64 prefaces are not included,[33] nor is Stephen Langton's work, while it does contain 14 prefaces[34] and IV Ezra[35] which were apparently not part of the 'Paris Bible'. Laura Light has emphasized that the 'Paris Bible' of the thirteenth century is more diverse than is sometimes thought and that other bible types of the thirteenth century need much more attention. In comparison, manuscript bibles from the fifteenth century have hardly been studied at all, apart from the five described by Schneider, and it is not quite clear what a 'Paris Bible' might mean in a fifteenth-century context, nor indeed if it is a helpful term to use for this period.

I shall therefore concentrate on texts which were available in printed form in the fifteenth century itself. The examination makes it clear that printers relied on the products of their colleagues, but that they also added material from manuscript sources. As we can place neither the texts of the Gutenberg Bible nor of later printed bibles in a context of fifteenth-century manuscripts, we must not forget that similarities between printed editions can arise because they have relied on similar, but as yet unstudied, manuscript material. When in doubt, I will talk about editions sharing a corpus of texts. My account of the printed editions can be, relatively, compressed, because details will be published in the catalogue of the Bodleian Library and because of the pioneering work of Quentin. However, merely referring to Quentin for this information is not possible, partly because he did not discuss many of the texts in question, and partly because my emphasis is not on establishing groups facilitating a description, but on a dynamic relation between groups of texts and their producers.

Sixteen editions contain the same selection of texts as the B42,[36] the edition from 1462,[37] and possibly others, with a number of textual emendations. The last edition to follow the B42 corpus is dated 'after 1480'. In several other editions the B42 corpus was retained while a few associated texts were added. Bernhard Richel's edition dated 'not after 1474'[38] included a marginal concordance to the Gospels and the Eusebian canons, the latter admittedly without the key reference numbers required to make it useful,[39] presumably intended to be added by hand. In addition he included a letter addressed to Jacobus Ysenach, and some verses extracted from Guido Vicentinus's *Margarita bibliae*.[40] In his edition dated 14 April 1478[41] Koberger provided a table of contents, numbered the Psalms, and modified headings to some giving brief indications of how they prefigure the life and death of Christ.[42] Marginal concordances, the canon tables, and tables of contents were all useful tools for biblical scholarship, and the interpretative notes on the psalms could also be useful in a pastoral context, all indications of the intended use of these bible editions.

A more radical change to the biblical corpus of the B42 is found in the 1471 edition printed in Rome by Sweynheym and Pannartz, the first to be printed outside German-speaking lands.[43] It has long been known that it depends on the Mainz 1462 edition, and also that it contains a number of additional texts. Appropriately for a Roman Bible it contains a dedicatory letter from Giovanni Andrea Bussi, the editor, addressed to pope Paul II.[44] He included the work known as *Ad Philocratem de lxx interpretibus*, ascribed to Aristeas,[45] in the translation of Matteo Palmieri, and a letter of dedication from Palmieri to Paul II. Having been commissioned by Giovanni Tortelli, Palmieri's translation was made in close association with the papal court of Nicolaus V and was first dedicated to Bartolomeo Malipiero, the bishop of Brescia, for whom Tortelli worked after the death of Nicolaus V.[46] The later dedication to Paul II reaffirms the close connection between the text and the humanist papal court. The letter of dedication and Palmieri's translation were first printed in Riessinger's edition of Jerome's letters.[47] The text on the translation of the Septuagint is highly relevant for the Bible, not least because Jerome himself in his prologue to the Bible refers to it.[48] There was a long-standing humanist interest in recovering for the West texts from the ancient Greek Christian tradition, exemplified by the work of Ambrogio Traversari.[49] The presence of the pseudo-Aristeas letter thus places the Roman Bible edition firmly in the Humanist circles around the papal court. Bussi himself attached great importance to pseudo-Aristeas, devoting a whole paragraph to the work in his letter to Paul II,[50] and even recording its presence in his summary list of the publications of Sweynheym and Pannartz. While the explicitly pro-Judaic pseudo-Aristeas did not make it into the mainstream of Latin bibles, it did become a standard part of bibles in Italian, and in that context the usefulness of the work was emphasized by the humanist Girolamo Squarzafico.[51] The humanist setting of the Roman Bible is emphasized by its visual appearance.[52]

The Roman edition also differs from the B42 text group in excluding IV Ezra. It is the first printed edition to be accompanied by Stephen Langton's *Interpretationes nominum hebraeorum*, a glossary of Hebrew names, a standard part of the 'Paris Bible' and an important tool for the scholarly study of the text.[53] A number of the 64 prefaces known from the 'Paris Bible' standard but not included in B42 were added in the Roman edition,[54] evidently adapting the biblical corpus to a tradition acceptable in Italy.

The Roman biblical corpus was only taken up once, by Johann Sensenschmidt in Nuremberg in 1475;[55] it would seem that German Bible buyers were used to the form known from the B42. It required the commercial onslaught from the Venetian presses to change their attitude: in his second edition from 1476,[56] a few vestiges apart, Sensenschmidt abandoned the Roman model, and reverted to the group based on Richel's Basel edition from 'not after 1474'.[57] However, apparently after he had printed the relevant sheets, he decided to follow the Roman edition in suppressing IV Ezra.[58] Like the first, his second edition contained Stephen Langton's *Interpretationes nominum hebraeorum*, although many surviving copies do not contain the five gatherings of forty-two leaves containing this text. Instead they are sometimes found with Koberger's edition from 1477.[59]

Richel's edition from 1477 is similar to his two earlier editions,[60] but contains a *registrum* of the books of the Bible and Stephen Langton's *Interpretationes nominum hebraeorum*. It is tempting to assume that this reflects a long-term impact of the Roman edition on bible editions from northern Europe, via Sensenschmidt's edition, but the text is too common in biblical manuscripts for us to draw this conclusion without a more detailed examination of the transmission of the text. However, Langton henceforth was a standard part of north-European-printed bible editions. For instance, it was included, whether from manuscript sources or based on an earlier printed edition, in the only fifteenth-century Parisian edition of the Latin Bible, dated to 'between 22 July 1476 and 21 July 1477',[61] although, as recorded by *GW*, this edition was mainly set from the Mainz edition of 1462.[62]

Zainer's 1480 edition from Ulm[63] is similar to Koberger's 1477 edition, but with Langton's *Interpretationes*, and, a new departure which we shall encounter later, expanded rubrics briefly summarizing each chapter of each book of the Bible, the *casus summarii*. Only the Song of Songs was without its *casus summarius*, because the interpretation was too controversial, as stated in a note preceding the book.

If the Roman edition of the Bible had little impact, two other Italian Bible editions entirely failed to influence the subsequent tradition, namely the editions from Piacenza (1475)[64] and from Vicenza (1476),[65] like Rome not commercial centres. The Vicenza edition was identified by Quentin as not belonging to the textual tradition of B42, and Denise Hillard in *CIBN*,[66] ever impressive, identified the Piacenza edition as being different from both the B42 tradition and the Vicenza edition.

On the other hand, the first Venetian edition, produced by Franciscus Renner in 1475, was to be of immense importance,[67] largely, no doubt, because Venice was the main European book exporting centre. Renner's edition depended, directly or indirectly, on the 1462 edition for some of its text. For instance, the 1462 edition mixed the readings of the two settings of B42, creating a distinctive text for Genesis 11: 13-14, as established by Paul Needham,[68] a reading found also in the Venice 1475 edition. It has been assumed that the Venetian edition depended on the Roman edition, which also has this reading.[69] However, on present evidence, this seems unlikely for the Venice edition shares a number of other features with the 1462 tradition which are not found in the Roman edition, IV Ezra for example. It also contains twelve prefaces which were not included in the Roman edition, and ten of these were not part of the 'Paris Bible'.[70] The prefaces shared by the Roman and the Venetian editions are not sufficient evidence of dependence, for they were widely available and, for instance, the prefaces to Chronicles in the Venetian edition are somewhat different from the Roman edition, and appear in a different order. The evidence thus points towards a use of a manuscript source jointly with a text in the 1462 tradition. This is of some importance for it is the beginning of a cultural and economic exchange where Venice-based printers relied on bible texts from German editions but modified and adapted what they found.

The Venetian selection of prefaces was to become part of the standard Bible for the rest of the century. In the course of only nine years, as many as thirteen editions followed this pattern.[71] Eleven are from Venice; a Naples edition from 1476 differed slightly.[72] In 1479 an edition[73] displayed what was to become a well-known pattern of Lyon printers making Venetian texts available in transalpine editions.

Likewise in 1479 Johann Amerbach, the Basel printer, took up the Venetian biblical corpus,[74] but adapted it to a pre-existing German tradition. As mentioned above, from Richel's edition 'not after 1474',[75] several German bibles contained a marginal concordance to the Gospels. Amerbach's edition of the Venetian texts contains a marginal concordance to the entire New Testament and each Gospel is preceded by a note on the contents of each chapter, called *registrum*.[76] Throughout the New Testament each chapter is divided into subsections, marked A to G. Perhaps the most important added text is the *capitulare lectionum et evangeliorum*,[77] indicating which passages of the Bible were to be read at what point of the liturgical year. The Amerbach edition also contains a number of mnemonic verses, one set of twelve lines on the order of the books of the Bible,[78] and one set on the recipients of the letters from the Evangelists and on the dates of the writing of the Gospels.[79] The first set of mnemonic verse is followed by the verses quoted at the opening of this article. Reinforcing the German trend of accumulation of texts well beyond that found in B42, Amerbach provided an apparatus which aimed to make the Bible much more useful for serious scholarly study for which memorization was an important part.[80]

Although several of these textual elements came to be much used, only one other edition of the Bible followed the pattern exactly, the one printed in Basel in 1485 by

Michael Wenssler.[81] Amerbach's own next bible edition was modified in several ways[82] and several later editions conformed to this new pattern.[83] This form was also followed outside German-speaking lands in Reinhart's and Philippi's edition from Lyon 1482.[84] More importantly, it had an impact on the Venetian editions of Johannes Herbort, who in his 1483 edition[85] incorporated the mnemonic verses on the order of the books of the Old Testament, and the notes on the contents preceding each Gospel. But he did not reproduce the other mnemonic verses, the verses beginning 'Fontibus e graecis ...', nor the tabulation enabling the Bible to be used for liturgical purposes. At the beginning he printed a letter from Franciscus Moneliensis, praising the edition, and at the end six hexameters by Quintus Aemilianus Cimbriacus.[86] Neither these additional verses nor Moneliensis's letter reappear in his edition from 1484,[87] where the verses on the order of the books of the Old Testament have been moved to the first leaf of the book; but in this edition we find the first Italian occurrence of the verses on the Greek and Hebrew sources which first appeared in Amerbach's edition.

The Venetian edition by Arrivabenus from 28 February 1487/8[88] incorporated the marginal concordance and the tables of contents for the Gospels and letters from the Basel editions, but excluded all mnemonic verse, the verses praising the edition ('Fontibus e graecis hebraeorum quoque libris ...'), and, like Herbort's Venetian editions, the *capitulare lectionum et evangeliorum*.

It would appear that in part Peter Drach's edition from 1489[89] followed the second Herbort edition, with the mnemonic verses on the order of the books of the Old Testament at the beginning.[90] Drach, however, decided to follow the Basel tradition in including the *capitulare lectionum et evangeliorum*, a choice indicating that this text was more useful in a north European context than in Italy where it was regularly excluded.

Basel editors continued to develop the Bible, supplementing it with more material facilitating its use for study. While Amerbach had placed a note on the contents of each chapter in front of each Gospel, calling them *registra*, Kesler's edition of 1487[91] added such tables, here *capitulationes*, to all works in the New Testament, except a few of the letters, mainly preceding each work, but in the case of Acts and Apocalypse coming after.[92] He also added a note on the translators and interpreters of the Bible.[93] The edition otherwise has elements known from Amerbach[94] and from Herbort.[95] Prüss's 1489 edition[96] added two brief passages providing further guidance to the Old and the New Testaments, *registrum librorum veteris testamenti* and *directorium novi testamenti*, but otherwise followed Kesler's 1487 edition.[97]

In his edition from 1491[98] Kesler conformed to his first edition,[99] although it seems that he had intended to present yet another change, extending the marginal concordance also to the Old Testament. This project was abandoned after only one sheet, and in some copies of the edition the marginal notes do not even occur there.[100] Where Kesler failed, Froben succeeded, for his edition, dated 27 June 1491,[101] contains a marginal concordance throughout. He printed a third version of the mnemonic verses on the order of the books,[102] and all these verses which in previous editions had been free standing are in this edition tied to a three-page *summarium* of the books of the Bible, yet another finding aid.

Although it is not possible to determine if it preceded Kesler's 1491 edition or came after it, we can conclude that printers were keenly aware of what their competitors produced and that the addition of useful features, such as a concordance, could be seen as advantage in a competitive market. That being said, Froben aimed at a different market from Kesler, if the size of the books is anything to go by: the Bodleian copy of Kesler's edition measures 310 × 220 mm, whereas Froben's measures 180 × 120 mm, the first truly small printed bible edition, a feature proclaimed by Froben himself.[103] Perhaps it is significant that Froben omitted *capitulare lectionum et evangeliorum*, the table enabling the Bible to be used in a liturgical context.

Froben's octavo bible soon made an impact on his competitors in Venice. Hieronymus de Paganinis produced an edition in 1492 evidently based on Froben's,[104] although the mnemonic verses which were found at the opening of Froben's edition were omitted, as was the *summarium*. Instead we find a new alphabetical table to the Bible, covering some twenty pages, composed by Gabriel Brunus, guardian of a Franciscan Convent of Venice,[105] followed by the note on the translators of the Bible and the note on the ways of interpreting scripture.[106] Like Froben's edition it contains a marginal concordance throughout the Bible. Preceding Stephen Langton's *Interpretationes* is a colophon praising the book and naming Petrusevangelus de Monte Ulmi as editor.[107]

Froben was, of course, not to be outdone and produced in 1495 an edition adding the alphabetical table of Gabriel Brunus, in a somewhat revised version.[108]

In 1494 Simon Bevilaqua, also in Venice, produced an edition[109] based on Paganinis' 1492 edition, adding a further finding aid, a table to the Bible in the form of mnemonic verse sometimes ascribed to Alexander de Villa Dei,[110] but also including the verses 'Fontibus e graecis ...' not seen in a Venetian edition since 1484.[111]

Yet another bible type had appeared in 1491, the year which saw the edition of both Kesler's folio and Froben's octavo. It was published not in Basel, but in near-by Freiburg im Breisgau, by Piscator,[112] and like Froben's 1491 edition it included a marginal concordance throughout the entire Bible and excluded the *capitulare lectionum et evangeliorum*.[113] However, it reached back to Zainer's 1480 edition, including the *casus summarii* to the books of the Old Testament,[114] whereas the *casus summarii* for the New Testament were replaced by the appropriate portions of the *capitulationes* or *registra* as they appeared first in Kesler's Basel edition from 1487.[115] It thus contains elements drawn from three different sources.

In 1497, in Strasbourg, Johann Grüninger produced an edition[116] which merged elements drawn from Froben's second edition with Piscator's version of the *casus summarii*.[117] They were also included in Pivard's 1497 Lyon edition,[118] which however followed Bevilaqua's edition from 1494 as a source for the introductory tables of contents, including the metrical mnemonic table sometimes ascribed to Alexander de Villa Dei, and using the form of Gabriel Brunus's table which was used in Venetian imprints. Pivard tried to give some order to this varied material by numbering the tables one to four, and he also added a prefatory note of his own, and he repeated this edition in January 1500/1.[119]

With Pivard's second edition we have reached the end of the fifteenth century, but we have not yet completed our picture of Latin Bible incunabula. We have seen how the Bible was increasingly surrounded by material making it easier to use for study and for reference. Although they have most often not been examined jointly with other bibles, editions which carry a full commentary are evidently part of this development. Three different sets of commentaries were published with Latin bibles in the fifteenth century: the *glossa ordinaria*, the *Postillae* of Nicolaus de Lyra, and the commentary of Hugo de Sancto Caro. The *glossa ordinaria* was the first to be published with the biblical text, by Adolf Rusch 'not before 1480', with the type of Johann Amerbach, and also with the financial involvement of Anton Koberger. It is not surprising that this was a collaborative enterprise for it is a truly gigantic book, of 1211 leaves printed on imperial folio and typically bound in four or five volumes, measuring half a metre in height. As far as the books of the Bible and the prefaces are concerned, the edition is independent of previous printed bibles. The gloss itself has been discussed in detail by Margaret Gibson,[120] who has described it as 'the classic analysis of Scripture: its method and outlook that of Late Antiquity – philosophically neoplatonist, and often more interested in the allegorical value of a text than in its literal meaning'.[121]

Already in 1481, probably just about a year later, we see the next printed bible with a commentary, now the *Postillae litterales* of Nicolaus de Lyra, printed in Venice by Johannes Herbort for the large Venetian consortium formed around Nicolaus Jenson.[122] Not quite as gigantic as the *glossa ordinaria*, copies being about 330 mm tall, this too was a very large-scale work, consisting of 1185 leaves, and not surprisingly for such a large-scale work was produced by a well funded consortium.[123] As for the text of the Bible, the edition is close to the Venetian tradition as we know it from Renner's edition from 1475 and onwards. It is preceded by a letter to Francesco Sanson, the general of the Franciscan order, written by Franciscus Moneliensis.

Editions of the *Postillae* published on their own appeared before they were printed jointly with the bible. The first edition was produced by Sweynheym and Pannartz in Rome 1471-2,[124] evidently in association with their bible edition of 1471. Giovanni Andrea Bussi, the editor, was working on the Lyra edition while the bible was being printed.[125] Also other separate editions of Lyra can be seen as companion volumes to bibles. Mentelin's edition 'not after 1472'[126] may well have been published in association with the edition of the Bible produced by the 'R-printer' around the same time.[127] Mentelin's edition became the basis for later separate editions of the *Postillae*. Importantly it was produced by Koberger, the prolific printer of Latin bibles, in 1481.[128] While editions which contain the complete *Postillae* belong with bible editions, economically as well as culturally, it is striking that those editions which consist only of sections of Lyra's *Postillae* cannot be linked to bible editions.[129]

In the Venetian edition of the Bible with Lyra, the text of the *Postillae* is, largely, the same as that printed by Koberger in 1481, and once again we can see a Venetian Bible production as both a response to a move by key German players in the bible market, and an innovation, for linking text and commentary was more radical than it might seem at first glance. Just as the Consortium's glossed edition was based not on a manuscript tradition of the Bible with gloss and text, but on two separate printed traditions, so also the layout was alien to the manuscript layout of glossed bibles, but similar to the one found in the Strasbourg edition of the *Glossa ordinaria*. The Consortium not only reacted to Koberger's edition of the *Postillae*, they also followed the pioneering layout introduced by Rusch for the *Glossa ordinaria*, a layout which Herbort, their printer had never used before, but which Nicolaus Jenson, a senior partner in the consortium, had used for legal works since 1474.[130] To us this may seem trivial but to contemporaries it was a surprising innovation: when they saw a printed edition of the

Bible with Lyra's *Postillae*, the Carthusians in Basel noticed that it looked like a law book.[131] The Consortium's innovation relied on their awareness of work by contemporary printers in Germany combined with their own practical experience: printing in Venice in the early 1480s was far removed from printing in Rome in the early 1470s where Sweynheym and Pannartz found it technically difficult to print marginal notes, not to mention a full scale commentary coordinated with the text of the Bible.[132]

Koberger responded to the new situation created by the Venetian Consortium: while he produced only one more edition of the plain Bible and no further separate edition of Lyra, he published four editions of the Bible accompanied by the *Postillae*, in 1485, 1486-7, 1493, and in 1497,[133] the same number of editions as those by all other fifteenth-century printers put together.[134]

Compared with the *glossa ordinaria*, the *postilla litteralis* of Lyra was aimed at a university audience of the high Middle Ages, carefully keeping apart the discussion of the literal meaning of the text based on a knowledge of Hebrew from allegorical or other interpretations. Lyra's use of the Hebrew text and in particular of the rabbinical interpretation of Rashi was criticised by Paul of Burgos (*c*. 1351-1425) in his *Additiones*, which were first included in Mentelin's separate edition of the text 'not after 1472', as was also Matthias Döring's defence of Lyra's method written in the 1430s.[135] This was not an ecumenical reaching-out to Jews, as is demonstrated by the simultaneous inclusion of Lyra's anti-Jewish treatise *Contra perfidiam judaeorum*, but it is difficult not to see this as part of an active debate about the use of the Hebrew text, partly played out in the context of the Council of Basel, as part of the background for Amerbach's verses quoted at the beginning of this article, programmatically declaring support for those who wanted to use Hebrew sources, another reminder of the presence in Basel in the same years of Reuchlin, who was to become involved in a polemic about the use of Hebrew books for Christian exegesis.

In 1495 Paganinus de Paganinis took the amalgamation of texts one step further, printing the text of the Bible with Lyra's *Postillae* jointly with the *glossa ordinaria*.[136] Not surprisingly there was a Basel response to this with the publication in 1498 of an edition of the Bible with the *glossa ordinaria* and with Lyra's *Postillae*, for the first time both *morales* and *litterales* together, edited by Sebastian Brant,[137] with a layout which displayed a technical virtuosity way beyond that of the earlier printers. By then Anton Koberger no longer published his editions of the Bible with Lyra's *Postillae*. Instead he undertook a new mammoth project, that of publishing, with Johann Amerbach, the Bible with the *Postillae* of Hugo de Sancto Caro, printed in seven volumes over a period of five years, from 1498 to 1502.[138]

In the first half of the fifteenth century some ninety manuscript pandects, containing all the books of the Bible, would have made a significant impact, but here we are talking about some ninety editions sometimes printed, as we have seen, in nearly a thousand copies. By the end of the century the Bible was available as it had never been before, as against manuscript bibles, almost exclusively containing all the biblical books, and with increasing amounts of scholarly apparatus enabling faster and better access to the texts.

COMPETITION AND DIVERSIFICATION

Bishops or heads of religious orders wished to ensure liturgical uniformity within their jurisdiction. When authorities imposed texts, they often assumed at least some financial responsibility for their production.[139] The Bible, on the other hand, was not subjected to attempts at imposing uniformity, and, correspondingly, editions were rarely sponsored.[140] Printers and publishers of the Latin Bible had to survive in a commercial world, and they both competed against one another and worked together. We need to get an impression of how their commercial relations affected the texts which they distributed.

Excellent German catalogues of incunabula published in the late twentieth century make it possible to get a glimpse of the situation, especially in southern Germany. Due to the history of the formation of their collections, information from the Bodleian Library and the British Library also has a bias towards south Germany. Unfortunately most of the French regional catalogues provide too little information, whereas *CIBN* gives good information on the important collection of the Bibliothèque Nationale de France. In Italy few collections have sufficiently detailed catalogues, although a number of smaller libraries do. Margaret Gibson could say that the *Glossa ordinaria* in southern Europe is still a closed book,[141] and Laura Light regretted the paucity of our knowledge of the late medieval biblical tradition in Italy: to some extent the same is true of incunable bibles.

While it is not possible to use the mere presence of an edition in a modern library as an indication of early distribution, some tentative conclusions may be drawn from the absence from a region of a group of editions, especially if another similar group of editions is well represented. Compared with the number of Italian editions which are present in Italian collections, the relative absence of Nuremberg or Basel editions of the uncommented Bible is striking, especially if one excludes locations in southern Tyrol. We have no reason to suppose that German editions have survived less well in Italian collections, and consequently we may conclude that there is no strong evidence for a substantial impact of north European bible editions on the Italian market,[142] once the Venetian bible production had begun. As far as present evidence goes, only Froben's octavo edition from 1491[143] may have had a significant impact on Italy, and that may explain why Italian printers were so rapid with their response to it. There is much less evidence for an Italian distribution of his second octavo edition.

The large commented editions present a different picture. After 1482 Koberger left the publication of the Bible on its own to others, and concentrated on the commented bibles. Indeed he had an involvement in all fifteenth-century north European editions of the commented Bible. Koberger's editions containing the *Postillae* of Lyra are better represented in Italian collections. This evidence will need to be examined in the light of information about individual copies, but the difference in the pattern of present day survival between the plain and the commented editions is so great that it is likely to be significant. It is undoubtedly true that Koberger had an interest in the Italian market, but it is plausible that a more powerful motivation for him to take up the Venetian model of combining Lyra and the Bible was to protect his own market share, in Germany and elsewhere in western Europe, against Italian exporters. This strategy is very understandable if one looks at the numerous copies of the 1481[144] and 1482-3[145]

Venetian editions of the Bible with Lyra's *Postillae* exported to Germany. Koberger's own four editions of the text[146] seem to have been successful in this respect, for the later Venetian edition, from 1489,[147] has left fewer traces in German libraries. The market impact of these editions can perhaps also be seen in the fact that the Venetian edition from 1495 appears to have had a relatively smaller impact on Germany than many Venetian editions of the Bible without commentaries.

Similarly, the two Strasbourg–Basel–Nuremberg ventures, from around 1480 and from 1498, producing the mammoth editions with the *Glossa ordinaria* and the text of the Bible, have left significant traces in Italian collections,[148] although nowhere near as much as the massively successful edition printed in Venice in 1495.[149] The 1498-1502 Amerbach–Koberger edition of the Bible with the commentary by Hugo de Sancto Caro also made a significant impact on Italian collections.[150] We can date when many copies of the 1498 *Glossa ordinaria* made their way into Italy. Although the book was produced by Froben and Johann Petri, it appears that the entire edition was bought by Anton Koberger. When his relative Hans Koberger went to Venice in 1501, he had with him three hundred copies of the work to swap for other editions.[151] Hans Koberger's visit to Venice was undertaken not only to sell his own firm's wares but, importantly, to buy books to take back to the north.[152] The Kobergers evidently had a product which they were confident would be of sufficient interest in the Italian market, but the cost to them of the Venetian books which they wanted to buy was not matched by the value of the books which Hans Koberger had with him: substantial amounts of cash were also involved. The Venetian book export was not merely in competition with north European printers: by acting as sellers of books produced by other printers, the northerners could get their share of the profit from Venetian editions of texts, law books for instance, which it was not worth their while to print.[153]

The Venetian export of books to Germany and to the rest of Europe is over-whelmingly documented,[154] but not all Venetian editions had the same impact on the German market. Leaving aside the two editions from the early 1480s of the Bible with the *Postillae* of Lyra, ISTC records 16 copies in German locations of Renner's edition from 1480,[155] 24 of his edition from 1483,[156] 21 of Herbort's from 1483,[157] and 22 of Herbort's from 1484,[158] but only three of Scotus's edition from 1480,[159] three of Nicolaus de Frankfordia's edition from 1485,[160] and none of Wild's edition from 1481,[161] the latter perhaps being destined more for the French market. Although these are raw figures and will include copies acquired later and exclude surviving copies which have been alienated from German collections, the variation between the figures is such that it is plausible to suggest that they reflect a different pattern of export for the editions from the two groups.

Frankfordia's edition presents an interesting possibility. It was the last edition to follow the original Venetian biblical corpus, and by 1485 editions with a much greater scholarly apparatus were common. Perhaps it looked old-fashioned in Italy and southern Germany. There are no recorded copies of it in Italian libraries, and the scarce surviving evidence points towards a possible distribution in northern Germany and the Netherlands, an area which also stuck to the rather simple B42 corpus of the Bible for longest, as evidenced by the Cologne Bible editions. Books from this area probably had a lower survival rate than books in southern Germany where religious institutions remained relatively stable until the Napoleonic wars. So perhaps we are not confronted with an edition which was not exported, but one with a very specific export market.

It must not be forgotten that the greatest export market for Venetian books was other Italian towns, as the raw figures of editions in Italian collections so clearly indicate. An important study of the structure of the Venetian trade within Italy has been made by Angela Nuovo, and the importation of printed books into Rome has been studied by Anna Modigliani and Paolo Cherubini.[162] When more information about the history of individual copies of the Bible in Italian collections is known it may even become possible to identify individual Venetian editions exported to specific areas, even within the area of present-day Italy.

In the five years from 1470 to 1475 some eight bible editions appeared. But then it seems that there was a dramatic change. In 1476 alone five editions appeared, and in the six years from 1476 to 1481 a maximum of 31 editions were published, the peak being 1479 and 1480. By contrast, for instance, only 15 editions were published between 1486 and 1491. Not taking into account the size of editions, format, paper size, etc., these figures cannot be used for an assessment of the financial commitments involved, but they provide a clear indication that the period around 1479 and 1480 was very active indeed in publishing Bibles.[163] In 1479 bibles were published in Basel, Cologne, Lyon, Nuremberg, and Venice. In 1480 bibles were published in Cologne, Nuremberg, Strasbourg, Ulm, and Venice. Cologne, a major book-producing centre, dropped out of the race after 1480. For the last twenty years of the fifteenth century Latin bibles were produced in a small number of major centres, south of the Alps nearly exclusively in Venice, north of the Alps in Nuremberg, Strasbourg and Basel, printers in the three cities often working together on major projects, in Lyon and only occasionally in a few other places.

The bi-polar nature of the competition between the large centres explains why few editions were produced outside the great book-producing centre. We have seen, for instance, that the Roman edition had only little impact on the textual development of the printed Bible in the fifteenth century, and that is matched by the relative absence of evidence for an early distribution of the edition along commercial channels, at least outside Italy. Several copies seem to have been owned by grand persons who had been to Rome and acquired the book there,[164] confirming a pattern for distribution of Roman books suggested by Lotte Hellinga.[165] Rome exported services not manufactured goods.

At a first glance it may be more surprising that there was only one fifteenth-century edition of the Latin Bible printed in Paris, an important centre for book production and trade. Denise Hillard has argued convincingly that this is due to a rapidly declining interest in the Bible at the University of Paris during the fifteenth century.[166] While this view is persuasive, the relation between university and the absence of bible editions was more complex. Once printing made books into a mass-produced product, the relation between international availability and local demand became a more commercially sensitive issue. With a university interest in a text the local market could possibly be big enough to warrant a production which might also be exported, but local demand is not necessarily enough: other texts more central to the curriculum of the University of Paris are also absent from the local production, such as the *Sententiae* of Petrus Lombardus or Thomas Aquinas's *Catena aurea*. Parisian printers did not compete in the area of these large university texts, being up against publishers who specialized in such works and who produced on a Europe-wide scale. If the local market was not strong enough to warrant local production, dealing in imported books might be a more viable option for the Parisian book producers/sellers. In general, the absence of a local edition may indicate availability from elsewhere, not necessarily a lack of interest.[167] We need to know more about bibles sold in Paris to be able to form an opinion about the use of the Bible in Paris.[168]

While only one edition of the Latin Bible was printed in Paris in the fifteenth century a number of editions appeared in Cologne, but there are no Cologne editions much after 1480, about the same time as Koberger gave up producing uncommented bibles, leaving that part of the market to competitors, in the main from Venice. The Cologne editions mainly followed the B42 biblical corpus, making no gestures towards the increasing scholarly apparatus found in other bible editions and they are unspectacular, compared with the handsome volumes from elsewhere. One of these comparatively humble editions survives only in a fragment,[169] a sign that the edition was in the hands of people who put the books to heavy use. This is confirmed by the often incomplete state of surviving copies of other Cologne editions. If Bible printing was viable neither in Paris nor in Cologne, two important book centres, versions of the biblical corpus produced in non-commercial centres like Piacenza and Vicenza stood absolutely no chance of surviving in this environment. The international nature of the book market made it impossible for local traditions of the biblical corpus to survive, but, as we have seen, this did not create a Europe-wide uniform Bible type: commercial pressure combined with a real or perceived demand for study aids created ever more diverse editions of the Bible, although this diversity no longer had a clear geographical aspect.

A trend which has been noticed in the development of the fifteenth-century printed Bible is the tendency towards producing smaller books. Paul Needham in particular has drawn attention to the importance of paper size when comparing editions. The B42 is a royal folio and measures some 420 mm high. The last Bible of the fifteenth century to be printed as a royal folio was, according to Paul Needham, Koberger's edition from 14 April 1480.[170] The first Venetian edition of 1475 was a chancery folio.[171] Many of the quarto editions from Venice measure only about 200 mm high.[172] This is much smaller than the small 'Parisian Bibles' of the thirteenth century, which often measured some 250-260 mm.[173] Froben's octavo measures some 180 mm. However, in the same year as Koberger produced his last royal folio uncommented Bible, he also took part in the production of the glossed Bible, an imperial folio, measuring some 500 mm. The production of large bibles for institutions did not cease – a more specialized product was created. The smaller printed bibles may be seen as a parallel to the relatively small manuscript bibles of the thirteenth century. In a very general way that is correct: smaller books may be cheaper, if neither lavishly decorated nor expensively bound, and may therefore be sold in more copies. But the similarities should not be over-emphasized. As against small manuscript bibles of the thirteenth century, the small printed bibles contained a substantial amount of scholarly apparatus in the form of tables and concordances, and there is no evidence to suggest that printers of small bibles in any way modelled their work on small manuscript bibles, whether in terms of content or design.[174] The mass production of bibles, small and large, must be understood as part of the product diversification which also marks the textual development of the Bible in the fifteenth century. Compared with manuscripts, printed bibles existed in a radically changed environment. They competed in a market of mass-produced items where diversity was no longer a possibility but an economic necessity. This new situation is emblematically expressed by Froben's marketing slogan for his new and better and smaller bible, quoted at the beginning of this article.

In the thirteenth century Venetian producers already copied luxury products from the east and exported them back to their countries of origin.[175] The Venetian success in marketing the German invention of printing is another example of this process, as is the specific case of the production and marketing of bibles. German printers played an overwhelming role in Venice from the introduction of printing until the mid-1480s,[176] part of a general interaction between Venice and Germany. Germans based in Venice must have had a better understanding of the German market for bibles. We have seen a continued Venetian interaction with printers based in Germany. The prefatory material of the 1475 Venetian Bible became standard throughout Europe in the fifteenth century, but otherwise most of the textual innovation to the biblical corpus was introduced by German printers. Innovations gained Europe-wide currency because they were taken up by printers in Venice who kept a close eye on what their German competitors did. German printers kept an eye on competitors in Venice, probably not so much to be able to export to Italy as to protect their share of the non-Italian market. Although Koberger withdrew from the production of uncommented bibles around 1480, in the bible market printers based in Venice never out-competed their colleagues based in Germany, unlike the way that, for a while, they dominated the market for texts by classical authors and for Roman law. Indeed, after 1485, when bibles were no longer produced by Germans based in Venice, the 21 bible editions produced in Germany vastly outnumber the seven editions from Italy.

The commercial necessity of ensuring or protecting a market must be a key explanation for the way in which printers modified their own bible editions as soon as new features were added by others.[177] Printers could not afford not to include texts which might tempt parts of their markets away, and the combination of textual evidence and evidence of the distribution of copies enables us to refine this picture of competition. Richard Goldthwaite has said that it is not easy to find manufactured products of value that were imported into Italy in notable quantities.[178] Certain editions of the glossed bibles evidently are an exception, while the picture holds true for printed bibles without commentaries.

There is thus a direct relation between economic necessity and the highly complex textual transfers across Europe which have been outlined above. We see how commercial pressure broke down regional specificity but did not lead to uniformity. On the contrary it made it possible throughout Europe to gain access to very diverse biblical corpora. In this perspective the rapid changes to the biblical corpus can also be seen as a function of product development – as expressed so clearly in Amerbach's promotional verses on the new qualities of his book. Whatever desire there might have been for uniformity, the commercial nature of bible production militated against it, manipulating the market to accept and expect innovation and generate continued demand by offering a diverse and ever improved product.

WHY DID PEOPLE BUY BIBLES?

The Bible in institutions – a tool for salvation

Some people wanted to buy bibles, and some could be persuaded that a new edition might be better than an older one; but this does not explain why a person might chose to buy a bible rather than any other object. To get an impression of some of the reasons, we must look in detail at the evidence which surviving copies provide about themselves. Even before printing was invented the collections of religious houses throughout Europe were replete with bibles; Pierre Petitmengin has talked about a glut.[179] At first sight that makes it even harder to understand why there was a great willingness to buy more bibles, but if we see how collections came about, the increased demand makes more sense. It is characteristic of late-medieval institutions that their libraries grew by donation.[180] In some instances books were bequeathed by members of the institution. This often meant a substantial accumulation of many copies of the same text. For instance, the fifteenth-century catalogue of the Augustinian canons at the Abbey of St Mary in Leicester records seventeen complete bibles, one *in refectorio*. Fifteen of the remaining sixteen have names of donors associated with them, mainly canons or friars at Leicester itself.[181]

It is sometimes assumed that the printed royal folio bibles of the fifteenth century were used for refectory reading.[182] This is evidently true of a few copies of the B42,[183] but it cannot be shown to be true for most surviving copies, nor for later editions, large or small. Nearly all copies of the B42 and later royal folio bible editions have survived because they have been in the ownership of religious institutions, but this does not mean that they were chosen by the institutions. In fact, none of the surviving copies of the B42 can be shown to have been bought by an institution, whereas many can be shown to have been donated at some point by private individuals. By and large the same holds true for later editions.[184]

Although in some cases we may assume that books were bought expressly to be donated, it is worth remembering that private persons donating bibles presupposes the existence of bibles in private ownership, a topic which deserves much more study. Apart from the books which have survived because they were donated to institutions, important evidence for private ownership of bibles can also be found in wills.[185]

Even if institutions did not often buy bibles, that does not exclude the possibility that, at least sometimes, they used the books which they were given – indeed on occasion they assessed the usefulness of donations with great care[186] – but to understand the economic function of bibles, it is important to concentrate on how and why they ended up in institutions.

Many surviving fifteenth-century printed bibles were presented by people associated with the receiving institution, continuing the tradition exemplified by St Mary's in Leicester. But as prices of books fell from the mid-1470s, people from outside were also increasingly in a position to donate books. This was often done in connection with the founding of chantries. Breviaries and other liturgical books would have been required for use at the numerous new altars which were erected to provide the requested liturgical services, and their link to the founding of chantries is more obvious.[187] Donated bibles played a different role in the same process.

The possibility of lay persons becoming associated with the activities of religious organizations reaches far back in the history of Christianity.[188] During the fifteenth century, the increasing importance of the doctrine of purgatory created an ever-wider market for participation in ecclesiastical services; one type of service could be bought in the form of an indulgence for oneself or for one's dearest whom one might wish to help through purgatory. In the relationship between a lay person purchasing and the Church providing a service, bibles as donations play a similar role. The pious and apparently frightened Martin Mergetheimer expressed it clearly when he gave a bible to the Benedictines of Ebersberg 'in order for prayers to be said for his soul for it not to be absorbed by hellish punishments and be deprived of the vision of God, which it confidently expects while bound by the chains of its body'.[189]

Numerous early printed bibles contain inscriptions which show that they were donated to institutions in return for annual masses or for prayers.[190] Relying on books which contain such explicit requests may underestimate the number of donations made with the expectation of a return in the form of prayers.[191] Such a stipulation could be made elsewhere, for instance in a will.[192] The stipulation could also be found in records belonging to the religious house in question. Thus the books donated by Johann Amerbach to the Carthusians of Basel did not normally contain an instruction to pray for him;[193] but the *Liber benefactorum* of the Basel Carthusians is organized by the calendar and lists all books and other items donated by Amerbach under 11 April, the day on which prayers were to be said for him.[194] Prayers were to be said on the same day for Nicolaus Kesler; for Jacobus Wolff de Pforzheim, Adolf Rusch, the Strasbourg printer, Lienhart Ysenhut, and Johann Froben, all on 12 April; for Johann Petri de Langendorff on 13 April.[195] For each of these printers there follows a list of their donations specifying the monetary value of each item.[196] The practice of donating books, as well as other items, in return for prayers was so widespread that one donor found it necessary to state that he gave a bible without expecting anything in return,[197] but even when no mass and no prayers were stipulated as a *quid pro quo*, the book was a public expression of private lay piety, not an expression of an institutional need for the book.

In part, the mass production of holy books presents a parallel to the enormous growth in the production of religious art in the fifteenth century which has been studied by Richard Goldthwaite:[198] consumers of religious art were not necessarily the institutions for which the art was destined, but private persons who commissioned a work of art in order to donate it in return for private masses or prayers. In pictorial art a physical expression of this lay encroachment on liturgical space and time might be the inclusion of the founder's portrait on an altarpiece. Donors of books did not gain the same visual recognition but it is, nevertheless, clear that if this part of the market for religious books was made up of benefactors and donors, it is not appropriate to search for an institutional need for the books. Even the concepts of use and usefulness are historically determined by cultural and economic factors. While donated bibles were not necessarily in use, say in a refectory, this does not mean that they were not useful books – only that they were useful within a context of a historically specific exchange between the secular and the holy spheres. Donated bibles were similar to a currency with which one could extend control over the fate of oneself or of one's dearest into the realm of the dead. This privatization of liturgical activities[199] depends on the late-medieval devotional desire for a personal involvement in religion, and was closely associated with the sale of indulgences. It is gratifying to remember that, along with school books, indulgences were the other main products from the press of Johann Gutenberg.

But donated bibles were not money. Although they do not reflect a choice of texts on behalf of the owning institution, they imply the view that bibles were suitable gifts to make in return for a religious service. The texts and the shared perception of their holiness were anything but irrelevant within the terms of the transaction. Donating, for instance, Ovid's *Ars amandi* in return for prayers for the soul of oneself would hardly have seemed appropriate. The texts of a donated book had a function, even if it differs from that which Christians today might expect of a Bible. Although it may have been particularly suitable, this function was not restricted to the Bible,[200] and we may have the explanation why so many books with monastic provenances show no signs of use: they were never intended to be read.[201]

The Bible for display of piety

Another aspect of the Bible as a consumer product is its function as an art object, putting on display not only the owner's wealth but also his piety –and of course providing pleasure and perhaps encouraging devotion at the same time. This is exemplified by Borso d'Este whose magnificent manuscript Bible was written and decorated between 1455 and 1461 and was displayed to visiting ambassadors even during its production. When Borso went to Rome to be vested with the dukedom of Ferrara he was accompanied by his Bible to demonstrate his 'piety and wealth, his liberality and his discrimination'.[202] A manuscript of the Bible with the *Postillae* of Lyra, written and decorated in Florence 1494-7 for Manuel of Portugal, probably to be donated to the royal monastery of Belem in Lisbon, is a glorious example of a combination of display and piety with the appropriation of liturgical time.[203]

While the bibles of Borso d'Este and Manuel of Portugal belong to the very expensive end of the market, printed bibles were decorated by artists who might also work on manuscripts, and they have their place in the same market for pious luxury.[204] There are numerous lavishly and expensively illuminated printed bibles, beginning with several copies of the B42,[205] for instance the copy now in Vienna which was very extensively decorated for a private owner,[206] although few printed books, if any, were as expensive as these two outstanding manuscripts.

We have seen how royal folio editions ceased to be published when the commented editions began to come out, a relatively high number of which are handsomely decorated: they took on the role of large bibles as suitable for supporting sumptuous decoration, for display and for donation.[207]

But many copies of smaller bibles were also decorated, perhaps vellum copies proportionally more often and more lavishly so,[208] but some paper copies have fine miniatures. Copies of some editions were more often decorated than others, the editions printed by Jenson in the late 1470s being among the most frequently decorated ones. An outstanding example is a copy of his 1476 edition now in the Bibliothèque Nationale de France.[209] This level of decoration is not unparalleled but unusual; still grand, but at a more normal level, is another vellum copy of Jenson's 1476 edition also in the Bibliothèque Nationale de France, in which only one page has historiation, an initial, and a roundel in the lower margin.[210]

Lilian Armstrong has listed thirteen copies of six editions of the Bible printed between 1477 and 1483 which can be attributed to a single Venetian miniaturist and his workshop, a clear indication that certain bible editions were decorated in significant numbers,[211] and she has argued convincingly that the introduction of printing brought more, not less, work to fifteenth-century Venetian miniature painters.[212] Decorated books, still expensive, could be produced in larger numbers, and a commercially graded hierarchy of decoration types can be identified.[213]

Handsome decoration of bibles has a long tradition and is not new to the fifteenth century, and magnates of the Church had long had bibles for pious display. But, within the context of the mass production of printed bibles, buying a book with illumination was becoming an option for a larger section of the population,[214] whether the aim was to donate it in return for patronage in this or the coming world, or to display piety in the lay sphere at home or in public. A decorated Bible would be a highly suitable donation from a prosperous person and it could be an equally suitable present for a prosperous person with whom one would want to establish good relations.[215] None of this denies that they also provided aesthetic pleasure and might encourage viewers or readers to greater devotion, but, seen from the point of view of the production and distribution of books, mass-produced illuminated bibles played their role in ensuring that the lay desire to express private piety was integrated into a religious, political, and economic system through an exchange of money, gifts, and services.

Bibles for study

While piety had a role in the creation of a market for the Bible as a luxury item, and while bibles were part of a commercial relationship between printers, donors, and the Church as a service-provider, this does not provide an exhaustive explanation for the function of the Bible in the market for religious books. Books were not used only for show, but also for the daily work in religious houses, in parishes, and in the studies of devout and learned men (and women). It could be argued that if they had not been perceived to be used mainly for such purposes, bibles could neither have served for the sumptuous display of religion nor for the purchasing of liturgical services.

Although relatively few books can be shown to have been bought by religious houses, this must not lead us to ignore the evidence that many bibles ended up there, no matter how. While the notion that bibles in institutions were nearly always used for refectory reading cannot be substantiated, there is good evidence that they sometimes were. It is known that large royal folio bibles could be used like that, but so were smaller ones, both quartos and octavos.[216] The evidence provided by actual books continually baffles our attempts to classify their uses according to external criteria.

Less remarked upon has been the use of the Bible for private reading and for study. It is nearly impossible to get to understand the private use of bibles: the surviving books tell us far too little.[217] In 1495 a Sicilian noblewoman owned seven books, one of which was a Bible,[218] if in Latin or Italian we do not know, nor do we know how she used it. We have better evidence for the use of the Bible for more or less learned study purposes. The textual development clearly indicates that printers thought it a good marketing strategy to make bibles ever more useful for study. The importance of bible studies is further underlined by evidence from individual copies of editions which did not provide study aids. The B42 text group is the least suitable for study purposes, perhaps, and yet it is evident that copies were used for this. Some copies of the B42 itself were used for serious study, as has been shown by Gerhardt Powitz.[219] The copy of the 1462 edition, also not particularly suited for study, now in the Morgan Library has numerous marginal manuscript corrections to the text.[220] We find as manuscript additions the *casus summarii*,[221] tabular concordances, the table of the Epistles and Gospels,[222] the extensive mnemonic verses ascribed to Alexander de Villa Dei,[223] the much shorter verses on the order of the books of the Bible,[224] and vernacular tables of contents.[225] Such additions are common and all are evidence that users engaged with the text of their bibles, and that in their work they needed heuristic, hermeneutic, or mnemonic tools.

The Bible could also be adapted for study purposes by adding printed material which to our eyes belongs to another edition. Thus the British Library's copy of Götz's Cologne edition from about 1478,[226] contains bound at the end of the first volume and at the beginning of the second volume *Vocabula Bibliorum ad litteralem eorundem intelligentiam admodum necessaria.*[227] One of the Bodleian copies of Frisner's edition from 1476 is bound with a copy of Richel's edition of Alphonsus de Spina's *Fortalitium fidei.*[228] The number of copies which contain Stephen Langton's *Interpretationes*, although it was not part of the edition in question, is too great even to begin listing. Equally the gatherings which contain this work often survive separately from bibles, to be used as a working tool with bibles which did not contain it. Seen from a consumer's point of view these adaptations reflect a situation where there was not a perfect market in bibles in which each user could buy the bible which met his specific demands.

The competitive marketing of the large commented bibles is an important part of the picture of the Bible as a tool for study. If the fifteenth century has been seen by students of manuscript bibles as a period of decadence, with little or no interest in the study of the Bible, the printed bibles tell a different story about the second half of the century. The main commentaries on the Bible had become available as they had never been before, and many other tools for biblical study were published separately from the Bible, often by printers who also produced bibles.[229] The evidence of the printed books amply testifies to a dramatically increased interest in the Bible and in the works which were used for its study. It is not possible to say that the printing of bibles was the cause of this, but it is obvious that such a massive distribution of bibles would not have been feasible without printing, and it is not too fanciful to suggest that the very availability of the texts played a role in creating both a market and an intellectual demand for bibles.

The notion that the popularity of the fifteenth-century printed Bible was somehow related to devotional reform, returning to the naked text liberated from its scholastic accretions, is not borne out by the evidence from the printed Bible.[230] On the contrary, it is interesting to note that many of the bibles which we do know to have been actively chosen on the part of institutions are copies of large editions providing the early- and late-medieval commentaries.[231] We saw above that the Carthusians in Basel looked upon the inclusion of Lyra's *Postillae* in the margins of a bible as something unusual, and it was a book which they were keen to acquire. In general they received as donations the books produced by Johann Amerbach, and therefore did not actively choose them, but they had asked Amerbach to procure a copy of the Bible with the *Postillae* for them.[232] The commented editions provided institutions with something which they had not had before, or at least not in that format. It was now possible to acquire complete sets of the important commentaries, which in manuscript form had mainly been available only in parts.

It seems clear that this level of biblical study would have to take place in the context of a religious institution, but we may not conclude that all bibles which show sign of study were institutional: a bible used for private study may have been used by a member of the secular clergy before it ended up in the institution which ensured its survival.[233] The evidence which we obtain from surviving copies about their use and the history of the textual development of the bibles jointly point towards the overwhelming importance of the Bible as an object of study in the late fifteenth century, often relying on study aids composed centuries earlier.

BIBLES FOR PARISH PRIESTS

We know that in Venice in 1478[234] Leonardus Wild printed 930 copies of a bible: *ISTC* records 93 surviving ones. It is reasonable to consider what happened to the remaining 90 per cent. While it is not possible to say to what extent patterns of survival have distorted patterns of ownership, there can be little doubt that books owned by a parish priest would have stood a relatively poor chance of surviving compared with lavishly illuminated books or with other books which somehow ended up in stable institutions. However, evidently, as the fifteenth century progressed, less expensive editions would have been more available to priests. The sumptuous vellum copy of the B42 now in the Huntington Library cost 100 Rhenish guilder, decorated and bound. In the 1490s you could buy a six-volume bible printed in folio on imperial paper, measuring about half a metre high, with several sets of glosses for the equivalent of about 15 Rhenish guilder,[235] or a set of the Bible with Lyra bound in three volumes for 8 Rhenish guilder.[236] A small folio bible could cost about 2 Rhenish guilder,[237] whereas a one-volume octavo bible, measuring 170 or 180 mm high, could be had for about half a Rhenish guilder.[238] The availability of cheaper books must have meant a broader customer base. Bearing in mind that remuneration, in money or in kind, varied from parish to parish, a price of half a Rhenish guilder brings the Bible into the reach of even the less well remunerated clergy, although it might still represent a serious outlay.

According to Denise Hillard several copies of the Lyon editions of the Bible were owned by priests in small parishes in the vicinity of Lyon, and they were sometimes passed on from one priest to the next.[239] Other examples of bibles owned by parish priests can be found in France, Italy, and elsewhere.[240] Here again the surviving evidence is skewed toward the wealthier part of the group. On closer examination, it becomes clear that some of these owners were pluralists who merely had a parish as a living, being in fact clergymen attached to great religious institutions.[241] The suspicion that wealthy people on occasion used titles which to us make them look like humble priests is also suggested by a relatively high number of surviving copies of expensive glossed bibles which, before they reached an institution, were owned by people who signed themselves as priests.[242] It must also be recalled that some parishes were wealthy institutions.[243] This of course does not mean that all bibles owned by parish priests can be dismissed as really having belonged to the wealthiest clergy.

If patterns of survival tend to make us underestimate the number of copies owned by parish priests, we can rely on other evidence which shows that, at least in north-western Europe, priests were increasingly expected to own a bible. Johannes de Westphalia's edition of the New Testament may be dated to 'after 1476' and he was thus among the last to follow the biblical corpus of the B42, if only in parts. He published his New Testament as a small quarto measuring only some 210 × 140 mm. There was not a strong tradition for producing the Latin New Testament as a separate unit, whether in manuscript or in print, and his publication was a significant innovation.[244] Johannes de Westphalia indicates a situation where the New Testament is perceived as the more important part of the Bible which would be adequate, if the whole book was too expensive. A shift from medieval Hebrew-centred biblical scholarship, for instance of de Lyra, towards Humanist Greek-centred New Testament scholarship is exemplified by Valla and by Erasmus.[245] With Johannes de Westphalia we see the same shift in the religious interest in the New Testament as an independent unit.

We saw above how far removed the donated bibles were from the world of sixteenth-century reform with its reading of the text of the Bible in a public liturgical context, although this is also a use of the Bible which grew out of the pious, lay encroachment on the activities of the Church. The separate publication of the New Testament, on the other hand, points in the same direction, a suggestion which is supported by Johannes de Westphalia in his introduction where he wrote:

There is a general demand that the holy scripture, in particular the part of the Bible which is called the New Testament, should be known to all men of faith, but in particular to those to whom pastoral care or the preaching of the word of God have been entrusted. But, in reality, it has been found that few have sufficient means to buy a whole Bible, and that many, even among the better off, take pleasure in portable books. Motivated by this, persuaded by the authority of my superiors, professors of holy theology, and also convinced by the keen interest of both regular and secular clerics, I ventured to publish this hand-book sized volume containing the whole New Testament, I hope with a good omen. May he who derives benefit from it approve of what I have done.[246]

Johannes de Westphalia mentioned that large bibles, presumably as against his smaller quarto volume, were beyond the means of many priests, and that he had therefore had encouragement from people in authority who wanted the Bible in the hands of priests and preachers and specified two situations in which a priest might have a use for his Bible: pastoral care, and preaching.[247] This challenges the accepted view that, before the Reformation, the Bible had no place in the religious life of parish churches. While missals and breviaries were easier to use for most liturgical purposes, it is worth remembering that it was not until 1570 that the Tridentine Church sanctioned the full missal as the exclusive textual basis for the celebration of the Mass.[248] Like Johannes de Westphalia's New Testament, both the cheaper, small-format bibles, and the appearance, first in Amerbach's 1479 edition, of the *capitulare lectionum et evangeliorum*, which enabled the Bible to be used for liturgical purposes, may be associated with the late-fifteenth-century reform movements of northern Europe with their evangelical aspirations. The *Capitulare* was often deliberately excluded by Venice-based printers from editions which otherwise relied on north European editions of the Bible. It is possible that the much used, and now often fragmentary, Cologne editions of the Bible should be understood in the same context. We know too little about daily practice to dismiss this and other evidence suggesting that the Bible had a place in the religious life of the parish.[249] There is much more work to be done to establish the extent of the late-fifteenth-century use of the Bible for preaching or for other work aimed at the lay population, but we may be irretrievably hampered by patterns of survival.

CONCLUSION

Useful texts catering for the intellectual needs of Bible students, the demand for objects for pious exchanges, and the economic necessities of marketing and distribution created by the mass production of books, have here been studied jointly to provide an overview of the specificity of the printed Bible in the fifteenth century.

Our examination of the textual relation between fifteenth-century editions has focused on the biblical corpus as a body of texts far from uniform but in rapid development. This focus was made possible by a clear methodological distinction between the textual critic's philological study of the transmission of texts and the study of texts as historical phenomena reflecting social, intellectual, and economic circumstances in which they were produced.

An examination of information derived from individual copies and from other sources has allowed a distinction to be drawn between buyers and owners, and this has highlighted a complex consumer culture in which the Bible, like other books and luxury items, could function as part of an economic transaction which consisted in a transfer of merits and of money or goods. This important aspect of the market for the printed Bible has not hitherto been taken into consideration. Another culturally related market was constituted by consumer demand for luxury goods, to be used as gifts to patrons or for private display.

These uses have implications for our understanding of the Bible as a corpus of texts. We know too little about how the Bible was used in the religious life of parishes, but the evidence which we have suggests that, as a commercial product, the Bible was deeply embedded in an exchange of goods, money, and merits between the Church and its members. Our evidence also suggests that textual diversity and innovation reflect consumer demand, based on the late-medieval tradition of Bible study, which enabled textual innovations to become a focus for competition between publishers who may even be seen to have created a continuing demand for a modified product, manipulating the demand for texts as part of a conscious programme of product development.

'VOLENTES SIBI COMPARARE INFRASCRIPTOS LIBROS IMPRESSOS ...'

PRINTED BOOKS AS A COMMERCIAL COMMODITY IN THE FIFTEENTH CENTURY[1]

JOHN L. FLOOD

ONE OF THE MOST critical points in the production, publication, and reception cycle of a book is that at which the finished product is launched into the world to meet its readers. If the contact is weak, the author's, printer's, and publisher's efforts have been in vain, and potential readers may remain ignorant of a book's very existence. This has been true at all periods, but establishing a link between producer and customer would have been particularly difficult in the age of incunabula, when the introduction of printing resulted in a major shift in the nature of the market for books.

Already by 1472 at the latest, the number of printed pages produced exceeded the number of pages written by scribes.[2] What impact did this increased output have on the book trade? The introduction of printing represented a first step in the direction of the mass-production that is an all too obvious feature of the book trade today when pulp novels, mail-order catalogues, advertising and travel brochures, and newspapers are often produced in their millions. As Marshall McLuhan (rather inelegantly) put it: 'Just as printing was the first mass-produced thing, so it was the first uniform and repeatable "commodity". The assembly lines of movable types made possible a product that was uniform and as repeatable as a scientific experiment.'[3] Not that the contemporaries immediately realized this: as late as 1485 and 1487 we hear of nervous or incredulous clerics at Regensburg and Freising laboriously checking hundreds of printed missals individually to see that they really were identical. At Freising, for example, five men were paid 400 Rhenish guilders for checking 400 copies of the Freising breviary which had already cost 2150 Rhenish guilders to print; this enormous outlay for checking each single copy, line by line, betrays the fact that the men involved were still thinking in terms of manuscripts which could very easily differ from one another in textual details.[4] They were accustomed to being cautious when dealing with multiple copies. Mass production as we know it was unimaginable in the fifteenth century.[5] When the Italian humanist Enea Silvio Piccolomini, later Pope Pius II but then in the service of the Holy Roman Emperor, attended the Diet of Frankfurt in October 1454, he was impressed by the claim of an unidentified 'vir mirabilis', a remarkable man (whether Gutenberg himself or one of his collaborators we do not know), to be able to supply a bible which might be read without spectacles and in 158 or 180 identical copies.[6] Though Enea Silvio clearly recognized that this represented a tremendous advance, neither he nor even Gutenberg himself will have envisaged the enormous print-runs that are fairly usual today. For all that the printing of 180 bibles represented a considerable increase over the output of scribes, we cannot yet call that mass production, even though the fifteenth century did furnish examples of something approaching it. Take indulgences, for example, for which *ISTC* has 308 entries under 'Indulgentia' alone. In May 1452 Cardinal Nicolaus Cusanus commissioned Heinrich Brack, Prior of St James's, Mainz, to arrange for 2000 copies of an indulgence to be ready within three weeks at most; Kai-Michael Sprenger has persuasively argued that this was achievable only if these were printed (and the word *expressio* is used, a term which, according to Sprenger's careful philological investigations, was then not used to mean 'issuing' or 'publishing' but, it seems, 'pressing out', that is 'printing') – and at this date only Gutenberg could have carried out the work; what is truly astonishing, if this interpretation is correct, is that the cardinal already recognised the potential of this untried art![7] Later we hear of other long print-runs: Jodocus Pflanzmann printed 20,000 certificates of confession, four to a sheet, for a church in Nördlingen in six weeks at Augsburg in 1480; in the same year the Augsburg printer Johann Bämler was paid 35 Rhenish guilders for 12,000 broadsides; and Johann Luschner, a German from Ulm who had previously worked at Barcelona, produced 142,950 indulgences for the Benedictine monastery at Montserrat over fifteen months in 1499 and 1500.[8] Other items for which there was a steady demand included almanacs and calendars, produced every year in Latin and German,[9] and books such as the *Mirabilia Romae* and the related *Historia et descriptio urbis Romae*.[10] How great a demand there was for the latter is indicated by the fact that, according to *ISTC*, in the jubilee year 1500 Rome printers produced no fewer than nine editions in Latin and nine in German.[11] Nor should we forget schoolbooks: Neddermeyer calculates that nearly half a million copies of 661 editions of various grammars were produced in the Holy Roman Empire alone before 1500.[12]

Leaving such slender products aside, we must remember that many early incunabula were in some sense unfinished, needing to be hand-rubricated, illuminated, even hand-illustrated, and of course bound, a state which represents a transitional stage between bespoke and speculative production, with a mass-produced text being tailored to the requirements of an individual customer, either in the original workshop or elsewhere; sometimes also the selection of texts bound up together in a composite volume might reflect the individual interests of a specific client.[13] Not only were there monastic presses (such as those at SS. Ulrich and Afra at Augsburg, the Benedictine monastery at Erfurt, and other houses at Lauingen, Marienthal, and Schussenried) which will have produced books needed for a particular community or associated communities,[14] there were printers like Peter von Friedberg at Mainz who produced some twenty-five books during the last decade of the fifteenth century of which thirteen were works of Abbot Johannes Trithemius of Sponheim and another six by Trithemius's friends, thus making the press more or less the Sponheim house publisher.[15]

But leaving aside specific needs and commissions such as these, we must recognize that it was a characteristic of printing that it created a particular problem unfamiliar to most medieval businessmen. In the medieval economy generally, most production had been to order, so the risk of being left with unsaleable stock was remote. This applied in large measure to the medieval book too: the manuscript was (with certain exceptions) essentially a bespoke item, books predominantly being produced to order or at least with a clearly defined customer-base in mind. This is, of course, not to overlook the flourishing trade in hand-written copies of texts in university towns like Bologna and Paris,[16] the production of books of hours for export, the international trade in second-hand manuscripts, or such practices as that whereby fourteenth-century French royal edicts were multiplied in the manner of chain letters, each recipient paying a scribe to make perhaps ten more copies for onward transmission.[17] Large numbers of indulgences were produced by hand, too.[18] Nor do we overlook the existence of scriptoria like that of Diebolt Lauber at Hagenau where, in the period 1420-70, copies of works of German vernacular literature were available more or less from stock.[19] Generally, however, a book would have to be specially commissioned from a scribe, either by the customer himself or through an agent.

While the multiple production of manuscripts was certainly the exception, it is nevertheless crucial to an understanding of the context in which Gutenberg was conducting his experiments at Strasbourg and later at Mainz. Presumably he was responding to a perceived need for a faster way of obtaining reliable multiple copies of texts rather than devising a technology which as yet had no immediate practical use; as Otto Fuhrmann put it, every church, Strasbourg Minster with its many altars included, needed missals, psalters, and bibles, all of which involved years of labour to write and cost a great deal of money.[20] What Gutenberg was trying to do was rationalize multiple production, in response to a demand (however poorly articulated) for more books. For if it took a scribe one man-year to write a bible, it took two man-years to write two bibles, and so on. The Alsatian chronicler Bernhart Hertzog specifically credits Gutenberg with enabling much time to be saved, so that 'in a single day two men can set and print more than, in former times, twenty or more scribes could write over a number of years'.[21] This is doubtless an exaggeration, but if we may accept Leonhard Hoffmann's calculations that it took six compositors and six pressmen thirteen and a half months to produce 180 copies of the 42-line Bible,[22] we must suppose that this was a rate of production much better than twelve scribes could have achieved in that time. By 1480 it had become clear that printing would soon have replaced manual reproduction as an efficient and cost-effective means of multiplying texts.[23] About this time also further significant economies were being achieved through the introduction of a new type of paper, specially designed for printing and cheaper to manufacture.[24]

One really fundamental change brought about by printing concerned the relation of the product to the customer. Though bibles, breviaries, and missals were often printed for a specific market (a bulk order for a particular diocese, for instance), seldom were individual books printed for the sole use of a specific customer (Maximilian's prayer book, printed in just ten copies by Schönsperger at Augsburg in 1513,[25] is a rare example). Printing was essentially a speculative enterprise. The identity of the reader, the end-user, now became an unknown factor, which made estimating print-runs and publishing printed books a hazardous enterprise. The printer found himself faced with the conundrum of how to take advantage of the low marginal cost of each additional copy produced without being left with unsaleable, unwanted merchandise.[26] Because the profit on each additional copy sold is high, there is a strong temptation to print an excessive number. The early printers already recognized this problem and attempted to reduce the risks by producing popular texts in familiar formats in the expectation, or at least the hope, that customers would be found for them. This explains not only the choice of texts – thus we find 28 editions of Cicero's *De officiis* before 1482[27] – but also the practice of modelling printed books on manuscripts.[28] The desire to benefit from the anticipated profits and to share the costs and minimize the potential risks led already around 1470 in Italy, slightly later in Germany, to the establishment of firm partnerships between financiers and printer-publishers.[29]

For all that even contemporaries like Nicolaus Cusanus hailed printing as 'a divine art',[30] the hard truth was that it called for earthly goods in abundance. Printing requires not only efficient organization of the workforce but also demands substantial capital investment, as is well known from the story of Gutenberg's own troubles.[31] Whereas one could set oneself up as a scribe for a modest outlay (the biggest expense would have been for vellum or paper which might in any case have been supplied by the customer),[32] we hear of sums in the region of seven hundred guilders being paid for purchase of the equipment for a printing shop at Augsburg around 1473 and at Basel around 1500[33] – equivalent to seven years' salary for Heinrich Steinhöwel, municipal physician at Ulm, or seven times the sum that was needed to acquire citizenship of Nuremberg in 1459. In many cases presses had to be financed by wealthy backers, particularly the Church – thus the 36-line Bible (*GW* 4202), printed at Bamberg not later than 1461, was almost certainly financed by Prince-Bishop Georg von Schaumburg, and similarly at Strasbourg Johann Mentelin, printer of the 49-line Bible in 1460 (*GW* 4203), was financed by Bishop Ruprecht von Pfalz-Simmern. In time another way in which printers could consolidate their financial base was through inheritance and marriage,[34] often within the trade: thus the Strasbourg printer Johann Schott was not only the son of a printer but his mother was a daughter of Johann Mentelin, and Johann Knoblouch, also of Strasbourg, married the widow of another local printer, Martin Flach the Elder (died 1500). Similarly Melchior Lotter of Leipzig married the daughter of his master, Konrad Kachelofen, who, before he took up printing about 1483, had been a well-to-do paper-merchant and tavern-keeper. In contrast, some early printers were seriously under-capitalized and hence their businesses were short-lived. Of more than a hundred firms operating in Venice before 1490 fewer than ten were still there in 1500. The experiences of these printers demonstrates that running such a business was not just (as the much quoted phrase has it) a *kunst*, but very much (as it were) an *aventur*, an adventure, too. Though the *Independent on Sunday* was wide of the mark when it called Gutenberg 'the Bill Gates of the fifteenth century',[35] we can at least say that the situation of that time has its parallel in the present age of incipient e-commerce, in the mushrooming and sudden demise of many so-called 'dotcom' companies.

A printer had to judge whether a project was commercially viable. In E. P. Goldschmidt's generalization, 'printing was from the start a commercial enterprise and, however often printers and publishers have lost their money in the past five centuries, there has never been a book that went to press unless the printer rightly or wrongly believed he could make a profit by printing it'.[36] Some printers, indeed, misjudged the market and paid the price,[37] but overall the industry matured with surprising rapidity, especially in Germany and Italy, where leading printers like Anton Koberger in

Nuremberg and Peter Drach of Speyer took on financiers, began to separate publishing and distribution from the actual printing side, and built up effective sales organizations, something that became essential if one aimed to satisfy more than a purely local market and hoped to outwit the competition. Drach, for instance, employed nearly fifty book-dealers and salesmen working in various towns in Germany and in Bohemia and Moravia over the last two decades of the fifteenth century, and was so wealthy that a loss of 500 guilders when one of them died meant little to him.[38] The more adventurous entrepreneurs traded with books other than those they had published themselves. For example, in a record dating from 1483 in a book at Corpus Christi College, Oxford, in which Thomas Hunt, stationer in that city, acknowledges receipt of a consignment of books from the booksellers Peter Actor and Johannes de Aquisgrano (identifiable with Johannes de Westfalia), the 65 titles listed included 13 printed at Lyon, 8 from Cologne, 3 from Brussels, 2 from Venice, and 1 each from Gouda, Strasbourg, Speyer, Milan, and Padua.[39]

Why did some printers succeed while others, who were perhaps equally capable as craftsmen, failed? The causes are many and various, but one important reason perhaps is that they did not all realize that the book, whether printed or manuscript, is different from most other commercial commodities. Unlike cabbages or pots and pans, the book also has a cultural, intellectual message: it mediates ideas. The sheer range of ideas contained in books meant that the printer, but above all the publisher and bookseller, needed a certain degree of education that went beyond what most other purveyors of commodities required. The printer-publisher needed linguistic skills, above all Latin (though, in Geldner's words, Peter Drach 'spent his whole life on a war-footing with Latin grammar'[40]), and the publisher-bookseller had to possess the requisite sound judgment for selecting books for their quality and interest. Successful publishers needed to be aware of existing intellectual currents and have a keen sense of likely future developments. Not least did they need to move cautiously between many competing claims from would-be authors for their attention and investment. They required long-term capital and, since this and their own capacities were not unlimited, they were forced to specialize, focusing on specific programmes: spreading oneself too thinly over too wide a range could be disastrous. A bit of luck was needed too. Despite all these uncertainties and difficulties, the book trade expanded rapidly, and the emergence of the printed book as a mass product soon came to be perceived as a threat in some quarters: already in 1479 Pope Sixtus IV authorized the theological faculty of the University of Cologne to examine the products of the newly established presses there.[41] And we soon find others complaining about the profusion of books: Sebastian Brant's *Narrenschiff* (Basel 1494) (GW 5041) pointedly opens with a chapter on 'Useless books' ('Von vnnutzen buchern').[42]

Access to finance and business acumen certainly played a large part in a firm's survival. Lotte Hellinga has shown how England's first printer William Caxton, canny businessman that he undoubtedly was, carefully prepared the ground to ensure that the enterprise was a success: he seems deliberately to have chosen to print those books the Continent could not supply ready-made, building up a market for books in English among the noblemen and merchant classes, an approach which gave English printing a unique national character from the start.[43] Caxton, of course, was a wealthy merchant, well-connected and not lacking in means, so *The Canterbury Tales*, the first major book printed at Westminster and undertaken as an independent venture, came into being in unusually fortunate circumstances.

Once a press had been set up, it needed to be kept busy if there was to be any hope of recouping the initial outlay. The press at Bamberg is a good example: the purpose of setting it up was to print the 36-line Bible, but thereafter, it seems, it was kept working with editions of such works as Boner's *Edelstein*, the *Ackermann aus Böhmen*, and Jacobus de Theramo's *Belial*. This is probably how the *Sibyllenweissagung* fits into Gutenberg's programme, and the same will apply also to the 46 undated Mainz editions of the *Ars minor* of Aelius Donatus, printed in the types of the 36- and 42-line bibles.[44]

Printing not only involves a very considerable initial investment and constant on-going expense: the returns may be very slow in coming. Peter Schöffer claimed that Gutenberg had spent over four thousand guilders before the first copy of the Bible was printed, approximately the cost of forty medium-sized houses in Mainz in 1450.[45] Much of this will have gone on what we would call research and development, on trial and error, and thus will not have produced a tangible return. Leonhard Hoffmann, who has investigated the likely actual production costs of the 42-line bible in some detail, calculated that sales may have realised a gross profit of almost 500 per cent, before Gutenberg's partner Fust took his cut and before repayment of loans and interest.[46] Of course, the general public may have benefited marginally from all this investment: just as we are told that without NASA's investment in space exploration there would have been no non-stick frying pans, seeing that 4375 calves ('a sizeable herd'![47]) would have to have been slaughtered to provide the parchment needed for 25 vellum copies of the Bible, veal must have been cheap in Mainz in the early 1450s – but the real problem (for all that Caxton could claim that some of his books '*anon* were sold to many and dyverse gentylmen'[48]) was that money resulting from sales trickled in only slowly, if at all. This of course was one of the reasons why the early printers tended to concentrate on established texts: there was always going to be a steady income from sales of the *Ars minor* of Donatus. Yet things could still go badly wrong. There is evidence to suggest that Sweynheym and Pannartz, the first printers in Rome, despite printing popular authors like Cicero, Augustine, Caesar, Virgil, Livy, and Pliny, were on the verge of bankruptcy in 1472. The list of books they produced between 1467/68 and March 1472 records 28 titles in a total of 12,475 copies, representing a huge investment.[49] How many of these books had meanwhile been sold we do not know, but it is note-worthy that many of their early books contain neither rubrication nor marks of ownership, which suggests that they were slow to find customers and were eventually disposed of as slow-movers, perhaps to be bought for adorning one's study rather than as books really to be read.[50] It is not that the choice of books to be printed was necessarily wrong; more probably the problem was with their under-developed business practices. Be that as it may, the last book Sweynheym and Pannartz printed jointly came out in May 1473; eighteen months later we find Pannartz printing on his own. Another case is that of the group of prominent Nuremberg citizens who lost a great deal of money over publishing the lavishly illustrated Latin and German editions of the Nuremberg Chronicle, printed for them by Anton Koberger in 1493. The reason for this was the unregulated competition that was a major problem for early publishing: the Augsburg printer Johann Schönsperger brought out markedly cheaper editions of the chronicle in 1496 (in German), 1497 (Latin), and 1500 (German) (*ISTC* is00310000, is00308000, and is00311000 respectively), with the result that as late as 1509, sixteen years after Koberger had originally published the books, 574 copies still languished on the shelves of agents throughout Europe, and furthermore even when copies had been sold payment had often not been received.[51] A fall in expected sales income would affect a publisher's ability to invest in future works. Koberger was also forced to sell books more cheaply than he would have wished. Thus he wrote to his Basel colleague Johann Amerbach (whose extensive correspondence throws considerable light on the difficulties with which contemporary publishers had to contend[52]) about the Hugo de Sancto Caro bible, *Biblia cum postillis Hugonis de Sancto Caro* (Basel: Johann Amerbach, for Anton Koberger, 1498-1502) (*GW* 4285; *ISTC* ib00610000), 'Please proceed slowly with the Hugo for truly it is selling slowly. I am writing to my agent herewith that he should quickly sell them cheap for I have set the price of the Hugo cheaper than I had expected to offer so that I can also sell it when the priests have so exhausted their funds on books that they don't want any more.'[53] Books represented a substantial outlay for many customers, hence their wheedling letters to booksellers.[54] Sometimes they might be allowed to pay by instalments: thus the Strasbourg priest Johannes Kuon was allowed to purchase Johann Mentelin's first Latin Bible (*GW* 4203), printed in 1460, in three instalments of four guilders each, payable at Christmas 1461, Easter, and All Saints' Day 1462. Credit played as great a role in this period as it does today,[55] reliance being placed on promissory notes, letters of credit, and bills of exchange, accounts being reconciled at fairs or through a network of business associates, friends, and acquaintances, bound together by personal knowledge and trust. Cash flow was a real problem for customers and publishers, then as now. The Strasbourg printer Adolf Rusch wrote to Amerbach, 'I am truly beset by ill fortune, and because of it my bag in which I kept my money and yours did not arrive.'[56] Koberger was forced to write to Amerbach, 'It is absolutely terrible for selling books anywhere in the country. I have completely shut down my workshop and am doing no printing at all.'[57] And: 'Please do not be annoyed with me because I did not pay you in full at Frankfurt; I truly was not able to do it because with war, pestilence, and scarcity, everything is so terrible everywhere that we can't do any business. You just would not believe that there isn't any money being made anywhere.'[58] Even if the books were successfully sold and payment duly received, the proceeds were not necessarily pure profit: often enough they had to be shared with a financier or go towards paying off debts in respect of initial capital investment – all this applied well enough to Gutenberg himself.

Success depended on knowing the market, what was likely to sell where. Thus on 16 November 1498 Anton Koberger told Johann Amerbach he had thought better of an earlier suggestion that Amerbach should send thirty copies of Nicolaus de Tudeschis's *Lectura super quinque libros Decretalium* (Basel, 1487-8) (*ISTC* ip00051000) to the Frankfurt fair: ten would suffice and the rest should be sent to Nuremberg, and none at all to Lyon: 'They do not sell.'[59]

So how did printers cope with this problem of high initial outlay and slow returns, high unit costs on short print-runs and potentially large profits on inherently risky large print-runs? One cannot generalize, because individual circumstances differed so much, but let us look briefly at three or four contrasting cases, not major operators like Koberger, Amerbach, or Froben, but more ordinary German incunable printers, and show how they tackled the problem. After all, it was men such as these who made up the vast majority of the printing trade. They tended to be conservative rather than innovative 'agents of change', catering for existing markets rather than creating new ones.[60]

One way was to invest modestly and to regard printing as a side-line, financed by some other business, as in the case of the Nuremberg printer Hans Folz. Folz was a barber-surgeon by trade, and it was this business that kept him afloat while he dabbled in printing; in no way could his modest output have kept a press continuously occupied.[61] Everything he printed he had written himself: *ISTC* lists 42 items, all in German, produced between about 1479 and 1488. They are all modest brochures of a type which existed in manuscript form in Nuremberg in the 1470s; he was thus perpetuating a format he knew. One wonders why he did not have his work published for him. Almost certainly no publisher in Nuremberg – such as Koberger – would have paid him for his poems which would at best have appealed to a limited local market and one that was as yet relatively untried when it came to book-buying. The only alternative would have been for him to have given the work to a jobbing printer who would have had to be paid, irrespective of whether the books sold or not. In any case, in this period, publishers would generally pay for scholarly editorial work and for proof correction, but rarely would they have paid an author a fee for the manuscript he produced himself.[62] Folz probably considered printing an intriguing new craft with which he, coming from a milieu of craftsmen anyway, was curious enough to want to experiment – today he would have been among the first to buy a new electronic gadget. In one of his poems, written before 1480 and containing what appears to be the oldest reference to Gutenberg's achievement in the German language, he boldly juxtaposes the unexpected novelty of the invention of printing with that of God's assumption of human form, though he recognized both benefits and dangers – even a sign of the coming of the Antichrist – in the widespread availability of books.[63] The very fact that Folz did not print for others surely indicates that his capacity was limited – he simply did not have the resources in terms of equipment or capital to take such work on. Nor, it seems, did he want to; he was not out to make serious money, even though as a writer he was concerned not only with purely literary but also with utilitarian texts (such as a plague tract and almanacs) which would be of interest to an urban readership.

Though he may have been intrigued by printing, Folz was not yet so forward-looking that he appreciated the essential difference between the medieval manuscript and the modern printed book, the bespoke nature of the former and the unknown customers for the latter. More so than the scribe, the printer-publisher had to make a real effort to find a market for his wares. This is where advertising comes in, whether by issuing posters and flyers inviting customers to come to inspect his products,[64] and/or by making more effective use of the title-page. Folz's books have their title on the verso of the first leaf, not on the recto, an arrangement which may serve to protect the title-page from getting dirty, but does mean that there is nothing at the front of the book to enable anyone immediately to identify it, let alone to attract anyone to purchase it. Things were rather different with another printer whom Folz possibly knew, Hans Sporer, first attested as a block-cutter in Nuremberg in 1471 and eventually (having fled that city after apparently kicking his wife to death) turning to printing small booklets at Bamberg between 1487 and 1494 and thereafter at Erfurt. His printing shop will have been as simple as can be: he used one size of type and the title pages were generally cut in wood.[65] Outfits such as this were generally dependent on jobbing work for other publishers, but in Sporer's case there seems to be no evidence of such an arrangement. He had always worked in the book trade, cutting wood blocks, but since he was no great artist he was presumably finding it difficult to make ends meet, especially after he quit Nuremberg. His situation was like that of the nineteenth-century blacksmith who, faced with the coming of the motor car, gave up shoeing horses to became a car mechanic and petrol-pump attendant. Sporer will have had precious little capital, so he, like Folz, concentrated on small cheap books[66] (though he does not seem to have written them himself).[67] Unlike Folz, Sporer recognized the importance of the title-page, printing the title on the first recto, with a woodcut, and – as far as I can see – actually inventing the rhyming title-page which became quite popular in sixteenth-century Germany.[68] The rhyming title was no great poetic achievement, but it was clearly designed to attract customers, especially when declaimed on the market-place by pedlars hawking the books for sale. Rhyming titles and poems incorporating acrostics, likewise designed to attract customers, were found with another small turn-of-the-century printer, too: Jakob Köbel of Oppenheim, most of whose books were popular mathematical, astronomical, legal, and historical works for the layman.[69] Köbel had studied at Heidelberg and indeed we find him selling and commissioning books there even before he completed his law studies. The son of a goldsmith, he married the daughter of a councillor at Oppenheim where he became town-clerk and official surveyor, and also ran the council's wine cellar, all of which doubtless helped him to finance his printing business too. In this respect he is reminiscent of Lucas Cranach the Elder at Wittenberg who, in addition to being court painter, also owned a pharmacy and a quarry and dealt in wine and in paper as well as financing a printing press in support of the Lutheran cause in the 1520s.[70]

The emergence of the regular use of the title-page is too wide-ranging a topic to be considered here,[71] but one aspect does deserve comment. That is the growth of the practice of employing laudatory adjectives in titles to make the book appeal even more readily to the customers.[72] Such devices can, in a sense, be traced back already to the earliest incunabula: for instance, the Mainz *Catholicon*, dated 1460, whose colophon extols 'this noble book' which has been 'printed and accomplished without the help of reed, stylus or pen but by the wondrous agreement, proportion and harmony of punches and types', or 'Presens Marci tulii clarissimum opus ...' ('this brilliant work ...'!) in Fust and Schöffer's Cicero, *De Officiis* of 1465.[73] A glance at some of the early vernacular books printed at Augsburg reveals all kinds of epithets underlining how 'useful', 'pleasing', or even 'exciting' the books will be found to be.[74]

Advertising to sell one's wares is one thing; the reverse side of the coin is protecting one's property. The growth in the use of privileges, especially imperial privileges, to protect one's books indicates that intellectual property had now become a tangible commodity.[75] But not only printers, authors too became jealous guardians of their rights; thus in 1511 we find the imperial chancery granting Albrecht Dürer a privilege in respect of his own writings.

The last printer I wish to discuss was much more ambitious than Folz, Sporer, or Köbel. This is the Strasbourg printer Johann Grüninger who, over a period of fifty years, from 1482 to 1532, one of the most interesting periods of German and European history, produced some five hundred books,[76] including religious tomes, scientific works, legal texts, humanist editions, works of popular literature and contemporary controversy, and practical handbooks, in Latin and in German, many of them richly illustrated. That his business lasted fifty years shows that overall he judged the market aright. Doubtless he was lucky in his backers and his contacts, but his astute choice of texts must have been a major factor in his success.

Grüninger seems to have established his business by printing rock-solid works for which there was a discernible market. Thus in 1483/84 he prints Peter Comestor's *Historia scholastica*, Ludolf of Saxony's *Vita Christi*, and a Latin bible. In 1484 he concentrates on collections of sermons, bringing out no fewer than four. His biggest coup seems to have been in 1485 when he landed the first of a series of contracts to print breviaries. The first was for the distant diocese of Breslau, and it led to commissions for some seventeen similar books over the next fourteen years for use in places such as Mainz, Constance, Hamburg, Olomouc, Münster, Osnabrück, Worms, and Strasbourg itself. Similarly the Nuremberg printer Georg Stuchs (active from 1484 to 1517) printed books for the dioceses of Regensburg, Salzburg, Prague, Olomouc, Cracow, Gran, Kammin, Naumburg, Magdeburg, Halberstadt, Hildesheim, Minden, Brandenburg, Meissen, Lübeck, Havelberg, Skara (in Sweden), Melk, and Linköping.[77] The great advantage of such commissions was that the customers bought the complete print-run: the printer did not have to bother about distribution and retail. But Grüninger was quite willing to experiment too, and 1485 also saw one of his most important innovations: his German bible, the tenth printed German bible (*GW* 4304), the first-ever handy-sized family bible: though in two volumes of about 460 leaves each, illustrated with 109 woodcuts, the format was only 280 × 200 mm, just half the size of previous bibles which had been royal folios measuring about 400 × 280 mm. This was an important milestone in bible design. Grüninger did not stop there. Living in Strasbourg, a major centre of German humanism, he made good use of his contacts.[78] To be sure, he published standard classics, in Latin and in German, but he also cultivated contemporary writers and, after the turn of the century, felt secure enough to publish their works. Thus already in the colophon of his 1512 edition of *Das Schiff des Heils* of Johann Geiler von Kaisersberg, the enormously popular preacher at Strasbourg cathedral, he announced his intention 'to print all the books of Doctor Keisersperg in the same format as the present volume', and indeed he did publish about fifteen editions of Geiler's works.

Grüninger's constantly evolving publishing programme cannot be examined in detail here, but the following lists show how different it looked in 1485, 1498, 1512, 1520, and 1524.

BOOKS ISSUED IN 1485

2 MAY: *Bible* [German].
Maneken, Carolus, *Formulae epistolarum*.
Angelus (Engel), Johannes, *Practica*
Balbus, Johannes, *Catholicon* [uncertainly assigned to Grüninger]
Breviarium Vratislaviense.
Gart der Gesundheit.

Lochmaier, Michael, *Sermones de sanctis cum vigintitribus Pauli Wann sermonibus. Vocabularius ex quo.*

BOOKS ISSUED IN 1498

12 MARCH: Horatius Flaccus, Q., *Opera.*
28 MARCH: *Bible, Euangelia mit vslegunge der glos.*
AFTER 19 MAY: Amsterdamis, Henricus (Hervicus) de, *Oratio funebris in Fridericum Bavariae Ducem, cum epistola Jacobi Wimphelingii ad Philippi comitis Palatini filios.*
1 AUGUST: Brant, Sebastian, *Varia carmina*, with Reuchlin, Johannes, *Scenica progymnasmata.*
15 OCTOBER: *Missale speciale.*
Wimpheling, Jacob, *Isidoneus Germanicus.*
Hortulus animae.
Prebusinus, Urbanus, *Oratio mordacissima.*
Wimpheling, Jacob, *Elegantiarum medulla oratoriaque precepta.*
Andreas Capellanus, *Amor, die Liebe*, transl. Johannes Hartlieb.

BOOKS ISSUED IN 1512

25 FEBRUARY: Brunschwig, Hieronymus, *De arte distillandi.*
31 MAY: Reisch, Gregorius, *Margarita philosophica noua.*
23 AUGUST: Geiler, Johann, *Schiff des Heils.*
7 SEPTEMBER: Geiler, Johann, *Predig der himelfart Mariae.*
24 NOVEMBER: Sachsenheim, Hermann von, *Die Mörin.*
Buch der Beispiele der alten Weisen.
Caesar, C. Julius, *Von seinen Kriegen.*
Coccinius (Köchlin), Michael, *De rebus gestis in Italia.*
Geiler, Johann, *Passion.*
Ma Sha Allah, al-Misri (Messahala), *Tractatus de compositione astrolabi.*

BOOKS ISSUED IN 1520

21 JANUARY: Murner, Thomas, *Ein christliche und brüderliche Ermanung.*
18 MARCH: Geiler, Johann, *An dem Ostertag hat … gepredigt von den dry marien.*
27 MARCH: Marcus von Lindau, *Frag und Antwurt der zehen Gebot*, [with] 31 AUGUST Marcus von Lindau, *Ein nützliche Leer und Underweisung waz und wy man betten soll.*
23 AUGUST: Geiler, Johann, *Narrenschiff.*
28 AUGUST: Adelphus, Johannes, *Barbarossa.*
10 NOVEMBER: Murner, Thomas, *Ein christenliche und briederliche Ermanung.*
24 NOVEMBER: Murner, Thomas, *Von Doctor Martinus Luters Leren vnd predigen.*
28 NOVEMBER: Fries, Laurentius, *Ein Kurtze Schirmred der Kunst Astrologie.*
13 DECEMBER: Murner, Thomas, *Von dem babstenthum.*

24 DECEMBER: Murner, Thomas, *An den Großmechtigsten vnd Durchlüchtigsten Adel tütscher nation das sye den christlichen glauben beschirmen.*

Adelphus, Johannes, *Barbarossa* (2nd edn).

BOOKS ISSUED IN 1524

5 JANUARY: Dietenberger, Johannes, *Der Leye.*

1 FEBRUARY: Cochlaeus, Johannes, *De fomite peccati.*

16 FEBRUARY: Tectonus, Theophilus, *Compendiosa Boemice seu Hussitane hereseos ortus & eiusdem damnatorum Articulorum descriptio.*

12 MARCH: Treger, Conrad, *Paradoxa centum.*

2 MAY: Dietenberger, Johannes, *Der Bauer, Obe die Christen mügen durch iere guten werck das hymelreich verdienen.*

28 JUNE: Dietenberger, Johannes, *Der Leye. Obe der gelaub allein selig macht.*

9 AUGUST: Cochlaeus, Johannes, *Von dem hoch gelerten geistlichen bischoff Jo. von Roffen ... zwen Artickel.*

22 OCTOBER: Cochlaeus, Johannes, *Ein christenliche vnnd nutzliche Sermon oder Predig sant Bernharts, von vnser lieben frawen.*

4 NOVEMBER: Cyprian, Saint, *Ein heilsamer Tractat S. Cypriani von einfaltigkeit der Prelaten vnd einigkeit der Kirchen*, trans. Johannes Cochlaeus.

Campegius, Laurentius, *Constitutio ad removendos abusus.*

Cochlaeus, Johannes, *Antwort auff Martin Luth. freueliche Appellation.*

Cochlaeus, Johannes, *De authoritate ecclesiae adverus Lutheranos.*

Cochlaeus, Johannes, *Ein Spiegel der ewangelischen Freyheit.*

Cochlaeus, Johannes, *Ob Sant Peter zu Rom sey geweßen.*

Cocles, Bartholomeus, *Ein Kurtzer bericht der gantzen Physionomey und Ciromancey.*

Dietenberger, Johannes, *Von Menschen Ler.*

Dietenberger, Johannes, *Widerlegung des Lutherischen Büchlins.*

Emser, Hieronymus, *Canonis missae contra Zwinglium defensio.*

Emser, Hieronymus, *Missae christianorum contra Lutheranum assertio.*

Felbaum, Sebastian, *Ein nutzliche Rede in lutrischen Sachen*, [with] Dietenberger, Johannes, *Christliche Unterweisung.*

Hohenlandenberg, Hugo von, Bishop of Constance, *Christenliche Underrichtung, die Bildnüsse und das Opffer der Meß betreffend.*

Luther, Martin, *Underrichtung auff etlich Artickel.*

In 1485 his output comprised mainly standard works, religious works, sermons, and handbooks; in 1498 there is a marked commitment to the classics (Horace) and especially Strasbourg humanism: Brant, Reuchlin, Wimpheling; in 1512 mostly books in German with Geiler von Kaisersberg prominent among them; in 1520 Geiler still, but now also works of two other local writers, Johannes Adelphus and the anti-Lutheran polemicist Thomas Murner; and in 1524 virtually nothing but anti-Lutheran polemics by Johann Cochlaeus and Johann Dietenberger. It was, in fact, Grüninger's support of Catholic polemicists that got him into trouble with the Strasbourg city authorities, who inclined to Protestantism, and nearly put an end to his business.

The case of Grüninger neatly shows how, as indeed with Caxton, if a printer took the trouble to research the market, he could make the business of books a going concern, even perhaps without being a great innovator. By the early sixteenth-century, publishing had, in the words of Edwin Hunt and James Murray, 'been transformed by the technological tinkering of a handful of Germans from a plodding and restrictive collection of copyists to a new agile industry preparing itself to meet the rising demands of an increasingly literate public'.[79]

ORATIONS CROSSING THE ALPS

HOLGER NICKEL

ORATIONS PRINTED IN THE incunable period are in some ways harbingers of the pamphlets of the Reformation. Mainly they consist of no more than a single gathering each (of two to eight leaves), but surviving editions are astonishingly numerous: they make up more than one per cent of the editions produced in the fifteenth century. In contrast to the pamphlets of the sixteenth century they rarely have a title-leaf with a promotional woodcut.

In 1998 I asked John Goldfinch to prepare a diskette containing all incunabula recorded on ISTC with the word 'oratio' in the title. He immediately sent it to me and I am grateful for his assistance with my book-historical examination of this genre. In order to focus on the contemporary orations that are of interest to me, I deleted all records relating to prayers and to speeches by classical authors. This left me with 350 editions. This method of identifying my primary material explains why I have not taken into account editions of orations with other titles, such as 'Panegyris' or 'Epistola', but I believe that they would not have changed the overall picture. It must not be forgotten that numerous orations are transmitted only in manuscript. They have been left out of consideration, as it would have been prohibitively time-consuming to identify and locate them.

It was not possible to read them all and to categorize them properly according to their contents. However, in order to evaluate them from the point of view of my specific interest, it was necessary to undertake some sort of classification. I used the sub-titles occurring after the word 'oratio' as a help to create an outline distribution. This provided me with the following textual groupings:

1 Addresses on ecclesiastical feast days (for instance Epiphany, Whitsun, Ascension Day, or All Souls)
2 Humble addresses to the pope from communes or lands subject to his secular powers
3 Funeral addresses of cardinals and other important persons
4 Addresses given at various official occasions

It is immediately clear that some of these orations have a secular, nearly professional character, not unlike the German 'Festrede'. Others might be termed sermons in English, addressing religious themes, the occasion of the oration being given as an ecclesiastical feast day.

In his detailed study of addresses 'coram papa inter missarum solemnia', John W. O'Malley consistently called the speakers 'preacher'.[1] However, he did not engage with the terminological question of the label 'sermon', although he demonstrated that the *genus demonstrativum*, as well as other aspects of classical rhetorical doctrine, had influenced the speakers. However, when looking at the sermons discussed by him, it might cause surprise that some authors, in addition to 'orationes', also published works which contain the word 'sermo' in their titles: Guillelmus Bodivit,[2] Bernardinus Carvajal,[3] Lionellus Chieregatus,[4] Johannes Antonius de Sancto Georgio,[5] Stephanus Thegliatius,[6] and so on.

For us 'sermo' is the normal Latin equivalent of 'sermon'. All manuscript and incunable librarians are familiar with the thick volumes containing late medieval Latin sermon collections. They are thought to be aids for priests[7], but it is difficult to imagine how they were used. A priest could not simply have read out such a ready-made sermon[8] from a manuscript or from a printed book, especially as he would have had to translate it into the vernacular. Did he extract key passages? I do not know what a 'normal Sunday sermon' to a lay audience might have sounded like, remembering that, later on in Germany, many clerics who had gone over to Lutheranism were found at visitations to be inadequate for their new task and were criticised as unsuited. Similar information comes from Italy. In the middle of the fifteenth century certain priests of the diocese of Pisa were reported not to possess a breviary, and, some hundred years later, their successors in the Mantua area got poor marks for their lack of education.[9] So what was the purpose of these collections? The language of the printed editions was only understandable by a Latinate audience, which indicates that they were used in monastic religious services. But, given the level of education, could all monks really follow Latin when it was read aloud? Perhaps these collections of sermons were used in religious houses for private reading. This is plausible, for it is easier to resolve the abbreviations of the printed edition when reading to oneself than when reading aloud, and religious houses had the means to buy the splendid quarto volumes. Admittedly, just as prayer books in old binding always show the dirt of unwashed fingers, more intensive reading ought to have made surviving copies grubby, so that antiquarian book dealers should only rarely have been able praise them as 'fresh' and 'without marks'.

However that may be, the orations-sermons which are discussed here must have been at the margins of ordinary church life. As distinct from the compendia, in the form in which they have reached us, they were composed to be recited to a Latinate audience on days which can be precisely determined. At the most, they got a stylistic polish after the public reading. The title 'oratio' was apparently intended to make a claim of a literary standing, for, then as now, it must have made anyone with a Humanist education think of classical orators, from Demosthenes to Cicero. Probably this association was of importance to the authors of the orations, and in this respect secular and clerical orations were similar.

The separate publication of each oration indicates the literary ambitions of their authors who wished to offer their works to the public one by one. It is unlikely that the reason for their separate publication should be sought in attempts to provide others with guidance for writing sermons. Compared with collections of sermons they would have been of little use in writing sermons which were to be given in the context of pastoral care and practical theology, for, at best, each was suited for one single Sunday of the ecclesiastical year. These orations could be useful models only indirectly through their formal structure, in the same way as classical orations could act as models. For the purpose of this study I therefore believe that I am justified in considering both sermons and orations which were composed for secular occasions. I shall use the word orations to cover both.

The home of these orations was Rome, a city in which remarkably few collections of sermons were published. More precisely, the essential central point for the orations was the Curia. Perhaps it was a point where literary and economic activities coincided: on the one side there was a concentration of education, ambition, and money, one the other the economic interests of the printers. Stephan Plannck and Eucharius Silber were the most prolific printers of orations. It was fundamental that the clerical target group earned more than, for instance, chaplains in early-sixteenth-century Milan who had an annual income of only 40 lire at their disposal, less than an unskilled worker.[10] Orators should be considered as the ecclesiastical elite: one even became pope: Enea Silvio Piccolomini.[11] Those who were allowed to present themselves before the pope or the cardinals on behalf of secular rulers, such as Matthias Corvinus[12] or Ferdinand and Isabella of Spain,[13] saw themselves as part of the establishment, ecclesiastical or secular, and they must have enjoyed this position – 'odi profanum vulgus'. Even if not stated, this Horatian phrase must have summed up a fundamental attitude of remoteness from all uneducated clergy. Socially, all concerned were nearly at the same level, including the dead who were commemorated in funeral orations. For instance Nicolaus Capranica[14] spoke at the funeral of Bessarion, the author of *Epistolae et orationes*;[15] Petrus Ransanus[16] spoke at the funeral of Franciscus de Toledo who himself had spoken at the funeral of Leonardo de Rovere,[17] and Raphael Brandolinus gave the funeral address of Guillelmus de Pereriis,[18] who had also been an orator himself.[19]

When a man had the honour of being chosen to be an orator he entered into a virtual competition with his predecessors. He would have wanted to study their works in order to understand his own level of competence and if possible to achieve a higher level of stylistic elegance. The audience would lose patience if the orations were too long,[20] so the printed editions were slender and could be bought in greater numbers: brevity made for cheap publications. For their part, printers ran hardly any financial risk if they produced a reprint, and could react fast to potential demand. They could anticipate sales with a great degree of certainty within this circle of persons: orators and their circles, and in addition Roman residents or visitors who saw a fascinating reminiscence of Cicero's days in the institution of the public oration.

In general, it is difficult for bibliographers to date reprints. When the type material cannot establish a range of dates, cataloguers often write 'not before/after' the day on which the oration was given. As for the orations, frequent reprints obscure the fact that apparently there were no 'star-orators' who performed very often. If I have counted correctly, Petrus Marsus is in the lead with five orations, followed by Martinus de Viana with four, and a long line of authors who had the privilege to perform three times. There is a single woman among the orators, Cassandra Fidelis.[21] Without a study of the relevant biographies I cannot determine if any orator was a child, as happened in a later period.[22]

The habit of giving public orations spread to other Italian cities. Thus, for instance, Leo Bentivolus[23], Gaspar Fantutius,[24] and Julianus Duciensis de Imola,[25] spoke before the University of Bologna; Bonifacius Bugellanus spoke before the 'academy' in Turin,[26] and Johannes de Margarit 'in senatu venetiarum'.[27] Other orations had more personal backgrounds: Petrus Simon Alatus spoke on the death of the wife of Hieronymus

Petrucci from Siena,[28] Baptista Mantuanus at the funeral of the duchess of Ferrara,[29] Bonifacius Bembus in praise of Ludovico Sforza,[30] and Thomas Ferrandus at the wedding of the duke of Mantua.[31] Whether as first editions or as reprints, we find orations printed in all the most important printing towns of Italy: Bologna, Brescia, Ferrara, Florence, Siena, Venice, Verona, etc., but also in smaller printing places like Cagli, Lucca, and Turin.

When we consider that, at least in the second half of the fifteenth century, these orations belonged to the intellectual world of Italian cities, we may be surprised to see that works by the same authors also appeared north of the Alps where, after all, social structures were very different. It is easy to see the movement from one place to the other in practical terms. Coming back from the Holy City, pilgrims had orations in their luggage, perhaps along with an edition of the *Mirabilia Romae*. Once at home they encouraged printers to offer an oration to a local audience. They could promise success to the printer if humanist thought had already found a fertile ground. But one thing must be said immediately: none of the imports was reprinted.

If we begin in Germany, among the printing towns Leipzig is in the lead with five transmitted orations, Bernardinus Carvajal,[32] Lionellus Chieregatus,[33] Jason de Mayno[34], Guillelmus de Pereriis,[35] and Christophorus Saucius Fanensis.[36] Next comes Nuremberg, where Peter Danhauser and, perhaps, Conrad Celtis played a role, with orations by Hermolaus Barbarus[37] and Cassandra Fidelis.[38] Passau,[39] Rostock,[40] Strasbourg,[41] Ulm,[42] and Erfurt[43] each saw the publication of one oration.

Perhaps the transmission of texts written in Italy failed to survive the change between the two cultural areas. Even if the ideology was fundamentally similar, social structures must have been noticeably different and many Italian themes must have seemed irrelevant a thousand kilometres to the north. If little remained of the social context of the oration, perhaps only the effort of the author and his rhetorical skill were noticed. This made it a difficult genre to appreciate. Perhaps orations written in northern Europe itself found a more ready audience.

To examine this, it seems most sensible to begin with names of authors again. The most successful author was Jacob Wimpheling, whose appreciation of the importance of public orations as part of a humanist education is known.[44] By him we have orations printed in Mainz,[45] Cologne,[46] Delft,[47] Speyer,[48] Augsburg,[49] and possibly Basel.[50] Wimpheling also edited the funeral sermon of the duke of Bavaria by Hervicus de Amsterdamis,[51] published by Grüninger in Strasbourg. Two orations are by Konrad Wimpina, both printed in Leipzig.[52] Also Trithemius got two orations into print, both in Mainz.[53] Other authors got only one oration into print. The greatest success was Geiler von Kaisersberg whose oration was reprinted in Strasbourg.[54] The remaining orations were printed in Freiburg,[55] Cologne,[56] Leipzig,[57] Mainz,[58] Strasbourg,[59] and Tübingen.[60]

With the oration of Wimpheling published in Delft we have already left the German-language area. Of relevance here is also the oration held by Hermolaus Barbarus before Frederick III and Maximilian,[61] likewise from the present-day Netherlands, printed in Alost. This oration was of particular importance in northern Europe, which is why Peter Danhauser edited it in Nuremberg (see above). It appeared also in Rome[62] and in Venice.[63] From France two orations are of interest, both printed in Paris, one by Beroaldus,[64] and the other by Gaguinus.[65] Here we see north European orations written in a city in which no southern orations were reprinted. Beroaldus came from the South, and Gaguinus was undoubtedly acquainted with south European practices. Were they the only ones to engage with the *genus demonstrativum*? It would be interesting to establish if orations printed in Italy were available in Parisian bookshops. Two orations by Petrus Cara printed in Lyon should also be mentioned.[66] Compared with the German-language area, France and the Netherlands are poorly represented in our material, while England and Spain are absent. In Germany Leipzig is the clear leader, followed by Mainz and Strasbourg.

The geographical distribution is not very surprising if we see the orations as witnesses of humanist aspirations. It is a parallel to the dominant position of Italy in the field of classical texts, noted already in the 1920s by Ernst Schulz who added that for northern Europe '... for each non-Italian edition of the classic we get about a dozen from Italy. Outside Italy classical texts are only printed to any extent in Paris, the Netherlands, and in Leipzig. In Germany Strasbourg also deserves to be mentioned, although a long way behind Leipzig.'[67] Also Rudolf Hirsch emphasised the role of Leipzig in the transmission of classical authors.[68] Schulz's observation on Paris and the Netherlands referred to classical texts, whereas the preponderance of Germany in northern Europe was specific to the genre of orations.

An interesting light on how the genre was spread from Rome to the north is thrown by the oration of Johannes Antonius Campanus, the Roman humanist and diplomat, held 'in conventu Ratisponensi', that is in Regensburg on the Danube, but printed in Rome.[69] There is indeed impressive evidence for a gradually increasing impact of the new learning in the north, which also bear witness to a coherent humanist community. Thus orations written in the north also fund their way south of the Alps. Bernhard Perger spoke at the funeral of Frederick III in Vienna, and it seems plausible that the Viennese edition[70] of his text was printed before both the Roman and the Leipzig editions.[71] Perhaps the most significant example is an oration by Johannes Reuchlin printed by Aldus Manutius, no less.[72]

It makes sense, as a conclusion, to cast a glance at how these texts were used five hundred years ago and how we deal with them today. It may come as a surprise that their use has not changed much. Today they stand as thin fascicles on the shelves of our libraries, and contemporaries must have kept them in much the same way – only then they probably lay flat, but still separately, the way they were acquired. In between came a period where they were bound together, whether by the first owner as he had acquired enough for a substantial volume or by collectors of later generations. We owe it to the tract volume that the editions survive at all, even if they were not 'originally part of a Sammelband', in the phrase of an important south German incunable catalogue.[73] Librarians have split up these volumes for the sake of tidy housekeeping, and antiquarian booksellers to improve their marketability. However, the tract volumes were created some five hundred years ago to make it possible to keep these little pamphlets, making them look like the collections of sermons. But they were used completely differently, as the orations offered little content which could be exploited at specific occasions, for one can hardly imagine that circumstances for two orations were sufficiently similar. The texts could be used for formal analytical training, and perhaps also for aesthetic appreciation. By being massed into a tract volume, not unlike a thick 'reader', these fifteenth-century productions must have challenged readers and authors to reassess their own habitual patterns of thought and to turn away from medieval Latinity and towards the stylistic and intellectual aspirations of antiquity. They gave pace to the change, improved the linguistic level, and spread a way of working and of thinking which may, after all, best be called humanist.

MIXING POP AND POLITICS

ORIGINS, TRANSMISSION, AND READERS
OF ILLUSTRATED BROADSIDES IN
FIFTEENTH-CENTURY GERMANY

FALK EISERMANN

I

DURING THE SIXTEENTH and seventeenth centuries the illustrated single-leaf broadside, in German 'Flugblatt', became one of the most widespread and multi-functional means of everyday communication throughout Europe.[1] Although the genre has been extremely popular with scholars of early modern culture in the past decades, its fifteenth-century origins and its initial development have not yet been adequately explored. The present paper will try to reconstruct some aspects of the early transmission of illustrated broadsides, focusing mainly on the ways in which authors chose their subjects, the structure of the printed texts, and the arrangement of words and images, as well as the question of potential predecessors of the illustrated broadside. Furthermore, I will discuss the scholarly commonplace that 'Flugblätter' are to be considered a nearly ubiquitous reading material, a medium directed at and reaching a wider audience than other literary productions in the incunable period.

Going through the select bibliography of a new book on the life and times of Johannes Gutenberg, I came across a well-known title: *The Printing Press as an Agent of Change* by Elizabeth Eisenstein. The printer's devil had decided to show off his more humorous talents, and had slightly altered the entry so that now it read *The Printing Press as an Agent of Chance*.[2] This would be an appropriate title for any study of the transmission of incunable broadsides. Working towards a new catalogue of incunable broadsides printed in Germany and the Netherlands,[3] I have studied much of the surviving material, and in doing so one truly learns to see the printing press as an agent of 'chance'. To begin with, a comprehensive survey is almost impossible when you are confronted with such fragile and often inconspicuous sources. Finding and cataloguing ephemeral printed works is difficult enough, but it is even more difficult to examine their backgrounds and contexts in order to find answers to some basic questions. For example, what were the author's or printer's intentions when they published a broadside? How many copies were actually made and distributed? Who read them – and why? For illustrated broadsides, few efforts have been made to clarify these issues; for all we know they fell from heaven.

There is something to be said for this suggestion. Shortly before noon on Wednesday, 7 November 1492, a large meteorite hit the ground near the Alsatian town of Ensisheim, causing a tremendous bang that could be heard as far away as Lucerne in

Switzerland, some 75 miles as the crow flies. Soon afterwards the remains of this space invader, weighing 260 pounds, were recovered from a wheat field and brought to Ensisheim.[4] This remarkable event, the first meteorite impact properly documented by contemporary sources, naturally received enormous public attention. Consequently, having been notified by regional authorities, on 26 November King Maximilian himself inspected the priceless specimen and decided that it should be preserved and put on display in the local church. He also ordered that henceforth no material be removed from the stone, but to no avail; today there are chopped-off parts of the meteorite in natural-history collections all over the world, and only a large fragment remains to be admired *in situ*.[5]

The 'Big Bang' of Ensisheim did not attract only royal interest. Quite rapidly the event became the subject of chronicles, scientific studies, and philosophical reflections all over Germany. The most important person to deal with the story was Sebastian Brant, the renowned humanist and later author of the *Ship of Fools*, the first German literary work to enter the ranks of world literature. Soon after the event, Brant, then dean of the faculty of law at the University of Basel, published a broadside entitled *Von dem Donnerstein gefallen im xcii iar vor Ensisheim*, in Latin *De fulgetra anni xcii*.[6] It features a woodcut of the meteorite penetrating the clouds on its way to the ground (Fig. 1). Beneath the image are two columns of text, the first dealing with the matter in 22 Latin distichs, the second presenting a German verse paraphrase. Both texts interpret the event as an incentive for Maximilian, who is directly addressed in the concluding paragraph, to take action against his impudent rival, Charles VIII of France. By marrying Maximilian's designated bride Anne de Bretagne, Charles had gained control of Burgundy, and there, too, the invaders heard the impact. It certainly made them tremble, as the Latin text states: 'Francia certe tremit', and the German elaborates 'Jn [the meteorite impact] forchtend die Frantzosen seer / Rechtlich sprich ich das es bedeut / Ein besunder plag derselben leut', expressing the wish that the impact would be a harbinger of political developments which would deal an even bigger blow to Maximilian's and the Empire's western arch-enemy.

Thus the broadside turns a recent prodigy into a political allegory, and it must be considered the earliest 'Flugblatt' according to the modern definition. Furthermore, the *Fulgetra* publication was not only a great leap forward in the history of printing, but also of the utmost importance within Brant's own work, since it was the starting-point of his career as 'arch-augur of the Holy Roman Empire'.[7] With the clever use of traditional set pieces, such as the address and dedication to the King, and the combination of classicizing Latin and the popular German *Knittelvers*, Brant established an innovative strategy of persuasion in a new multifunctional medium. In the following decade he became the centre of an expert discourse on natural or historical phenomena and their significance for the fortunes of the Empire and the emperor. He fairly regularly published broadsides which depicted a particular incident, and offered explanations, prophecies, and political admonitions, often directed and addressed to the emperor himself. Consequently, after Maximilian had triumphed over a French army at Salins on 17 January 1493, Brant must have felt that the chain of events he had predicted in the *Fulgetra* had started to unfold. 'Within an hour', as the colophon states, he composed a poem about the battle to celebrate the victory and to explain its political implications; this, of course, was printed as a broadside.[8] After a quiet year, 1494,

Fig. 1. Sebastian Brant, *Von dem Donnerstein gefallen im xcii iar vor Ensisheim (De fulgetra anni xcii)*. [Basel: Michael Furter for] J[ohannes] B[ergmann], after 7 November 1492]. *GW* 5023. (Basel, Öffentliche Bibliothek der Universität.)

which saw the publication of only three religious broadsides expressing Brant's personal piety,[9] the following year again brought dramatic developments which fuelled his imagination. In the spring of 1495 he praised the papal and royal cooperation of the Holy League of Venice in the *Congratulatio de confoederatione Alexandri VI cum Maximiliano*.[10] In September of the same year, Siamese twins were born near Worms, where, as it happens, the most important Imperial Diet of the later Middle Ages had just ended. As Brant hoped that the Diet would turn out to be a breakthrough for Maximilian's reform plans, the poem celebrated the rare coincidence of the mysterious birth and, as he saw it, the unification of the German Empire, in both Latin and vernacular poems entitled *Von der wunderbaren Geburt des Kindes bei Worms* or *De monstruoso partu apud Wormaciam*, which were printed as broadsides and small illustrated booklets.[11] Throughout the following years Brant kept publishing similar items, but with the turn of the century this specific part of his work came to a sudden halt. Around 1500 it had become evident that Maximilian's high-flying reform plans had broken down; even worse, he had suffered a serious defeat in the Swabian war of 1499, which led to the secession of the Swiss confederation. This not only diminished the power and territory of the Empire but also affected Brant's personal situation. Although it was not immediately clear whether Basel would join the confederation or remain part of the Empire, Brant, an 'ardent admirer of Maximilian and imperial patriot, who was always dreaming of expansion of the Empire',[12] left for Strasbourg in the autumn of 1500. Three broadsides featuring a text called *Pacis in Germanicum Martem naenia Martisque contra pacem defensio*, a disputation between Peace and War which was triggered off by the disastrous course of events, were to be his last sophisticated project in this medium.[13] After the Swiss defeat, Brant must have come to the conclusion that he, too, had lost his personal propaganda war.

The *Fulgetra* broadsides, as indicated, were the starting-point for a remarkable innovation involving the broadside genre and the printing press as a whole. Their main formal characteristic is the presence of an image, placed prominently above the text and dominated by an unusual and eye-catching iconography. The Latin text uses elaborate rhetorical strategies and allegorical language, whereas the vernacular is in a more popular mode; nevertheless, both versions are full of learned metaphors and historical allusions. They both focus on a single objective: to convince prospective audiences to support their leader, Maximilian, in the difficult political situation of the early 1490s. Due to the stylized character and strategies of persuasion employed in early illustrated broadsides, texts were far more important than images in transmitting the author's intentions, although we know that Brant himself designed some of the pictures and instructed woodcutters about motifs and iconographical details. But in general, the depiction of events like the meteorite impact is used to catch the eye, and the words offer interpretations which go far beyond the depicted scene and the actual relevance of the event in question. Furthermore, these broadsides always name high-ranking persons as their immediate addressees, another clever move to make a recipient feel that by reading the poems he would become part of a high-level discourse – and who could resist such a temptation?

Thus the overall display of 'pictura' and 'poesis' and the suggestive structural subtext were designed to catch the viewer's attention quickly, and to direct it towards a well-defined communicative aim. This turns the broadside into a propaganda billboard, in terms not so much of its actual use as of its intended effect. Due to the mixture of popular prodigy and political allegory it could even arouse the interest of those who normally could not or would not read such a publication.

II

Astonishingly enough, to my knowledge no one has ever examined what might have inspired Sebastian Brant in a technical sense, or where he might have come across the idea of communicating his concerns in the form of a single-leaf illustrated broadside when he sat down to compose and publish the *Fulgetra*.

Before, during, and after the establishment of typography proper, woodcuts and small images – e.g. 'Heiligenbildchen' or 'Kleine Andachtsbilder' combined with prayers, indulgences, and the like – were a widespread genre.[14] These rather unsophisticated but nonetheless enormously popular products were usually made and disseminated by craftsmen going by the name of 'Briefmaler' or 'Kartenmacher', as is evident in sources from monasteries and German cities like Augsburg, Basel, Nuremberg,[15] and Ulm. They are often regarded as predecessors of, and even models for, letterpress broadsides, but although some religious texts and images are preserved in both woodcuts and in letterpress,[16] the overall number of examples of such a double (or triple where manuscripts are also involved) transmission is relatively small, and the parallel seems to have been restricted to the religious genres mentioned above. In contrast to the general assumptions of scholars, I do not think that printers were particularly eager to copy the motifs and texts of those wide-spread religious woodcuts; rather, the use of the printing press led to the development of new and different types of literacy, and products of the printing press were certainly designed for different audiences. Roughly thirty years after Gutenberg's invention, the printing press had overcome a number of initial problems and economic crises. Printers had established their craft and gathered sufficient experience in marketing strategies as well as practical knowledge of technical and compositional skills. Although early woodcut culture may have provided some of those skills which were exploited by letterpress printmakers as well, the influence of the woodcut on the printing press was not overwhelming, nor were there close interrelations between the two types of broadsides with regard to typological aspects, choice of motifs, contents, and communicative aims. When viewed in the more general context of typographic culture, I would rather stress that the momentum of the 'letterpress broadside' medium – one might speak of the 'auto-dynamics' of the press – was important in the formation of the innovative medium of the illustrated broadside. To cut a long and well-known story short, throughout the fifteenth century the introduction of the press, its ongoing improvement, and the functional differentiations of printed matter not only added considerably to the attractiveness of the genre, but also brought into being two largely different types of illustrated broadsides, the popular single-leaf woodcut, mostly on religious subjects, and the letterpress print with which we are dealing, which relied heavily on the impact of the written word.

Nevertheless the emergence of the illustrated (letterpress) broadside as a medium in its own right was slow and unmistakably experimental during the early years of the printing press. Before the success of the *Fulgetra*, printers were not over-eager to publish material like this, as is evident from Appendix B. The overview shows twenty-three numbers representing about forty editions of illustrated broadsides published in Germany until 1492 which can (at least in certain aspects) be compared with humanist broadsides. The first to experiment with a combination of words and images on a single leaf was Günther Zainer, the first Augsburg printer and creator of an influential style of book illustration.[17] From a small number of broadsides still extant with full-scale images from his workshop, the verse narrative *The evil woman fighting the devils* may serve as an example.[18] It shows what was to become the classical page design of vernacular books from his and other printing houses: an oblong woodcut which could be called a scenic head rule, covering the width of the type area, followed by a double column of didactic text in the vernacular, each verse starting on a new line (Fig. 2). The anonymous poem itself was not originally written for publication in print but taken from a manuscript tradition probably of Augsburg origin. Alternative compositional modes include the insertion of an image into a text, as in Zainer's edition of the religious poem *Syben tagzeit unser frowen* (c. 1475), and the 'Bilderbogen', the earliest surviving letterpress example of which is a *Ten Commandments* sheet by an anonymous printer probably from Basel.[19] This design, which of course owes its existence to well-established modes of pictorial presentation, became popular for catechetical purposes and multi-scenic narratives; Brant himself varied the layout in his *Vita s. Onophrii* broadside of 1494.[20] As a collaborator with printers in Basel, as an editor and an author, and as someone who worked within a web of erudite colleagues and friends, he was certainly familiar with all the various aspects and developments of contemporary book and broadside illustration. He might also have known works like the *Zeichen der falschen Gulden*, eleven editions of which were published to warn against a large-scale counterfeiting campaign in Göttingen in 1482; six of those eleven editions are from Augsburg or Ulm.[21] This is an early specimen of an illustrated newsletter print or 'Neue Zeitung', a genre which, by the way, was not as popular with the printing press as some handbooks suggest, at least in the fifteenth century.

While the Swabian cities of Augsburg and Ulm dominated the production of illustrated broadsides before 1492, as is evident from Appendix B, the locations given in Appendix A show that in its initial phase the humanist broadside was almost exclusively a phenomenon of the upper Rhine, coming mainly from printing houses in Basel and Strasbourg. Furthermore, most of the broadsides in question were published by competitive workshops located in strongholds of press activity: Bergmann von Olpe and Amerbach in Basel, Grüninger and Prüss in Strasbourg. Others who jumped on the bandwagon, such as the *Fulgetra* pirater Greyff of Reutlingen, were also experienced workers running efficient enterprises. When one compares the lists below (Appendices A and B), it also becomes evident that the majority of editions in Appendix B are anonymous, while all the broadsides listed in Appendix A bear their author's name. This shows a general tendency of humanist writing, of course, and is therefore not restricted to broadsides alone, but in terms of shaping the new medium it became a significant characteristic. Even writers of lesser reputation than Brant, Konrad Celtis, or Jakob Locher, such as the semi-obscure Johannes Panecianus in his *Ode to Saint Leopold*,[22] felt the urge to display their names in prominent places such as headings or colophons. By doing so, they certainly hoped to attract the attention of potential sponsors as well as to introduce themselves to the inner circles of the current cultural

Ich kam auff ein gewilde weyt
Do sach ich zů der selben tzeit
Ein ubel weyb das ist war .
Strepten mit des teuffels schar
Es geschach auff ein morgen frů
Die teuffel sẽctẽ dẽ ubeln weib zů
Mit mangerley schalckhait
Einer schwůr auff seinen eyd
Er wölt grousse ding began
Wölt das vbel weib allein bestan
Sie hyelten gegen einander
Die teuffel mit prem pancr
Das ubel weib stůnd allein dort
Vnd sprach greuwcliche wort
Wol der ir teuffel alle gemein
Seydt gewůß vnd auch klein
Wir wöllen an annder reyssen
Zerren grymmen vnd reyssen
Sie zerriß in kurtzer stund
Der teuffel mer dann tausunt
Ir aller meyster der lag tot
Do hůb sich angst vnd not
Vber das ubel weib also
Wc we sie thůt vns allen also
Do sprach ein teuffelischer man
Von dem strept sullen wir lan
Vnnd wider in die helle faren
Da můge wir vns wol bewaren
Vnd do sie in die helle komen
Ir einer sprach bey namen
Vñ were wir lenger hie gewese
Vnser keiner wer vor ir genesen

Von der bösen.vnseligen öyet
Ir aller syn in das tv ryet
Wol vns lieben gesellen mein
Das wir also enttunnen sein
Wann wer mit ubeln weiben
Sein tzeit můß hye verrtreyben
Dem wer vil weger der tod
Denn das er köme in solhe not
Ist sie ubel vnnd arg von art
Weim das er ye geboren wart
Ist er traurig so ist sie fro
Wil er denn sunst sie will so
Wil er gen sie wil lauffen
Wil er steelen sie wil rauffen
Wil er traben sie wil tzelten
Wil er kpfeln sie wil schelten
Wil er essen sie wil trincken
Wil er springen sie wil hincken
Wil er denn ligen sie wil sitzen
Wil er auffsten sie wil schwitzen
Wil er denn kalt sie wil heyß
So er sie nart sp läst sy ein scheiß
Sy gat tzů einem pfaffen
Also kan sie es geschaffen
Darumb wer ein ubel weyb hab
Der thů sich ir bey tzeit ab
Vnnd fůre sie da in die hellen
Zů den teuffelischen gesellen
Das ist von den ubeln weyben
Die tugenthafften leyd vertreyben
Des das ubel weyb nit enkan
Darumb hasset sie yederman

Fig. 2. *The evil woman fighting the devils.* [Augsburg: Zainer, *c.* 1473]. Einbl. 709. (Leipzig, Universitätsbibliothek.)

Fig. 3. Leonhard Clement, *Elegia ob victoriam Turci*. [Strasbourg: Matthias Hüpfuff, before 1 September 1498]. (Einbl. 849. Ansbach, Staatsbibliothek.)

and political debate. Another minor humanist and clergyman, Leonhard Clement of Ulm, having published an *Elegia ob victoriam Thurci* in Strasbourg in 1498 (Fig. 3),[23] became the addressee of a counter-statement by Brant, *Thurcorum terror et potentia*, which – as far as we know – was not published as a broadside but was included in the *Varia Carmina*, thus making Clement's name known to a wider audience than he himself might ever have hoped to reach. In general, the humanist broadsides abolished anonymity, and their producers seem to have realised the genre's potential as a means not only of political but also of personal propaganda. This display of authorial self-consciousness soon rubbed off on non-humanist authors like Nikolaus Wolgemut. In 1500 he published an illustrated broadside featuring a rhyming vernacular admonition to Maximilian, boasting the author's name in both the heading and the concluding verse: 'O kunig hab dich selbs in gutter hutt / Also spricht Niclauß Wolgemudt.'[24] The urge to present one's name was also felt by printers as broadsides also came to be seen as advertisements for workshops; in this regard, Brant's publications with Bergmann were obviously trend-setting. Both *Fulgetra* piraters, Prüss in Strasbourg and Greyff in Reutlingen, not only replaced Bergmann's initials, which appear in most of the colophons of his original editions of the Brant broadsides, with their own names, they also plagiarized Bergmann's motto 'Nüt on ursach' verbatim.[25] All these efforts show that after 1492 the illustrated broadside had rapidly obtained a certain reputation as an effective means of propaganda, a reputation which was doubtlessly linked to Brant's overall reputation as 'arch-augur of the Holy Roman Empire'. He could rightfully be described as the most influential author of the later fifteenth century.

Apart from illustrated broadsides dealing with contemporary events like the *Zeichen der falschen Gulden*, there was another successful type of broadside which may have inspired Brant in certain ways: the so-called almanacs.[26] Calculated for one specific year, they combined calendrical data and instructions for blood-letting with a varying account of astronomical prognostications and other predictions. From the early 1470s onwards, a great number of almanacs was published year after year, soon to be embellished by woodcuts, which turned the almanac into one of only a few incunabula-specific types of text which became enormously popular in the fifteenth century. Almanacs show a general tendency to experiment with new illustrative and compositional ideas, thus in certain aspects preceding Sebastian Brant's 'Flugblätter'. Moreover, calendars regularly depicted and described remarkable astronomical phenomena, sometimes combined with predictions on political or social matters. A spectacular celestial event prior to the Ensisheim meteorite, a total eclipse of the sun which occurred on 16 March 1485, was often described in almanacs computed for this very year, and also provoked contemporary comments like the following distich: *Bis dedit octo dies forte et tot Martius horas / Versus ad occiduas sol tenebrosus aquas*, 'a weak effort in itself', as one scholar has pointed out, but nevertheless it was translated into the following almost unintelligible German: *Nach zehen sexs Mertz stund ouch tag / Vil kleines schins die sun hie pflag*.[27] These couplets were actually written by Sebastian Brant himself, who did indeed produce occasional verse before the *Fulgetra*, which remained unpublished in his time. Hence, we can assume that Brant was familiar with the task of interpreting or commenting on celestial and astronomical phenomena; like everyone else in his time he must have been familiar with almanacs as main sources of everyday 'hygiene', of popular medicine, and of calendrical and household information in the German towns in the later Middle Ages. In terms of layout and modes of publication, they share a number of characteristics with the broadsides in question: illustration (which due to competition became almost compulsory in almanacs from the 1480s onwards), periodicity (in the case of the broadside, this was not linked to certain calendrical dates, but incident-related), and combinations of pragmatic forecasts and prognostic interpretations.

Furthermore, there is another possible interrelation, perhaps even more convincing, between the broadside medium 'almanac' and the literary efforts of upper Rhenish humanists like Sebastian Brant. His home cities, Strasbourg and Basel, were strongholds of almanac production in the fifteenth century; but there was also a specific local tradition of calendars, the so-called Lunation tracts. These were basically 'a curious combination of political exhortation and calendrical data'.[28] Structured like an almanac through the use of the sequence of new moon conjunctions of one specific year, these short poems of twelve or thirteen stanzas appealed to political leaders and society as a whole to take action against their respective enemies, meaning either the Turks or the French; other texts made in the same way contained didactic and prognostic information. These texts were regularly published in print, starting with the famous *Türkenkalender* booklet of 1454, and there are at least four broadsides, all from Basel and Strasbourg: an early anonymous poem from Basel[29] was followed by three Strasbourg editions, namely the *Neumondkalender für 1478* (Fig. 4), Hans Erhart Tüsch's *Poetischer Neumondkalender für 1482*, and later a similar text for the year 1500.[30]

Hence, there were various representations of calendrical media related to, and dependent on, the printing press in the upper Rhine area in the late fifteenth century. Their outstanding popularity was certainly an incentive to produce similar publications modelled on these types of calendars. Although Lunation tracts were not illustrated, and although we cannot be absolutely sure whether Brant knew any of these publications, it is possible that in their mixture of popular calendrical presentation and political predictions, their use of verse for purposes of propaganda and prognostication, and their design and layout, calendrical texts from the cultural capitals of the upper Rhine might have had some impact on Brant's idea to publish illustrated broadsides featuring political-prognostic-didactic verse in an event-related sequence. I stress that this is a hypothesis which needs further consideration.

The general layout as introduced in the *Fulgetra* became a characteristic feature of Brant's broadside output, and other humanists followed suit. Jakob Locher, an old friend of Brant's, published a laudatory poem *In faciem Aquilae et laudem Maximiliani romanorum regis* dedicated to the King, after having been named 'poeta laureatus' in 1497;[31] two years later, following another monstrous birth in November 1499, he commented on various relevant issues in a broadside called *De monstruoso puero nato in oppido Rhayn*. According to Locher, the prodigy was to be interpreted as a divine reminder that in Germany, as in Italy and France, the foundations of social life were endangered, if not already crumbling, something which was not only a threat to the majesty of the German Empire, but also a portent of chaos and, ultimately, the end of the world.[32] The range of topics presented in illustrated broadsides also included pious material, as in the texts of Celtis, Panecianus, and Reuchlin, and medical treatises and allegories like those of Theodoricus Ulsenius.[33]

The broadsides by Brant's fellow humanists, however, were all written in Latin, indicating that they were directed towards certain erudite in-groups. Unlike his Latin publications, Brant's German texts, at least up to about 1500, were obviously not used as models by other authors. This may be due to the fact that after the tremendous success of the *Ship of Fools* he had become an authority on vernacular verse with whom nobody could or would compete. From highly complicated, almost encoded allegories like the *Sow of Landser* and the *Foxhunt*,[34] it is evident that his vernacular compositions, too, became more and more sophisticated, and we may speculate as to whether he sometimes expected too much of his audience. But who, we must now ask, were the audience?

III

Scholars dealing with the subject of audiences of illustrated broadsides normally do not hesitate to stress one specific point – that these works were produced in great numbers and hence found a wide range of readers belonging to various social groups: noblemen,

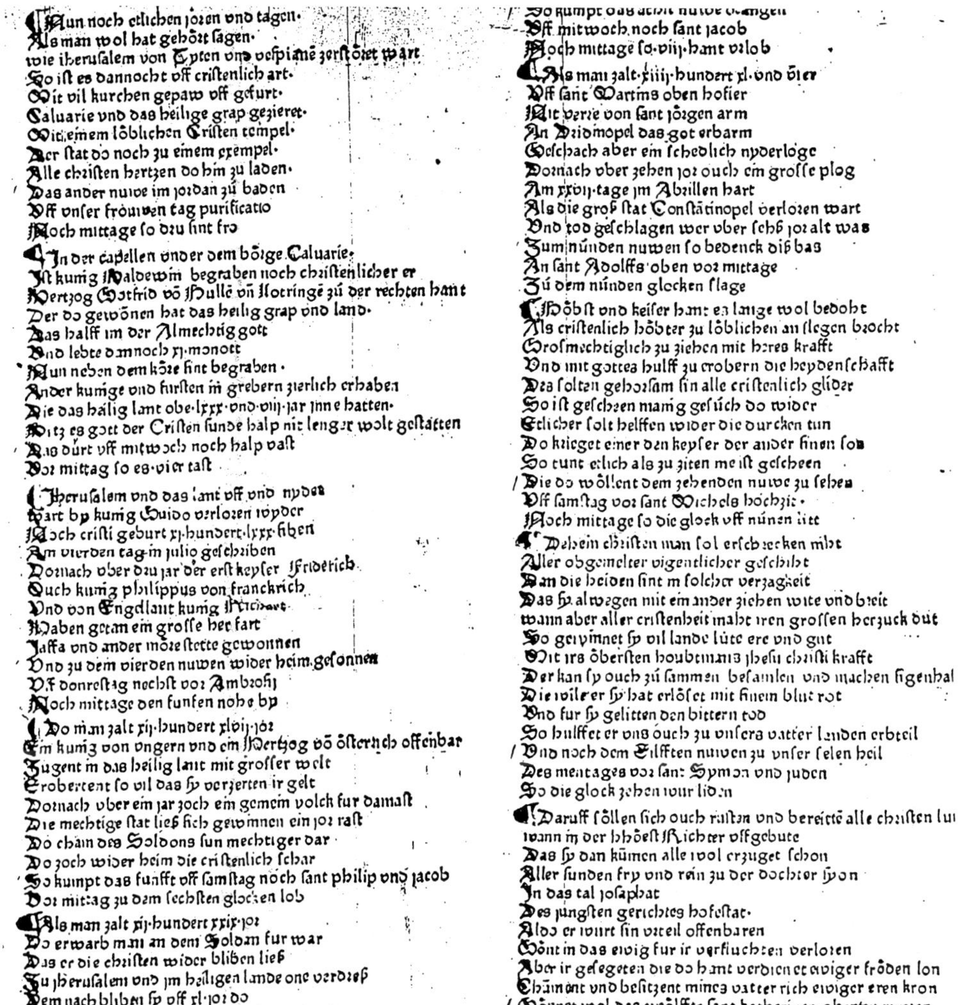
Nun noch etlichen joren vnd tagen·
Als man wol hat gehört sagen·
wie iherusalem von Tyten vnd vespiane zerstöret wart
So ist es dannocht vff cristenlich art·
Mit vil kurchen gepaw vff gefurt·
Caluarie vnd das heilige grap geziert·
Mit einem löblichen Cristen tempel·
Der stat do noch zu einem exempel·
Alle christen hertzen do hin zu laden·
Das ander nuwe im jordan zu baden
Vff vnser frouwen tag purificatio
Noch mittage so dru sint fro

In der capellen vnder dem börge Caluarie·
Ist kunig Baldewin begraben noch christenlicher er
Hertzog Gotfrid vō Bulle vn̄ Lotringē zū der rechten hant
Der do gewonen hat das heilig grap vnd land·
Das halff im der Almechtig gott
Vnd lebte dannoch xj·monott
Nun neben dem köre sint begraben·
Ander kunige vnd fursten in grebern zierlich erhaben
Die das hälig lant obe·lxxx·vnd·viij·jar jnne hatten·
Bitz es gott der Cristen sunde halp nit lenger wolt gestatten
Das dürt vff mitwoch noch halp vast
Vor mittag so es·vier tast

Iherusalem vnd das lant vff vnd nyder
Wart by kunig Guido verloren wyder
Noch cristi geburt xj·hundert·lxxx·siben
An vierden tag in julio geschriben
Domach vber dru jar der erst keyser Friderich
Ouch kunig philippus von franckrich
Vnd von Engellant kunig Richart
Haben getan ein grosse her fart
Jaffa vnd ander mörestette gewonnen
Vnd zu dem vierden nuwen wider heim gesonnen
Vff donrestag nechst vor Ambrosij
Noch mittage den funfen nohe by

Do man zalt xij·hundert xviij·jor
Ein kunig von vngern vnd ein Hertzog vō österrich offenbar
Zugent in das heilig lant mit grosser welt
Erobertent so vil das sy verzerten ir gelt
Domach vber ein jar zoch ein gemein volck fur damast
Die mechtige stat lies sich gewinnen ein jor rast
Do cham des Soldons sun mechtiger dar
Do zoch wider heim die cristenlich schar
So kumpt das funfft vff samstag noch sant philip vnd jacob
Vor mittag zu dem sechsten glocken lob

Als man zalt xij·hundert xxix·jor
Do erwarb man an dem Soldan fur war
Das er die christen wider bliben liess
Zu jherusalem vnd jm heiligen lande one verdriess
Dem nach bliben sy vff xl·jor do
Bitz das die heiden mit jnen machten mordio
Das obe funff tusent christen dott bliben
So ist das sechste nuwe an geschriben
Dem sontage vor sant Erasmy
Noch mittage den sechsten nohe by

Noch christi geburt xij·hundert·xl·vnd viij·jor rast
Gewan kunig ludwig von Franckrich damast
Aber wie er sin selbs hatt gepflegen
Er ist do by vom Soldon nider gelegen
Vnd ist darnach chein christenlich volck gon jherusalem kume
Dan in Bilgerins wise mit cleinem sumen
Das heilige grap vnd lant zu gesehen
In gleit vnd in liden vil gesmechen
Vmb gelt noch der heiden willen

So kumpt das achte nuwe ...
Vff mitwoch noch sant jacob
Noch mittage so·viij·hant vrlob
Als man zalt·xiiij·hundert xl·vnd vier
Vff sant Martins oben hofier
Mit verre von sant jörgen arm
An Dridinopel das got erbarm
Geschach aber ein schedlich nyderlöge
Domach vber zehen jor ouch ein grosse plog
Am xxvij·tage jm Abrillen hart
Als die gros stat Constātinopel verloren wart
Vnd tod geschlagen wer vber sechs jor alt was
Zum nünden nuwen so bedenck dis bas
An sant Adolffs oben vor mittage
Zu dem nünden glocken slage

Römsch vnd keiser hant es lange wol bedoht
Als cristenlich höbter zu löblichen an siegen brocht
Grosmechtiglich zu ziehen mit heres krafft
Vnd mit gottes hulff zu erobern die heydenschafft
Des solten gehorsam sin alle cristenlich glider
So ist geschehen manig gesüch do wider
Etlicher solt helffen wider die durcken tun
Do krieget einer den keyser der ander sinen son
So tunt etlich als zu ziten me ist geschehen
Die do wöllent dem zehenden nuwe zu sehen
Vff samstag vor sant Michels hochzit·
Noch mittage so die glock vff nünen lite

Dehein christen man sol erschrecken nit
Aller obgemelter eigentlicher geschiht
Wan die heiden sint in solcher verzagkeit
Das sy alwegen mit ein ander ziehen wite vnd breit
wann aber aller cristenheit inalre iren grossen herzuck dut
So gewinnet sy vil lande lüte ere vnd gut
Mit irs öbersten houbtmans jhesu christi krafft
Der kan sy ouch zu sammen besamlen vnd machen eigenhaf
Die wile er sy hat erlöset mit sinem blut rot
Vnd fur sy gelitten den bittern tod
So hulffet er vns ouch zu vnsera vatter landen erbteil
Vnd noch dem Eilfften nuwen zu vnser selen heil
Des mentages vor sant Symon vnd juden
So die glock zehen wur liden

Daruff söllen sich ouch rüsten vnd bereiten alle christen lu
wann in der höchsten Richter vffgebute
Das sy dan kümen alle wol erzuget schon
Aller sunden fry vnd rein zu der dochter syon
In das tal josaphat
Des jungsten gerichtes hofestat·
Aldo er wurt sin vrteil offenbaren
Gönt in das ewig fur ir verfluchten verloren
Aber ir gesegeten die do hant verdienet ewiger fröden lon
Enphönt vnd besitzent mines vatter rich ewiger eren kron
Gönnet wol das zwölffte sant katherinen oben zu xj·oren
Noch mittag frölich on alles truren

Das helff vns die kunnigin aller barmhertzkeit
Ir kunnigklich erbermde begnode vns wite vnd breit
Vnd erwerbe das vff aller erden kreis
Einhellig werde lobelich gesungen Cristeleis
Vnd das salue Regina jr zu hoher ere
Vnd das alle menschen leben noch euangelischer leré
Die vs jrs suns munde sint geflossen·
Der sin heliges blut vmb menschlich hat vergossen·
Der helff vns ouch allen zu ewiger selikeit
Amen sy vns von dem drizehen nuwen geseit
Vff den heligen Crist abent vor mittage
Balde noch dem Eilfften slage·

Fig. 4. *Poetischer Neumondkalender für das Jahr 1478*. [Strasbourg: Heinrich Eggestein]. *GW* 1330. (Berlin, Staatsbibliothek zu Berlin – Preußischer Kulturbesitz.)

craftsmen, peasants, academics, learned and lay people of every description, even illiterates who could only look at the pictures and had the texts explained to them by someone who could read. On the other hand, and this is quite intriguing, little has been done, at least to my knowledge, to collect information about actual readers of broadsides by looking at the provenance of extant copies or at related documents.[35] In short, evidence is scarce while speculation and hypotheses are abundant.

Although Brant's *Fulgetra* broadside was very successful, with at least one official reprint and two pirated editions published within a short span of time, there is no information whatsoever about the actual print run of this or any other of his single-leaf editions. The same is true for Celtis, Locher, Ulsenius, and other humanists as well as popular authors of the fifteenth century like Hans Folz, Jörg Preining, and others, who produced broadsides. It has been claimed that the various *Fulgetra* editions were disseminated in two thousand to four thousand copies,[36] but for all we know the print-run might have been considerably higher or dramatically lower, so any other guess is as good as this. Given the fact that almost all available data on print runs of broadsides are related to non-literary texts such as indulgences and official proclamations, and considering that these data are quite inconsistent, no estimate or projection can claim to offer reliable insight.[37] Furthermore, even if figures were known, they would not tell us much about any item's actual audience, but by late medieval standards the illustrated broadside by no means qualifies as a medium of mass communication.[38] Distribution of prints in huge quantities is known from indulgence campaigns only: in 1480, Johannes Bämler delivered about 10,000 copies of various imprints for an indulgence to the city of Nördlingen, and Jodokus Pflanzmann, also of Augsburg, added 20,000 'confessionals' for the same purpose; a preacher travelling from Lübeck to Scandinavia brought with him 20,000 'formae absolutionis' in 1489, and in the following year 50,000 of these forms were sold within seven months in the Austrian monastery of Vorau; a Franciscan commissioned 10,000 letters of indulgence in Seville in 1493, along with 50,000 'verónicas' on parchment; and finally, Johann Luschner of Barcelona produced some 200,000 printed indulgences for the indulgence campaign of the monastery of Montserrat in 1499.[39]

There are, however, two means of obtaining information about the recipients of broadsides. We can check secondary sources for comments on broadsides, and we can also turn our attention to surviving copies of the broadsides themselves.

Correspondence, for example, can be a valuable source. On 4 January 1496, in Speyer, Jakob Wimpfeling wrote a letter to Konrad Celtis complaining that he was unable to get hold of a copy of Brant's poem on the alliance between Maximilian and pope Alexander VI; the text in question must have been *De Alexandri VI confoederatione cum Maximiliano facta congratulatio*, published after 1 April 1495.[40] Wimpfeling states that he left the poem behind when he moved from Strasbourg to Speyer, and he describes the town as a bad place for books and erudition, clerics leading dissipated lives and being intellectually uninterested. Enclosed, he continues, Celtis would find a copy of Brant's poem on the miracle birth, mentioning that Brant himself had sent this *charta* to Speyer from Basel.[41]

Wimpfeling also owned a manuscript copy of the Latin text on the Siamese twins, preserved in the 'Wimpfeling codex', a private archive of this famous humanist, now in Uppsala University Library.[42] Other manuscript copies of Brant's 1495 poem, taken

Von einer wunderbarn geburt bey Worms in einem dorff birster geuant. Jm ia
vö Christ geburt.M.CCCC.vi wdin dē rcu.An dē ädern tag des wintermöds

SO laszen wir die alten m ere stä
sint ein mal wir newe selbs han
Do kei.er otto ein keiser was
ein frau ein zwistirnigs kint genas
vö keiser otto als er dz reich zespalt
wart er abe von dem reich gezale
Sint ein mal auf dyse stund.
t wenig frde m a.   sechs bundt
Am iügstē der kung vö frackrich.
zu romedg herzogē berif zu   urch
Auf das er machte ewigen   fride.
zwischen allen des reichs gelide
Czum ersten macht er steren ras
den fursten und des reiches last.
Und wie dz rich an uritschaft were
ti he er scharf auf mein ere
Dye fursten dauchte solch ordē ue.
der kunig trugs auch ein hoe mut
Aber leider do beschossen ware d rot.
hat grosses zeichen gesendet got
wan nahet bey worms sind gebon
zwey kint mit einer stirne voru
Sy haben alle glide recht.
wie es ist in menschliche geschlecht
Hund oben an der styrne stande.
gen die haubt gar fast bey ander.
wie wol sy haben zwen leibe.
muszen doch ä einem haubt beleibe

Ich gelaub got vö himelreich hoch
hab es gethan durch vor bedacht.
Das auf zweyen leibn ein haubt
sich wunderbar do hat erzeigt.
An zweifel es zeichet einigkeit.
des babsts kunigs und cristēheit
Bedeut auch en alle zwang.
erlosung es durche krichner land.
Ich freu mich vms d cristēheit wille
des babsts vö kunigs vö edler hildu
Das sy got erweler hat
unter in solche guttat erst an gat
Ich hoff got in hellem trone
mach dy werlt im untertane.
Gleich dy kint mit einer sterne
zweyē leibē dyenē gerne
will auch vermeine ritter vö baure
und alle dy des reichs ere laure.
Ich hoff in volgē stet und lande
den die zwunder wirt bekant
Vū ob sy funde ungehorsam gelied.
das dem haube nicht hilff ethede
Schnitē fleissig vū wurffen das abe
das es ewige bein trage
Unter des erentreicher kuig werd
must du lebē als läg nestor ungesern
An einē rat vnd milte iar
verging dy cristēheit gätz vn gar.

Gedruckt in dem iare nach Christi geburdt.M.CCCC.
in dem rcvi Am dinstag nerhst Narh Letare.

Fig. 5. *Von einer wunderbarn geburt bey Worms.* [Erfurt: Printer of Hundorn], 15 March 1496.
GW 5709. (Munich, Bayerische Staatsbibliothek.)

either from the broadside or the booklet edition,[43] are preserved in manuscripts in Munich, Augsburg, and Strasbourg.[44] Around 1500, Hieronymus Streitel, an Augustinian hermit who collected contemporary documents of historical interest along with other material, owned the *Hymnus de sancto Ivone* broadside[45] as well as manuscripts of the *Deformed sow of Landser* and the Worms poem (in German), both decorated with woodcuts which had been cut out of prints.[46] Another Streitel manuscript contains a version of the Gugenheim monster poem.[47] It is intriguing to see these broadside texts circulating widely – in manuscript form. Considering Wimpfeling's complaints about the lack of broadsides in Speyer, one might find that the printed matter in question was not as widespread and readily available as is often assumed, but had to be circulated amongst interested recipients who had to copy the texts if they wanted them to be available for further use.

As for the surviving copies of humanists' broadsides, apart from Wimpfeling, Celtis, and Streitel, only a few other contemporary owners are known. In 1511, the Augustinian hermits of Ramsau in Bavaria owned one of the *Fulgetra* copies; Hartmann Schedel, the famous composer of the 1493 *Chronicle*, like Streitel an assiduous and dedicated collector of illustrated prints and related matter, owned the Latin *Sow of Landser* along with a copy of the Celtis broadside *In vitam divi Sebaldi carmen* and a lot of other single-sheet material.[48] Another famous humanist, Konrad Peutinger of Augsburg, owned copies of Brant's *Congratulatio* and *De pestilentiali scorra*, and a unique *Carmen theologicum ad Johannem Geiler de Kaisersberg* by Johannes Reuchlin, printed by Martin Schott in Strasbourg, c. 1495-9, all of which were pasted down in the covers of editions of Italian juridical texts from his library.[49] Humanist broadsides are often found as paste-downs in book bindings, but the careful way this was done and the state of preservation indicate that they were not used as binder's waste. Their primary purpose was either to function as decorative (or entertaining) elements within the books, or else they were attached to the bindings to prevent their loss. Quite often, as in Peutinger's case, the carrier volumes contain legal works, indicating a university or at any rate an educated background even where we do not know the names of their owners.

Considering these data and leaving aside the argument of chance, we can assume that the main recipients of early illustrated broadsides produced by Sebastian Brant and others were humanist friends and colleagues of the authors and thus members of the already mentioned erudite in-groups, not primarily vast anonymous audiences.[50] As of now, there is little proof that before the Reformation illustrated broadsides were produced in large numbers. Most of the recipients we know of were humanists themselves. Wimpfeling, Celtis, Schedel, Peutinger, and others from this circle were regular recipients of Brant broadsides; many of them were certainly included in Brant's distribution network, perhaps comparable to today's mailing lists for offprints. A second group of readers consisted of people like Hieronymus Streitel who compiled contemporary news and stories for documentary purposes, or who were simply curious. Thus, the illustrated broadside as generated by humanists in the late fifteenth century was not primarily a popular or folkloristic medium even in German, let alone in Latin. It was rather a means of communication circulating within, and probably largely restricted to, certain elites.[51] It may be noted that, although many of the broadsides themselves were addressed to high-ranking personalities, members of the court or the king himself, nothing seems to be known about the reception of the broadsides within these circles.

Nonetheless, this medium of elite culture did come to be transformed into a medium of 'popular' culture. Again, there are no data concerning quantity to illustrate that point; it would seem that the popular 'Flugblatt', not unlike the earliest illustrated broadsides of the 1470s and 1480s, had a rather slow start. At least during the incunable period and following Brant's landmark editions, only a small number of illustrated single-leaf prints qualify as 'popular' in terms of their language, their style and their arrangement of words and images, 'popular' here basically meaning 'simpler' than their humanist forerunners.[52] Apart from Brant's publications, for example, three other broadsides dealing with the Worms miracle birth of 1495 came out soon after the event, all in the vernacular: two Erfurt editions, one by an anonymous printer and one by Hans Sporer, and a Strasbourg edition by Johannes Prüss, who had also reprinted Brant's *Donnerstein*.[53] The only copy of the Prüss edition, a fragment of eleven lines with an illustration, is lost. From the few incoherent quotes available through the entry in *GW* 10579 it is evident, though, that it dealt with the matter in an interesting way: line [1]: [...] 'wie das hie gemollet ist Horch zů jung vnd alt/ wier stón all in gottes gewalt ...' line [4]: '... wer daß kint ye hat gesehen/ by wurmß am ryn geboren ...' line [10]: '... die der beůcher sient gelert. den [...]en leyen nit zů gehórt. AMEN.' The beginning (or heading) refers to the illustration ('wie das hie gemollet ist'), line [4] indicates the subject of the publication, and the concluding couplet hints towards a differentiation between learned and lay audiences, using a literary topos of restricted information for the *simplices*. The phrase might have read: 'We leave the interpretation of this prodigy to the experts, because it is not appropriate for lay people to learn more and speculate about such things' – a rather crude opposition which certainly did not meet Brant's intentions. Unfortunately, nothing more is known about this edition's intention or impact. Sporer's version is preserved in one complete copy, but nevertheless consists of only nine lines and a woodcut.[54] Its main characteristic is the use of a large-scale title type, Sporer's typeface 2:168G, and as far as we know, it is the only broadside ever published by this itinerant printer, a fact which may indicate that this project failed economically.[55] The anonymous Erfurt edition of 15 March 1496, some six months after the event, offers an extraordinarily downgraded, even faulty narration of the miracle birth and its implications (Fig. 5).[56] Clearly making use of one of Brant's Latin texts, the printer not only simplified the sophisticated original layout quite drastically; the text was also changed in a way that can only be described as bizarre, moving the Worms Diet to Rome and transforming Maximilian, Brant's original addressee, into the king of France, of all people. Prodigies were also used as sermon material, and in at least one case we know that a preacher used illustrated broadsides (or at least, closely related printed matter) for this purpose. The Augustinian Canon Balthasar Boehm (d. 1530) noted in his 'Sermones de tempore' manuscript that a 'nuncius' had come to Nürnberg, reporting the appearance of crosses the colour of blood in the skies over Maastricht and the Limburg countryside on 23 May and again on 10 August 1501: 'nuncius testisque pervenit ad Nürbergam portans secum huiusmodi figuras ... "hec omnia scripta et depicta venerunt ad nos in hanc inpressa" ... Czu wissen aller mennichlich daß dyse figur plutfarb von himel gefallen'.[57]

IV

Although the example of the Worms prodigy shows some interaction between humanist discourse and more 'popular' presentations, it is evident that the latter lacked the erudition and political impetus typical of Brant's broadsides. Thus, the follow-up publications on the 1495 miracle birth indicate that the 'Flugblatt' was about to become a popular medium some time after its invention. Still, caution is called for. Relatively little is known about the development of the illustrated broadside in the first two decades of the sixteenth century, the immediate pre-Reformation period. This knowledge gap clearly reflects the traditional boundaries of academic disciplines and the established focal points of scholarly interest, for neither incunabulists nor historians of early modern history, theology, and literature have paid much attention to what could be called a cultural and typographic interregnum between the end of the incunable period and the beginning of the Reformation.[58] Only the vast number of similar prints on all kinds of matters from about 1520 onwards is sufficient proof that humanists had ignited a development with (now obvious) far-reaching cultural consequences. Technical means as well as skills of woodcutters and printers (though not necessarily the skills of the authors) improved significantly in the following decades, and the implications of the medium changed dramatically in the course of the Reformation. The basic rules of layout, textual presentation, and subtextual purposes of broadsides as developed by Brant, however, remained the same for centuries to come. If we accept the evidence of chronology, we must assume that it was Sebastian Brant who triggered this highly momentous innovation of late medieval and early modern communication.

Brant and others who published illustrated broadsides from the 1490s onward introduced an innovative mixture into public communication by combining political discourse and elements of popular culture, thus reorganizing the medium of the illustrated broadside according to their specific aims and purposes. It is obvious that the broadside as a medium of communication represents an important link between medieval and early modern culture. However, during the fifteenth century broadsides in general were basically a means of traditional communication. In the first fifty years of printing, a vast number of well-established text types – such as indulgences, calendars, and charters, to name the most important ones – dominated the output of broadsides from presses in Germany and elsewhere. The illustrated humanist broadside represented a late and somewhat isolated tendency within the overall framework of the 'Einblattdruck' genre. From the incunabulist's point of view, the question whether the printing press was an agent of change, as Elizabeth Eisenstein saw it, and whether this is true for all the various and divergent sorts of texts that were produced and reproduced in its initial phase, is still subject to discussion. Unfortunately Eisenstein's arguments as well as results achieved by other scholars are these days often reduced to catchy slogans. One concept dominating today's discussion is the so-called 'media revolution' which is presumed to have immediately followed Gutenberg's invention. Having taken a closer look at the development of printing in the first five decades after Gutenberg, however, one must come to the conclusion that it was certainly not a 'revolution' which took place.[59] The average output of early presses shows neither a rapid nor a continuous development from 'old' to 'new' which would justify such sweeping statements. Every single text, and even more the various genres, one of them being the illustrated broadside, must be considered with regard to their respective traditions, origins, developments, and consequences. A central problem is to assess whether traditional or innovative aspects dominated; the problem remains unsolved, given the fact that we are dealing with about thirty thousand incunable editions existing in hundreds of thousands of copies, a very small number of which have been researched comprehensively. Nonetheless, more often than not the invention of the press is judged globally as the one and only decisive factor of innovation, as the single outstanding achievement dividing medieval from modern culture. But even an innovative medium like the illustrated broadside, which brought about considerable communicative changes, needed time to unfold and is unthinkable without an ingenious mind like Sebastian Brant's. Unlike the 'Donnerstein' of Ensisheim, the innovations of the printing press did not fall from heaven, nor did its products always cause big bangs.

APPENDIX A: ILLUSTRATED BROADSIDES BY HUMANISTS

Sebastian Brant

1   *The Ensisheim meteorite*, Latin and German texts on one sheet, after 7 Nov. 1492. [Basel: Michael Furter for] J[ohannes] B[ergmann], 2 editions (*GW* 5023, 5020); pirate editions: [Reutlingen] Michael Greyff (*GW* 5021), and [Strasbourg] Johannes Prüss (*GW* 5022)

2   *The Battle of Salins*, German. [Basel: Furter for] J. B[ergmann], after 17 Jan. 1493 (*GW* 5024)

3   *Ad divum Sebastianum martyrem*, Latin. [Basel:] J. B[ergmann], 1494 (not in *GW*)[60]

4   *Vita sancti Onophrii* and *De variis heremi cultoribus*, Latin. [Basel:] J. B[ergmann], 1494 (*GW* 5026)

5   *Hymnus de sancto Ivone*, Latin. [Basel: Johannes Amerbach, *c*.1494] (*GW* 5025)

6   *De Alexandri VI confoederatione cum Maximiliano facta congratulatio*, Latin. [Basel:] J. B[ergmann, after 1 April 1495] (*GW* 5027)

7   *Birth of a deformed child at Worms*, after 10 Sept. 1495. Editions: [Augsburg: Johannes Schönsperger], German (*GW* 5029), [Basel: Bergmann], Latin (not in *GW*); German and Latin texts also published as booklets

8   *De inundatione Thybridis*, Latin. [Basel:] J. B[ergmann, after 4 Dec.] 1495 (*GW* 5033)

9   *The deformed sow of Landser*. German and Latin editions, both [Basel: Bergmann] after 1 Mar. 1496] (*GW* 5034, 5035)

10   *Birth of a two-headed goose and a deformed sow at Gugenheim in Alsace etc.* German and Latin editions, both [Basel: Bergmann, April or May 1496] (*GW* 5036, 5037)

11   *De pestilentiali scorra*, Latin. [Basel: Bergmann, before 18 Oct 1496] (*GW* 5038)

12   *The Foxhunt*, German. [Basel:] Bergmann, 1497 (*GW* 5039)

13   *Pacis in Germanicum Martem naenia Martisque contra pacem defensio*. Latin: [Basel:] Bergmann, 1499 (*GW* 5040) and [Strasbourg: Bartholomäus Kistler, *c*.1499/1500]; German: [Basel:] Bergmann, 1499

Others[61]

Konrad Celtis
14   *In vitam divi Sebaldi Carmen*. Two editions, both: [Basel, J. Bergmann, *c*.1493-1495] (*GW* 6464 and a variant)

15 *Ad divam dei genitricem sublevatis aegritudinibus gratiarum actio.* [Vienna: Johannes Winterburg, 1498] (GW 6462)

Leonhard Clement
16 *Elegia ob victoriam Turci.* Two editions: [Strasbourg: Matthias Hüpfuff, before 1 Sept. 1498] (*Einbl.* 849) and [Strasbourg: Johannes Grüninger, c. 1500-1506] (unrecorded)

Jakob Locher
17 *Carmen 'In faciem Aquilae et laudem Maximiliani romanorum regis'.* [Strasbourg: Grüninger, c. 1497] (ISTC il00260000)
18 *De monstruoso puero nato in oppido Rhayn.* [Basel:] Bergmann, after 17 Nov. 1499 (ISTC il00258500)

Johannes Panecianus
19 *Ode ad divum Leopoldum.* Vienna: Jo[hannes] W[interburg, c. 1500] (*Einbl.* 1074)

Johannes Reuchlin
20 *Carmen theologicum ad Johannem Geiler de Kaisersberg.* [Strasbourg: Martin Schott, c. 1495-99] (ISTC ir00153300)

Theodoricus Ulsenius
21 *In epidemicam scabiem vaticinium.* Two editions: Nuremberg [Hans Mair], 1 Aug. 1496, and [Augsburg: Johannes Froschauer c. 1498] (*Einbl.* 1467, 1466)
22 *Speculator consiliorum.* [Nuremberg: Kaspar Hochfeder or Georg Stuchs, c. 1497] (*Einbl.* 1394)

APPENDIX B: NON-HUMANIST ILLUSTRATED BROADSIDES, c. 1472-1492 [62]

1 *Advice against the Black Death*, German verse. Two editions, both: [Augsburg: Günther Zainer, c. 1472] (*Einbl.* 1180, 1181)
2 *The evil woman fighting the devils*, German verse. [Augsburg: Zainer, c. 1473] (*Einbl.* 709)
3 *Syben tagzeit unser frowen*, German religious poem. [Augsburg: Zainer, c. 1475] (ISTC im00269000). The same woodcut in Latin editions of Enea Silvio Piccolomini, *Carmen sapphicum de passione Christi*, c. 1477 (Zainer, unrecorded), and *Passionis Jesu Christi via contemplationis est quadruplex*, [Augsburg: Ludwig Hohenwan[g], and [Johannes Blaubirer, c. 1481-6] (*Einbl.* 1485, 1486)
4 *Ten Commandments*, German. [Basel? unidentified printer, c. 1475] (GW 10576)
5 *Zwölf Früchte des Holzes des Lebens*, German. [Augsburg: Zainer, c. 1475] (GW 10414)
6 *Secunda aetas mundi*, Latin. [Nuremberg: Anton Koberger, c. 1475] (GW 446/10)
7 Johannes Tiberinus, *Epitaphium gloriosi pueri Simonis Tridentini novi martyris*, Latin verse. [Trent: Albrecht Kunne, c. 1476] (unrecorded)
8 Sixtus IV, *Indulgence for St Odilienberg*, Latin. [Strasbourg: Heinrich Eggestein, 1480] (*Einbl.* 1340)
9 *Pater noster, Ave Maria, Credo*, German. [Nuremberg:] Friedrich Creussner [c. 1480] (*Einbl.* 1473)
10 *Prayers to Saints*, various editions in Latin and German, beginning around 1480 in Basel and Ulm, e.g. *Salve sancta facies*, Latin [Ulm: Johannes Zainer d. Ä., c. 1482] and German [Ulm: Konrad Dinckmut, c. 1482] (*Einbl.* 1287 and 643)

11   *Figura exprimens mysterium eucharistiae*, Latin. [Augsburg: Johannes Blaubirer, *c.* 1481-6] (*GW* 9892)[63]

12   *Zeichen der falschen Gulden* ('How to recognise false coins'), German. Eleven editions (*Einbl.* 1562-1569a and some unrecorded prints, mostly from Swabia or Bavaria, 1482 and slightly later)

13   *Advice against the Black Death*, German verse. [Reutlingen: Michael Greyff, *c.* 1482] (*Einbl.* 1520)

14   *Temptationes daemonis temptantis hominem de septem peccatis mortalibus*, Latin. [Strasbourg: Printer of the Breviarium Ratisponense, *c.* 1482] (*Einbl.* 1454)

15   *O mors quam amara est memoria tua*, Latin. [Memmingen: Albrecht Kunne, *c.* 1483] (*Einbl.* 1020)

16   *Relics of the church of Waver*, Dutch. [Southern Netherlands: unidentified printer, *c.* 1483] (*ISTC* ih00009800)

17   Hieronymus, *Narratio vitae quam tenuit in eremo*, Latin. Two editions: [Basel: Martin Flach, *c.* 1485] and [Memmingen: Kunne, not before 1486] (*Einbl.* 688, 689)

18   *Valver van der munte* (coin regulations), Dutch. [Leuven: Ludwig Ravescot, 1487] (*ISTC* iv00090260)

19   *Gemein Nutz* ('The common good'), German. Memmingen: Kunne, 1487 (*Einbl.* 1045)

20   *Benedicite and Gratias*, German prayers. Nuremberg: Hans Hoffmann, 1490 (*GW* 3813)

21   Hans Folz, *Branntweinbüchlein* and *Die Rechnung Ruprecht Kolbergers* (two editions), German verse (*GW* 10121, 10150, 10151); Folz?, *Verkundung des engelischen Grußes* (Ave Maria explanation in German verse; *Einbl.* 1477). All: [Nuremberg: Printer of Rechnung Kolbergers, *c.* 1491][64]

22   *Arbor vitae with prophecies from the Old Testament about the crucifixion*, Latin. Ulm: Johannes Reger, 1492 (*GW* 2314)

23   *Rosary contemplations*, German. [Nuremberg: Anton Koberger], 1492 (*GW* 4187)

LIBRI IMPRESSI BIBLIOTHECAE MONASTERII SANCTI EMMERAMMI

THE INCUNABLE COLLECTION OF ST EMMERAM, REGENSBURG, AND ITS CATALOGUE OF 1501

BETTINA WAGNER

IN THE MID-FIFTEENTH CENTURY, even a widely travelled humanist like Aeneas Sylvius Piccolomini showed himself considerably impressed with the attractions of the city of Regensburg, where he had stayed during the diet against the Turks in 1454:

In Boiaria vix opidum reperias cuius munditias non magnopere admirere Saltzburga ... Maior tamen ea est Ratispona, beatissimi apostoli Petri delubro et ponte, quo Danubius transmittitur, lapideo, et pluribus sanctorum ecclesiis, memoranda: Atque in primis Sancti Emmerami monasterio, in quo Leo Pontifex Maximus beatum Dionisium ex Parisiis pro furto deductum iacere effirmat.[1]

Among the three sites of interest mentioned by Aeneas Sylvius, the monastery takes pride of place. It surpasses even the venerable cathedral church of St Peter, probably the most important example of Gothic architecture in southern Germany, which had been covered only a decade before with new roofs and had thus become usable,[2] and the twelfth-century stone bridge, for a long time the only crossing-point of the Danube between Ulm and Vienna.[3] Even though the city was already on the edge of economic and political decline when Aeneas Sylvius visited, the monastery still vigorously claimed international importance. Way back in the eleventh century, this ambition had become embodied in the relics of St Denis, said to have been furtively abducted from his resting-place near Paris and transferred to Regensburg, where they were rediscovered in 1052 by Pope Leo IX.[4] This legend, clearly familiar to Leo's successor-to-be, served the double purpose of marketing the monastery of St Emmeram as the German counterpart to St Denis near Paris and thus demonstrating its spiritual eminence, and of putting the royal city of Regensburg on a par with the political centre of France herself. The story persisted in local historiography well beyond the end of the Middle Ages: as late as 1750, one of the last abbots, Johann Baptist Kraus, attempted to prove the relics genuine.[5]

From the early Middle Ages,[6] Regensburg had been the intellectual centre of the east Franconian Carolingians (notably of emperor Arnulf of Carinthia) as well as the main settlement of the Duchy of Bavaria (Stammesherzogtum Bayern). In the high Middle Ages, it acquired the epithet of *urbs populosissima*, being inhabited by about fifteen thousand people from various nations who benefitted from the free city's exemption from taxes and other services to the Empire and from its excellent trade connections to Italy. By the fifteenth century, however, this precarious balance between various interest groups had become unstable. The emperor made growing financial demands on the city because of its exposed geographical location as an outpost against threats posed by Hussites and Turks. The Bavarian dukes of Wittelsbach endeavoured to make use of the city as a stronghold in their competition with the Habsburgs and thus tried to break the city's independence through economic repression. In addition, Augsburg and Nuremberg grew to become strong competitors with a better position both for the production and for the distribution of goods. The fifteenth century was thus a crucial period in the history of the city: its relations to the Duchy of Bavaria and the Empire were shaped then, a development which culminated in 1492, when its status as imperial city was reaffirmed, albeit on much worse terms than before.

Around 1500, Regensburg was rich not only in craftsmen and tradesmen, but also in clerics. 230 secular clerics, 66 monks, and 85 nuns lived in the city just before it turned protestant;[7] they constituted about three per cent of the total population. St Emmeram was not the only Benedictine house in the city,[8] but the oldest, and indeed one of the oldest in southern Germany, deservedly referred to as *terra Benedictina*. The presence of the order in an urban centre and centre of secular power meant that it could draw on generous endowments and maintain a high level of intellectual and cultural life. Its history of almost eleven hundred years had begun with the burial of the bishop and martyr St Emmeram in Regensburg in the seventh century and the foundation of the diocese by Boniface in 739; for the first 250 years of its existence, the monastery was headed by abbot-bishops after the Anglo-Saxon model and functioned as a cathedral monastery. Its intellectual activities are reflected in the existence of a scriptorium, continuously attested since the ninth century, and by the scholarly and literary achievements of several monks, especially in the eleventh century, when the monk Arnold compiled a life of St Emmeram and a history of the Regensburg monastery,[9] the astronomer Wilhelm, later abbot of Hirsau, created an astrolabe and defended natural science,[10] and the author and calligrapher Otloh wrote his partly autobiographical *Liber de temptatione cuiusdam monachi*.[11]

From early on, the academic centre of the monastery was its library,[12] which was first referred to in 879 and may have been housed in a separate room already under abbot Wolfgang in the tenth century;[13] it probably remained the only academic library in Regensburg for the next 200 years. The richness of its holdings is testified not only by outstanding treasures like the famous Codex aureus[14] and the only surviving copy of the plays of the nun Hrotsvit von Gandersheim,[15] but also by the surviving catalogues[16] which attempted to organize the collection and make it accessible.

The earliest catalogue was compiled before 993 under abbot Ramwold (975-1000).[17] At that time the library already contained 513 books; 80 more were added in the first decades of the eleventh century.[18] Only a small proportion of them was produced in the scriptorium of St Emmeram; some of the oldest manuscripts had been imported from Britain, others from France (like the Codex aureus) or Italy or from German monasteries like Fulda and Benediktbeuern. Acquisitions were determined not only by liturgical needs and theological interests – the library also boasted numerous classical texts: works by Aristotle, Cicero, Cato, and Seneca, a commentary on Vergil, as well as

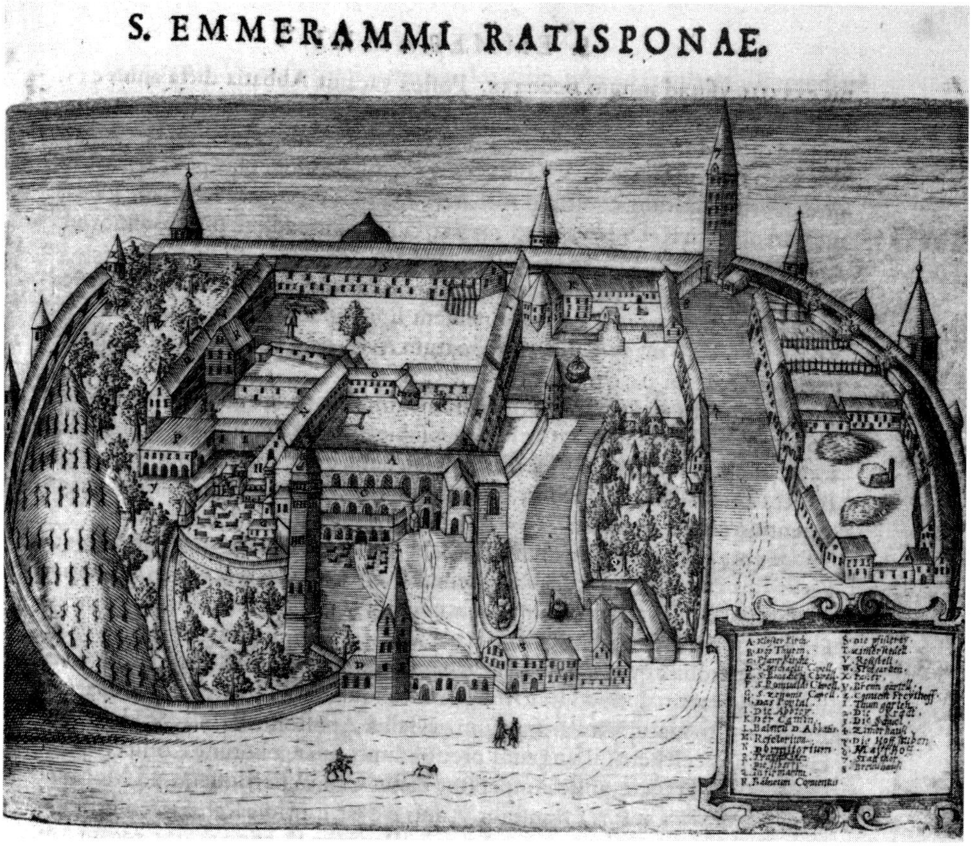

Fig. 1. The medieval buildings of St Emmeram, Regensburg, as depicted in Carl Stengel's *Monasteriologia in qua insignium aliquot monasteriorum familiae S. Benedicti in Germania, origines, fundatores, clarique viri ex eis oriundi describuntur eorundem idaeae aeri incisae oculis subijciuntur.* Augsburg, 1619. The library building is on the far left, marked with the letter P. (Munich, BSB, 2 H.mon. 15 d/Beibd.1-1)

more recent authors like Walahfrid and Alcuin.[19] Of the manuscripts listed in the first catalogue, about a hundred survive.

After the monastery had become immediately subject to the Emperor ('reichsunmittelbar') in 1295 and exempt from the bishop's influence in 1326, the collection of books increased considerably. This was largely the merit of abbot Albert von Schidmüln (1324-58), who not only purchased books on his journeys to France, but also had a new library building (Fig. 1) erected, as we are told in the preface to the comprehensive catalogue of 1346:[20] 'constructa est hec liberia ... ad laudem et gloriam Dei et sanctorum suorum et ad utilitatem omnium studere volencium in eadem'.[21] Following the model of the Sorbonne, the 236 volumes listed in the catalogue were kept on 32 desks, thus making Schmidmüln's library the earliest German library with this arrangement.[22] The catalogue takes up only six leaves of the manuscript[23] and is supplemented with book-lists of all the other male monasteries of Regensburg

181

(the Dominicans, Franciscans, Augustinian hermits, as well as the Benedictines from Prüfening and the Carthusians from Prüll), which brings the total of volumes described to more than 1100. The result is an early union catalogue comparable with the nearly contemporary *Registrum Anglie de libris doctorum et auctorum veterum*, which is however larger in scope and organized from the perspective of the text, not the holding institution.[24] Like the *Registrum*, the Regensburg catalogue reflects a policy of co-operation and liberal access among the libraries covered, not only for local users, but probably also for scholars from outside. Further evidence of a stimulating intellectual climate are the donations made by monks in the mid-fourteenth century; the expansion of the library was however stifled by a financial crisis and a subsequent decline in the number of monks.

Nevertheless, the collection of St Emmeram was the only one of the libraries covered by the catalogue to survive into the fifteenth century without substantial losses – even though outside users continued to be admitted and were even allowed to borrow books.[25] In 1435 Ambrogio Traversari was the first Italian humanist to visit the library and to comment on the large number of manuscripts.[26] After the monastery adopted the Kastl reform in 1452, the library grew further, partly due to the employment of professional scribes. The monastic reform involved not only the return to the strict rule and more severe administrative and financial control, but also demanded measures relating to the intellectual life: the inner and outer school for the *pueri oblati* and the city pupils[27] respectively were to be run separately, and one monk at a time should be sent to university. While the university connections of St Emmeram were comparatively short-lived[28] and never developed into a close link with an individual university, unlike the association of the Melk reform houses with the university of Vienna, several monks attended the universities of Leipzig and Ingolstadt (founded in 1472) in the incunable period: Hermann Poetzlinger gained an MA from Leipzig, where he matriculated in 1456, and later worked as teacher in the monastery school; he died in 1469, leaving a total of 110 manuscripts, some of which he had brought from Leipzig, to the convent.[29] Johannes Vogel de Ebern studied in Leipzig from 1457 to 1465;[30] Johann Tegernpeck attended the same university from 1464 onwards; he was probably the first to buy printed books for the library.[31] The lawyer Nikolaus Bernauer († 1531) had studied in Ingolstadt and became professor there in 1485, four years before joining the monastery; he predominantly collected texts related to Dionysius Areopagita.[32]

When Tegernpeck became abbot in 1471, the library was still arranged as in 1347, but the number of manuscripts had increased by about 100; the total came now close to 350 books. A new catalogue was drawn up by prior Konrad Pleystainer in 1449/52,[33] but provided insufficient space to keep track of new acquisitions made over the next thirty years,[34] a period during which the monastery started seriously purchasing printed books. At the same time, the number of scholarly visitors[35] from outside was on the increase – ranging from historians like Hartmann Schedel over theologians like Johannes Eck to philologists like Conrad Celtis – and the lack of an updated catalogue soon proved cumbersome. Improved finding aids were as necessary as were checklists for the books borrowed by users – after all, Celtis never returned the unique manuscript of the *Ligurinus* which he had obtained from the monastery of Ebrach after publication of the first edition in 1507, probably because it had been worn to pieces in the printing workshop.[36]

Consequently, Pleystainer's catalogue was abandoned, and his colleague Laurentius Aicher (prior 1482-1507) undertook the first steps towards a revision. Preservation issues seem to have been of particular concern during this period: more than 150 manuscripts from all periods and innumerable incunables were rebound in the monastery workshop,[37] and many of them were chained (Fig. 2). Aicher rearranged the books and often entered the shelf-mark and a brief summary of the contents on the front pastedown. The shelf-mark system consists of two numbers separated by a dot, the first one ranging from 1-60, the second one from 1-10 (thus allowing for a maximum of 600 volumes); they are still frequently found in the surviving books.[38] There is however no contemporary catalogue based on this system.

When the avid book-collector Erasmus Münzer (1493-1517) succeeded Tegernpeck as abbot, this situation was to be resolved.[39] The task of compiling a new catalogue was given to Aicher's assistant Dionysius Menger (prior 1507-30),[40] who chose a much more efficient approach. After taking responsibility on 20 May 1500, he had the catalogue[41] completed within a year, on 29 May 1501. The existence of two fifteenth-century inventories from St Emmeram (Pleystainer's and Menger's) illustrates how much the collection increased after the advent of printing. With its cut-off date of 1501, the scope of Menger's catalogue neatly coincides with the end of the incunable period as it is defined today; it probably constitutes one of the oldest incunable catalogues *avant la lettre*. When comparing the information provided in it to modern bibliographies and the surviving incunables,[42] the following questions ought to be considered:

Did acquisitions of printed books focus on any particular subjects? How did incunables relate to the manuscripts already in the library? Where were the editions printed? How and when were the books acquired? Who used them?

Menger's catalogue is divided into three groups of books, each of which is arranged systematically. The first part lists the *libri in pergameno* (fols 1ʳ-39ᵛ, completed on 10 April 1501), the second one manuscripts on paper (fols 48ʳ-73ʳ, completed on 31 October 1501), the final one printed books (fols 84ʳ-100ᵛ). The main section of the latter describes *libri impressi in papiro*[43] which were bound and chained and was finished on 29 May 1501. The speed at which Menger must have worked is particularly impressive, as he includes very detailed descriptions of the contents, external appearance, and sometimes provenance of a total of more than 700 volumes.[44] In the incunable section alone, 202 printed volumes are listed under the numbers A1 to L5,[45] each letter comprising 20 numbers. The numbers show no relation to Aicher's shelf-mark system; curiously, unlike those shelf-marks, they can only rarely be found in the surviving books.[46] Each volume of a multi-volume work is given a separate number,[47] but nevertheless, the number of editions is slightly higher (230) than that of volumes, as the library contained many composite volumes in which several editions were bound together, a fact noted by Menger with the recurrent phrase: 'Hec omnia in uno parvo volumine et bona impressione sed diversa sicut et materia diversa est.'[48] The reasons for assembling different editions are not always obvious: while identical size was a prerequisite, the contents do seem to have played a role,[49] as well as the place of printing (and possibly source and date of acquisition by the monastery), as is shown by items from the same press, sometimes even printed in the same year, which were bound together.[50]

Fig. 2. Lower cover of a chained binding from the St. Emmeram workshop (Kyriss 29). (Munich, BSB, 2° Inc.c.a. 638; Menger *MBK* p. 376, 7572-4)

The catalogue follows the systematic arrangement commonly used in monastic libraries, starting with editions of the Bible (including concordances and commentaries), followed by standard theological reference works like commentaries on Petrus Lombardus (A20-B7, B11-13, B17-18), works by church fathers (B19-C12), expositions of the Psalter and the New Testament (C13-C20), saints' lives (D6, D8-10), and sermons (E15-F11) – mirroring the pastoral tasks of the monks. From F12 on, numerous composite volumes without a clearly identifiable thematic aspect are listed; they combine theological treatises with school texts and carmina (F14), often by contemporary authors like Burkard von Horneck (F14), Johannes Trithemius (G8-10), and Conrad Celtis (G9). Section H contains law-books, followed by works on natural history and historiography including editions of classical authors (I11) and even translations of works by Herodotus, Plotinus, and Plato (I12, I16, I17). Apart from their translators, Lorenzo Valla and Marsilio Ficino, other Italian humanists are represented: the library contained works by Petrarch (K3) and Francescus Philelphus (K6). A philological interest in the Greek language is demonstrated by the presence of a bilingual edition of the *Erotemata* by Constantinus Lascaris (K14) as well as a Greek-Latin dictionary (K15). Very occasionally, texts in German including a German-Latin dictionary appear in the catalogue (F14, F16, K8, K20). Most German books were however intended for the use of the lay brothers and are therefore listed in the separate section *Libri Inpressi Pro Conversis in Vlgari Lingua*.[51]

While the manuscripts in the library form 'das Bild einer ordentlichen mittel-alterlichen Klosterbibliothek, an welcher die Theologie natürlich den überwiegenden Anteil hat'[52] and which had not been expanded systematically since the mid-fourteenth century, the acquisitions of printed books reflect a revival of scholarly interests which took place considerably earlier than in other Benedictine houses – even if more than half the collection falls into the categories of theology and law. A good selection of Italian and a few examples of German humanist literature were acquired to complement the source editions of classical texts, but a truly modern approach was adopted only by individual members of the convent like Erasmus Daum[53] whose collection was integrated into the library after his death in 1504.

The catalogue is outstanding not just for its scope and contents, but also for the very precise descriptions of the books given. Menger listed all the texts contained in a book, including editions bound together; often following the title-pages or tables of contents in the books themselves (cf. figs 3 and 4). Beyond this, he regularly provides more precise textual information like the number of parts and other sub-divisions and the incipit of a text, sometimes even referring to a quire signature where a text starts or an index can be found.[54]

Menger was not just a careful and systematic textual scholar, but also an apt codicologist: his descriptions of the physical appearance of the books are a unique source for the codicological terminology of the time. The size of each book (*magnus, regius, maior, mediocris, parvus, parvissimus*) is given, sometimes even its paper size: volumes in royal (large) folio are described as *in magno / bono regali papiro* (A16); the term for folio books is *arcus modus* (M15 and *MBK* p. 380, 7724-5); *textpleter* (*MBK* pp. 376-7, 7574-80) or simply *text* (L18) normally refers to quarto books; *regelpletel* to small quarto or octavo; *halbregelpletel* means small sizes. Attention is drawn to handwritten additions to printed books (K6, K10). Sometimes Menger even analyses the quire structure of manuscripts and gives a sort of collation;[55] scripts are classified by both age and legibility.[56] Similar criteria are applied to printing types: the quality of printing is described as *optima, bona, mediocris* or *parva impressio*, sometimes even as *legibilis impressio sed minus correcta*.[57] Very rarely, illustrations are mentioned: for the Gerson edition (L18-20), Menger notes the presence of the portrait of Gerson by Dürer:[58] 'unaqueque pars habet picturam sive effigiem eiusdem [Gersonis] in principio'.

Menger sometimes indicates the country of printing (*Ytalica impressione*),[59] but only in rare cases place of printing or date.[60] Of the 50 surviving editions which have so far been identified, most (36) were printed in the German-speaking area, 13 in Italy, and one in France (Lyon). Among the German editions, products of the presses at Strasbourg (10), Cologne (7), Nuremberg(5), Basel (4), Memmingen, and Leipzig (3 each) dominate; in addition, the collection contains individual incunables from Augsburg, Esslingen, Hagenau, Ingolstadt, Mainz, and Reutlingen. Among the Italian presses, Venice stands out (9 editions); one edition each was printed in Bologna, Brescia, Florence, and Treviso. This profile of less than a quarter of the collection may not be representative, as it is affected by the chance of survival,[61] but nevertheless it shows the importance of trade routes for the building of a collection; personal connections like university membership (Leipzig, Ingolstadt) and other journeys (Münzer's stay in Augsburg, see below) seem to have played a less important role.

Copy-specific information is limited to binding description and sometimes provenance information. Bindings are described in varying levels of detail.[62] About half the surviving incunable volumes still have their original bindings. Most of them (19) were bound in the monastery workshop (Kyriss 29), the rest in other Regensburg binderies,[63] in Augsburg[64] or in Leipzig.[65] The known volumes provide an insight into the precision of the catalogue descriptions. While Menger sometimes emphasizes only the quality of the binding (*bene inligato*: A16), he often also mentions the colour of the leather and the number of clasps: I8, described as *rubeo corio obducto*, was bound in red sheepskin in the monastery workshop, L18-20 in white pigskin (*albo corio obducto*), M11 (*glauco corio vitulino obducto cum fibulis*) in blind-tooled calf, with metal clasps and catches as well as (now lost) centre- and corner-pieces, but calf could also be described as *fusco corio sive glauco vitulino*.[66] The meaning of *nigro corio obducto* (K7) is not quite clear – the catalogue entry might refer to a volume now in the BSB, which is however bound in pigskin. Quarter bindings are described as *albo corio usque ad medium obducto*.[67] Occasionally, attention is drawn to volumes with particularly attractive bosses and clasps: in the case of the *vocabularius poeticus Iuniani liber magnus et Ytalicae inpressionis cum fibulis et clausuris optimis*[68] both the chain and the other metal work survive to the present day in spite of the potential danger to neighbouring volumes.

Conveniently, Menger also gives some information about the users and former owners of these books. On fol. 1ᵛ, he draws up a list of the inhabitants of the monastery in 1501 which was to be used for the annual distribution of books on Ash Wednesday. Apart from the abbot, the Christian names of 27 monks and 4 converts are given, with years of death added to some of them later.[69] This compares with a number of 12 priests and 6 *pueri* in 1452, severely reduced in 1463, when the convent was hit by the plague and 6 patres and 9 converts died within a month.[70]

The reason why Menger listed some books separately may have been that not all the books were housed in the library: six printed schoolbooks[71] were probably kept in the room used for teaching, the German books intended for lay brothers[72] possibly in some sort of common room. Furthermore, some members of the convent had personal reference collections in their cells which were integrated into the library only after their deaths. The most remarkable private collection and the first to be added to the library after Menger had completed his catalogue of printed books was the one assembled by Erasmus Daum († 1504), an admirer of Conrad Celtis: he owned just under 40 printed volumes, including post-incunables, in addition to numerous manuscripts with a strong emphasis on classical and humanist literature.[73] For some years, the numbering of the main catalogue was continued for new accessions; the last volume to be numbered is N9. N6, an edition of Boninus Mombritius's *De dominica passione*, is the first volume associated with another owner than Daum, frater Marcus Feckel, who died in 1505.[74] Frater Kilian, who may have been the convent doctor, owned a volume with several medical works, the *Summa collationum* by Johannes Gallensis and Rolewinck's *Fasciculus temporum*.[75]

Avicenna's *Canon medicinae* was given in 1508 by the local apothecary Nicolaus Vischpach in memory of his deceased wife.[76] Other donors were the priest Gabriel Stadler († 1507),[77] Conrad Leutenpeck,[78] and the monastery's *provisor* Wolfgang Doeler.[79] Frater Christophorus Hoffmann († 1534), the most talented author among the monks, inherited several books from his uncle Nicolaus Örtlein († 1498).[80] On various occasions Menger recorded books purchased by abbot Erasmus. In 1510 the abbot attended the diet at Augsburg;[81] just before Christmas 1515 he gave the convent a set of the works of Gerson together with a vellum antiphonar originally owned by the nuns from Obermünster;[82] the following year he purchased an Italian edition of the works of Raphael Volateranus and the works of Origines.[83]

The list of printed German books which were set aside for the use of the four lay brothers comprises 28 items bound in 15 volumes.[84] No places or dates of printing are given, but some texts were definitely not published before 1501, and donations were recorded until at least 1515. One of the German books (*liber depictus per totum continens primo artem memorandi 4 ewangelia. Item apokalipsis, liber genesis, ars moriendi*) is highly likely to have been a block-book, as three of the texts are known to have been printed as block-books; the *Ars memorandi quattuor evangelia* was not printed in any other form in the incunable period. The rest are predominantly biblical texts like a German bible, a plenary, and collections of legends: two editions of the German *Vitas patrum*, books about the Antichrist and St Wolfgang (bishop-saint of Regensburg), and legendary lives of Christ and Mary. Other volumes of religious content are the collection of examples published under the title *Seelen-Wurzgarten*, theological works by church fathers, Bonaventura and Geiler von Kaisersberg, monastic texts like the rule of St Benedict, the *consuetudines monialium* and the union bull of the Franciscan order issued by Pope Leo X in 1517, pastoral handbooks like a *Beichtspiegel* and another *Ars moriendi*, as well as a treatise on the joys of the chosen and the pains of the damned. More secular interests are catered for by travel books, albeit with religious motivations (in the case of handbooks for pilgrims to Trier and Jerusalem), and even by some works of more entertaining character like Aesop's fables, a *Ritterbuch*, and even the story of Melusine translated from the French version by Couldrette – hardly appropriate reading matter for monks. Practical needs are fulfilled by 'Sachliteratur' on the art of distilling and a calender. A considerable number of the books are illustrated, the presence of illustrations being sufficient to make a book useful even for the illiterate lay brothers: an illustrated manuscript which contains various Latin passions of Christ is listed in the first section of Menger's catalogue with the note: 'et hunc librum habuerunt conversi, et hoc propter picturam, cum tamen eis alias in nullo deserviat, quia omnia in Latino scripta sunt, que in eo continentur'.[85]

Most German books were given to members of the convent. The German bible[86] was given by the mother of the monk and professor Nikolaus Bernauer *ob amorem filii et utilitatem conversorum*. A copy of the German *Vitas patrum* was donated by a *matrona Walpurg nomine*, perhaps the *Leben der heiligen Altväter* which is now in the University Library of Würzburg.[87] Three editions (including Murner's *Schelmenzunfft* first printed in 1512) were bought by a new convert from Rosenheim; in 1515, Frater Dionysius gave a small book containing the legend of Wolfgang bound with the *Seelen-Wurzgarten*.

Even though books continued to be added to the library, the number of printed books acquired seems to have diminished in the sixteenth century compared with the preceding decades. Printed books did not only enter the library, but were also disposed of at a rather early stage. In some cases this may be due to the presence of duplicates which Menger noted. When listing editions of Lactantius's *Opera*, a collection comprising *De divinis institutionibus*, *De ira dei* and various *Carmina*, he remarks that one Italian edition had been bought by abbot Johannes Tegernpeck (i.e. before 1494) and another, slightly different one by his successor Erasmus Münzer.[88] It is conceivable that the greater ease with which duplicates could be identified in the new catalogue made it easier to select books to be sold and thus helped to make the library more efficient. In 1502, an incunable which had been bought by Tegernpeck in 1488 was sold by Nicolaus Bernauer to a *magister* Petrus. The volume contains the 1486 editions of the *Liber sextus Decretalium* and the Clementine Constitutions in a St Emmeram binding and is now in the BSB, having been previously owned by the monasteries of Füssen and Polling.[89]

Dionysius Menger died in 1530, and his death coincided with the end of the medieval library history of St Emmeram. While the monastery was comparatively little affected by the Reformation (and indeed later developed into a Counter-Reformation stronghold), Regensburg turned Protestant in 1542; and an inventory of church treasures had been drawn up by the Protestant city council already before that date. After being plundered by Swedish troops in 1633, the monastery flourished again in the eighteenth century, when a new library building was erected by the Asam brothers. The printed catalogue of 1748 lists 922 manuscripts, and the holdings of printed books are estimated to 20-25,000 volumes.[90] The historical collection was in the first rank among south German monastic libraries; for that reason, it was consulted by visitors like Mabillon in 1683 as well as by several monks who worked as university professors in Salzburg and Ingolstadt, and continued to grow as a modern research collection with holdings not only in the areas of archaeology, church music and pedagogy, but also sciences (meteorology and mechanics).

The dispersal of the library took place in 1811/12. Unlike the other 36 Bavarian Benedictine abbeys, St Emmeram escaped secularization in 1803. The monastery was given to the family of Thurn und Taxis as a compensation for the loss of income which they had previously obtained from the running of postal services in Germany. The family had resided in Regensburg since the mid-eighteenth century, and the Asam library offered itself as a spacious and representative replacement for their own library building, which had burnt down in 1792. There was however no great interest in the scholarly and theological reading-matter amassed by the monks of St Emmeram over a period of more than a thousand years.[91] After the monks had left, the Codex aureus and other manuscripts were brought to Munich. Today, the nearly 1100 manuscripts from St Emmeram form one of the largest collections from any individual Bavarian monastery at the BSB.[92]

The incunables were of much less interest to the Munich library, which was already inundated by large numbers of printed books acquired from monasteries dissolved a decade earlier. Therefore, only 78 incunable editions from St Emmeram are kept in the BSB today. The largest part of the collection is still kept very near their original home, in the Staatliche Bibliothek Regensburg, the successor institution of the Reichsstädtische Bibliothek (later Kreisbibliothek).[93] A considerable number of incunables must have been sold as duplicates by either library. Nearly twenty incunables with a St Emmeram provenance are to be found in the collections of the Bodleian; ten are in the British Library; four are now kept in Cambridge.[94] Not all of them can be identified with books in Menger's catalogue; only if original bindings and composite volumes have been preserved and if Menger's information on the texts matches the edition in case, a high degree of certainty can be achieved.[95]

APPENDIX

SURVIVING INCUNABLES WHICH MATCH ENTRIES
IN MENGER'S CATALOGUE

In the following list, transcriptions from Menger's catalogue are based on the relevant passages in *MBK*. Descriptions of the editions are taken from *BSB-Ink* for Munich copies, as *BSB-Ink* gives full information on the texts contained which can be matched up with Menger's information. For copies in British and other libraries, the *ISTC* entries are reproduced. Each edition is identified with a number in Hain or *GW*. References to local incunable catalogues are given after the shelf-mark; copy-specific information has been standardized and sometimes expanded by consultation of the originals.

A16, A17, A18, A19

Item doctoris irrefragabilis Anglici Alexandri de Ales ordinis minorum Parisius sepulti prima pars summe theoloice, et incipit: 'Quoniam, sicut dicit Boecius in libro de trinitate' etc., habens tabulam in principio, et est bona inpressio in magno regali papiro bene inligato. A 16. Item 2a pars summe eiusdem doctoris incipit: 'Completis tractatibus de hiis, que pertinent ad speculacionem' etc., in omnibus aliis similis priori etc. A 17. Item 3a pars summe eiusdem doctoris incipit: 'Tota Christiane fidei disciplina' etc., similis priori in omnibus aliis. A 18. Item 4ta pars summe eiusdem doctoris incipit: 'Dictum est supra de redemptore, qui est per graciam redemptor' etc., in aliis omnibus similis aliis partibus 3bus etc., et tantum pronunc de eiusdem doctoris scriptis habemus. A 19.
Identifiable with: Cambridge, UL, Inc. o. A. 7.2 [863] (Oates 997)
Alexander de Ales: Summa universae theologiae (Partes I-IV).
Nuremberg: Anton Koberger, 1481-2. 2°.
GW 871.

Binding: Bound in 4 volumes. Contemporary pigskin, vols 1, 2, and 4 bound in the workshop Kyriss 29; two metal clasps each, bosses lost; formerly chained; with shelf-mark inscription *e1*, *e2*, and *e4*. Vol. 3 bound in a different workshop.

Provenance information: Regensburg, St Emmeram, vols 1, 2, and 4 with purchase inscriptions by Erasmus Münzer. – John Emench Edward Dalberg-Acton (1834-1902). – Bought by Andrew Carnegie and given by him to John Morley (1838-1923), who presented the books to the University of Cambridge.

B8 (Figs 3 and 4)

Item libri et tractatus sancti Bonaventure quamplurimi, et primo breviloquium eiusdem sancti doctoris, et incipit: 'Flecto genua mea ad patrem' etc. Item soliloquium de 4 mentalibus exerciciis anime devote. Itinerarium mentis in Deum. Lignum vite. Utilissima epistola, que est quasi quedam regula et institucio omnium pie et spiritualiter in Christo vivere volencium et distingwitur in 2V memoralia. Libellus de reduccione arcium ad theologiam. Parvum bonum vel regimen consciencie, quod vocatur fons vite. Centiloquium. Pharetra. Tractatus de paupertate Christi contra magistrum Wilhelmum. Tractatus de V festivitatibus pueri Iesu. Epistola ad dominam Blankam reginam Hyspanie de regimine anime. Epistola ad magistrum innominatum eliminans errorem contra regulam beati Francisci. Epistola de eo, quod Christus et discipuli et apostoli incesserunt discalciati. Epistola, in qua sanctus Bonaventura minister generalis mandat, ut fratres sui ordinis caveant a frequencia discursuum, ab importunitate questuum, a sumptuositate edificiorum, librorum, vestium ac ciborum, a predicacione contra prelatos contra laycis et a litigiosa invasione sepulturarum et testamentorum. Epistola ad ministros provinciales et custodes de reformandis fratribus sui ordinis. Liber de tribus ternariis peccatorum infamibus. Tractatus de 7 gradibus contemplacionis. Viginti passus de informacione spiritualis vite ac virtute et profectu religiosorum. Sermones de X preceptis, quos sanctus Bonaventura Parisius predicavit ad clerum. Apologia pauperum adversus eorundem calumniatorem. Exposicio oracionis dominice. Oracio in vitam et merita eiusdem sancti Bonaventure per insignem iuris utriusque doctorem Octavianum de Martinis etc. Hec omnia in uno volumine mediocri ac bona inpressione, habens registrum in primo folio etc. B 8.

Identifiable with: Oxford, Bodleian Library, Auct. 4Q 3.1 (Proctor 683, Sheppard 510)

Bonaventura, S: Opuscula. Add: Octavianus de Martinis: Oratio in vitam et merita S. Bonaventurae.

Strasbourg: Martin Flach (printer of Strasbourg), 31 Oct. 1489. 2°.

GW 4647.

Binding: Contemporary calf, bound in the workshop Kyriss 29; clasps and bosses lost; formerly chained; with shelf-mark inscription *e13* and manuscript title.

Provenance information: Regensburg, St Emmeram, Benedictines. – Bought by the Bodleian Library in 1861.

B9

Item centiloquium sancti Bonaventure et incipit: 'Ecce descripsi eam tibi tripliciter' etc., et sunt partes 4 etc. Item epistola eiusdem, que est quasi regula et institucio omni pie et spiritualiter in Christo vivere volenti etc. Libellus de reduccione arcium ad theologiam. Libellus de tribus ternariis peccatorum infamibus. Apologia pauperum. Eliminacio erroris cuiusdam magistri contra regulam sancti Francisci etc., et sunt epistole 4 eiusdem sancti Bonaventure. Item epistola eiusdem ut supra omnium in Christo pie vivere volencium. Item viginti passus de virtutibus bonorum religiosorum. Liber de reduccione arcium ut supra. De tribus ternariis ut supra. Exposicio oracionis dominice. De 7 gradibus contemplacionis. Laudismus de sancta cruce, quem cecinit venerabilis Bonaventura episcopus cardinalis cordis de visceribus. Item corona beate virginis, et primo ponitur tabula alphabetica, et est liber notabilis. Et est sciendum, quod plures sermones possunt formari precipue de beata virgine et eciam aliis festivitatibus ex stellis coronarum XII supradictis beate virginis, et pro forma habentur aliqui in fine libri annotati etc. Hec omnia in uno mediocri volumine ac inpressione. B 9.

Identifiable with: Heidelberg, Universitätsbibliothek, Q 1554-2 qt.[96]

Bonaventura, S: Opuscula (lacking fols 1-122 of part I).

[Cologne]: B.D.V. (Bartholomaeus de Unkel) [and Johann Koelhoff, the Elder], 1484[-85]. 2°.
GW 4644.

Corona B.M.V.

[Strasbourg: Printer of the 1483 'Vitas Patrum', *c.* 1485]. 2°.
GW 7572.

Binding: Contemporary pigskin, bound in the workshop Kyriss 29; one of two clasps and all bosses lost; formerly chained; with shelf-mark inscription *e14* and manuscript table of contents on front pastedown.

Provenance information: Regensburg, St Emmeram. – Rev. J. Whelan. – Nicolaus Trübner (1817–84). – Donated by Trübner to Heidelberg University in 1885.

B18

Item textus sentenciarum, et sunt libri 4, in fine libri registrum bonum secundum ordinem alphabeti habens, et est impressio mediocris in mediocri volumine. B 18.

Identifiable with: München, BSB, 2° Inc.s.a. 801 (*BSB-Ink* P-379,1)

Petrus Lombardus: Sententiarum libri quattuor.

[Basel: Bernhard Richel, *c.* 1482]. 2°.
H 10185.

Binding: Contemporary pigskin, bound in the workshop Kyriss 29; two clasps lost; title-label with initial in red.

Provenance information: Regensburg, St Emmeram.

C5

Item opus questionum divi Augustini et primo questiones in heptateucon, id est opus variarum questionum super 7 libros primos biblie. Item questionum novi et veteris testamenti libri III. Item questionum ewangeliorum libri III. Item questionum octoginta trium liber unus. Item questionum LXV Orosii eiusdem dyalogus, qui est liber unus. Questionum octo Dulcicii liber 1. Item questionum Laurencii de fide, spe et caritate enchiridion. Item inquisicionum Ianuarii et de consuetudinibus ecclesie libri II. Questionum Honorati de gracia novi testamenti liber 1. Questionum V Hylarii libellus unus. Questionum sex contra paganos ad Deogracias liber 1, et omnium istorum indices et retractaciones in faciebus posite. Hec omnia in uno mediocri volumine et optima inpressione et incipit liber: 'Eodem tempore scripsi libros questionum' etc. C 5.

Identifiable with: Cambridge, MA, Harvard University, Houghton Library, Inc. 8613 (Walsh 3801)

Augustinus, Aurelius: Opus quaestionum. Ed: Augustinus de Ratisbona, Jodocus Badius Ascensius.

Lyon: Johannes Trechsel, 25 Apr. 1497. 2°.
GW 2915.

Binding: Contemporary pigskin; claps; bosses lost; formerly chained.

Provenance information: Regensburg, St Emmeram, bought by Erasmus Münzer in 1499. – Richard Ashhurst Bowie (1836-87). – Gift of Mrs E. D. Brandegee († 1956).

C18

Item continuum sancti Thome de Aquino super 4 ewangelistas sive ewangelia in magno et regio

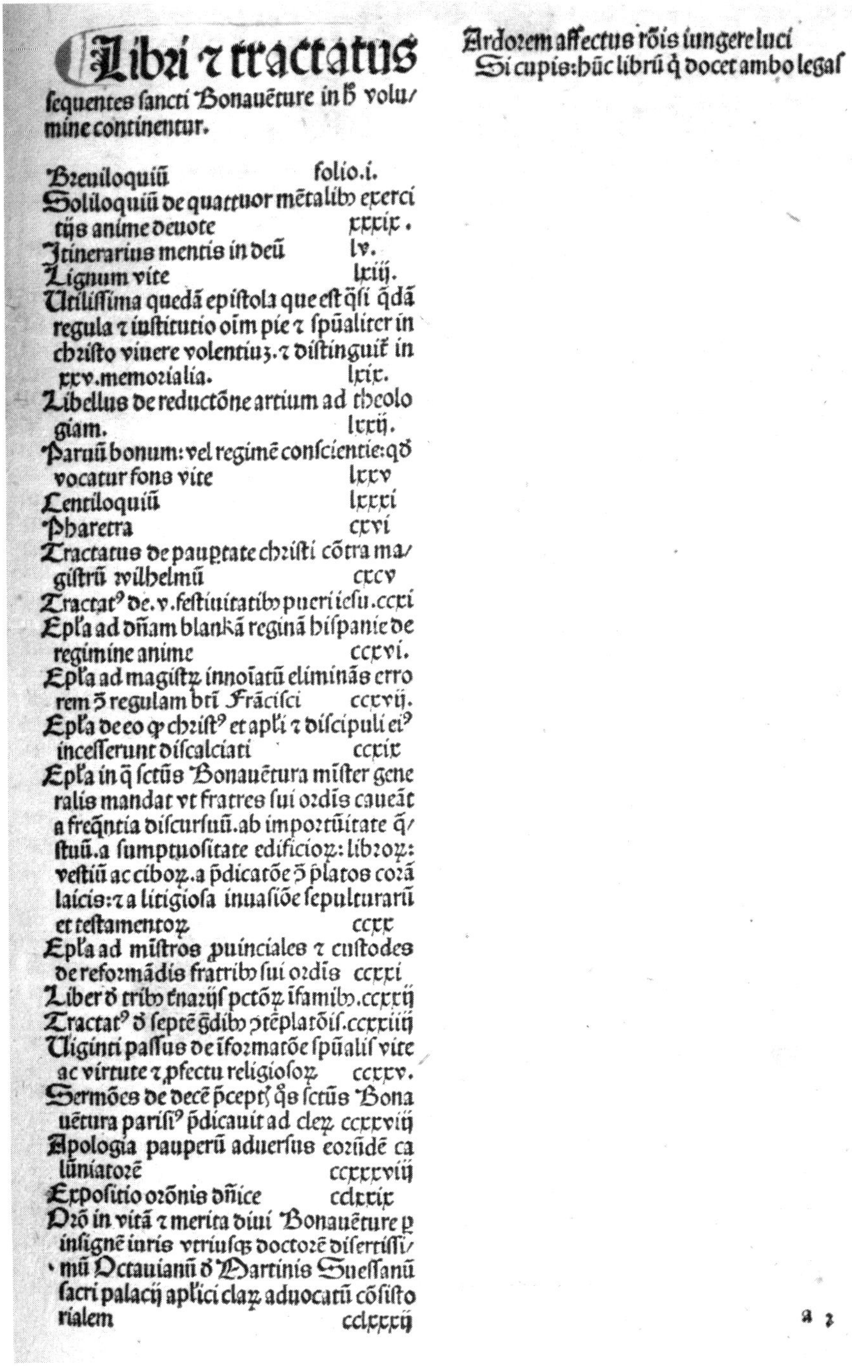

Libri ⁊ tractatus sequentes sancti Bonaueture in ḃ volu/mine continentur.

Ardorem affectus rōis iungere luci
Si cupis:hūc librū q̃ docet ambo legaſ

a ⸝

Fig. 3. Table of contents of Bonaventura's Opuscula, printed Strasbourg: Martın Flach (printer of Straßburg), 31 Oct. 1489 (GW 4647). (Munich, BSB, 2° Inc.c.a. 2225, fol. a2[ra])

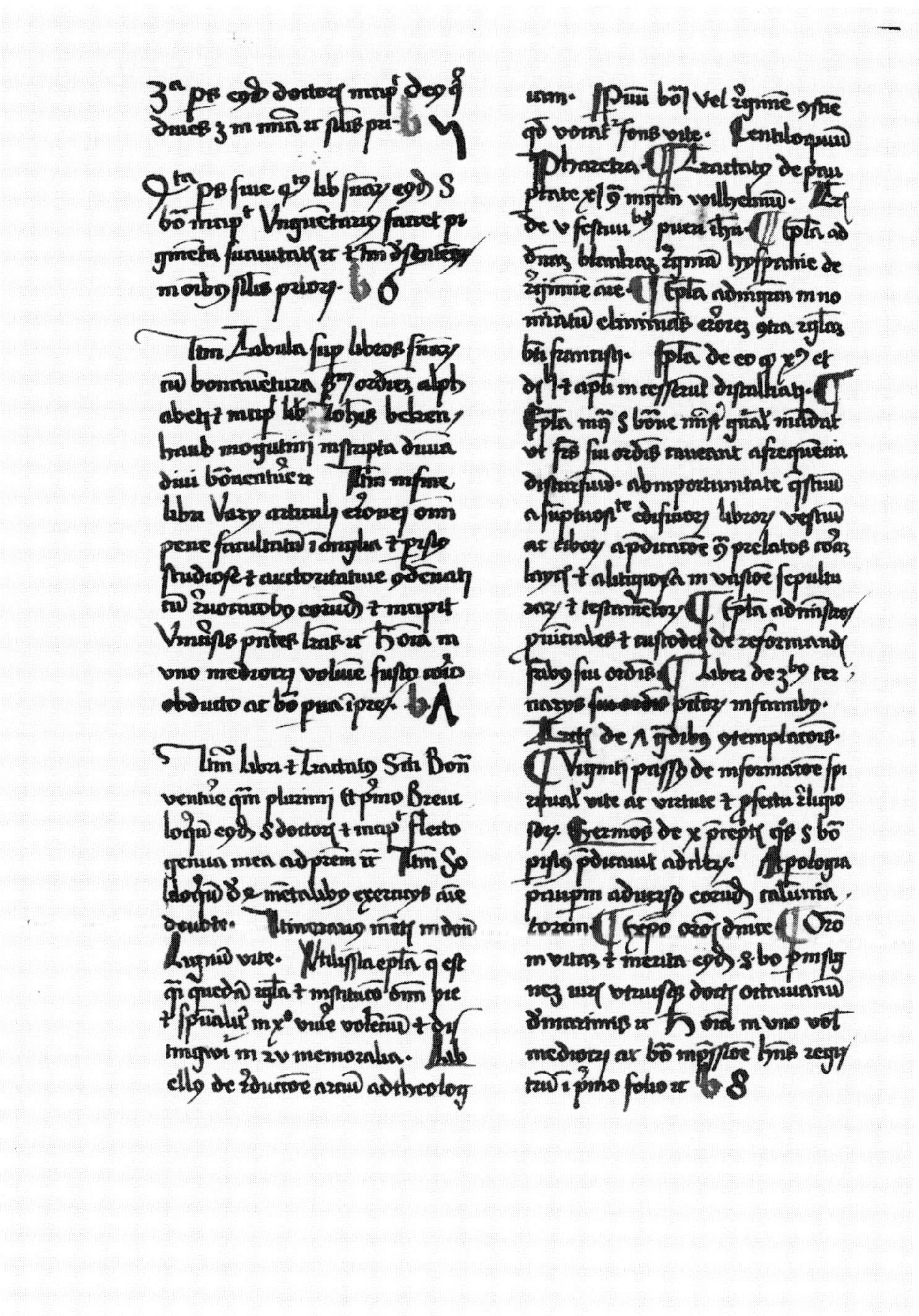

Fig. 4. Menger's catalogue entry for Bonaventura's Opuscula (B8). (Munich, BSB, Clm 14675, fol. 85v)

volumine et bona inpressione, et incipit: 'Sanctissimo ac reverendissimo patri domino Urbano pape quarto etc. frater Thomas de Aquino' etc. C 18.
Identifiable with: Oxford, Bodleian Library, Auct. 6Q inf. 2.21 (Proctor 2477, Sheppard 1775) Thomas Aquinas: Catena aurea super quattuor evangelistas.
[Esslingen: Conrad Fyner, 1475?]. 2°.
HC 1329.
Binding: Rebound in the nineteenth century with the supralibros of the Bodleian Library; old title-label on front pastedown.
Provenance information: Regensburg, St Emmeram.

D5

Item prima pars summe Alberti Magni de 4 coequevis una cum secunda eius, que est de homine, in uno volumine mediocri, et incipit liber: 'Queritur de creaturis et primo de creacione' etc. Et prima pars habet registrum suum in principio libri, 2a pars vero in fine. D 5.
Identifiable with: Oxford, Bodleian Library, Auct. 4Q 3.33 (Proctor 5621, Sheppard 4700) Albertus Magnus: Summa de creaturis.
Venice: Simon de Luere, for Andreas Torresanus, de Asula, 19 Dec. 1498; 16 Feb. 1498/99. 2°.
GW 779.
Binding: Contemporary pigskin, bound in the Regensburg workshop Kyriss 138; two metal clasps; bosses lost; formerly chained; title-label on front cover.
Provenance information: Regensburg, St Emmeram, bought by Erasmus Münzer in 1501. – Leonhard Seitz (1739-1842). – Bought from his legacy by his pupil Joseph Edmund Hoeß. – Bought by the Bodleian Library in 1861.

D15

Item 4tum speculum dicitur hystoriale, et dividitur in duas partes, prima pars continet libros XVI, et incipit: 'Secundum Augustinum nono decimo libro de civitate Dei' etc., habens tabulam in principio secundum alphabetum etc. D 15.
Identifiable with: München, BSB, 2° Inc.s.a. 1213 i (1 (*BSB-Ink* V-202,3)
Vincentius <Bellovacensis>: Speculum historiale. P. 1-4. 2°.
[Strasbourg: The R-Printer, i.e. Adolf Rusch, c. 1473]. 2°.
C 6245.
Binding: Contemporary pigskin, bound in the workshop Kyriss 29; formerly chained; inscription of Aicher's shelf-mark 59.4 and manuscript title.
Provenance information: Regensburg, St Emmeram.

D17, D18, D19, D20

Item prima pars summe Anthonini archiepiscopi Florentini ordinis predicatorum, et incipit: 'Quoniam reverendissimus pater et eximius' etc., et est bona inpressio in magno volumine. D 17.
Item 2a pars summe Anthonini incipit: 'Tu contribulasti capita draconum in aquis' etc., per omnia similis priori. D 18. Item 3a pars summe Anthonini incipit: 'Astitit regina a dextris et' etc., in omnibus similis priori. D 19. Item 4ta pars summe Anthonini incipit: 'Benediccionem dabit legislator' etc., per omnia priori similis. D 20.
Identifiable with: München, BSB, 2° Inc.c.a. 3290 b (*BSB-Ink* A-601,4)
Antoninus Florentinus: Summa theologica. P. 1-4. Mit Tabula von Johannes Molitoris.
Strasbourg: Johann Grüninger, P. 1: 4 Sept. 1496; P. 2: 24 Apr. 1496; P. 3: 6 March 1496; P. 4: 12 Aug. 1496. 2°.
GW 2192.
Binding: Bound in 4 volumes. Pigskin, sixteenth century.
Provenance information: Regensburg, St Emmeram.

E4

part I:

Item confessionale eiusdem in parvo volumine et legibili inpressione, et incipit: 'Defecerunt scrutantes scrutinio' etc. Item in eodem sermo beati Iohannis Crisostomi de penitencia, qui incipit: 'Provida mente et profundo cogitatu'. Item regule ad cognoscendam differenciam inter peccatum mortale et veniale Heinrici de Hassia doctoris famosissimi, deinde registrum super confessionale Anthonini.

Identifiable with: London BL, IA.11022 (BMC II 602)

Antoninus Florentinus: Confessionale: Defecerunt scrutantes scrutinio. Add: Johannes Chrysostomus, Sermo de poenitentia, together with Henricus de Hassia: Regulae ad cognoscendum differentiam inter peccatum mortale et veniale.

Memmingen: Albrecht Kunne, 1483. 4°.

GW 2097.

part II:

Item tractatus solemnis de arte et vero modo predicandi ex diversis sanctorum doctorum scripturis et principaliter sancti Thome de Aquino parvo tractatulo suo quodam recollectus, et incipit: 'Communicaturus meis desiderantibus' etc. [...] Hec omnia in uno volumine diversa tamen inpressione. E 4.

Identifiable with: London BL, IA.11024 (BMC II 603)

Thomas Aquinas: De arte praedicandi.

Memmingen: Albrecht Kunne, 1483. 4°.

HC 1362.

Binding: Calf, eighteenth century.

Provenance information: Regensburg, St Emmeram. – Augustus Frederick, Duke of Sussex (1773-1843). – Bought by the Bodleian Library in 1844.

F2

Item sermones thesauri novi de sanctis per circulum anni, et incipit: 'Relictis retibus secuti sunt eum' etc., in omnibus similis priori etc. F 2.

Identifiable with: München, BSB, 2° Inc.c.a. 1948 e (2 (*BSB-Ink* S-349,7)

Sermones *Thesauri novi* de tempore et de sanctis. P. 1-2.

Nuremberg: Anton Koberger, P. 2: 20 Feb. 1487. 2°.

CR 5409 = C 5415

Binding: Contemporary pigskin.

Provenance information: Anonymous purchase inscription on fol. 225 (Nn7)b: *Jtem 1499 In die walpurge* [1.5.] *Emi pro xiiij solidis ambas partes*. – Regensburg, St Emmeram.

F14

part I:

Item tractatus de virtutibus Alberti Magni episcopi Ratisponensis, qui alias vocatur paradisus anime, et incipit: 'Sunt quedam vicia, que frequenter' etc.

Possibly identifiable with: Oxford, Bodleian Library, Auct. 5Q 6.37 (Proctor 2812, Sheppard 2015)

Albertus Magnus: Paradisus animae, sive Tractatus de virtutibus.

Memmingen: [Albrecht Kunne, about 1488, not after 1496]. 4°.

GW 704.

Binding: Half calf, nineteenth century.

Provenance information: Regensburg, St Emmeram. – Duplicate from the Royal Library, Munich, no. 1904 in list of duplicates in quarto. – Acquired by the Bodleian Library between 1847 and *c.* 1892, probably in 1850.

another part:
Item Iesuida Ieronimi de Vallibus Paduani medicinc doctoris clarissimi una cum divino Lactancii Firmani carmine divino de resurreccione Domini, et incipit: 'Maxime celicolum supera' etc. […] Hec omnia in uno parvo volumine et bona inpressione sed diversa sicut et materia diversa est. F 14.
Possibly identifiable with: München, BSB, 4° Inc.s.a. 1903 (*BSB-Ink* V-50,1)
Vallibus, Hieronymus de: Jesuida. – Daran: Venantius <Fortunatus>: De resurrectione domini. [Ingolstadt: Georg Wirffel the Younger and Marx Ayrer, 1497]. 4°.
H 15841*.
Binding: Pasteboard, nineteenth century.
Provenance information: Regensburg, St Emmeram.

G6

part I:
Item tractatus de mendicitate spirituali venerabilis magistri Iohannis de Gerson cancellarii Parisiensis, et incipit: 'Incipit secretum colloquium hominis contemplativi' etc. […] Hec omnia in uno parvo volumine ac legibili inpressione usque ad medium obducto albo corio. G 6.
Identifiable with: München, BSB, 4° Inc.s.a. 873 (*BSB-Ink* G-156,1)
Gerson, Johannes: De mendicitate spirituali.
[Cologne: Ulrich Zell, not after 1472]. 4°.
GW 10838.
Binding: Pasteboard, nineteenth century.
Provenance information: Regensburg, St Emmeram.

G15

Item stellarium corone benedicte Marie virginis in laudem eius pro singulis predicacionibus elegantissime coaptatum, et incipit prologus: 'Quoniam, ut ait beatissimus ille Gregorius maximus, indignus est dandis' etc., et sunt 12 libri. Item liber Alberti Magni de adherendo Deo et ultima et superna perfeccione hominis ad Deum quantum possibile est, et incipit: 'Cogitanti mihi aliquid ultimate' etc. Item contemplaciones devotissime Iohannis de Turrecremata cardinalis quondam Sancti Sixti, que in parietibus circuitus Marie Minerve nedum litterarum caracteribus verum eciam ymaginum figuris ornatissime descripte atque depicte sunt, et incipit: 'Admiranda et laudanda tue dispensacionis gracia' etc. Hec omnia in uno mediocri volumine sed diversa inpressione. G 15.
Identifiable with: Oxford, Bodleian Library, Auct. 4Q 4.31 (Proctor 3194, Sheppard 2237)
Pelbartus de Themeswar: Stellarium coronae beatae Mariae virginis.
Hagenau: Heinrich Gran, for Johannes Rynman, 2 May 1498. 2°.
HC 12563* = H 12566.
Binding: Contemporary pigskin, bound in the Regensburg workshop Kyriss 138; two catches, clasps and bosses lost; formerly chained; title-label with red initial. According to an inscription on the front pastedown, originally bound with Albertus Magnus, *De arte praedicandi*; Thomas Aquinas, *De modo praedicandi*; Albertus Magnus, *De adhaerendo Deo*; Johannes de Turrecremata, *Contemplationes*.
Provenance information: Regensburg, St Emmeram. – Bought by the Bodleian Library in 1884.

G18

part I:
Item tractatus sacerdotalis de sacramentis deque divinis officiis et eorum administracionibus, et incipit: 'Medice, cura te ipsum' etc.
Identifiable with: München, BSB, 2° Inc.c.a. 1814 l (*BSB-Ink* N-85,1)

Nicolaus de Blonie: De sacramentis. Prolog mit Mandat von Stanislaus Ciolek, Bischof von Posen.
[Strasbourg: Johann Prüss], 21 Oct. 1486. 2°.
HC 3250.
part II:
Item concordancie biblie et canonum cum titulis decretalium tociusque iuris civilis, et incipit: 'Concordancie auctoritatum sacre scripture' etc.
Identifiable with: München, BSB, 2° Inc.c.a. 1814 l /1 (*BSB-Ink* I-604,2)
Johannis, Johannes: [Memoriale Decreti <Ausz. P. 1>] Concordantiae bibliae et canonum. – Daran: [Modus legendi abbreviaturas in utroque iure] Libellus hic primis iurium alumnis utilissimus: titulos utriusque iuris solicitissime collectos cum modo allegandi legendique continens.
Basel: Nikolaus Kessler, 22 June 1487; 12 July 1487. 2°.
HC 9416. H 15600 (2).
part III:
Item summa rudium autentica, et incipit: 'Quia varia dicta sanctorum et contrarie oppiniones doctorum' etc. Hec omnia in uno mediocri volumine et bona inpressione. G 18.
Identifiable with: München, BSB, 2° Inc.c.a. 1814 l /2 (*BSB-Ink* S-637,1)
Summa rudium. – Darin: Henricus <de Frimaria, der Ältere>: De decem praeceptis.
Reutlingen: Johann Otmar, 1487. 2°.
HC 15172*.
Binding: Contemporary pigskin, bound in the workshop Kyriss 29; two clasps; formerly chained.
Provenance information: Regensburg, St Emmeram. – Regensburg, Kreisbibliothek.

I8

Item kalendarium Kinsperger et incipit: 'Aureus hic liber est' etc., in mediocri volumine et rubeo corio obducto etc. I 8.
Identifiable with: München, BSB, 4° Inc.c.a. 85 m (*BSB-Ink* R-69,1)
Regiomontanus, Johannes: Kalendarium. Mit Gedicht auf das Werk Aureus hic liber est. …
Venice: Bernhard Maler, Peter Löslein, & Erhard Ratdolt, 1476. 4°.
HC 13776.
Binding: Contemporary red sheepskin, bound in the workshop Kyriss 29; bosses lost.
Provenance information: Regensburg, St Emmeram.

I9

Item Plinii Secundi Novocomensis in naturalibus hystoriis libri 37 in uno magno regali volumine et bona Ytalica inpressione, et incipit Ius: 'Libros naturalis hystorie novicium' etc. Et hunc librum dedit huic loco Ulricus Prossinger licentiatus anno Domini 1492 etc. I 9.
Identifiable with: München, BSB, Res. 2° A.lat.b. 512 (*BSB-Ink* P-606,3)
Plinius Secundus, Gaius: Historia naturalis. Mit Brief an Marcus und an Tacitus von Gaius Caecilius Plinius Secundus. Mit Exzerpten zu Plinius aus De viris illustribus des Gaius Suetonius Tranquillus, dem Apologeticum des Quintus Septimus Florens Tertullianus und dem Chronicon des Eusebius Caesariensis. Mit den Annotationes in Plinium (Plinius-Kommentar Version B: Correctiones) von Philippus Beroaldus.
Venice: Marinus Saracenus, 14 May 1487 or rather 14 June 1487. 2°.
HC (+ Add.) 13096.
Binding: Pasteboard, nineteenth century.
Provenance information: Ulrich Prossinger. – Regensburg, St Emmeram.

I12

Item Herodotti Halecarnasei hystoriographi patris historie traduccio e Greco in Latinum per virum eruditissimum Laurencium Valensem libri novem, habentes tabulam in principio libri et incipit primus: 'Herodotti Halicarnasei historie explicacio hec est' etc., et est bona inpressio Ytalica in mediocri volumine. I 12.

Identifiable with: München, BSB, 2° Inc.c.a. 3064 a (*BSB-Ink* H-122,2)
Herodotus: Historiae <lat.> Aus dem Griech. übers. von Laurentius Valla. Mit Widmungsbrief an Nicolaus Rubeus, Venice 30.3.1494, hrsg. von Antonius Mancinellus.
Venice: Johannes & Gregorius de Gregoriis, »8 March« [rather: not before 30 March] 1494. 2°. HC 8472.
Binding: Contemporary pigskin, bound in the workshop Kyriss 29; two clasps; formerly chained.
Provenance information: Regensburg, St Emmeram, bought by abbot Erasmus Münzer in 1498.

I16

Item Plotinus de omnibus philosophie mysteriis, et sunt libri 54 in mediocri volumine, et bona Ytalica inpressione distincti in 6 enneades, unicuique enneadi 9 libros tribuens, et tabulam invenies B 1 etc., et incipit prohemium libi: 'Magnus Cosmus senatus consulto patrie pater' etc. I 16.

Identifiable with: München, BSB, Res. 2° A.gr.b. 874 (*BSB-Ink* P-620,3)
Plotinus: Enneades <lat.> Mit Vita Plotini von Porphyrius. Aus dem Griech. übers. und mit Kommentar von Marsilius Ficinus. Mit Widmungsvorrede an Lorenzo de' Medici und an die Leser und Brief an Piero de' Medici von Marsilius Ficinus.
Florence: Antonio Miscomini for Lorenzo de' Medici, 7 May 1492. 2°.
HC 13121.
Binding: Contemporary pigskin, bound in the workshop Kyriss 29; formerly chained; title-label.
Provenance information: Regensburg, St Emmeram, bought by abbot Erasmus Münzer in 1498.

I17

Item opera Platonis a Marsilio Ficino Florentino traducti, et primo ponitur vita ipsius Platonis genealogia et genesis, et incipit: 'Divina providencia fortiter attingens omnia' etc., et sunt libri in numero 58 etc. Item theologia Platonica folio 338. de inmortalitate animarum, et incipit: 'Plato philosophorum pater, magnanime' etc., et sunt libri 18, et post finem librorum ponitur tabula librorum theologie Platonice etc. Hec omnia in uno mediocri volumine et bona inpressione. I 17.

Identifiable with: München, BSB, 2° Inc.c.a. 2605 (*BSB-Ink* P-569,1)
Plato: Opera <lat.> Aus dem Griech. übers., mit Kommentar, Vita, Tabula, Vorrede an Lorenzo de' Medici und an den Leser von Marsilius Ficinus. – Daran: Ficinus, Marsilius: Theologia Platonica de immortalitate animorum. Mit Gedicht auf das Werk von Naldus Naldius.
Venice: Bernardinus de Choris and Simon de Luere for Andreas Torresanus, 13 Aug. 1491. 2°.
HC 13063.
Binding: Contemporary pigskin; two clasps; formerly chained.
Provenance information: Regensburg, St Emmeram.

K6

part I (printed):
Item libri XVI epistolarum Francisci Philelfi, et incipit primus: 'Quod nihil aput me duxerim antiquius' etc., et est bona inpressio Ytalica in mediocri volumine etc.
Identifiable with: Oxford, Bodleian Library, Auct. P 5.17 (Proctor 6976, Sheppard 5778)
Philelphus, Franciscus: Epistolae (16 Bücher).
Brescia: Jacobus Britannicus, 7 May 1485. 2°.
HC(+ Add) 12933

Binding: Half calf, nineteenth century; bound for Kloß.
Provenance information: Regensburg, St Emmeram. – Georg Franz Burkard Kloß (1787-1854). – Bought by the Bodleian Library in 1835.
part II (manuscript):
Item translacio nova quinque librorum ethicorum, et primo ponitur oracio magistri Nicolai Bernawer Ratisponensis in laudem et preconium moralis philosophie, specialiter in X libros ethicorum Aristotelis etc. Isti libri sunt scripti per eundem magistrum etc. Hec omnia in uno mediocri volumine etc. K 6.
Identifiable with: München, BSB, Clm 14993a (Catalogus codicum latinorum Bibliothecae Regiae Monacensis secundum Andreae Schmelleri indices, ed. by Carolus Halm et al. Vol. 2/2 Codices num. 11001 – 15028 complectens. Munich 1876, p. 257)
'Aristotelis ethicorum ad Nicomachum libri VI interprete Leonardo Aretino, cum glossis Joh. Bernauer Ratisbonensis. Praemissa est eiusdem Bernaueri oratio, Ingolstadi a. 1485.' (138 fols)
Binding: Pasteboard, nineteenth century.
Provenance information: Nicolaus Bernauer († 1531). – Regensburg, St Emmeram.

K7

Item Anicii Manlii Torquati Severini Boecii viri nominis celebritate quam memorandi textus de Philosophie consolacione cum edicione commentaria beati Thome de Aquino ordinis predicatorum, et incipit: 'Philosophie servias oportet, ut tibi contingat' etc. Et est bona parva inpressio in mediocri volumine nigro corio obducto etc., habens multum de papiro non scripto in fine libri etc. K 7.
Possibly identifiable with: München, BSB, 4° Inc.c.a. 1187 (*BSB-Ink* B-609,1)
Boethius: De consolatione philosophiae. Mit Kommentar von Pseudo-Thomas Aquinas. Nuremberg: Anton Koberger, 8 June 1495. 4°.
GW 4559.
Binding: Contemporary pigskin, bound in the Augsburg workshop Kyriss 81.
Provenance information: Inherited by Christoph Hoffmann († 1534) from his uncle Nicolaus Örtlein († 1498): *Hunc libellum legauit Dominus Nicolaus örtlein prespiter quondam in opido Rothenburg* [o. d. Tauber] *Auunculo suo carissimo confratri Christophoro professo apud almum Emmeranum Ratisbonae.* – Regensburg, St Emmeram.

K10

Item nova translacio librorum ethicorum, et incipit: 'Aristotelis ethicorum libros' etc. Item in fine breve scriptum quod incipit: 'Preciosa sunt interdum parvi corporis' etc. Hec in uno volumine mediocri et legibili inpressione rubeo corio obducto. K 10.
Identifiable with: London, British Library, G.8005 = IB.580 (BMC I 53)
Aristoteles Ethica ad Nicomachum. Add: Politica; Oeconomica (Tr: Leonardus Brunus Aretinus). Leonardus Brunus Aretinus: Epistola ad dominos Senenses (with reply).
[Strasbourg: Johann Mentelin, before 10 Apr. 1469]. 2°.
GW 2367.
Binding: Calf, eighteenth century. Bound with 12 leaves with manuscript text, inc.: [P]reciosa sunt interdum parui corporis … (= copy of Pars III).
Provenance information: Regensburg, St Emmeram. – Legacy of Sir Thomas Grenville (1755-1846) to the British Museum.

K11

Item textus omnium tractatuum Petri Hispani, eciam sincathegrewmatum et parvorum logicalium cum copulatis secundum doctrinam divi Thome Aquinatis iuxta processum magistrorum Colonie in bursa montis regencium, et incipit: 'Circa inicium sumularum Petri

Hispani, in quibus breviter' etc. Et est parva bona inpressio in volumine mediocri etc. K 11.
Possibly identifiable with: München, BSB, 4° Inc.s.a. 112 d /1 (*BSB-Ink* L-23,1)
Lambertus de Monte: Copulata omnium tractatuum Petri Hispani etiam syncategorematum et parvorum logicalium ac trium modernorum secundum doctrinam Thomae Aquinatis cum textu. [1–3].
Cologne: [Heinrich Quentell], [1]: 7 Apr. 1490; [2]: 6 Apr. 1490. 4°.
H 8703.
Binding: Contemporary pigskin, bound in the workshop Kyriss 29; formerly chained.
Bound second with München, BSB, 4° Inc.s.a. 112 d (*BSB-Ink* A-253,1)
Alexander <de Villa Dei>: Doctrinale. P. 1-4.
Cologne: Heinrich Quentell, P. 1: 13 Aug. 1491; P. 2: 23 June 1491. 4°.
GW 1124.
Provenance information: Regensburg, St Emmeram. – Regensburg, Kreisbibliothek.

K15

Item diccionarium Grecum copiosissimum secundum ordinem alphabeti cum interpretacione Latina, et incipit: 'Αγής infrangibilis' etc. Item Cirilli opusculum de diccionibus, que variato accentu mutant significatum, secundum ordinem alphabeti, cum interpretacione Latina, et incipit: 'Agens penultima acuta' etc., circa litteram L 1 cum reliquis, quorum titulos habes in primo folio libri. Hec omnia in uno mediocri volumine. K 15.
Identifiable with: München, BSB, 2° Inc.c.a. 3470 (*BSB-Ink* C-691,2)
Crastonus, Johannes: Dictionarium graecum cum interpretatione latina.- Daran: Johannes <Philoponus>: De dictionibus quae variato accentu mutant significatum cum interpretatione latina. – Ammonius <Alexandrinus>: De differentia dictionum <griech.>. – Instructio vetus praefectorum militum <griech.>. Mit Erklärung der griech. Partikel ἤ und ὡς. – Mit lat. Widmungsbrief an die Studenten und lat. Vorwort zum Index an den Leser von Aldus Manutius. Mit griech. Gedicht von Scipione Fortiguerra und von Marcus Musurus. Mit Privileg.
Venice: Aldus Manutius, Dec. 1497. 2°.
GW 7814.
Binding: Contemporary calf, probably bound in the Leipzig workshop Kyriss 103.
Provenance information: Regensburg, St Emmeram, bought by abbot Erasmus Münzer in 1501.

L1

Item cronica Nurenbergensis in magno regali volumine ac bona inpressione habens. L 1.
Identifiable with: National Trust, Saltram House, S/2[97]
Schedel, Hartmann: Liber chronicarum.
Nuremberg: Anton Koberger, 12 July 1493. 2°.
HC 14508*.
Binding: Contemporary pigskin, bound in the workshop Kyriss 29; bosses lost; formerly chained.
Provenance information: Regensburg, St Emmeram.

L18, L19, L20

Item prima pars operum Gersonis, et primo ponitur inventarium eorum, que in operibus eiusdem continentur, et incipit: 'Abbas noster Iesus Christus', postea epistola eiusdem ad germanum suum ordinis Celestinorum, deinde annotacio titulorum operum eiusdem, ultimo incipit prima pars operum eiusdem: 'Scrutari scripturas exhortabatur olim Iudeos Christus, Johannis V.' etc. Et una queque pars habet picturam sive effigiem eiusdem in principio, et est bona inpressio text modus albo corio obducto cum clausuris et fibulis. L 18.
Identifiable with: München, BSB, 4° Inc.c.a. 646 (*BSB-Ink* G-185,5)
Gerson, Johannes: Opera.

[Nuremberg: Georg Stuchs], P.1: 22 Nov. 1489; P.2.: 1 Aug. 1489; P.3: 21 Oct. 1489. 4°.
GW 10716.
Binding: Bound in 3 volumes. Contemporary pigskin, bound in the workshop Kyriss 29; bosses lost; title-labels with shelf-marks *P3*, *P4*, *P5*; on the first leaf of each volume, the shelf-marks *L 18*, *L 19*, *L 20* in red and black.
Provenance information: [Erasmus Daum († 1504)]. – Regensburg, St Emmeram. – Magister Georg Ludwig Glatthorn (seventeenth/eighteenth century). – Polling, Augustinerchorherrenstift during the reign of provost Franz Töpsl, 1744.

M11

Item Richardum de duodecim patriarchis et de mistica archa glauco corio vitulino obducto cum fibulis. [M 11]
Possibly identifiable with: Oxford, Bodleian Library, Auct. 1Q 6.20 (Proctor 7602, 7603, Sheppard 2445, 2444)
Richardus de Sancto Victore: De arca mystica. Add: De duodecim patriarchis, sive Benjamin minor.
[Basel: Johann Amerbach], 1494. 8°.
HC(+Add) 13912
Binding: Contemporary blind-tooled calf; with clasps and catches, bosses lost.
Provenance information: [Erasmus Daum († 1504)]. – Regensburg, St Emmeram. – J. T. Hand (fl. 1835-7). – Bought by the Bodleian Library in 1837.

M15

Item fasciculum temporum a quodam Carthusiense conpilatum, et incipit: 'Generacio et generacio laudabit' etc. Arcus modus non ligatus. M 15.
Possibly identifiable with: Oxford, Bodleian Library, Broxb. 19.6 (Proctor 563, not in Sheppard)
Rolewinck, Werner: Fasciculus temporum.
[Strasbourg: Johann Prüss, not before 1490]. 2°.
HC 6916*.
Binding: Contemporary quarter calf, bound in the Regensburg workshop Kyriss 44; with clasp.
Provenance information: [Erasmus Daum († 1504)]. – Regensburg, St Emmeram. – Georg Franz Burkard Kloß (1787-1854). – Ernst Philip Goldschmidt (1887-1954). – Albert Ehrman (1890-1969). – Donated to the Bodleian Library by John Ehrman in 1978.

N3

part I:
Item Platina de honesta voluptate ac valitudine, et sunt libri XI una cum tabula, et incipit primus: 'Errabunt et quidem vehementer' etc. [...] Hec omnia in uno volumine simili priori in omnibus cum una clausura. N 3.
Identifiable with: München, BSB, 4° Inc.c.a. 1680 (*BSB-Ink* P-564,1)
Platina, Bartholomaeus: De honesta voluptate et valetudine. Gewidmet Kardinal Bartholomaeus Roverella.
Bologna: Johannes Antonius de Benedictis, 11 May 1499. 4°.
HC 13056.
Binding: Pasteboard, nineteenth century. Inscription of shelf-mark N 3 in red and black on a1r.
Provenance information: [Erasmus Daum († 1504)]. – Regensburg, St Emmeram.

N7

part I:
Item liber de remediis utriusque fortune prospere et adverse conpilatus per quendam Adrianum

Carthusiensem, et sunt libri duo, prologus primi incipit sic: 'Quondam michi meditati' etc. ...
Identifiable with: München, BSB, 4° Inc.s.a. 20 (*BSB-Ink* A-27,1)
Adrianus Cartusiensis: De remediis utriusque fortunae.
[Cologne: Ulrich Zell, *c.* 1472]. 4°.
GW 227.
part II:
Item consolaciones theologie Iohannis de Tambaco sacre theologie professoris, et sunt 15 libri, et incipit prologus: 'Quoniam secundum apostolum quecumque scripta sunt ad nostram doctrinam' etc. Hec omnia in uno parvo volumine albo corio usque ad medium obducto cum una clausura, mediocris inpressio et legibilis. N 7.
Identifiable with: München, BSB, 4° Inc.s.a. 20/1 (*BSB-Ink* I-523,1)
Johannes de Tambaco: De consolatione theologiae. Kurze Fassung.
[Mainz: Peter Schöffer, *c.* 1470-5]. 4°.
HC 15235.
Binding: Pasteboard, nineteenth century. Inscription of shelf-mark N 8 in red and black.
Provenance information: Regensburg, St Emmeram.

N8

part I:
Item conclusiones de diversis materiis moralibus valde utiles Iohannis Gerson cancellarii Parisiensis, et incipit prologus: 'Agamus nunc interim, quod natura' etc. [...] Hec omnia in uno parvo volumine, in omnibus similis priori. N 8.
Identifiable with: München, BSB, 4° Inc.s.a. 867 a (*BSB-Ink* G-137,1)
Gerson, Johannes: Conclusiones de diversis materiis moralibus.
[Cologne: Ulrich Zell, *c.* 1472]. 4°.
GW 10734.
Binding: Pasteboard, nineteenth century. Inscription of shelf-mark N 7.
Provenance information: Regensburg, St Emmeram.

N9

Item epistola beati Augustini doctoris eximii ad beatum Cirillum secundum Ierosolomitanum episcopum de magnificenciis beati Ieronimi, et incipit: 'Gloriosissimi Christiane fide adthlete sancte matris ecclesie lapidis angularis' etc. Item epistola sancti Cirilli ad beatum Augustinum de miraculis beati Ieronimi incipit: 'Venerabili viro episcoporum eximio' etc. Item epistola beati Ieronimi ad Susannam lapsam. 'Puto levius esse crimen, ubi homo peccatum suum ultro confitetur' etc. Item epistola sancti Ieronimi ad Eliodorum. [...] Hec omnia in uno parvo volumine, per omnia similis priori. N 9.
Identifiable with: München, BSB, 4° Inc.s.a. 244 (*BSB-Ink* A-912,1)
Augustinus, Aurelius <Pseudo->: Epistula ad Cyrillum Hierosolymitanum de magnificentiis Hieronymi. – Daran: Cyrillus <Hierosolymitanus, Pseudo->: Epistula ad Augustinum de miraculis Hieronymi. – Hieronymus, Sophronius Eusebius <Pseudo->: Epistula ad Susannam lapsam. – Hieronymus, Sophronius Eusebius: Epistula ad Heliodorum.
[Cologne: Ulrich Zell, *c.* 1470]. 4°.
GW 2949.
Binding: Modern pasteboard; old title-label. Inscription of shelf-mark N 9 in red and black on fol. a1ʳ.
Provenance information: Regensburg, St Emmeram.

MBK p. 373, 7433-7439 (without shelf-mark)

part I:

Item luminare maius, secundum alios lilium medicine, et incipit: 'Electuarium de aromatibus' etc.

Identifiable with: München, BSB, 2° Inc.s.a. 850 (*BSB-Ink* M-129,1)

Manliis, Johannes Jacobus de: Luminare maius. – Daran: Augustis, Quiricus de: Lumen apothecariorum.

Venice: Albertinus Rubeus Vercellensis, [not before 1501]. 2°.

HR 10709 (incl H 2117).

part II:

Item practica Bordonii, dicta lilium, et tractatus eiusdem de urinis, et incipit liber Ius: 'Interrogatus a quodam Socrates' etc., liber 2us incipit: 'Quia bona corporis disposicio' etc.

Identifiable with: München, BSB, 2° Inc.s.a. 850 /1 (*BSB-Ink* B-336,1)

Bernardus de Gordonio: Practica seu Lilium medicinae: De ingeniis curandorum morborum; De regimine acutarum aegritudinum; De prognosticis; De urinis; De pulsibus.

Venice: Bonetus Locatellus for Octavianus Scotus, 22 Dec. 1498. 2°.

GW 4084.

part III:

Item Cornelius Celsus et incipit: 'Ut alimenta sanis corporibus agricultura' etc. Hec omnia in uno volumine albo corio obducto per totum cum fibulis et clausuris, et fuit fratris Kiliani.

Identifiable with: München, BSB, 2° Inc.s.a. 850 /2 (*BSB-Ink* C-210,1)

Celsus, Aulus Cornelius: De medicina.

Venice: Philippus Pincius for Benedictus Fontana, 6 May 1497. 2°.

GW 6459.

Binding: Contemporary pigskin, bound in the workshop Kyriss 29; formerly chained.

Provenance information: Frater Kilian († between 1505 and 1508). – Regensburg, St Emmeram. – Regensburg, Kreisbibliothek.

MBK p. 374, 7452-7459 (without shelf-mark)

Item anno Domini 1508. in die sancte Elisabeth magister Nicolaus Vispach apothecarius tradidit nobis pro requie uxoris sue Marthe Avicennam in maiori volumine mediocris impressionis, divisum in duas partes, ac fusco corio obductum cum fibulis et clausuris, et prima pars continet III libros, primum, 2m et 4tum, et incipit primus: 'Inprimis Deo gracias agemus' etc. 2a pars continet II libros, 3m et quintum, et incipit primus: 'Inquit Galienus: "Intencio in creando", in fine libri multum de papiro vacuo.

Identifiable with: München, BSB, 2° Inc.s.a. 131 (*BSB-Ink* A-956,2)

Avicenna: Canon medicinae <lat.> Lib. 1–5. Aus dem Arab. übers. von Gerardus Cremonensis.

[Strasbourg: The R-Printer, i.e. Adolf Rusch, before 1473]. 2°.

GW 3114.

Binding: Contemporary calf, bound in Regensburg, St Emmeram; formerly chained; title-label with shelf-marks O2 and O3.

Provenance information: Nicolaus Vischpach: *Magister Nicolaus Vispach, Apothecarius tradidit hunc librum S. Emeramo per manus fratris Christofforj in profesto S. Elisabeth* [18.11.] *1508 ob Requiem uxoris sue marthe etc.*

MBK p. 376, 7572-7574 (without shelf-mark)

Item vocabularius poeticus Iuniani liber magnus et Ytalice inpressionis cum fibulis et clausuris optimis, et fuit fratris Erasmi Tawm Australis.

Identifiable with: München, BSB, 2° Inc.c.a. 638 (*BSB-Ink* M-66,3)

Maius, Junianus: De priscorum proprietate verborum. Mit Widmungsvorrede des Autors an Ferdinand I., König von Neapel, und Brief an Erzbischof Henricus Languardus.

Treviso: Bernardus de Colonia, 1477. 2°.

H 10540.

Binding: Contemporary pigskin, bound in the workshop Kyriss 29; bosses; chain; on upper cover, inscription of Aicher's shelf-mark *36.9* and title-label with shelf-mark *J 5*. (See ill. 2).

Provenance information: Erasmus Daum († 1504). – Nicolaus Bernauer († 1531): *Iste liber est Nicolai Bernawer quem comparauit pro 2 fl. et 2 1/2 sol.* – Regensburg, St Emmeram. – Windberg, Prämonstratenserabtei.

MBK pp. 376-377, 7574-7580 (without shelf-mark)

part I:

Item vita Christi a sancto Bonaventura edita, et incipit: 'Inter alia virtutum'.

Identifiable with: München, BSB, 4° Inc.s.a. 378 b (*BSB-Ink* B-683,3)

Bonaventura <Pseudo->: Meditationes vitae Christi.

[Strasbourg: Johann Grüninger, *c.* 1496]. 4°.

GW 4754.

part II:

Item idem de castitate et mundicia sacerdotum et ceterorum altaris ministrorum.

Identifiable with: München, BSB, 4° Inc.s.a. 378 b /1 (*BSB-Ink* B-679,1)

Bonaventura <Pseudo->: De castitate et munditia sacerdotum. Mit Anhang.

Leipzig: Melchior Lotter, 21 May [14]99. 4°.

GW 4718.

part III:

Item exposicio misse misteriorum Christi passionem devotissime figurancium etc.

Identifiable with: München, BSB, 4° Inc.s.a. 378 b /2 (*BSB-Ink* B-28,3)

Balthasar de Porta: Expositio mysteriorum missae. – Darin: Vallibus, Hieronymus de: Jesuida <Ausz.> – Mit Schlußgedicht Huchuc quisquis eris …

Leipzig: [Gregor Boettiger, 14]94. 4°.

GW 3221.

part IV:

Item paradisus anime Alberti Magni.

Identifiable with: München, BSB, 4° Inc.s.a. 378 b /3 (*BSB-Ink* A-192,1)

Adrianus Cartusiensis: Paradisus animae sive de virtutibus. Mit Gedicht Laus deo caeli …

Strasbourg: Martin Flach, 10 July 1498. 4°.

GW 706.

part V:

Item tractatus de erroribus philosophorum in fide Christiana etc. Hec omnia in uno parvo volumine textpleter fusco corio sive glauco vitulino cum fibulis et clausuris. Et fuit fratris Erasmi Australis.

Identifiable with: München, BSB, 4° Inc.s.a. 378 b /4 (*BSB-Ink* W-88,1)

Wimpina, Conradus: Tractatus de erroribus philosophorum in fide christiana Aristotelis commentatoris Avicennae et Alkindi cum confutationibus eorundem. Mit Vorrede und Nachwort an den Leser.

[Leipzig: Gregor Boettiger, 1493]. 4°.

H 16206.

Binding: Contemporary calf, bound in the Augsburg workshop Kyriss 81; title-label with red initial.

Provenance information: Erasmus Daum († 1504). – Regensburg, St Emmeram. – Regensburg, Kreisbibliothek.

MBK p. 380, 7724-7725 *(without shelf-mark)*

Partes tres Alexandri cum commento, arcus modus albo corio usque ad medium obducto cum una clausura, 1486 Basilee inpressi.
Identifiable with: München, BSB, 2° Inc.c.a. 1704 g *(BSB-Ink* A-248,1)
Alexander de Villa Dei: Doctrinale. [1-4]. Mit Kommentar von Ludovicus de Guaschis.
Basel: Nikolaus Kessler, 20 Aug. 1486. 2°.
GW 998.
Binding: Contemporary half pigskin, bound in the workshop Kyriss 29; one clasp.
Provenance information: Regensburg, St Emmeram. – Regensburg, Kreisbibliothek.

MBK p. 384, 7863 *(without shelf-mark)*

Item vitas patrum, et incipit prologus libri: 'In Gottes namen amen. Der ewig Got'. Sed liber: 'Es fraget ein brueder sand Anthoni' etc., fusco corio per totum obducto cum una clausura in magno volumine cum effigiis sanctorum patrum, et hunc librum dedit quedam matrona Walpurg nomine huic loco.
Possibly identifiable with: Würzburg, UB, I.t.f. 339 (Hubay, Würzburg 1111)[98]
Hieronymus: Vitae sanctorum patrum, sive Vitas patrum. [German] Leben der heiligen Altväter. [Augsburg: Johann Schönsperger, about 1485?]. 2°.
C 2966
Binding: Contemporary blind-stamped dark brown leather.
Provenance information: Matrona Walpurg. – Regensburg, St Emmeram, with date 1648.

NOTES

TEMPORARY MATRICES AND ELEMENTAL PUNCHES IN GUTENBERG'S DK TYPE

1 This work was done in collaboration with Paul Needham, Scheide Librarian, with the generous support of William H. Scheide and Princeton University.

2 Harry Graham Carter, *A View of Early Typography up to about 1600* (Oxford, 1969).

3 *Danse macabre* [Lyons: Mathias Huss], 18 Feb. 1499 [/1500?]. GW 7954.

4 Among the earliest unambiguous surviving references to punches is Nicolaus Jenson's will of September 1480 (Carlo Castellani, *La stampa in Venezia* (Venice, 1889 [1973 reprint]), pp. 85 et seq.) mentioning among Jenson's bequests '... ponzoni cum quibus stampantur matrices, cum quibus matribus fiunt littere ...'.

5 The camera back is a 4 × 5″ Phase One PowerPhase, with a 6000 × 8400 pixel scan area and 12-bit internal colour depth (www.phaseone.com). The printed area of the *Bulla Thurcorum* measures 10 × 16.5 cm, yielding a scan resolution of ~500 pixels/cm (or ~1200 dpi). We have used a ReproGraphic copystand, view camera, and tungsten lighting from Tarsia Technical Industries (www.ttind.com). All analysis software is our own, written in C++ and Matlab™ (www.mathworks.com).

6 Charlton Hinman, *The Printing and Proof-Reading of the First Folio of Shakespeare* (Oxford, 1963).

7 For an overview, see Kenneth Rose, 'Deterministic Annealing for Clustering, Compression, Classification, Regression, and Related Optimisation Problems', *The Proceedings of the IEEE*, 86(11) (1988), 2210-39.

8 Janet Ing, *Johann Gutenberg and His Bible* (New York, 1988), p. 78.

9 Catharina Senensis, *Epistole*. Venice: Aldus Manutius, Romantus, '15' [i.e. not before 19] Sept. 1500. GW 6222.

10 *Biblia sacra, Hebraice, Chaldaice, Græce, & Latine*. Antverpiæ: Christoph. Plantinus: 1569 [1571]-73.

11 *Lo Inferno di Dante Alighieri fiorentino* [Chelsea: Nella stamperia di Ashendene, 1902].

12 Gerard Meerman, *Origines typographicae* (The Hague, 1765), I, 26.

13 Paul Needham, 'Johann Gutenberg and the Catholicon Press', *Papers of the Bibliographical Society of America*, 76 (1982), 395-456.

14 Stanley Nelson, Smithsonian Institution, personal communication.

TRADITION AND RENEWAL

1 H. M. Nixon, 'Caxton, His Contemporaries and Successors in the Booktrade from Westminster documents', *The Library*, 5th ser., 31 (1976), 305-26, esp. the section 'Caxton bequests' (pp. 314-17). Not until 1496 was a settlement of the will made. Nixon discusses the problems in identifying the 'legends' bequeathed to St Margaret's, Westminster, and the 'birth of our lady' and Life of St Katherine, given by Caxton's executors to the Fraternity of the Assumption of the Blessed Virgin Mary at St Margaret's.

2 'In Caxtons hous' in *The twelve profits of tribulation*, Duff 400, datable '1499, after 10 July', on the basis of the state of device C and the type. In a dated edition in: William Lyndewode, *Constitutiones provinciales*, 31 May 1496, Duff 279: 'In domo caxston'.

3 See for example the instances quoted by J. H. Baker, 'The Books of Common Law', in *History of the Book in Britain, Volume III, c.1400 to 1557*, ed. by L. Hellinga & J. B. Trapp (Cambridge, 1999), pp. 411-32, esp. pp. 425-7 (John Rastell's inventory, 1538, William Powell's inventory, 1553).

4 E. Gordon Duff's numeration of types is followed throughout, as it will be in *BMC*, vol. xi. Proctor's numeration of Wynkyn de Worde's type is different, but in all later literature Duff's numeration is used.

5 First used in *The Royal Book*, Duff 366, last in the second edition of pseudo-Bonaventura, *Meditations on the Life of Christ*, Duff 49.

6 In Clement Maydeston, *Directorium sacerdotum*, Duff 292, with type 6. Its last use as a main text type was in 1485 (*Paris and Vienne*, Duff 337) and in the undated page-for-page reprint of the *Quattuor Sermones*, Duff 299, STC 17957 (note), according to the chronology proposed by P. Needham, *The Printer and the Pardoner* (Washington DC, 1986) printed in 1487.

7 Wynkyn de Worde Type 1: 99 G, used in *The Golden Legend*, Duff 410 and in *The Life of St Katherine*, Duff 403.

8 The large woodcut initial T is illustrated as Pl. XII in Duff. Two of the smaller initials in Lotte Hellinga, 'Wynkyn de Worde's Native Land', in *New Science out of Old Books: Studies in Manuscripts and Early Printed Books in Honour of A. I. Doyle*, ed. by Richard Beadle & A. J. Piper (Aldershot, 1995), pp. 342-59 (Pl. 57).

9 Wynkyn de Worde Type 7: 103 G, used only in Duff 57. For the evidence indicating that de Worde maintained his connections with printers and typefounders in Holland see note 8 above, L. Hellinga (1995).

10 Illustrated in W. & L. Hellinga, *The Fifteenth-Century Printing Types of the Low Countries* (Amsterdam, 1966), Pls 61-4. Also in Lotte Hellinga, *Caxton in Focus* (London, 1982), pp. 73-6.

11 *The Chastising of Goddes Children*, Duff 85; *The Treatise of Love*, Duff 399. Whether the proof-sheet for *The Book of Courtesy*, Duff 54, with device B, is evidence for the printing of a full edition is unascertainable.

12 Walter Hylton, *Scala perfectionis*, Duff 203 and peudo-Bonaventura, *Meditations on the Life of Christ*, Duff 50.

13 Hodnett 237-308 (and some others), 309-33, 214-36.

14 R. B. McKerrow, *Printers' and Publishers' Devices in England and Scotland 1485-1640* (London, 1913), no. 1. Caxton's device has been illustrated many times, e.g. George D. Painter, *William Caxton: a Quincentenary Biography* (London, 1976), p. 159.

15 Mary Erler, 'Devotional literature', in *The Cambridge History of the Book in Britain*, vol. III, as note 3, pp. 495-525, esp. pp. 500-3.

16 Duff 182 and 183.

17 Duff 90, 253, 284, 102, 114.

18 The date reads: 'the .viii. daye of Ianeuer the yere of oure lorde Thousande. CCCC.lxxxxviij And in the .xiii. yere of the reynge of kynge Henry the vii'. The thirteenth year of Henry VII's reign ended on 21 August 1498. The formulation of the imprint date is therefore a strong argument for dating the book in 1498. However, since the state of the type is not found in any of the books dated in the calendar year 1498, it is generally assumed that the regnal year was mistaken, and that the date should be read as 8 January 1498/9.

19 O. D. Macrae Gibson, 'Wynkyn de Worde's *Marlyn*', *The Library*, 6th ser., 2 (1980), 73-6. One of the four forms of capital I which he distinguished is the occasional use of wrong-fount I of Type 8 that strayed into the type-cases of Type 4. Margaret Lane Ford, 'A new addition to the corpus of English incunabula: Wynkyn de Worde's *Proprytrees & Medicynes of Hors* (c.1497-98), *The Library*, 7th ser., 2 (2001), 3-9.

20 W. W. Greg, 'The Early Printed Editions of the Canterbury Tales', *Publications of the Modern Language Association*, 34 (1924), 737-61. William F. Hutmacher, *Wynkyn de Worde and Chaucer's Canterbury Tales: a Transcription and Collation of the 1498 Edition with Caxton 2 from the General Prologue through the Knight's Tale* (Amsterdam, 1978). [Costerus: Essays in English and American language and literature NS 10.] See also Thomas J. Garbáty, 'Wynkyn de Worde's "Sir Thopas" and other Tales', *Studies in Bibliography*, 31 (1978), 57-67.

21 The changeover occurs between the end of the Tale of the Prioress and the beginning of Chaucer's Tale, on r2ª. This is a difference of one quire with the changeover surmised by Ford (between quires p and q).

22 Satoko Tokunaga, 'The Sources of Wynkyn de Worde's Version of "The Monks Tale"', *The Library*, 7th ser., 2 (2001), 223-35.

23 *The Riverside Chaucer*, 3rd edn, ed. by Larry D. Benson (Oxford, 1988), p. 1118.

24 Duff 236.

ILLUSTRATIONS IN PARISIAN BOOKS OF HOURS

1 *Early Illustrated Books: a History of the Decoration and Illustration of Books in the 15th and 16th Centuries* (London, 1893), p. 181; see also his article on 'The Illustrations in French Books of Hours, 1485-1500', *Bibliographica*, 3 (1897), 430-70.

2 Pollard, *Early Illustrated Books*, 178. Claudin, I 240-1: Du Pré's Hours of 1488 'sont d'un intérêt capital pour l'histoire de la gravure en France, car elles nous font connaître d'une manière certaine le procédé par lequel les images ont été exécutées'.

3 The Vérard editions date from 21 August 1486 (*ISTC* ih00324100) and 7 July 1487 (*ISTC* ih00349600); both are small in dimension, with text set 17 lines to the page. The woodcuts (approximately 75 × 60 mm) apparently belonged to Vérard. A different series of woodcuts was used for the edition of 18 February 1487/8 (*ISTC* ih00357900), with text set 23 lines to the page.

4 *ISTC* ih00359630. Two copies are known, one in Berlin, Staatsbibliothek zu Berlin Preussischer Kulturbesitz (imperfect), the other in Wrocław, Biblioteka Uniwersytecka. The text is set in a single column of 35 lines to the page.

5 *ISTC* ih00359640. Two copies are known: Paris, BNF Rés. B.27672 and Chantilly, Musée Condé 909 (XIV.C.4). The text is set in two columns of 28 lines each.

6 *ISTC* ih00369360. Printed by Du Pré for Antoine Caillaut, it is dated *c*.1491 in *CIBN* according to the state of the printer's mark. The only known copy is in Paris, BNF Rés. Vélins 1643.

7 In the Berlin copy, the repertoire occupies fols 1ʳ-2ʳ and is followed by an almanach (fol. 2ᵛ) and the 'Blason des armes de nostre redemption' (fols 4ʳ-4ᵛ). Although the original gathering undoubtedly consisted of four leaves, the third is now missing. I am very grateful to Dr Wolfram Kardorf of the Staatsbibliothek zu Berlin, for details about this copy. In the Wrocław copy (*IBP* 2856), the repertoire is found in the last gathering which, according to the catalogue, consists of only two leaves. Since the incipits cited for fols 87ʳ and 88ᵛ correspond to the description of fols 1ʳ and 4ᵛ of the Berlin copy, the conjugate leaves 2-3 must be missing from the gathering. Consequently, the repertoire is also incomplete, consisting of only the first two pages (fols 1ʳ-1ᵛ).

8 In quoting from the editions of Hours, I have expanded abbreviations, standardized punctuation and capitalization in conformance with modern usage, added an *accent aigu* on final tonic *e*, and distinguished between *i* and *j*, *u* and *v*.

9 These dimensions are provided by *IBP* according to the copy in Wrocław. The Berlin copy

lacks the leaf bearing this woodcut which begins the Office of the Virgin. Only two other woodcuts of this size are used in the edition: David and Goliath on fol. A1^r to begin the Penitential Psalms, and the Feast of Dives on fol. B1^r for the Office of the Dead.

10 The woodcuts used at the beginning of the other major divisions of the Hours are in fact slightly smaller (9 lines high) than those used for the individual psalms (10 lines high), and they seem stylistically to constitute a separate set.

11 One wonders whether this impatience applies only to the introductory material, rather than to the liturgical texts themselves, and whether the language used for the table – French, instead of Latin – is at all relevant. It should also be noted again that in one copy of this edition the table is bound at the end of the volume, not at the beginning, so that its information would not delay the reader's recitation of the hours. Whatever the printer's intention may have been for the placement of this gathering, its independent signature subjected it, more than others, to the will of the binder.

12 The two large woodcuts of David and of the Feast of Dives are used in later editions, but I have not yet determined whether they appear in some of the editions dated as '*c.*1488' or 'pre-February 1489'.

13 One of the omitted images is the prophet Micheas who is used in the book to announce alternate texts for Tuesday and Friday. An inscription next to his picture on fol. e3^r reads: 'le prophete Micheas au v. chapitre. de Micheas'. This image precedes that of the prophet Isaiah, and should be no. 33 in the set of 37. Since it was not used in the earlier edition of March, it was not included in the repertoire. Its absence from the table of the May edition seems to be an oversight, caused perhaps by copying the earlier repertoire without verifying the presence of the woodcuts within the book.

14 Similar treatment is given to the large woodcuts for Prime, Terce, Sext, None, Vespers, and Compline which replace the smaller woodcuts of the March edition. Each cut measures 80×46 mm, but is expanded to 103×70 mm by the addition of three rectangular pieces, above and on each side. None of these large woodcuts is cited in the repertoire.

15 For the description of this image in the repertoire of March 1487/88, see p. 33 above and Fig. 1.

16 For the identification of various series of woodcuts used by Du Pré, Caillaut, and others, based on careful stylistic analyses, see the recent dissertation by Isabelle Delaunay, 'Echanges artistiques entre livres d'heures manuscrits et imprimés produits à Paris (vers 1480-1500),' diss. Univ. de Paris IV Sorbonne, 2000, II, 357-64.

17 The iconographic sources and designs of Du Pré's woodcut series demand a fuller investigation than I have yet been able to complete, but the project is under way.

18 From the 'vignes' or grapevines used to decorate the margins of manuscripts.

19 'Et premierement en la pagee [sic] ensuyvante l'istoire de l'Annunciation est prefiguree la nativité Nostre Dame ...'

20 For the use of Rome; *ISTC* ih00364200. About this edition, see my article 'Vérard's Hours of 8 February 1489/90: Prologue, Table, and Typological Borders', *Papers of the Bibliographical Society of America*, 87.3 (1993), 337-62.

21 Marcel Desjardin, 'Les Livres d'Heures imprimés en France aux XVème et XVIème siècles: Essai d'iconographie', 1940-47, unpub. ts., Paris, BNF Réserve des Imprimés, p. 37.

22 *ISTC* ih00359642. The Morgan Libary copy of this edition does not contain the repertoire, and I have been unable to locate the copy described by Desjardin.

23 I am extremely grateful to the owner (P. van Hooff) for allowing me to examine this book and for providing reproductions of some of its pages.

24 The first large woodcut depicting God creating the angels (112×78 mm) is followed by four L-shaped borders featuring God standing to create the stars, moon, and birds. A large woodcut (114×78 mm) of the creation of Adam and Eve concludes the series. For a repro-

duction of the latter, albeit surrounded by different borders, see John Macfarlane, *Antoine Vérard* (London: 1900; rpt. Geneva: Slatkine, 1971), pl. L.

25 For the use of Rome, although cited in BMC VIII, 75 as 'secundum usum Armoricane'. *ISTC* 00360500; copies in Florence, Biblioteca Nazionale Centrale, Inc.G.6.1; London, BL, IA 41096 (impf.); Millau, Bm Rés. XV 12.

26 Vérard's text is printed, however, in two columns of 35 lines each whereas Du Pré uses 30 long lines to the page.

27 The prologues are reprinted in my study, *Anthoine Vérard, Parisian publisher, 1485-1512: Prologues, Poems, and Presentations* (Geneva, 1997), pp. 222-5. See also 'Vérard's Hours of February 20, 1489/90 and their Biblical Borders', *Bulletin du bibliophile*, 2 (1991), 299-330. I have discussed typological borders in editions by other printers in 'Biblical Typology in the Borders of French Books of Hours (1488-1510)', *ACTA*, 15 (1990), 101-20.

28 For reproductions of the border with guide letters, see pp. 305, 310, 321 in 'Verard's Hours and their Biblical Borders', as note 27.

29 There are, however, two different designs. The first has individual cuts for each prophet, which are separated by blocks of text, printed vertically; the second places both prophets within the same block, with a single block of text to the outer side, next to the lateral border piece.

30 The Nativity border is used on fol. g7^v with the following texts: (above Moses) 'Figure de Moyse et du buysson. Exode iii;' (below Moses) 'La nativité nostre Seigneur Jesucrist;' (next to the prophets below): 'Figure de la verge de Aaron. Numeri .xvii / Par la verge de Aaron est figuree la nativité'.

31 For the Nativity, the texts are: 'Peperit filium suum primogenitum / Parvulus natus est nobis / Et filius datus est nobis / Et regnabit in eternum'.

32 Two of the fifty anti-types are lacking: nos 8 (the Presentation of Christ) and 19 (Christ's entry into Jerusalem). For reproductions, see my articles 'Biblical Typology', p. 107, as note 27, and 'Verard's Hours and Typological Borders', p. 347, as note 20.

33 Examples of Pigouchet's three sets are reproduced in my article 'Printing and Reading the Book of Hours: Lessons from the Borders', *Bulletin of the John Rylands University Library of Manchester* (1999), 194-7. For other examples of typological borders, see Claudin II, 63 (Le Rouge); II, 245 (Jehannot); II, 270-1, 275-6 (Kerver); II, 351 (Chappiel); II, 414-15 (Vérard).

34 Gilles and Germain Hardouyn apparently acquired some of Jean de Coulonce's borders since they are used, among miscellaneous pieces, in an edition for the use of Rome, *c.* 1510 (Lacombe 204), as reproduced in a recent sale catalogue (Andrew Stewart, cat. 57 [2000], item 44, back cover).

35 Copies in Cambridge, MA, Harvard, Typ Inc 3209; London, BL, IA.14003; New York, PML, ChL 578.

36 San Marino, HEHL, RB 55794; Goff H-242.

37 For examples, see Claudin II, 34-9.

38 These sets are reproduced in Claudin II, 52-3.

39 *A Catalogue of a Collection of Early French Books in the Library of C. Fairfax-Murray* (London, 1910), II, 1078.

40 Milan, Biblioteca Nazionale Braidense Gerli 1387.

41 San Marino, HEHL RB 88372.

42 Chapel Hill, University of North Carolina Library (*) Incun. ND3363.K4 C3.

43 See note 1 above.

Notes

BOOKS OF HOURS

1 I would like to thank the Gladys Krieble Delmas Foundation for a travel scholarship that has allowed me to consult a number of unique exemplars of Roman Hours in northern Italy.

2 The *Corpus Codicum Liturgicorum Latinorum*, a database being compiled by Laurent Cavet from the late Dom Beyssac's unpublished notes and with the support of Fr P.-M. Gy, lists 4884 manuscript Books of Hours. *CCLL* gathers together information on the Hours of the Virgin and other offices such as Office of the dead, Offices of the three Days before Easter, Offices of the four Sundays in Advent, Office of the Annunciation, and Office of the Assumption. It is a work in progress and does not include Books of Hours in private collections, but it is the best and most systematic survey available at the moment. I would like to thank Mr Cavet for providing this data for me.

3 The full list of fifteenth-century Hours provided by *ISTC* includes 12 editions that are still recorded as being of unknown use. Some of these, in fragmentary form, will probably remain unidentified, but others are identifiable if they contain sufficient data from either the Office of the Virgin or of the dead; for example *Horae* (unknown use). Paris: [Jean Du Pré (printer of Paris), for] Antoine Vérard, 21 Aug. 1486. 8°. *CIBN* H-257 (reassigned by Denise Hillard to [Antoine Caillaut], *ex informatione* Nicolas Petit) is actually use of Rome. By the same method, the fragment of the *Horae: ad usum Sarum* (Salisbury) [Paris: Philippe Pigouchet, *c*.1495]. 8°. Duff 189; *STC* 15883; reassigned to [Paris: Jean Barbier, *c*.1510], of which only four leaves are known in the Bodleian Library (Inc. f.F1.1495.1) containing a portion of Matins and Lauds of the Office of the dead, can be properly identified as being of the use of Sens. The presence of the responsories 'Credo quod' in the first lesson, 'Qui Lazarum' in the second, 'Heu mihi' in the third, and 'Memento mei deus' in the sixth lesson implies the use of that town; see K. Ottosen, *The Responsories and Versicles of the Latin Office of the Dead* (Aarhus, 1993), p. 156. It certainly excludes the use of Sarum, to which this fragment has been previously attributed probably because of the catch letter 'S' on fol. G_1^r. But 'S' is used to mark the use of Sens also in the *c*.1513 edition of the Hours for the use of Sens which were printed in Paris for Simon Vostre; see P. Lacombe, *Livres d'Heures imprimés au XVe et au XVIe siècle conservés dans les bibliothèques publiques de Paris. Catalogue* (Paris, 1907), no. 249.

4 M. B. Winn, 'Vérard's Hours of 8 February 1489/90: Prologue, Table, and Typological Borders', *Bibliographical Society of America*, 87 (1993), 337-62, at 337 gives an estimated number of 1585 editions printed in the fifteenth and sixteenth centuries based on H. Bohatta, *Bibliographie der Livres d'Heures des 15. und 16. Jahrhunderts*, 2nd edn (Vienna, 1924). See now Virginia Reinburg, 'Books of Hours', in *The Sixteenth-Century French Religious Book*, ed. by A. Pettegree, P. Nelles & P. Conner (Aldershot, 2001), pp. 68-82, for an interesting analysis of Books of Hours as an aspect of social, economic, cultural, and religious life of fifteenth- and sixteenth-century France.

5 See Kristian Jensen, p. 116, in this volume.

6 Hours of Roman use were printed also in the Netherlands, starting from the edition assigned to [Pafraet, between 1477 and 1479] (*ISTC* no: ih00357298), Germany, and Spain.

7 P. Needham, 'Venetian printers and publishers in the fifteenth century', *La Bibliofilia*, 100 (1998), 157-74, 167 no. 2. Hereafter in brackets in the main text.

8 During the 1470s, however, he also printed two bibles, a Roman breviary, and a Roman missal. Between 1481 and 1482 another bible, two Franciscan breviaries, a Dominican breviary, a Roman diurnal, and another Book of Hours were printed for the partnership that Jenson had formed with Johannes de Colonia and others.

9 The analysis of the saints listed in the litanies of another Milanese liturgical imprint, *Rituale Ambrosianum*. [Milan: Leonardus Pachel and Uldericus Scinzenzeler, *c*.1478]. 4°. *ISTC* no:

i00200400, without a calendar, has allowed Magistretti to identify its manuscript exemplar as coming from the Milanese basilica of Santo Stefano in Brolo; see M. Magistretti, 'Di due edizioni sconosciute del Rituale dei Sacramenti secondo il rito Ambrosiano', in *Miscellanea Ceriani* (Milan, 1910), pp. 87-120, at 97 and 99-101 the litanies. Zarotus's prolific output includes a substantial number of liturgical imprints, especially Roman and Ambrosian, but also Dominican and Humiliate missals, Ambrosian breviaries, and a Roman psalter.

10 Including a bible, two Franciscan missals and a Dominican one, a Roman diurnal, a breviary for the Franciscans, one for the Celestines, and one for the use of the diocese of Valencia.

11 In addition, he himself printed a missal for the diocese of Chalon-sur-Saône in 1500, while three Roman Hours and a Roman breviary were printed for him in Lyon in 1499 and 1500.

12 T. Gasparrini Leporace, 'Nuovi documenti sulla tipografia veneziana del Quattrocento. I. Un'edizione finora sconosciuta della Società "Zuan de Cologna, Nicolò Jenson e compagni"', in *Studi bibliografici: atti del convegno dedicato alla storia del libro italiano nel V centenario dell'introduzione dell'arte tipografica in Italia. Bolzano, 7-8 ottobre 1965*, Biblioteca di Bibliografia Italiana, 50 (Florence, 1967), pp. 25-46, at 25-7. Needham 188 no. 34.

13 While this was his only Book of Hours, Arrivabenus produced one bible, three Roman breviaries, one breviary for the Franciscans, two for the Cistercians, a diurnal, and three Roman missals, either alone or in association with other printers.

14 Leoviler's small output of 12 editions includes, apart from the Hours, a Franciscan breviary of 1486 and a number of little-known devotional texts, both in Italian and Latin, as well as a manual of arithmetic for merchants.

15 These are set within the context of a breviary for the use of the diocese of Capua, a Roman missal, and four editions of minor liturgical works, including the Miracles of the Virgin, a rosary in Italian, and the manual for the Baptistery of Naples.

16 *Oratio s. Anselmi. Domine deus meus si feci ut essem reus tuus, numquid facere potui ut non essem effectus tuus ... Cognosce ergo in me quod est tuum et absterge quod est meum*; a selection of passages from the first and second meditations of Anselm; see Anselm, *Opera omnia*, ed. by F. S. Schmitt, 6 vols (Edinburgh, 1946), III 79-82.

17 *Oratio s. Gregorii. O domine Iesu Christe adoro te in cruce pendentem ...*; see V. Leroquais, *Les Livres d'Heures manuscrits de la Bibliothèque Nationale*, 2 vols (Paris & Mâcon, 1927-43), II 346 no. xxxvii, a set of seven prayers that can be found arranged in different order.

18 Io, 18,1-19,42.

19 Leroquais, as note 17, II 346 no. xxi.

20 Leroquais, as note 17, II 346 no. xxxviii.

21 For which see J. Sonet, *Répertoire d'incipit de prières en ancien français* (Geneva, 1956) and E. Brayer, 'Livres d'heures contenant des textes en français', *Bulletin d'information de l'Institut de recherche et d'histoire des textes*, 12 (1963-4), 31-102.

22 *Dictionnaire de spiritualité ascétique et mystique: doctrine et histoire*, 1- (Paris, 1937-), VII, 1 410-31.

23 M. M. Smith, *The Title-Page: Its Early Development 1460-1510* (London, 2000), pp. 25-34, where a few exceptions arc discussed.

24 *The Oxford Companion to the Year*, ed. by B. Blackburn & L. Holford-Strevens (Oxford, 1999), pp. 752-61, 809-15, 829-32, 846-7, and see the Glossary.

25 M. B. Winn, 'Printing and Reading the Book of Hours: Lessons from the Borders', *Bulletin of John Rylands University Library of Manchester*, 81/3 (1999), 177-204, at 178-9.

26 During the sixteenth century Venetian printers continued to print Roman Hours, although not in any great quantity when compared with the hundreds of editions which continued to emerge from the Parisian printing shops. Data for the sixteenth century has to be based on Bohatta, *Bibliographie der Livres d'Heures*, as note 4; because of Bohatta's unclear division

between Hours and *Officia B.M.V.*, and because his information is often based on sales catalogues rather than on books located in public libraries, his work is of only limited use today.

27 So far I have noticed some text in Italian only in de Boninis's 1481 edition (no. 15), Torresanus's 1481 (no. 17), and de Spira's 1494 (no. 41) and 1498 (no. 53) editions.

28 P.-M. Gy, 'L'Unification liturgique de l'Occident et la liturgie de la Curie Romaine', *Revue des sciences philosophiques et théologiques*, 59 (1975), 601-12, at 601-2. Liturgical matters, and in particular the reform of the breviary and missal, were debated at the 25th session of the Council; see E. Weber, *Le Concile de Trente et la musique de la réforme à la contreréforme*, Musique-Musicologie, 12 (Paris, 1982), pp. 103-26.

29 Gy, *L'Unification*, as note 28, 608.

30 Gy, *L'Unification*, as note 28, 609.

31 By 1570 of the 116 French dioceses 84 had printed for the local use either a breviary or a missal or both; see ibid. 611.

32 *Officium Beate Marie Virginis nuper reformatum*. Rome: In Aedibus Populi Romani, 1571. 12°. Bohatta, *Bibliographie der Livres d'Heures*, as note 4, no. II 187.

33 *Officium Beate Marie Virginis nuper reformatum*. Antwerp: C. Plantin, 1573. 8°.

34 The calendar of the Papal Court (1260) was edited by S. J. P. Van Dijk, *Sources of the Modern Roman Liturgy: the Ordinals of Haymo of Faversham and Related Documents (1243-1307)*, 2 vols, Studia et Documenta Franciscana, 1-2 (Leiden, 1963), II 364-84. Van Dijk, *The Ordinal of the Papal Court from Innocent III to Boniface VIII and Related Documents*, Spicilegium Friburgense, 22 (Fribourg, 1975), pp. 59-85 contains the text of a calendar revised by Cardinal Giovanni Gaetano Orsini (later Nicholas III) *c.*1255; this calendar was officially abolished during his papacy, but it left traces in the thirteenth-century books of the Papal Court and, later, in several local and regional customs of central Italy. For the analysis of fifteenth-century calendars these texts will have of course to be complemented with the newly venerated feasts, in particular those of the Franciscans and Dominicans.

35 A.-G. Martimort, 'Missels incunables d'origine Franciscaine', in *Mélanges liturgiques offerts au R. P. Dom Bernard Botte O.S.B. de l'Abbaye du Mont César a l'occasion du cinquantième anniversaire de son ordination sacerdotale (4 juin 1972)* (Louvain, 1972), pp. 359-78, at 378.

36 See the introduction to the *Breviarium Romanum*, GW 5101-5177.

37 Martimort, as note 35, p. 360.

38 G. Mercati, *Appunti per la storia del Breviario Romano nei secoli XIV-XV tratti dalle 'Rubricae Novae'* (Rome, 1903) [extract from *Rassegna Gregoriana*, Fasc. 9-10 – Settembre-Ottobre 1903]. Menth warned that such distinction might be more difficult to make in the missals, as a number of Roman missals were produced by Franciscans working for the editors, and that they inserted in their missals, destined for the secular churches, feasts proper to the Franciscans and Augustinian Hermits.

39 Mercati, *Appunti*, as note 38, 3-4; L. Armstrong, 'Nicolaus Jenson's Breviarium Romanum, Venice, 1478, Decoration and Distribution', in *Incunabula: Studies in the Fifteenth-Century Printed Books, Presented to Lotte Hellinga*, ed. by M. Davies (London, 1999), pp. 421-67, at 422 and 461.

40 Simon prof (4 Feb.), Faustinus et Iovita (15 Feb.), Secundus (1 June), Apparitio beati Marci ev (25 June), Marina (17 July), Fantinus (31 July), Moyses (4 Sept.), Zacharia (6 Sept.), Magnus (6 Oct.), Iustus (2 Nov.), Prosilonius (for Prosdocimus 7 Nov.), Maurus (21 Nov.), Bassus (5 Dec.). In particular the Aquileiese feasts Cancius Cancianus et Cancianilla (31 May), Hermacora et Fortunatus (12 July), and Euphemia Dorothea Tecla et Herasma (3 Sept.), the four virgins venerated in Aquileia on 19 Sept. with an octave; see *Breviarium*

Aquileiense. Venice: Franciscus Renner, 1481. 4° and 8°. *GW* 5257; and Venice: Andreas Torresanus, de Asula, 29 July 1496. 8°. *GW* 5258. Relics of the four saints were transferred to Venice *c*. 1200, where a church was dedicated to them; see S. Tramontin, A. Niero, G. Musolino, & C. Candiani, *Culto dei santi a Venezia*, Biblioteca Agiografica Veneziana (Venice, 1965), p. 312.

41 *Culto dei santi*, as note 40, p. 280; G. Cattin et al., *Musica e liturgia a S. Marco*, 3 vols (Venice, 1990), p. 32.

42 The patriarchate of Aquileia dates back to the third century. In 568 the Lombard invasions forced the patriarchate to take refuge in Grado, which from the early seventh century rivalled Aquileia as the new patriarchate. The territory of Aquileia came under Venetian domination in 1420, while the patriarchate of Grado was transferred to Venice in 1451; see *Patriarcato di Venezia*, ed. by S. Tramontin, Storia religiosa del Veneto, 1 (Padua, 1991), pp. 21-83 and *The Oxford Dictionary of the Christian Church*, ed. by F. L. Cross & E. A. Livingstone, 3rd edn (Oxford, 1997), pp. 94-5 and 1686-7.

43 P. Chiesa, 'Santi d'importazione a Venezia tra reliquie e racconti', in *Oriente Cristiano e Santità*, ed. by S. Gentile, Biblioteca Nazionale Marciana 2 luglio – 14 novembre 1998 (Milan, 1998), pp. 107-15, at 109.

44 We have no liturgical manuscripts of the ninth and tenth centuries for St Mark, nor for Venice in general (Cattin, *Musica e liturgia*, as note 41, p. 32). The earliest Venetian liturgical document is a *Missale plenum votivum et Rituale*, in use at Torcello and datable between 1054 and 1084 (Bologna, Biblioteca Universitaria, ms. 2679). Its calendar (fols 4-10) was edited by Stefano Borgia, *Kalendarium Venetum saeculi XI ex cod. Ms. Membranaceo Bibliothecae S. Salvatoris Bononiae* (Rome, 1773), a copy of which is bound with the manuscript (ex informatione Dott.ssa Laura Miani). This important manuscript is not mentioned by Cattin, who refers only to its calendar. The liturgical sources analysed by Cattin date otherwise to the thirteenth century, and may represent material a couple of centuries older.

45 As Cattin, *Musica e liturgia*, as note 41, p. 29 remarks, only by analysing the liturgical witnesses of the cathedral of Venice will it be possible to evaluate the extent to which the *consuetudines* of St Mark, ducal chapel and State Church, were distinctive from the diocesan liturgy of Venice; such analysis may also allow a more precise identification of the contribution of the liturgy of Grado, if this can still be quantified. For the customs of the cathedral church see B. Betto, *Il capitolo della basilica di S. Marco in Venezia: statuti e consuetudini dei primi decenni del sec. XIV (In appendice un confronto con il capitolo della cattedrale di S. Pietro di Castello fino al sec. XVI)*, Miscellanea erudita, 44 (Padua, 1984), pp. 194-253.

46 Cattin, *Musica e liturgia*, as note 41, pp. 38-40.

47 For the Venetian cult of Old Testament saints, to whom churches were dedicated from the eleventh century onwards, see *Culto dei santi*, as note 40, pp. 155-80; it is always significant the passage from the *Summa de ecclesiasticis officiis* of Johannes Beleth († 1182): 'Et nota, quod festa sanctorum ueteris testamenti ut Abraham Ysaac et Iacob et Dauid et Daniel et aliorum per Greciam et Venetiam coluntur, et ibi habent ecclesias'; ed. by H. Douteil, CCCM, 41-41A (Turnhout, 1976), p. 244 (Pl. 202, col. 134C).

48 As Chiesa points out, the acquisition by western churches of relics of saints that were already venerated locally would augment an already established tradition; if, on the other hand, the relics were of saints not known locally, they would be treasured and only generically would they augment the fame of the foundation; see Chiesa, `Santi d'importazione', as note 43, p. 109.

49 P. Chiesa, 'Recuperi agiografici veneziani dai codici Milano, Braidense, Gerli ms. 26 e Firenze, Nazionale, Conv. Soppr. G.5.1212', *Hagiographica*, 5 (1998), 219-71, at 257.

50 Chiesa, 'Santi d'importazione', as note 43, p. 110.

51 Chiesa, 'Recuperi', as note 49, 220-1.

52 On Pietro Calò († 1348) Prior of the Dominican convent of San Giovanni e Paolo (Zanipolo), Venice, in 1328 see *DBI* XVI 785-7, T. Kaeppeli, *Scriptores Ordinis Praedicatorum medii aevi*, 4 vols (Rome, 1970-93), III 220-1 no. 3215; the *Legendarium* survives only in three manuscript exemplars; see Chiesa, 'Recuperi', as note 49, 219 n. 1; an index of the collection of saints in C. De Smet et al., 'Le Légendier de Pierre Calò', *Analecta Bollandiana*, 29 (1910), 5-116. On Pietro Nadal († between 1400 and 1406), Bishop of Jesolo (1370-1400/6) see Chiesa, 'Recuperi', as note 49, 220 n. 2. See also *Bibliotheca Hagiographica Latina, Novum Supplementum*, Subsidia Hagiographica, 70 (Brussels, 1986), nos 9039 and 9040. The *Catalogus sanctorum et gestorum eorum ex diversis voluminibus collectus* was first printed in Vicenza: Henricus de Sancto Ursio, Zenus, 12 Dec. 1493. Folio. *ISTC* no. in00006000. The information provided on the life and cult of saints in this article will at times refer to the Latin martyrologies of Jerome, Florus, Adon, and Usuard, for which see: *Martirologium Hieronymianum*, ed. by J. B. De Rossi & L. Duchesne in *Acta SS. Novembris*, t. II/1 (Brussels, 1894, repr.); J. Dubois & G. Renaud, *Édition pratique des martyrologes de Bède, de l'Anonyme Lyonnais et de Florus*, IRHT, Travaux preparatoires (Paris, 1976); *Le Martyrologe d'Adon*, ed. by J. Dubois & G. Renaud (Paris, 1984); *Le Martyrologe d'Usuard*, ed. by J. Dubois, Subsidia hagiografica, 40 (Brussels, 1965). For all of them see *Les martyrologes du moyen âge latin*, ed. by J. Dubois, Typologie des sources du moyen âge occidental, 26 (Turnhout, 1978).

53 For an analytical description of the extant liturgical manuscripts from St Mark see Cattin, *Musica e liturgia*, as note 41. Some other fifteenth- and sixteenth-century liturgical manuscripts from Venice are listed in B. Baroffio, 'Codici liturgici italiani datati o databili 1400-1550 inventario sommario', in *Liturgia in figura*, ed. by G. Morello & S. Maddalo (Rome 1995), pp. 335-44: Book of Hours 1468 (Rome, Biblioteca Apostolica Vaticana, Ross. III); Book of Hours 1481 (Vicenza, Biblioteca Comunale, G.2.7.28); breviary 1473 (Oxford, Bodleian Library, Douce 314); missal 1461 (Oxford, Bodleian Library, Canon. Liturg. 331); pontifical 1405 (Manchester, John Ryland Library, MS. 479). To my knowledge a systematic inventory of Venetian liturgical sources has not yet been compiled.

54 As defined in note 34.

55 The entries marked with an asterisk can be found in the sanctoral of St Mark, although not necessarily with a proper office.

56 *Bibliotheca Sanctorum*, 15 vols (Rome, 1961-2000), V 991-2 [hereafter abbreviated *BSS*]; *Culto dei santi*, as note 40, 124 and 292; her body was preserved in a church dedicated to her in Torcello.

57 *BSS* V 483-92; martyr saint of Brescia with Giovita; some of their relics were placed in San Giorgio, Aquileia, in the ninth century.

58 *BSS* VI 1176-7; *Culto dei santi*, as note 40, 129 and 292; the martyr of Nicomedia, whose body was translated to Pozzuoli and then to Naples; in Venice she was co-titular of a church with St Pantaleon.

59 *BSS* II 966-7; *Culto dei santi*, as note 40, 116 and 322; according to the *passio* reported by the Venetian hagiographers Calò and Nadal, he was a bishop of Nicaea; the body is believed to be preserved in Cupra Marittima (Marche), and his cult developed along the Adriatic coast from the Marche up to Venice (Malamocco in particular); he is also the patron saint of sailors. A church was dedicated to him in Venice in sestiere di San Marco, and he also appears in the mosaics of St Mark; see *Culto dei santi*, as note 40, 148.

60 *BSS* IV 786-7; *Culto dei santi*, as note 40, 309; Donatus, bishop of 'Euraea', Epirus, is venerated on 30 Apr. in the Byzantine Synaxaries, and on 7 Aug. in the West (with a clear confusion with the homonymous bishop of Arezzo who is also venerated on that date); his

relics were stolen from Cephalonia by the Venetians in 1126 and then translated into the monastery of Santa Maria in Murano by the Doge Domenico Michiel. In Murano he is venerated on 30 Apr., his Byzantine date; see E. Follieri, 'S. Donato vescovo di Èvria in Epiro', in *Byzantina Mediolanensia*, ed. by F. Conca, Medioevo Romanzo e Orientale. Colloqui, 3 (Messina, 1996), pp. 165-75, at 174-5. The account of his translation is recorded by Pietro Calò and by Andrea Dandolo (*Andreae Danduli Ducis Venetiarum Chronica per extensum descripta aa. 46-1280*, book IX, cap. 12, ed. E. Pastorello, *RIS*, XII (Bologna, 1938), 236) but the date is not given. Considering that he appears on 13 Mar. not only in Jenson 1474 calendar, but also in Girardengus's 1481 and in De Spira's 1494, 1495, and 1497, I wonder whether this is the date of his translation.

61 *BSS* XI 1043-7; *Culto dei santi*, as note 40, 139; the cult of Sigismundus was probably imported to Venice from Aquileia, where he received a double feast; in Venice he appears among the saints in the mosaics in the entrance of the church of St Mark, but was added there at a later date.

62 *BSS* VIII 1150-65; *Culto dei santi*, as note 40, 87-8; the church in sestiere di Castello, which was founded in the eleventh century and originally dedicated to the saints Liberalis and Alexis, was entitled to Marina in 1231 when her body was brought to Venice from Constantinople.

63 *BSS* VIII 300-7; *Culto dei santi*, as note 40, 120 and 311; the Franciscan canonized in 1317, titular of the church dedicated to him, San Alvise, in sestiere di Cannaregio.

64 *BSS* IX 604-49; *Culto dei santi*, as note 40, 168-9 and 313; venerated in Venice on 4 Sept. and titular of a parish church in sestiere di San Marco; Moyses was probably also the titular saint of the cathedral of Venice, later dedicated to St Peter (San Pietro di Castello).

65 *BSS* VI 1345-9; *Culto dei santi*, as note 40, 223-4 and 316; titular of a church in sestiere di Castello.

66 *BSS* VI 15-19; *Culto dei santi*, as note 40, 118 and 317; a church was dedicated to him in sestiere di San Marco.

67 *BSS* X 1186-93; *Culto dei santi*, as note 40, 20, 103, and 319.

68 *BSS* VI 1046; Giovanni Orsini (twelfth century) bishop and patron saint of Traù, now Trogir, Dalmatia, whose body was translated to Venice; Chiesa, 'Recuperi', as note 49, 251.

69 *BSS* IX 228-31; *Culto dei santi*, as note 40, 103, 160-1, and 321; bishop and patron saint of Parenzo, now Poreč in Croatia, part of the old patriarchate of Grado, he is venerated in Venice in the church of Sant'Angelo in sestiere di San Marco.

70 *BSS* V 597-600; patron saint of Foligno, where he is venerated as a bishop on this day.

71 Possibly one of the twelve martyrs of Smyrna, of whom Polycarpus is the one generally remembered by the martyrologies on 26 Jan. Germanicus is recorded on 19 Jan. by the Martyrology of Adon; see *BSS* VI 229-30.

72 *BSS* XI 958-9; bishop of Scythopolis (Beth Shean), Palestine, he is generally venerated on 21 Feb.

73 *BSS* IX 393-5; generally venerated on 20 Feb.

74 Probably a latinized form for the Byzantine Polieutus. On 5 Dec. the patriarch of Constantinople († 970) of that name is remembered in the Byzantine Synaxaries. Another Polieutus, martyr of Melitene, Armenia, was also venerated in the West; the martyrology of Jerome and Florus list him on 14 Feb., Adon and Usuard on 13 Feb., moreover on 1 Apr. the martyrology of Jerome records the dedication of an oratory to Polieutus in Ravenna; *BSS* X 995-9.

75 *BSS* XI 768-71; one of the Forty Martyrs of Sebaste, Palestine, who are venerated on 9 Mar.

76 *BSS* X 746-62; *Culto dei santi*, as note 40, 296.

77 He was probably the parish priest of San Giovanni Decollato in Venice, who lived between the end of the thirteenth and the beginning of the fourteenth century; *BSS* VI 856-7.

78 i.e. Dedication of the Lateran basilica in Rome; see P. Jounel, *Le Culte des saints dans les basiliques du Latran et du Vatican au douzième siècle*, Collection de l'École française de Rome, 26 (Rome, 1977), 49.

79 The liturgy of the Canons of the cathedral of Lucca influenced that of the Canons of the Lateran in the twelfth century; see P.-M. Gy, 'L'influence des chanoines du Lucques sur la liturgie du Latran', *Revue des sciences religieuses*, 58 (1984), 31-41, reprinted with some variation in P.-M. Gy, *La Liturgie dans l'histoire* (Paris, 1990), pp. 127-39. Despite the fact that in the thirteenth century the Canons of the Lateran had to adopt the liturgy of the Papal chapel, manuscripts retaining a heavier Lucca influence continued to circulate. For the sanctoral of Lucca see M. Giusti, 'L'Ordo Officiorum della cattedrale di Lucca', in *Miscellanea Giovanni Mercati*, II, Studi e Testi, 122 (Vatican City, 1946), pp. 522-66.

80 Milan, Biblioteca Braidense, Gerli ms. 26; see Chiesa, 'Recuperi', as note 49, 223 and following.

81 Chiesa, 'Recuperi', as note 49, 254-5. The presence should be noted in Venetian calendars of saints from, or venerated in, southern Italy e.g. Sabinus (8 Feb.), bishop of Canosa; Castrensis (11 Feb.), bishop of Sessa; Iuliana v (16 Feb.), whose body was translated to Pozzuoli then to Naples; Hermolaus (27 Feb.), venerated in Benevento; Fantinus (31 July), the Calabrian saint; Ruffus (27 Aug.), martyr of Capua; Victorinus (5 Sept.), buried in Naples; Felix ep (24 Oct.), venerated in Nola; Felix (15 Nov.), bishop of Nola. Cattin, *Musica e liturgia*, as note 41, pp. 39-40, has also pointed out a good number of concordances between the fourteenth-century antiphonaries of St Mark (Venice, Archivio di Stato, P. s., Reg. 114-18) and a late-twelfth- or early-thirteenth-century monastic antiphonary from Benevento (Benevento, Biblioteca Capitolare, ms. 21).

82 Translatio Francisci (25 May); Stigmata Francisci (17 Sept.); Translatio Clare (2 Oct.); Translatio Ludovici cf (8 Nov.). The entry for a Dominus ep (7 May) is so far unidentified, while Dedicatio Petri et Pauli (18 Nov.) is Roman, from the Lateran tradition.

83 Not found in the previous edition is the entry for *Iustus m (2 Nov.), bishop of Trieste, a feast imported to Venice from Aquileia, where the saint came from; Iustus was venerated in the patriarchal chapel in San Pietro di Castello with a double feast and he is also venerated in St Mark; *BSS* VII 33; *Culto dei santi*, as note 40, 20 and 318.

84 *BSS* XI 820; the martyr from Asti who is generally venerated on 30 Mar. His body was translated in 1237 (or 1284 according to Cattin) to the isle of San Erasmo, later known as San Secondo, where there was a convent of Benedictine nuns which was given to the Dominicans in 1534; in Venice the saint is also commemorated on 1 June, the day of his translation to the city; see F. Corner, *Notizie storiche delle chiese e monasteri di Venezia e di Torcello* (Padua, 1758), pp. 274-81, and Cattin, *Musica e liturgia*, as note 41, III 105. Secundus is present in all the Venetian editions I have examined so far, with the exception of Jenson's 1474 and 1475.

85 *BSS* VIII 546-50; Bishop of Oderzo and Eraclea, Veneto, his body was transferred on 6 Oct. 1206 to the Venetian church of San Geremia in sestiere di Cannaregio, where he is co-titular; see Chiesa, 'Recuperi', as note 49, 230. He is also venerated in St Mark, where he appears among the saints in the mosaics of the entrance of the church; see *Culto dei santi*, as note 40, 139-40.

86 The cathedral of Lucca is dedicated to St Martin. The dedication is generally remembered on 6 Oct.; this discrepancy, however, can be found in old Lucchese books and is due to the commemoration on 8 Oct. of St Reparata, to whom was dedicated the old cathedral of Lucca: see Giusti, 'L'Ordo', as note 79, 537 n. 72, 558, and 562. It is unfortunate that the church of St Mark was also dedicated on this day (see Cattin, *Musica e liturgia*, as note 41, II 158-9), creating ambiguity in entries such as 'Dedicatio s Mar' in the calendars of other Venetian Hours.

87 They do not contain the following saints, which Girardengus derived from Jenson: Sabinus, Germanicus, Ugo, Severianus, Simon, Iulianus, Romanus, Sixtus pp (15 Apr.), Juvenal, Dedicatio s Martini. They do include the Venetian Fantinus, who is found neither in Girardengus's edition, nor in Jenson's. Moreover, only the first of Hamman's editions includes Cyriacus (2 Apr.), who is not found in Girardengus's but in Jenson's; while Hamman's second and third editions include the Dedicatio Salvatoris (9 Nov.), which can be found in Jenson's 1474 and in Girardengus.

88 *BSS* VI 732-40; Johannes Damascenus, not included in the medieval western martyrologies, but in Nadal, apparently on 6 May. His relics were apparently in Constantinople by the fifteenth century.

89 See n. 84.

90 *BSS* VI 1164-8; a saint from Carthage, whose relics were taken to Corsica, and thence to the Tuscan isle of Gorgóna and to Brescia in 763, and placed in San Salvatore, the church of the famous Benedictine monastery; Giulia is also patron saint of Livorno, where the first church was dedicated to her in commemoration of a stop of the relics in the journey to Brescia.

91 *BSS* XII 1443-6; the father of St John the Baptist; his relics were apparently translated to Venice on this date; see Cattin, *Musica e liturgia*, as note 41, III 77.

92 *BSS* XII 1280-1; *Culto dei santi*, as note 40, 314; old titular saint of the church of San Moisè in Venice.

93 *BSS* XII 286-8, the martyr of Caesarea generally venerated on 2 Apr.; a relic of the saint was in the parish church of San Tomà in sestiere di San Polo; Chiesa, 'Recuperi', as note 49, 233-4.

94 *Horae ad usum Romanum.* Lyon: [Jacobinus Suigus and Nicolaus de Benedictis], for Boninus de Boninis, de Ragusia, 20 Mar. 1499. (*ISTC* no ih00399360) In the Lyon calendar can be found the following five additions: Longinus (15 Mar.), Patritius (17 Mar.), Ioseph (19 Mar.), Nicolaus de Tolentino (10 Sept.), finally a very early example of the spread of the cult for Simon from Trent, whose death in 1475 was blamed on the Jews of that city. Promoted by the Franciscans, his cult immediately spread, although it never reached official recognition (*BSS* XI 1184-8).

95 *Biblioteca Hagiographica Graeca*, ed. by F. Halkin, Subsidia Hagiographica, 8 (Brussels, 1957) and *BHG Novum Auctarium*, ed. by F. Halkin, Subsidia Hagiografica, 65 (Brussels, 1984), 1508 and 1509; E. Follieri, *La vita di San Fantino il Giovane*, Subsidia hagiographica, 77 (Brussels, 1993), 373-98; F. Follieri, 'I santi dell'Italia greca', in *Oriente Cristiano e Santità*, ed. by S. Gentile, Biblioteca Nazionale Marciana 2 luglio – 14 novembre 1998 (Milan, 1998), pp. 93-106, at 95 and 101.

96 E. Follieri, 'Il culto di san Fantino a Venezia', in *San Marco: Aspetti storici e agiografici*, ed. by A. Niero (Venice, 1996), pp. 504-19.

97 *Breviarium Romanum.* Venice: Nicolaus Jenson, [before 6 May] 1478. Folio. *GW* 5101.

98 His body was preserved in the cathedral of Lucca, where an altar was dedicated to him; generally venerated in Lucca on 1 Sept.; Giusti, 'L'Ordo', as note 79, 534-5, 540, 561, 566, etc.

99 Probably the Tarpetus martyr of Pisa venerated in Lucca; Giusti, 'L'Ordo', as note 79, 556; alternatively perhaps, the Provençal saint with the same name (fr. Tropez), whose cult, together with that of Maxima of Fréjus, extended to Friuli; *BSS* XII 627 and see below n. 102.

100 Giusti, 'L'Ordo', as note 79, 558; on the celebration of Hilarius of Poitiers on this date in Lucca, where he is co-titular of the high altar in the Cathedral of San Martino, see E. B. Garrison, 'Three Manuscripts for Lucchese Canons of S. Frediano in Rome', *Journal of the Warburg and Courtauld Institutes*, 38 (1975), 1-52, at 17.

101 *BSS* IV 1012-16; Eleutherus is venerated as Bishop of *Illiricum*, and had a church dedicated

to him in Parenzo, Dalmatia, where he is venerated on this date; the saint is named 'Eleuitius' in de Spira's editions.

102 *BSS* IX 12-13; the friend of St Tropez.

103 *BSS* IX 40-1; Maximianus was venerated in Cittanova then also in Parenzo following the unification of the two dioceses in 1443; when Parenzo was temporarily united to the patriarchate of Venice in 1451 the relics of the saint were translated to the church of San Canziano by a member of the Badoer family who lived in that parish.

104 *BSS* X 1333; Quirinus bishop of Siscia, now Sisak, Croatia; some of his relics were in Aquileia, where he is venerated on this date with a double office; see *Breviarium Aquileiense*. Venice: Franciscus Renner, de Heibronn, 1481. 4° and 8°. *GW* 5257; and Venice: Andreas Torresanus, de Asula, 29 July 1496. 8°. *GW* 5258.

105 *Culto dei santi*, as note 40, 139-40; in Venice Foca appears among the saints in the mosaics in the entrance of the church of St Mark; he is also the patron saint of sailors.

106 The ducal chapel before the construction of St Mark was dedicated to St Theodorus, whose body was apparently translated to Venice in 1096; he is generally venerated on 9 Nov.; *Culto dei santi*, as note 40, 91-5; Chiesa, 'Recuperi', as note 49, 232. The entry is in red in de Ragazonibus's edition.

107 Bishop of Pavia; his ashes were brought to St Mark in 1479; Cattin, *Musica e liturgia*, as note 41, II 86.

108 Actually Eufrasia, of Alexandria, venerated on this date in the martyrologies of Florus, Adon, and Usuard; see Cattin, *Musica e liturgia*, as note 41, II 98.

109 *BSS* IX 574-5; from the Martyrology of Jerome and in Nadal.

110 *BSS* VII 104-5; King of Burgundy and Orleans, fifth century; 'Gandarnus' in de Ragazonibus's edition, 'Grondanus' in de Spira's.

111 *BSS* IV 638-9; in Usuard's martyrology; his body from Rome was given by Innocent III (1198-1216) to Emericus, Prior of St Denis, Paris.

112 *BSS* XI 1097-1100; the *catholicos* of Seleucia, whose veneration was introduced to the West on this date by Florus, later followed by Adon (who claims that the saint lived in Apulia; Cattin, *Musica e liturgia*, as note 41, II 109) and Usuard.

113 *BSS* XII 1142-6; not remembered in the old martyrologies other than Nadal.

114 *BSS* IV 1194-5; venerated in Sardinia with Felix, Priamus, and Felicianus.

115 *BSS* VII 1351-2; Abbot of La Croix, near Évreux. His relics were moved to Saint-Germain-des-Prés, Paris, in the ninth century.

116 *BSS* XII 1487-9 probably one of the companions of the better-known saint Zoilus, martyr of Cordoba. Zostus and Zoilus both appear on this date in the calendar of the 1562 edition of the Roman breviary. Venice: Johannes Variscus & Socii; H. Bohatta, *Bibliographie der Breviere, 1501-1850* (Leipzig, 1937), no. 247.

117 The fourteenth-century saint from Montpellier, who is venerated as patron saint against the plague. During the epidemic of 1477 a confraternity in honour of the saint, the Scuola di San Rocco, was founded in Venice. In 1485 the Venetians supposedly acquired relics of the saint in Voghera; see *BSS* XI 264-73 and E. Fusaro, *San Rocco nella storia, nella tradizione, nel culto, nell'arte, nel folklore ed a Venezia* (Venice, 1965).

118 Martyr of Capua or Ravenna (Cattin, *Musica e liturgia*, as note 41, II 146); in de Spira's editions the saint is called Ruffinus.

119 *BSS* V 586-7 bishop of Thibiuca or Tubzak, near Carthage, today Zoustina, venerated in Venosa, Apulia, and Nola, Campania.

120 Regulus, Hilarius, Eleutherus, Maxima, Maximianus, Quirinus, Foca, Fantinus, Victor, Magnus, Iustina, Sirus, Policarpus, Alexander, Longinus, Patritius, Iohannes heremita, Isidorus, Symeon, Iulia, Desiderius, Vincentius, Leufridus, Panthemius, Eustachius, Rochus, Anastasius, Ruffus, Serapia, Victorinus, Marianus, Germanus, Lupus, Apolinaris,

Eustachius, Florentius, Severinus, Felix (24 Oct.), Felix (15 Nov.), Pontianus, Sostenis, Albinus, Cassianus, Valerianus.

121 Florentius, Satyrus, Alexander, Montanus, Johannes heremita, Dyonisius, Symeon, Iulia, Philippus, Leufridus, Zostus et Zoilus, Partenius, Eustachius, Anastasius, Victorinus, Syrus, Philippus (13 Sept.), Marianus, Germanus, Lupus, Eustachius, Felix, Albinus, Cassianus, Paulus (12 Dec.), Gratianus.

122 See above n. 116; the calendar is edited for comparative reference in Cattin, *Musica e liturgia*, as note 41, 465-93.

123 I would like to thank my colleague Helen Dixon for transcribing the calendar of the Hours for me.

124 *Missale Romanum*. Milan: Antonius Zarotus, 6 Dec. 1474. Folio. *ISTC* no: im00688450. Ed. by R. Lippe, Henry Bradshaw Society, 17 (London, 1899).

125 The body of the Persian martyr saint Jacobus Intercisus was brought to Italy and his head was kept in St Peter since the time of Eugenius IV (1431-1447); see Jounel, *Le Culte des saints*, as note 78, 48 n. 82

126 Such as Severus (30 Apr. *BSS* XI 992-3) Bishop of Naples, Ianuarius (19 Sept., Bishop of Benevento but patron saint of Naples *BSS* VI 135-51), and Asprenus (3 Aug. *BSS* II 507-11), first Bishop of Naples and one of the city's 47 patron saints, ranking second after Ianuarius.

127 Agnellus's relics were preserved in the cathedral of Lucca; Giusti, 'L'Ordo', as note 79, 561 n.178.

128 Only the following entries have not been included: Geminianus (29 Jan.), Faustinus (15 Feb.), Metranus (26 Feb.), Romanus (20 Mar.), Albinus (24 Mar.), Petrus (29 Mar.), Cyriacus (2 Apr.), Sixtus pp (15 Apr.), Petrus (29 Apr.), Theodora (13 May), Iuvenal (21 May), Marina (17 July), Iustina (7 Oct.). Interestingly, it is evident that an attempt has been made to correct some of the entries: Bonifatii (11 Feb.) instead of Bonitii, Hipoliti (28 Feb.) instead of Polioti, Sixti pp (6 Apr.) instead of Celestini pp.

129 *Horae ad usum Romanum*. Paris: Philippe Pigouchet, 21 Nov. [1487?]. 8°. *ISTC* no: ih00358000.

130 *Horae ad usum Romanum*. Paris: Philippe Pigouchet, [c. 1493-6]. 8°. *ISTC* no: ih00370600.

131 We find entries such as Basilius (14 June), Fantinus (31 July), Prosdocimus (7 Nov.), and Maurus (21 Nov.).

132 Herculianus (1 Mar.) Bishop of Perugia, Anselmus (18 Mar.) Bishop of Lucca, the dedication of the basilica of San Salvatore (9 Nov.), and of that dedicated to Peter and Paul (18 Nov.).

133 *Horae ad usum Romanum*. Paris: Philippe Pigouchet, [c. 1489?]. 8°. *ISTC* no: ih00364000.

134 *Horae ad usum Romanum*. Valencia: [Printer of Officium B.V. Mariae], 7 Nov. 1486. 4°. *ISTC* no ih00357880.

135 Claudius (6 June), Abbot of Condat; Martialis (30 June), Bishop of Limoges; and Gratianus (18 Dec.) Bishop of Tours.

136 *Horae ad usum Baiocensem*. (Bayeux). Paris: [Etienne Jehannot], for Pierre Regnault at Caen, 31 Oct. 1497. 8°. *ISTC* no: ih0033949.

137 *Horae ad usum Cenomanensem*. (Le Mans). [Paris: Etienne Jehannot], for Jean Poitevin, 20 Feb. 1498/99. 8°. *ISTC* no: ih00343300.

138 *Horae ad usum Parisiensem*. (Paris). [Paris: Etienne Jehannot], for Jean Poitevin, 15 May 1498. 8°. *ISTC* no: ih00353500.

139 *Horae ad usum Rothomagensem*. (Rouen). [Paris: Etienne Jehannot], for Pierre Regnault at Caen, [c.1497]. 8°. *ISTC* no: ih00418800.

140 Jehannot printed 37 Books of Hours, 18 for the use of Rome, out of an output of 148 editions. Pigouchet printed 95 Books of Hours, 55 for the use of Rome, out of an output of 180 editions.

141 *Horae ad usum Romanum.* Paris: Antoine Vérard, 10 Apr. 1489. 8°. *BMC* VIII 75.

142 C. Péligry, *Catalogues Régionaux des incunables des bibliothèques publiques de France. III. Bibliothèques de la Région Midi-Pyrénées* (Bordeaux, 1982), 420 (Millau, BM, Rés. XV. 12).

143 *Horae ad usum Romanum.* Add: Jean Quentin: *Examen de conscience* [Paris: André Bocard, *c.*1500]. 8°. *ISTC* no: ih00411300.

144 *Horae ad usum Romanum.* [Paris]: Etienne Jehannot, [*c.*1499]. 8°. *ISTC* no: ih00401300.

145 *Breviarium Lingonense.* [Venice?: s.n. post 1500?]. 8°. *CIBN* B-830; *ISTC* no: ib01164030. 4 fragments of *Proprium de tempore, pars hiemalis. Breviarium Lingonense.* Paris: [Thielman Kerver? for] Simon Vostre [*c.*1505]. 8°. *CIBN* p. 417: *pars aestivalis* only. *Breviarium Lingonense.* Paris, [Thielman Kerver, *c.*1505]. 8°. *CIBN* p. 417: *pars hiemalis* only. See also L. Marcel, *Les livres liturgiques du diocèse de Langres* (Paris and Langres, 1892), pp. 126-8.

146 In the sixteenth century, the breviary for the use of Langres was printed in 1536 (Bohatta, *Bibliographie der Breviere,* as note 116, no. 2356), 1560 (Bohatta, *Bibliographie der Breviere,* no. 2357), etc. The missal for the use of Langres was printed in 1517 (W. H. J. Weale, *Bibliographia liturgica: Catalogus missalium ritus latini ab anno M.CCCC.LXXIV impressorum,* ed. by H. Bohatta (London & Leipzig, 1928), no. 536), 1520, etc.

147 *Psalterium latinum cum hymnis et precibus.* Venice: [Bernardinus Stagninus, de Tridino]; [Baptista de Tortis?]; [Antonius de Zanchis], 30 Dec. 1495. 16°. *ISTC* no: ip01051000.

148 Corner, *Notizie storiche,* as note 84, 133-46. On the convent, suppressed in 1810, see also *S. Lorenzo,* ed. F. Gaeta, Fonti per la storia di Venezia. Sez. II – Archivi ecclesiastici – Diocesi Castellana (Venice, 1959). The oldest list of the relics preserved in the Venetian churches was compiled by Pietro Nadal and can be found in a manuscript copy of his *Catalogus* (Biblioteca Apostolica Vaticana, Cod. Vaticano Ottob. Lat. 225, fols 322A^v-322B^r), in a section not included in the printed editions of the text; see the transcription in Chiesa, 'Recuperi', as note 49, 267-71. On the revenues of the convent and its wealth, particularly in the sixteenth century, see also J. G. Sperling, *Convents and the Body Politic in Late Renaissance Venice* (Chicago & London, 1999), *ad indicem.*

149 Chiesa, 'Recuperi', as note 49, 237.

150 The body of Simeon the prophet was translated from Constantinople to Venice in 1204; on 4 Feb. 1318 the relics were transferred into the church of San Simeone Grande in sestiere di San Polo; see P. Chiesa, 'Ladri di reliquie a Costantinopoli durante la quarta crociata. La Traslazione a Venezia del corpo di Simeone profeta', *Studi Medievali,* s. III, 36 (1995), 431-59, at 433, at 451-9 the text of the translation, preserved only in the manuscript Milan, Biblioteca Braidense, ms. Gerli 26, fols 71^r-74^v; see Chiesa, 'Recuperi', as note 49, 227.

151 *BSS* III 945; i.e. Castrensis, Bishop of Sessa, Campania.

152 *BSS* V 65-7; martyr in Nicomedia and generally venerated on 27 July, relics in San Simeone Grande, Venice and in Benevento, Campania, where it was venerated on 7 Feb.; see Chiesa, 'Recuperi', as note 49, 228.

153 *BSS* VII 1293-1302; *Culto dei santi,* as note 40, 295 and 296; Leo IX, Pope, who was the titular saint of the church of San Lio in sestiere di Castello. It should also be remembered that the Greek saint Leo, whose body was moved from Samo to the isle of Malamocco, and in 1109 to the monastery on the island of San Servolo in Venice, was venerated in Venice as a bishop of the city on 29 Apr. (*BSS* VII 1228).

154 *BSS* XII 124-7; a Greek hermit, whose body was brought to Venice in the eleventh century and placed in the female convent of San Zaccaria; Chiesa, 'Santi d'importazione', as note 43, 111.

155 *BSS* VIII 50-52; probably a Greek saint, venerated in San Lorenzo on 13 Sept. and on 7 July, the day of the *inventio* of his body in San Lorenzo, together with St Barbarus; Chiesa,

'Recuperi', as note 49, 231.

156 *BSS* V 10-21; *Culto dei santi*, as note 40, 82-4 the bishop and the deacon of Aquileia, patron saints of Venice and titular saints of the parish church of San Marcuola; bones in San Lorenzo.

157 *BSS* X 959-61.

158 *BSS* VIII 5-9; the patron saint of Treviso, where he is venerated on 27 Apr.; his body, together with those of Tabra, Tabrata and Theonistus were moved to Torcello in 639 and from there to San Lorenzo.

159 Chiesa, 'Recuperi', as note 49, 240.

160 A finger of the patriarch of Alexandria in San Lorenzo; Chiesa, 'Recuperi', as note 49, 241.

161 African saints whose relics were supposedly in Treviso; a bone of the former in San Lorenzo.

162 A foot in San Lorenzo.

163 Her body in San Lorenzo.

164 *Breviarium Benedictinum (Monialium S. Laurentii de Venetiis)*. Venice: Antonius de Zanchis, 22 Mar. 1497. 8°. *GW* 5187; Vicenza, Biblioteca Civica Bertoliana, Inc. G.3.4.30.31. All the saints listed above are also present in the calendar and litanies of this edition.

165 D.E. Rhodes, 'Antonio Zanchi of Bergamo Printer or Publisher at Venice and Mantua', *Gutenberg-Jahrbuch* (1956), 141-4, reprinted in *Studies in Early Italian Printing*, ed. by D. R. Rhodes (London, 1982), 149-52.

166 Rhodes, 'Antonio Zanchi', 149 n. 2.

167 Rhodes, 'Antonio Zanchi', 150-2, and F. Ascarelli & M. Menato, *La Tipografia del '500 in Italia*, Biblioteca di Bibliografia Italiana, 116 (Florence, 1989), 183, 345-6.

168 *Diurnale Benedictinum Monialium Monasterii Sancti Zachariae Venetiarum*. Venice: Antonius de Zanchis, 28 Sept. 1496. 8°. *GW* 8510; Rhodes, 'Antonio Zanchi', as note 165, 150 no. 1.

169 *Legenda del beato Zanebono*. Mantua: Antonius de Zanchis, [1512?]. 8°. Rhodes, 'Antonio Zanchi', as note 165, 152 no. 13.

170 *Martyrium S. Theodosiae virginis*. Venice: Antonius de Zanchis, 22 Dec. 1498. 4° and 8° (A-H). *ISTC* no: ito0147500.

171 *Missale monasticum secundum ordinem Camaldulensem*. Venice: Antonius de Zanchis, 13 Jan. 1503. Folio. Rhodes, 'Antonio Zanchi', as note 165, 152 no. 11.

172 London, British Library, C.24.f., fol. 294: 'Absolutum Venetiis felicissimi diui Michaelis archangeli et sancti Matthie apostoli auspiciis, necnon almificorum patrum Benedicti et Romualdi, ac eiusdem ordinis monachorum sub Petro Delphino Veneto Generali. Cura uero et impensis Antonii de Zanchis de Bergomo. Regnante inclyto Duce Leonardo Lauredano. Idibus Januarii .M.D.III'. The calendar contains Venetian feasts.

173 Pietro Dolfin (1444-1525); abbot of San Michele, Murano, in 1479; General of the Camaldulese Order 1480-1514; *DBI* 40 565-71.

174 *Breviarium Camaldulense*, ed. by Petrus Delphinus. Florence: Antonio di Bartolommeo Miscomini, 13 Apr. 1484. 8°. *GW* 5191; according to W. A. Pettas, 'The Cost of Printing a Florentine Incunable', *La Bibliofilia*, 75 (1973), 67-85, at 69, 300 copies were printed of this breviary; E. Barbieri, *Il libro nella storia* (Milan, 1999), 13-14. In 1514 Dolfin commissioned from the Venetian Bernardinus Benalius a second edition of the Camaldulese breviary; Bohatta, *Bibliographie der Breviere*, as note 116, no. 1309; *Le edizioni italiane del XVI secolo* (=EDIT16), III (Rome, 1993), C611; Barbieri 14 n. 37. We should remember that in this period de Zanchis was in Mantua.

175 Venice, Biblioteca Nazionale Marciana, Lat. III 170 (2453); Barbieri 18-22.

176 An asterisk indicates the editions that I have been able to examine so far.

READING LITURGICAL BOOKS

1 Paul Saenger, 'Books of Hours and the Reading Habits of the Late Middle Ages', *Scrittura e Civiltà*, 9 (1985), 239-69; S. J. P. van Dijk, 'Medieval Terminology and Methods of Psalm Singing', *Musica Disciplina*, 6 (1952), 9-26; Diana M. Webb, 'Woman and Home: The Domestic Setting of Late Medieval Spirituality', in *Women in the Church: Papers Read at the 1989 Summer Meeting and the 1990 Winter Meeting of The Ecclesiastical History Society*, ed. by W. J. Sheils & Diana Wood (Cambridge, Mass., 1990), pp. 159-73.

2 My own research has focused on liturgical incunabula which contain music, the major genres being the missal, gradual, psalter, and antiphonal, and this paper will refer only briefly to the breviary. See Mary Kay Duggan, *Italian Music Incunabula* (Berkeley, 1992); *Music Incunabula of German-Speaking Lands*, in progress.

3 *The Sixteenth and Seventeenth Centuries*, Fontana Economic History of Europe, ed. by Carlo M. Cipolla, II (New York, 1974), p. 38. The estimate of the clerical and religious population is cited in Werner Sombart, *Die vorkapitalistische Wirtschaft* (Munich, 1928), I:1, 161. Sombart tells us that the percentage was probably higher than 5% for women. In 1552 in Florence, 15-16% of the female population were nuns. Elissa Weaver, 'Spiritual Fun: a Study of Sixteenth-Century Tuscan Convent Theater', in *Women in the Middle Ages and the Renaissance: Literary and Historical Perspectives*, ed. by Mary Beth Rose (Syracuse, NY, 1986), p. 175.

4 Erwin Iserloh, 'The Inner Life of the Church: the Urban Parish', in *A History of the Church, IV: From the High Middle Ages to the Eve of the Reformation*, ed. by Hubert Jedin & John Dolan, trans. by Anselm Biggs (New York, 1986), pp. 566-7.

5 Francis Rapp, *L'Église et la vie religieuse en Occident à la fin du Moyen Age*, 6th edn (Paris, 1999), chap. IX, 'La Réforme', pp. 207-25; Duggan, 'Politics and Text: Bringing the Liturgy to Print', *Gutenberg-Jahrbuch*, 76 (2001), 104-17.

6 For the repertoire of incunable breviaries, see *GW* 5101-5518, and *The Illustrated ISTC on CD-ROM*, 2nd edn (Reading: Primary Source Media in association with The British Library, 1998). Statistics on missals and psalters are taken from *IISTC* and my own research.

7 Editions of the liturgical psalter (239) include those with the complete repertoire of 150 psalms and printed references or space for manuscript references to the antiphons, hymns, etc., required for the performance of the hours of the Divine Office. The total does not include editions of commentaries on the psalms (by, for example, Nicolaus de Lyra, Alanus de Rupe, Bonaventura, Bernard of Clairvaux, Driesche, or Nitzschewitz), psalters of the Blessed Virgin Mary, psalters of a few pages for teaching children, or scholarly texts in Greek or multiple languages.

8 Keeping in mind Roger Chartier's cautions concerning the difficulty of measuring either reading or writing skill ('The Practical Impact of Writing', in *A History of Private Life*, ed. by Philippe Ariès & Georges Duby, 5 vols (Cambridge, Mass., 1987-91), III, *Passions of the Renaissance* (1989), ed. by Roger Chartier, trans. Arthur Goldhammer, pp. 111-12), we learn from Rolf Engelsing that in about the year 1500 in German lands three to four per cent could read; in the towns that percentage rose to ten or even thirty per cent (*Analphabetentum und Lektüre: Zur Sozialgeschichte des Lesens in Deutschland zwischen feudaler und industrieller Gesellschaft* (Stuttgart, 1973), p. 20). David Cressy estimated that in 1500 in England one per cent of women and five per cent of men could read (*Literacy and the Social Order* (Cambridge, 1980), p. 177).

9 The unique extant copy of the *Psalterium* attributed to Augsburg printer Johann Schönsperger about 1495 (*ISTC* ip0105220) was owned by Prioress Ursula Dättingen. Printed on vellum, it is richly illuminated in the south German style. London, Victoria and Albert Museum, R. C. F. 20.

10 Multiple copies of the two incunable editions of the *Rituale ambrosianum* remain at the Milan cathedral; see Duggan, *Italian Music Incunabula*, as note 2, p. 269.

11 Michel Aubrun, *La Paroisse en France des origines au XVe siècle* (Paris, 1986), *passim*; Jacques Toussaert, *Le Sentiment religieux en Flandre à la fin du Moyen-Age* (Paris, 1963), pp. 563-5; Louis Pérouas, *Les Limousins, leurs saints, leurs prêtres, du XVe au XXe siècle* (Paris, 1988), pp. 18-30.

12 'Quo opere expleto debeat et teneatur ex eo cuilibet librum habere exposcenti pro quatuor florenis rhenensibus colligatum tradere et assignare. Quapropter prefatarum ciuitatis et diocesis nostrarum prelatos ecclesiasticosque et beneficiatos ac subditos nostros pie et paterne amonemus et in domino exhortamur quatinus ipsi ad emptionem siue comperationem predictorum librorum missalium taliter se studeant preparare ...,' *Missale Herbipolense*. [Würzburg: Georg Reyser, 1481] (*ISTC* im00663900), fol. 12^r, preface of Rudolph von Scherenberg, Bishop of Würzburg.

13 Abbot Martin Senging (d. 1485) of Melk in 'De uniformitate Divini Officii', a section of *Tuitiones pro observantia Regulae S. P. N. Benedicti ex Concilio Basileensi*, said: 'Also lay people, in particular the literate, would be much edified by hearing a uniform liturgy, where before they were scandalized by the prevailing discord. Many might join our order who otherwise would remain secular. Otherwise they enter other orders, in consideration of the great diversity [of our liturgy] ... or they might enter an order in which uniformity is observed, such as the Carthusian, the Cistercian, and all the mendicant orders.' 'Populus quoque, maxime litteratus, aedificaretur multum audiens uniformitatem, ubi alias scandalizatus fuit de discordia: multique intrarent Religionem, qui alias manent seculares, aut intrant alias Religiones, considerantes tantam diversitatem ... aut intrarent ordinem aliquem, in quo servatur uniformitas, ut sunt ordo Cartusiensis, Cisterciensis et omnes ordines mendicantium.' Melk, Codex lit. N. 16, printed in *Bibliotheca ascetica antiquo-nova*; ed. by Bernhard Pez (Farnborough, 1967; reprint of the 1723 edition), VIII, 543.

14 Roger Chartier describes that kind of reader in a very different context, that of the reader of the *bibliothèque bleue*, who belonging to a primarily oral society would have 'a manner of reading that was more recognition than true discovery'. 'Avant-propos: La culture de l'imprimé', in *Les Usages de l'imprimé*, ed. by Roger Chartier *(XVe-XIXe siècle)* (Paris, 1987), pp. 7-20.

15 The introduction to the 1499 *Graduale* is discussed in Giuseppe Massera, *La 'Mano musicale perfetta' di Francesco de Brugis dalle prefazioni ai corali di L. A. Giunta (Venezia, 1499-1504)*, Biblioteca degli 'Historiae musicae cultores', 18 (Florence, 1963).

16 Robert Bonfil, 'Reading in the Jewish Communities of Western Europe in the Middle Ages', in *A History of Reading in the West*, ed. by Guglielmo Cavallo & Roger Chartier; trans. by Lydia G. Cochrane (Amherst, 1999), 149-78.

17 The Mass of the Dead in German in a prayer book printed in Augsburg by Gunther Zainer, 1471 (*ISTC* ig00112700); a commentary on the Mass in German [Nuremberg: Friedrich Creussner, not after 1482] (ia01395000). There are two bilingual Latin/German liturgical psalters: one with the the Postilla moralis of Nicolaus de Lyra [Strasbourg: Printer of Ariminensis = Georg Reyser?, *c.* 1474] (*ISTC* ip01066000); Augsburg: Erhard Ratdolt, 1494 (*ISTC* ip01067000).

18 In a memorial to the Fifth Lateran Council (1512-1517) two Camaldolese hermits, Paolo Giustiniani and Pietro Quirini, requested that the epistles and gospels read at Mass be translated into the vernacular. Nelson H. Minnich, 'Erasmus and the Fifth Lateran Council (1512-17)', reprinted in his *The Catholic Reformation: Council, Churchmen, Controversies* (Brookfield, VT, 1993), X:50, from *Erasmus of Rotterdam, The Man and the Scholar: Proceedings of the Symposium Held at the Erasmus University, Rotterdam, 9-11 November 1986*, ed. by Jan Sperna Weiland & Willem Th. M. Frijhoff (Leiden, 1988).

19 The translation of the Brigittine breviary is attributed to the first half of the fifteenth century; *The Myroure of oure Ladye*, ed. by J. H. Blunt, Early English Text Society, extra series 19 (London, 1873). Pynson first printed *The Myroure* in 1516. The use of the work is discussed by Ann M. Hutchison in 'Devotional Reading in the Monastery and in the Late Medieval Household', in *De Cella in Seculum: Religious and Secular Life and Devotion in Late Medieval England*, ed. by Michael G. Sargent (Cambridge, 1989), pp. 215-27.

20 Staatsbibliothek zu Berlin Preussischer Kulturbesitz, Inc. 2654 8° (*ISTC* ip01076000).

21 The annotations of Cardinal Guglielmo Sirleto (1514-85) for the reforms of the Council of Trent can be found in a copy of a *Missale Romanum*. Venice: Johannes Baptista Sessa, 8 October 1497 (H 11412*, *ISTC* im00712000); see Duggan, *Italian Music Incunabula*, as note 2, no.105. A picture of the fifteenth-century ecclesiastical editor at work, books spread out on desk and shelves, was painted by Giovanni di Paolo (*c.*1403-82) as *Saint Jerome appearing to St Augustine* (Berlin, Gemäldegalerie; reproduced in Geneviève Hasenohr, 'L'Essor des bibliothèques privées aux XIVe et XVe siècles', in *Histoire des bibliothèques françaises*, 4 vols (Paris, 1998-1992), I: *Les bibliothèques médiévales du VIe siècle à 1530*, ed. by André Vernet, pp. 215-63, planche 17, p. 256).

22 David Ewing Duncan, *Calendar: Humanity's Epic Struggle to Determine a True and Accurate Year* (New York, 1998).

23 Incunable examples of the printed portion of the *Missale itinerantium* include an octavo of 16 leaves (Cologne: Retro Minores [Martin von Werden?]) 11 October 1499 (*ISTC* ie00132000); a quarto of 22 leaves ([Cologne: Heinrich Quentell, *c.*1500]) (*ISTC* im00731890); an octavo of 28 leaves ([Cologne:] Heinrich Quentell, 1500 'ad medium Aug.') (*ISTC* im00731900).

24 Universitäts- und Stadtbibliothek, Cologne, Ennen 233. *Missale itinerantium* [Cologne: Heinrich Quentell, *c.*1500] (*ISTC* im00731890). Indulgence granted by Cardinal Nicolaus de Cusa on fol. [xlviii].

25 Staatsbibliothek zu Berlin Preussischer Kulturbesitz, 2anDy 355 R.

26 *A Critical Edition and Study of Frère Robert (Chartreux) Le Chastel perilleux*, by Sister Marie Brisson, Analecta Cartusiana, 19-20 (Salzburg, 1974), I, 109-11.

27 Jeannine Quillet, 'Quelques textes sur la prière de Chancelier Gerson', in *La Priére au Moyen Age: Littérature et civilisation* (Paris, 1981), p. 425. Relevant works by Gerson include *De meditatione cordis, De oratione et valore eius, Initiation à la vie mystique*, and *De arte moriendi*.

28 S. J. P. van Dijk, 'Medieval Terminology', as note 1 above. By the sixteenth century recitation had become the norm for performance of the Hours of the Office.

29 John Moorman, *A History of the Franciscan Order from its Origins to the Year 1517* (Oxford, 1968), p. 507.

30 *Speculum vitae B. Francisci et sociorum ejus; opera fratris, Guil. Spoelberch* (Antwerp, 1620), part i, cap. 4, as quoted in J. J. Jusserand, *A Wayfaring Life in the Middle Ages (XIVth Century)*, trans. by Lucy Toulmin Smith (London, 1889), p. 292.

31 London, BL, Cotton MSS, Domitian A. XVII, reproductions of fols 122^v and 177^v in *Musikgeschichte in Bildern*, III: *Musik des Mittelalters und der Renaissance*, Lieferung 8: *Musikleben im 15. Jahrhundert*, E. A. Bowles (Leipzig, 1977), Abb. 105-6.

32 The *Psalterium*, Cologne: Conrad Winters de Homborch, 1482 (*ISTC* ip01043000) left blank space before the psalms for the manuscript text and plainchant of antiphons. In one extant copy that space is carefully filled in (Paris, BNF, Rés. B2787), in another only the manuscript text of antiphons was entered, with space carefully measured out for plainchant (Paris, BNF, Vél. 923) (see *CIBN* P-658), and in a third empty space remains (New York Public Library, *KB 1482). Reproduced in Duggan, 'The Psalter on the Way to the Reformation: the Fifteenth-Century Printed Psalter in the North', in *The Place of the Psalms in the Intellectual*

Culture of the Middle Ages, ed. by Nancy Van Deusen (Albany, NY, 1999), figs 8.7-8.9.

33 See notes on copies in Duggan, *Italian Music Incunabula*, as note 2. For example, a copy of the *Missale Romanum* printed in Venice by Nicolaus de Frankfordia in 1485 (*ISTC* im00700000) ends with 53 leaves of manuscript sequences (Batchelder Coll., Library of Congress, Washington, D.C.).

34 *Psalterium*. Ulm: Johann Zainer, [*c.* 1480] (H 13475*; *ISTC* ip01041500). Staatsbibliothek zu Berlin Preussischer Kulturbesitz, Inc. 2631,3. 8°: manuscript roman plainchant for psalm tones on fols [131]-[133] in bottom margin.

35 *Psalterium*, Dutch. Deventer: Jacobus de Breda, Mar. 26, 1494 (*ISTC* ip01049800). Museum Meermanno-Westreenianum, The Hague, 1F15.

36 *Psalterium*. Cologne: Conrad Winters de Homborch [about 1482] (*ISTC* ip01043000), New York Public Library, KB 1482. Duggan, 'The Psalter on the Way to the Reformation', as note 32, figs 8.9, 170.

37 Geneviève Hasenohr, 'Religious Reading amongst the Laity in France in the Fifteenth Century', in *Heresy and Literacy, 1000-1530*, ed. by Peter Biller & Anne Hudson (Cambridge, 1994), pp. 205-21; see also her 'L'Essor des bibliothèques privées aux XIVe et XVe siècles', as note 21.

38 See, for example, the breviary of Queen Isabella of Castile (London, BL, Add. MS. 18851); Christopher de Hamel, *A History of Illuminated Manuscripts* (London, 1994), fig. 195, p. 215.

39 Diana M. Webb, 'Woman and Home': as note 1 above.

40 *Navicula* S. Ursulae (German). [Strasbourg: Heinrich Knoblochtzer, *c.* 1482] (*BMC* I 91; *ISTC* iu00076500); Strasbourg: Johann (Reinhard) Grüninger [not before 1496] (iu00077000); Strasbourg: Bartolomaeus Kistler, 1497 (iu00077200).

41 *Ain schöne Tagweis wie Maria ist Empfangen* [Ulm: Johann Reger, *c.* 1497-8], (*ISTC* ia00747800); Rolf Wilhelm Brednich, *Das Liedpublizistik im Flugblatt des 15. bis 17, Jahrhunderts*, Bibliotheca bibliographica Aureliana, 55 (Baden-Baden: Koerner, 1974), p. 28, Abb. 9; 'Ave Preclara', translated into German by Sebastian Brant ([Basel?: J. Bergmann, about 1496?]); for a facsimile, see Paul Heitz, *Einblattdrucke des XV. Jahrhunderts in Krakau* (Strasbourg, 1942), no. 15.

42 See, for example, Chapter III, 'Psalm Books', in Donald Krummel, *English Music Printing 1553-1700* (London, 1975), pp. 34-78.

43 Andrew Hadfield, 'National and International Knowledge: the Limits of the Histories of Nations', in *The Renaissance Computer: Knowledge Technology in the First Age of Print*, ed. by Neil Rhodes & Jonathan Sawday (London, 2000), p. 109.

44 Kate van Orden, 'Cheap Print and Street Song Following the Saint Bartholomew's Massacres of 1572', in *Music and the Cultures of Print* (New York: Garland Publishing, 2000), pp. 275-6.

45 François Lebrun, 'The Two Reformations: Communal Devotion and Personal Piety', in *A History of Private Life*, see note 8, p. 73.

46 Chap. XII, 'Reading as Poaching', in Michel de Certeau, *The Practice of Everyday Life*, trans. by Steven Rendall (Berkeley, 1984), pp. 165-76.

47 Duggan, 'The Psalter on the Way to the Reformation', as note 32, fig. 8.13.

48 Eight monks share five psalters at the Vespers of the Dead in the Book of Hours of René d'Anjou (Paris, about 1410, BL, MS. Egerton 1070, fol. 54^v; *Musikleben im 15. Jahrhundert*, as note 31, Abb. 107, p. 117. Only one of a group of nuns holds a psalter at the Vespers of the Dead while priests in their stalls sing from two large books (psalter? antiphonal?) (Book of Hours, Ghent or Bruges, *c.* 1450; fig. 189, Christopher de Hamel, *A History*, as note 38, p. 208). A group of five secular clerics, one with glasses to assist in reading, sing beside the casket in a Paris Book of Hours, fifteenth century (London, BL, MS. Harley 2971, fol. 109^v;

Musikleben im 15. Jahrhundert, as note 31, Abb. 95, p. 109).

49 The incunable psalter printed in Strasbourg by Johann Prüss about 1498 (*BMC* I 127) shows a group of four secular clergy singing from a large book (Duggan, 'The Psalter on the Way to the Reformation', as note 32, fig. 8.3, p. 162). A group of four Franciscans sing within the 'C' in a Bolognese manuscript psalter of the early fifteenth century (London, Private Collection), Christopher de Hamel, *A History*, as note 38, p. 222. A group of three nuns sing within the 'C' of a northern breviary (London, Private Collection, fol. 58^r); *The Art of the Book: Its Place in Medieval Worship*, ed. by Margaret M. Manion & Bernard J. Muir (Exeter, 1998), fig. 30.

50 Six clerics sing before a lectern at a Mass in the chapel of Philip the Good (1396-1467) while the duke himself reads in a private prayer tent at the side, as painted in an illumination (fol. 9^r) of his manuscript *Traité sur l'oraison dominicale*, Brussels, Bibliothèque Royale, MS 9092; *The Art of the Book*, as note 49, fig. 89. A dozen or more range themselves in front of a giant book at Emperor Maximilian's Mass at Augsburg in an engraving by Hans Weiditz of 1519; 'Chorbuch', in *Musik in Geschichte und Gegenwart*, 2 (1952), cols 1343-4. Twelve singers are pictured before a choirbook in the gradual of King Jan Olbracht of Poland (about 1500, Cracow, Biblioteka Kapitulna, Ms. 42, fol. 17^v; *Musikleben im 15. Jahrhundert*, as note 31, Abb. 97, p. 109). Nine kneel before the choirbook during the consecration of the Mass at the court of Queen Eleanor of France; titlepage of Attaingnant's *Viginti missarum musicalium*, Paris, 1532; reproduced in Daniel Heartz, *Pierre Attaingnant, Royal Printer of Music: a Historical Study and Bibliographical Ctalogue* (Berkeley, 1969), pl. VIII. In the text of *Les très riches heures* of the Duc de Berry, illuminated between 1485 and 1489, is an illumination for Christmas showing a nobleman kneeling before a prie-dieu in a curtained niche, two noblewomen sitting in the foreground with open books, the priest with missal on the altar, and five singers in the choirstalls before a choirbook, with two small books open on the desk below; *Musikleben im 15. Jahrhundert*, as note 31, Abb. 104.

51 The Carolingian poem *Krist* already describes Mary as reading the psalter at the Annunciation. A summary of Annunciation iconography is in G. Schiller, *Iconography of Christian Art*, trans. by J. Seligman, I (London, 1971), pp. 33-52. See also D. M. Robb, 'The Iconography of the Annunciation in the Fourteenth and Fifteenth Centuries', *Art Bulletin*, 18 (1936), 480-526.

52 Papal procession in *Musikleben im 15. Jahrhundert*, as note 31, Abb. 114, p. 123. *Légende et miracles de Saint Hubert*, by David Aubert for Philip the Good, Bruges, 1463, ibid., Abb. 117, p. 125. The woodcut from the *Processionarum Predicatorum*. Venice: Johannes Emericus, de Spira, for Lucantonio Giunta, 1494 (*ISTC* ip00998000) is reproduced in Victor Masséna Essling, *Études sur l'art de la gravure sur bois à Venise: Les livres à figures vénitiens* (Florence, 1907-14), Première partie, Tome II, no. 1208.

53 Albert Châtelet, *Rogier van der Weyden: Problèmes de la vie et de l'oeuvre* (Strasbourg, 1999), pp. 133-4. The painting now hangs in the Koninklijk Museum voor Schone Kunsten in Antwerp.

54 Chevrot's will specifically mentions a large and beautiful Bible, law books, the *De consolatione* of Boethius (in both Latin and French), and the *Speculum regum*. To his secretary he left a small Bible and *De vita Christi* in three volumes. For the will, see Lucien Fourez, 'L'Evêque Chevrot de Tournai et sa Cité de Dieu', *Revue belge d'archéologie et d'histoire de l'art*, 23 (1954), 102-10. A chapel inventory of 1477 shows that the new chapel was equipped with illuminated missals, a gradual, and a book of organ music, as well as with relics, altar cloths, and vestments.

55 An early form of the catechism is found in a French manuscript of *L'Ordinaire des crestiens* (1468), which defines the genre: 'Catechiser vault autant à dire comme instruire ou enseigner les fondemens et articles necessaires de nostre saincte foy, car ceulx qui doivent estre baptisez

et promettre garder la foy et les commandemens en doivent premierment estre enseignez.' See Marc Venard, 'Présentation du thème du colloque', *Aux origines du catéchisme en France*, ed. by Pierre Colin (Paris, 1989), p. 13. The work was printed in Paris nine times between 1490 and 1500, usually in folio (*ISTC*).

56 Such plaques became common across Europe in the middle of the fifteenth century in an effort to regularize the vernacular languages of the prayers and commandments. In 1450 Cardinal Nicolaus de Cusa, the papal legate, granted an indulgence to those who recited the correct form from such a plaque and broadsheets of such contents were printed as incunables. See Hans Jürgen Rieckenberg, 'Die Katechismus-Tafel', *Deutsches Archiv für Erforschung des Mittelalters*, 39 (1983), 556-76; Harmut Boockman, 'Über Schrifttafeln in spätmittel-alterlichen deutschen Kirchen', *Deutsches Archiv für Erforschung des Mittelalters*, 40 (1984), 210-24. The *Virgin in the Church*, an Antwerp painting by the Master of 1499, shows such a plaque in a gothic church; reproduced in *The Art of the Book*, as note 49, fig. 91. Pierre Gasnault reviews the similar *Croix de par Dieu* in '*La Croix de par Dieu au XVIe siècle*, in *Aux origines du catéchisme en France*, ed. by Pierre Colin (Paris, 1989), 13-27.

57 A grilled niche at the Cathedral of Le Mans is surmounted with the inscription 'Magister Guillelmus Thebardi, huius ecclesie canonicus, dedit istud breviarium pro usu indigencium'; reproduced in *Histoires des bibliothèques françaises, I: Les Bibliothèques médiévales du VIe siècle á 1530*, ed. by André Vernet (Paris, 1989), p. 369, with illus. In 1294 an inventory of books at the Cathedral of Angers included a 'psalterium vetus quod erit in craticula'.

58 Willibald Sauerländer, 'Gedanken über das Nachleben des gotischen Kirchenraums im Spiegel der Malerei', *Münchner Jahrbuch der bildenden Kunst*, 45 (1994), 167; Jacques Toussaert, as note 11, p. 89.

59 František Šmahel noted that, because of the demand for new clergy following the plague of the mid-fourteenth century, standards for the command of Latin among clergy were lowered and pastoral manuals were written in Czech; 'Literacy and Heresy in Hussite Bohemia', in *Heresy and Literacy*, as note 37, pp. 244-5. The Serbian and Catalan psalters survive in unique copies, the latter saved in the files of the Inquisition after the destruction of 999 copies seized from a Valencia bookseller (Duggan, *Italian Music Incunabula*, as note 2, pp. 267-8).

60 For illustrations of the Mass of the Dead in German. Augsburg: Zainer, 1471; and the complete Proper of the Mass in German (Nuremberg, about 1482), see Duggan, 'Politics and Text', as note 5, figs 3-4.

61 Simon van Venlo, *Boexken van der officien ofte dienst der missen*, printed in facsimile with a commentary (Antwerp, 1982), 2 vols.

THE HAND ILLUMINATION OF VENETIAN BIBLES

1 I wish to thank Kristian Jensen for asking me to participate in the conference at which this paper was presented. I am also grateful to Giordana Mariani Canova for asking me to speak in her seminar on bible illustration at the University of Padua in the spring of 2000, thereby leading me to address this topic. Also providing invaluable assistance by translating that lecture was Federica Toniolo to whom I am also indebted. For support of my research, I thank the National Endowment for the Humanities for a Fellowship for College Teachers, and Wellesley College for the funding of a sabbatical leave and for research funds from the Mildred Lane Kemper Chair.

2 *Biblia italica*. Venice: Giovanni Ragazzo for LucAntonio Giunta, 15 October 1490 (*GW* 4317). The 1490 bible is discussed in all major studies of Italian woodcuts: see especially Victor Masséna, Prince d'Essling, *Les livres à figures vénetiens de la fin du XVe siècle et du commencement du XVIe*, 3 parts in 6 vols (Florence, 1907, 1914), no. 133 (hereafter Essling); and Lilian Armstrong, 'Il Maestro di Pico: un miniatore veneziano del tardo Quattrocento',

Saggi e Memorie di Storia dell'Arte, 17 (1990), 7-39 and ill. on 215-53. On Michelangelo's use of the narrative scenes see Edgar Wind, 'Maccabean Histories in the Sistine Ceiling', in *Italian Renaissance Studies*, ed. by E. F. Jacob (London, 1960), pp. 312-13; and Charles Hope, 'The Medallions of the Sistine Ceiling', *Journal of the Warburg and Courtauld Institutes*, 50 (1987), 200-4.

3 Throughout the paper the word 'illustration' will indicate a narrative scene or figures alluding to the text, and 'decoration' will indicate the painted motifs without narrative content. I will also sometimes use the term 'frontispiece' to indicate elaborately painted first text-pages, while acknowledging that the term is often reserved for the verso opposite an opening text-page. See Margaret M. Smith, *The Title Page: its Early Development 1460-1510* (London, 2001).

4 On the relationship of Bible texts to that of the Gutenberg bible see Paul Needham, 'The Text of the Gutenberg Bible', in *Trasmissione dei testi a stampa nel periodo moderno*, II, ed. by Giovanni Crapulli (Rome, 1987), pp. 43-84; and Needham, 'The Changing Shape of the Vulgate Bible in Fifteenth-century Printing Shops', in *The Bible as Book: the First Printed Editions*, ed. by Paul Saenger & Kimberly Van Kampen (London, 1999), pp. 53-70. See also Kristian Jensen, pp. 118-25 in this volume.

5 *Biblia latina*. Rome: Conradus Sweynheym and Arnoldus Pannartz, [not before 15 March], 1471 (GW 4210).

6 Luigi Balsamo has pointed out that the 1471 Sweynheym and Pannartz Bible is the only Latin Bible to be printed in the fifteenth century in roman type rather than in gothic ('La Bibbia in Tipografia', in *La Bibbia a stampa da Gutenberg a Bodoni*, exhibition catalogue, ed. by Ida Zatelli (Florence, 1991), pp. 13-38, esp. at p. 16).

7 Maury Feld, 'Sweynheym and Pannartz, Cardinal Bessarion, Neoplatonism: Renaissance Humanism and Two Early Printers' Choice of Texts', *Harvard Library Bulletin*, 30 (1982), 286-8 (lists editions 1465-73).

8 Manchester, John Rylands University Library (hereafter Rylands), 14787, fol. 1ʳ.

9 For typical Roman white vine-stem borders see *Gutenberg e Roma: le origini della stampa nella città dei papi (1467-1477)*, ed. by Massimo Miglio e Orietta Rossini (Naples, 1997), figs 39-40.

10 *Biblia italica*. Venice: Vindelinus de Spira, 1 August 1471 (GW 4311). On Malerbi see Edoardo Barbieri, 'La fortuna della *Biblia* vulgarizata di Nicolò Malerbi', *Aevum*, 63 (1989), 421ff; and Edoardo Barbieri, *Le Bibbie italiane del Quattrocento e del Cinquecento*, 2 vols (Milan, 1992), esp. I, pp. 15-35.

11 Recorded vellum copies are: Berlin, Staatsbibliothek Preussischer Kulturbesitz, 2.Inc.3630 (perg), Vol II only; Göttingen, Staat- und Universitäts Bibliothek; New York, PML, 26983-4 (ChL ff722); BnF, Rés. Vélins 19 (only Part I, fols 1-11 on vellum); Wolfenbüttel, Herzog August Bibliothek, 2° 151, 2 vols; Wrocław, Biblioteka Uniwersytecka, XV.F.297, Part I only. See also Michael Kotrba, 'Malermis italienische Bibel 1471: Unbekanntes Werk ferraresischer Buchmalerei in Venedig', in *Zentralbibliothek, Zürich: Schatzkammer der Überlieferung*, ed. by Alfred Cattani & Bruno Weber (Zürich, 1989), pp. 30-3, 152-3.

12 Manchester, John Rylands University Library, 17102, Vol. I, fol. 11ʳ.

13 Wolfenbüttel, Herzog August Bibliothek, Sig. 2° 151, Vol. I, fol. 1ʳ. See *The Painted Page: Italian Renaissance Book Illumination 1450-1550*, exhibition catalogue ed. by Jonathan J. G. Alexander (Munich, 1994), p. 170, no. 82 (entry by G.Mariani Canova with earlier bibliography on Franco de'Russi).

14 New York, PML, PML 26983-4 (ChL ff722), Vol. II, fol. 3ᵛ.

15 Lilian Armstrong, *Renaissance Miniature Painters and Classical Imagery: the Master of the Putti and His Venetian Workshop* (London, 1981), pp. 19-26, 106-7; *The Painted Page*, as note 13, pp. 166-7, no. 81 (entry by L. Armstrong, with earlier bibliography); *La miniatura*

Notes

a Padova dal medioevo al settecento, exhibition catalogue ed. by G. Canova Mariani (Modena, 1999), pp. 295-7, no. 117 (entry by Maria F. P. Saffioti & G. Canova Mariani).

16 Illustrated in colour in *The Painted Page*, as note 13, p. 167.

17 G. Mariani Canova, *La miniatura veneta del Rinascimento* (Venice, 1969), fig. 22.

18 Modena, Biblioteca Estense, MS V.G.12-13 (= Lat. 422-3). For an overview of Franco de'Russi see Federica Toniolo 'Franco de'Russi' in Hermann J. Hermann, *La miniatura Estense*, ed. by Federica Toniolo, intro. by G. Mariani Canova, trans. by Giovanna Valenzano (Modena, 1994), pp. 221-30. For Franco's role in the *Bible of Borso d'Este* see Federica Toniolo, 'La Bibbia di Borso d'Este: Cortesia e magnificenza a Ferrara tra Tardogotico e Rinascimento', in *La Bibbia di Borso D'Este: Commento al codice*, (volume accompanying the facsimile edition), (Modena, 1997), Vol. II, pp. 295-497, esp. 401-11.

19 Vatican City, Biblioteca Apostolica Vaticana (hereafter BAV), MS Barb. lat. 613. See *Biblioteca Apostolica Vaticana: Liturgie und Andacht im Mittelalter*, exhibition catalogue ed. by Joachim M. Plotzek & Ulrike Surmann (Cologne, 1992), pp. 310-17, no. 64; G. Mariani Canova, 'La miniatura e le arti a Ferrara dal tempo di Niccolò III alla Bibbia di Borso', in *La Bibbia di Borso d'Este: Commentario*, as note 17, pp. 246-8; and *I Vangeli dei Popoli: La Parola e l'immagine del Cristo nelle culture e nella storia*, exhibition catalogue ed. by Francesco D'Aiuto, Giovanni Morello, & Ambrogio M. Piazzoni (Città del Vaticano, 2000), pp. 367-72, no. 97 (entry by Antonio Manfredi).

20 Only Part II survives in the Berlin copy (see note 11). J. B. B. van Praet stated that Vol. I of this copy was in the Biblioteca Corsini, Rome, but no copy is listed in ISTC which incorporates a recent census of copies in Italian libraries, including the Corsini (*Catalogue des livres imprimés sur vélin de la Bibliothèque du Roi* (Paris, 1822), Vol. I, p. 40). I am most grateful to Dr Holger Nickel for information about the decoration of the Berlin copy. For identification of the Malipiero coat of arms, see E. Morando di Custoza, *Libro d'arme di Venezia* (Verona, 1979), no. 1848.

21 On the Pico Master see: Lilian Armstrong, 'Il Maestro di Pico', as note 2.

22 Rovigo, Biblioteca dell'Accademia dei Concordi, Silvestriana Inc. 234-5. See G. Ferraresi, *Il beato Giovanni Tavelli da Tossignano e la riforma di Ferrara nel Quattrocento*, 4 vols (Brescia, 1969), Vol. 2, p. 158 (illustrates beginning of *Genesi*, Part I, fol. 13^r).

23 Zürich, Zentralbibliothek, II.6; folio 1^r is illustrated in colour by Kotrba who suggests that the owner was Antonio Priuli, Proveditore of the Venetian army in Friuli in 1472 (as note 11, p. 153, note 8), and dedicatee in 1469 of a manuscript by Lorenzo Spirito. Martin Lowry has noted that Jenson's *Scriptores Re Rusticae* of 1472 (H 14564) was dedicated to one Piero di Marco Priuli. He suggests that Piero Priuli must have invested in the new industry of printing (*Nicholas Jenson and the Rise of Venetian Publishing in Renaissance Europe* (Oxford, 1991), pp. 83-4).

24 The Pico Master woodcut in the 1490 Giunta edition is illustrated in Essling, as note 2, I, I, p. 124 (No. 133).

25 *Biblia italica*. [Venice: Adam de Ambergau], 1 October 1471 (*GW* 4321).

26 For a recent short survey of bible illustration with essential bibliography see Kathryn A. Smith, 'Bibles', in *Leaves of Gold: Manuscript Illumination from Philadelphia Collections*, ed. by James R. Tanis, exhibition catalogue (Philadelphia: Philadelphia Museum of Art, 2001), pp. 21-4.

27 The scheme is frequently found in small Parisian thirteenth-century bibles that circulated widely; see Christopher De Hamel, *A History of Manuscript Illumination*, 2nd rev. edn (London, 1994), pp. 118-23. For Bolognese examples see *Duecento: Forme e colori del Medioeve a Bologna*, exhibition catalogue, ed. by Massimo Medica (Vicenza, 2000), cat. nos 65-7, 92, 104, 113-14.

28 Vienna, Österreichische Nationalbibliothek (hereafter ÖNB), Inc. 6.B.2 (2 vols). Herman J.

Hermann, *Die Handschriften und Inkunabeln der italienischen Renaissance*, 2. *Oberitalien: Venetien* (Leipzig, 1931), pp. 74-8, nos 46-7, and pls XXV (Vol. I, fol. 10ᵛ: Four Days of Creation) and XXVI (Vol. II, fol. 1ʳ, Solomon).

29 Manchester, John Rylands University Library, 3071. See T. F. Dibden, *Biblioteca Spenceriana*, 4 vols (London, 1814-15), Vol. I, pp. 63-4, no. 31 (calling the images coloured drawings); Essling, as note 2, Part I, Vol. I, pp. 118-19, No. 131; and Part III, pp. 56-7; Lamberto Donati, 'I fregi xilografici stampati a mano negl' incunabuli italiani', *La Bibliofilia*, 74 (1972), 304-11 and 75 (1973), 155-6. The full opening with woodcuts is illustrated in colour in Kristen Lippincott, *The Story of Time* (London, 2000), p. 18.

30 Armstrong, *Renaissance Miniature Painters*, as note 15, pp. 28-9 and 121, no. 32 (with further bibliography).

31 On woodcut borders see Donati, 'I fregi xilografici', as note 29, (1972), 157-64, 300-27; (1973), 124-74; Armstrong, *Renaissance Miniature Painters*, as note 15, pp. 26-9; and L. Armstrong, 'The Impact of Printing on Miniaturists in Venice after 1469', in *Printing the Written Word: the Social History of Books, circa 1450-1520* (Ithaca, NY, 1991), pp. 192-200.

32 Venice, Biblioteca Nazionale Marciana (hereafter BNM), Inc. 112-13. See *Le Civiltà del Libro e la stampa a Venezia: Testi sacri ebraici, cristiani, islamici dal Quattrocento al Settecento*, exhibition catalogue, ed. by Simonetta Pelusi, Civiltà Veneziana Studi, 51, (Padua, 2000), pp. 141-2, no. 61 (entry by Maria Cristina Fazzini).

33 Paris, BnF, Rés. Vélins 96-7 (*CIBN* B-450). The initials were illuminated by Antonio Maria, but the marginal decoration and miniatures were added later by a French miniaturist. For recent literature on Antonio Maria da Villafora see *La miniatura a Padova*, as note 15, pp. 377-97.

34 Princeton, NJ, Princeton University Library, Scheide Library, Goff B-639. The Genesis opening text-page is surrounded by a white vine-stem border and the reserved spaces of the left side are filled with gold intials imbedded in white vine-stems. The requisite 'N' is correctly provided, and a capital 'E' is inserted although not required by the text. The first space on the right has been filled by an image of God the Creator hovering over a sphere. I am grateful to Dr Paul Needham for bringing this copy to my attention.

35 ÖNB, Inc. 6.B.2, Vol. II, fol. 1ʳ (Hermann, as note 28, Pl. XXVI). This heretofore not mentioned connection is supported by comparing the Vienna King Solomon to both the Solomon of Shooting at Father's Corpse and the youthful King Alexander the Great at the beginning of I Maccabees in the Morgan De Spira bible (26984, fol. 3ᵛ and 162ʳ respectively).

36 *Biblia latina*. Venice: Franciscus Renner de Heilbronn and Nicolaus de Frankfordia, 1475 (*GW* 4216).

37 Copies of the 1475 Renner *Biblia latina* measure about 280 (269) × 190 (193) mm (11 × 7½ in.), instead of the 390 × 280 mm (15½ × 11 in.) of the 1471 De Spira bible.

38 Dallas, Southern Methodist University, Bridwell Library. See Eric White, *Bold Beginnings: the Art of the Illuminated Initial in the Bridwell-DeBellis Collection of Fifteenth-Century Italian Printing*, exhibition catalogue (Dallas, TX, 1998), no. 28, with colour reproduction.

39 Illuminated copies on vellum: Chantilly, Musée Condé, XII, G. 38, fol. 1ʳ: St Jerome in his Study, North Italian miniaturist (Chantilly, Musée Condé, Cabinet des Livres, *Imprimés anterieurs au milieu du XVIᵉ siecle* (Paris, 1905), no. 264); Paris, BnF, Rés. Vélins. 903-4; Vol. I, fol. 1ʳ: St Jerome and his lion, Venetian miniaturist, unidentified arms (*CIBN* B-377). An illuminated copy on paper is Rome, Biblioteca Casanatense, Vol. Inc. 876; fol. 1ʳ: North Italian miniaturist, St Jerome reading, unidentified coat of arms.

40 BL, IB 19845, fol. 1ʳ: Flemish miniaturist, St Jerome dictating to Brother Ambrosius, full border with roundels of God Blessing, a prophet (?), and the Virgin Mary; last text page, name of owner: Willem Moreal of Bruges, 1479; New York, PML, PML 16592 (ChL 783+),

fol. 1ʳ [a1ʳ]: German miniaturist, decorative initial and marginal extensions.

41 Numbers based on *ISTC*.

42 *Biblia latina*. Venice: Franciscus Renner & Nicolaus de Frankfordia, 1476 (*GW* 4223); *Biblia latina*. Venice: Nicolaus Jenson, 1476 (*GW* 4222).

43 *Biblia latina*. Venice: Nicolaus Jenson, 1479 (*GW* 4238).

44 Manchester, John Rylands University Library, 9382 (illuminated by Girolamo da Cremona; for discussion, see below); Modena, Biblioteca Estense, L. B. I, 15 (illuminated by Antonio Maria da Villafora, Olivetani arms; Mariani Canova, *La miniatura veneta*, as note 17, p. 160, no. 104, and figs 105a, b, 151); New York, New York Public Library, [*KB] 1476.Bible.Latin (Neapolitan illumination); Paris, BnF, Rés. Vélins 81 (illuminated by the Pico Master for San Giorgio Maggiore, Venice); Paris, BnF, Rés. Vélins 80 (illuminated by Spanish miniaturists for Juan de Zuñiga, Grand Master of the Order of Alcantara; F. Avril, *Bibliothèque Nationale: Manuscrits enluminés de la péninsule iberique* (Paris, 1983) pp. 138-41, no. 154 and Pls LXXXVIII-XC); Ravenna, Inc. 31 (illuminated by Girolamo da Cremona for 'B. Agostini'; see below); United Kingdom, Private Collection (illuminated by Antonio Maria da Villafora); Washington, DC, Library of Congress.

45 On Jenson's prominence in relation to illuminated incunables see L. Armstrong, 'The Hand-Illumination of Printed Books in Italy 1465-1515', in *The Painted Page*, as note 13, pp. 35-47, with previous bibliography. See also Lowry, *Nicholas Jenson*, as note 23, pp. 82-7.

46 *Ravenna: La biblioteca Classense*, I, *La città, la cultura, la fabbrica*, ed. by Marco Dezzi Bardeschi (Bologna, 1982), colour illus. of fol. a5ʳ on p. 125. On the Agostini see: L. Armstrong, 'The Agostini Plutarch: an Illuminated Venetian Incunable', in *Treasures of the Library: Trinity College Dublin*, ed. by Peter Fox (Dublin, 1986), pp. 86-96. On Girolamo da Cremona see *The Painted Page*, as note 13, cat. nos 93-6, 99, 101, 123; and *La miniatura a Padova*, as note 15, nos 144-5, 150.

47 For a recent discussion of the Jenson 1476 Pliny, see Paul Needham, 'Concepts of Paper Study', in *Puzzles in Paper: Concepts in Historical Watermarks*, ed. by Daniel W. Mosser, Michael Saffle, & Ernest W. Sullivan, II (London, 2000), pp. 1-36.

48 Manchester, Rylands, 9382. I am grateful to Jonathan Alexander for directing my attention to the Rylands Bible many years ago, and for attributing the illumination to Girolamo.

49 Dresden, Sächsische Landesbibliothek, Inc. 2°.2876. See H. Deckert, *Katalog der Inkunabeln der Sächsischen Landesbibliothek*, Zentralblatt für Bibliothekswesen, Beiheft 80 (1957), no. 122, pls 10-11. On Ugelheimer see below.

50 Vienna, ÖNB, Inc. 8.E.10, on vellum (Herman, as note 28, pp. 117-25, no. 96 and Pls XXVIII, 2-3, and XXXVIII). The historiated initials are attributable to the Pico Master, but the Genesis frontispiece is by another unidentified Venetian miniaturist.

51 *Biblia* [Low German]. Cologne: [Heinrich Quentell, about 1478 ?] (*GW* 4307) and *Biblia* [Low German], Cologne, [Heinrich Quentell, about 1478?] (*GW* 4308). The classic study of the Cologne bible presuming the date of 1478 is: S. Corsten, 'Die Kölner Bilderbibeln von 1478', *Gutenberg-Jahrbuch*, (1957), 72-93. Recently however, William Sheehan has proposed a date of 1472 based on an *ex-libris* in the Vatican Library copy of *GW* 4308 (Inc. Ross. 283-4; William Sheehan, *Bibliothecae Apostolicae Vaticanae Incunabula*, Studi e testi, 380-3 (Città del Vaticano, 1997), B-296; hereafter Sheehan). See also William Sheehan, 'Frederick, a Cleric from Cologne, Antonio Urceo, Geroldus de Bonzagnis and three anonymous rubricators', in *Miscellanea Bibliothecae Apostolicae Vaticanae*, VI, *Collectanea in honorem Rev.mi Patris Leonardi Boyle*, Studi e Testi, 385 (Città del Vaticano, 1998), pp. 569-76; and *I Vangeli dei Popoli*, as note 19, p. 385, no. 104.

52 The 1476 Renner example (see note 42) in Florence is Biblioteca Marucelliana, R.a.373 (*La Bibbia a stampa da Gutenberg a Bodoni*, as note 6, pp. 92-3, cat. no. 10 [entry by Milka Ventura Avanzinelli]). *Biblia latina*. Venice: Franciscus Renner de Heilbronn, 1480 (*GW*

4241): copies with Pico Master illumination are Chicago, Newberry Library, Inc +4177, on vellum, three pages illuminated with borders and miniatures (Armstrong, 'Il Maestro di Pico', as note 2, p. 34, no. 56, fig. 30); London, BL, C.9.b.12, on vellum (fig. 10; and Armstrong, 'Il Maestro di Pico', as note 2, p. 34, no. 54); Venice, BNM, Inc. Ven. 756 (Armstrong, 'Il Maestro di Pico', as note 2, p. 34, no. 55; and G. Castiglione, ''Frixi et figure et miniadure facte de intajo': Tra silografia e miniature in alcuni incunaboli veneziani', *Verona illustrata*, 2 (1989), 19-27, esp. p. 25 and figs 14-16); Vienna, ÖNB, Inc. 23.F.22 (Hermann, as note 28, pp. 142-4, no. 104, and Pl. XLV, 1).

53 See notes 38, 52.

54 Armstrong, 'Il Maestro di Pico', as note 2, fig. 30.

55 Bibles illuminated by the Pico Master or his workshop with variant decorative schemes include: *Biblia latina*, Jenson, 1479: United Kingdom, private collection, copy on vellum, fol. a5ʳ with arms of the Della Rovere family (without papal tiara or cardinal's hat), God the Creator partially repainted (*The Estelle Doheny Collection Part I: the Fifteenth Century Books including the Gutenberg Bible* (New York: Christie, Manson and Woods, 22 Oct. 1987), lot 91, colour pl.); two copies of the *Biblia italica*. Venice: Antonio di Bartolomeo Miscomini, 1477 (*GW* 4312): Bologna, Biblioteca dell'Archiginnasio, 16.H.III, 14-15, fol. aa2ʳ: frontispiece to Genesis with miniature of God the Creator (illustrated in colour in C. Pedretti, *Leonardo: Studies for the Last Supper* (Ivrea, 1983), fig. 92); and Vienna, ÖNB, Inc. 5.D.22, fol. aa2ʳ (11ʳ): Genesis with architectural frontispiece and scenes of Creation (Hermann, as note 28, pp. 109-10, no. 88, and Pl. XXXV; Armstrong, 'Il Maestro di Pico', as note 2, no. 42, and fig. 20); and *Biblia italica*. Venice: Gabriele di Pietro, 26 Nov. 1477 and 15 Jan. 1477 [1478] (*GW* 4313): Vienna, ÖNB, Inc. 7.F.23, Vol. 2 only, with Nativity (Hermann, as note 28, pp. 108-9, no. 87, and Pl. XXXIV, 1). A Venetian miniaturist known as the Master of the Rimini Ovid illuminated a copy of the 1478 Leonardus Wild *Biblia latina* (*GW* 4233): London, BL C.9.c.5; and a copy of the *Biblia italica*. Venice: Johannes Rubeus Vercellensis, 1487 (*GW* 4316): Vienna, ÖNB, Inc. 11.F.22. Elaborate borders and a miniature of the Creation of Eve were painted by a French miniaturist in a vellum copy of the Jenson 1479 *Biblia italica* (BnF, Rés. Vélins 82).

56 *Biblia latina cum postillis Nicolai de Lyra*. Venice: [Johannes Herbort de Seligenstadt], for Johannes de Colonia, Nicolaus Jenson et Socii, 31 July, 1481 (*GW* 4286).

57 *Biblia latina cum postillis Nicolai de Lyra*. Venice: Franciscus Renner de Heilbronn, 1482-3, in three parts (*GW* 4287).

58 Since the 1480 edition has no indication of printer or place of printing, its printing history has been much debated. In the *ISTC* it is cited as *Biblia latina. With the Glossa Ordinaria of pseudo-Walafrid Strabo* [Basel: Johann Amerbach, for Adolf Rusch & Anton Koberger, not after 1480]; and also recorded as: [Strasbourg: Adolf Rusch, for Anton Koberger] (*GW* 4282). See *Biblia Latina cum Golssa Ordinaria: Facsimile Reprint of the Editio Princeps, Adolf Rusch of Strassburg, 1480/81*, ed. by Karlfried Froehlich & Margaret T. Gibson, 4 vols (Turnhout, 1992); and Karlfried Froehlich, 'An Extraordinary Achievement: the *Glossa ordinaria* in Print', in *The Bible as Book*, as note 4, pp. 15-21.

59 J. P. Gumbert, 'The Layout of the Bible Gloss in Manuscript and Early Print', in *The Bible as Book*, as note 4, pp. 7-13; and Froehlich, as note 58.

60 Lowry, *Nicholas Jenson*, as note 23, pp. 137-72.

61 BAV, Membr. II, 6-9 (Sheehan, as note 51, B-280).

62 BAV, MS Vat. Lat. 263, fol. 1ᵛ; see *Umanesimo e Padri della Chiesa*, Biblioteca Medicea Laurenziana, 5 febbraio-9 agosto 1997, exhibition catalogue ed. by Sebastiano Gentile (Rome, 1997), no. 84, illus p. 332. Another incunable illuminated by the same Roman miniaturist is the Origines, *Contra Celsum*, printed in Rome by G. Herolt in 1481 and destined for the Venetian Doge Giovanni Mocenigo (Lotte Hellinga, 'Il console Joseph Smith collezionista

a Venezia per il mercato inglese', *La Bibliofilia*, 102 (2000), fig. 5 colour illustration). On Ravaldi and the Theophylact see also *The Painted Page*, as note 13, no. 37 (entry by Jonathan Alexander).

63 Ursula Baurmeister, '1481: a False Landmark in the History of French Illustration?: the Paris and Verdun missals of Jean Du Pré', in *Incunabula: Studies in the Fifteenth-Century Printed Book Presented to Lotte Hellinga*, ed. by Martin Davies (London, 1999), pp. 469-91, esp. p. 483, citing H. Forgeot, *Jean Balue, cardinal d'Angers (1421?-1491)* (Paris, 1895).

64 *Special Collections at Brown University: a History and Guide* (Providence, RI, The Friends of the Library of Brown University, 1988), p. 46 (illus. in colour).

65 Padua, Biblioteca Capitolare, Inc. 103 (E. Govi, *Librorum XV Saec. Impressorum. Index. Patavinae Cathedralis Ecclesiae Capitularis Bibliotheca* (Padua, 1958), pp. 35-6, no. 103). On Barozzi see: F. Gaeta, 'Barozzi, Pietro', in *DBI*, VI, pp. 510-12. On Antonio Maria see note 33.

66 Florence, Biblioteca Medicea Laurenziana, Inc. 3.29 a-d. See Angela Dillon Bussi, 'I libri decorati di Girolamo Rossi: Illustrazione libraria a Venezia nella seconda metà del Quattrocento', *Verona illustrata*, no. 2 (1989), 29-51, esp. no. 6, 46-9, colour pl. V and figs 28-31; *La Bibbia a stampa da Gutenberg a Bodoni*, as note 6, no. 19, and colour pl. on p. 21; and Armstrong, 'Il Maestro di Pico', as note 2, no. 60, and fig. 31.

67 Dillon Bussi catalogues ten illuminated incunables owned by Rossi, and others have been located subsequent to her 1989 publication (as note 66, pp. 29-32 and 42-51).

68 New York, PML, PML 16872-5 (ChL f905); see Armstrong, 'Il Maestro di Pico', as note 2, p. 34, no. 61.

69 BAV, Inc. Ross. 1157-9 (Sheehan, as note 51, B-281; Armstrong, 'Il Maestro di Pico', as note 2, 22-3, 35, no. 70, and figs 32-3).

70 *Breviarium*: Oxford, Bodleian Library, MS Canon. Lit. 410, fol. 1^r (Armstrong, *Renaissance Miniature Painters*, as note 15, fig. 91); Petrus de Abano, *Expositio problematum Aristotelis*. Venice: Johannes Herbort, 1482: The Hague, Koninklinjke Bibliothek, 169.D.2, fol. 2^r (Armstrong, 'Il Maestro di Pico', as note 2, fig. 27; *The Painted Page*, as note 13, no. 99, entry by L. Armstrong; *La miniatura a Padova*, as note 15, no. 150, entry by G. Canova Mariani).

71 Paris, BnF, Rés. Vélins 111-14 and 957 (*CIBN* B-428). Rés. Vélins 111: Judges to Chronicles, but misbound so that Chronicles precedes Judges (normally Chronicles would be the first book of the second volume in a 1481 *Biblia latina cum postillis*). Rés. Vélins 112: I Ezra-Ecclesiasticus; Rés. Vélins 113, Isaiah-II Maccabees; Rés. Vélins 114, Matthew-Apocalypse; and Rés. Vélins 957, only one gathering, Nicolaus de Lyra's *Quaestiones disputatae contra Hebraeos*.

72 The fullest discussions of the Ugelheimer incunables are: *The Painted Page*, as note 13, nos 96-101 (entries by L. Armstrong); and *La miniatura a Padova*, as note 15, nos 145, 148 (entries by A. De Marchi) and 146-7, 149-51 (entries by G. Canova Mariani).

73 See note 72.

74 The Hague, Koninklijke Bibliothek, Inc. 169 D 3 and Inc. 169 D 1 respectively (*La miniatura a Padova*, as note 15, nos 151 and 149 respectively).

75 On Bordon see bibliography cited in *The Painted Page*, as note 13, nos 97, 104, 118 (entries by L. Armstrong); and *La miniatura a Padova*, as note 15, nos 146-7, 151-2 (entries by G. Canova Mariani); 171-2, 175 (entries by H. K. Szepe); 173-4 (entries by G. Baldassin Molli).

76 *La miniatura a Padova*, as note 15, no. 149; and see note 73.

77 T. Laguna Paul, *Postillae in Vetus et Novum Testamentum de Nicolàs de Lyra. Biblioteca Universitaria de Sevilla, MS. 332/145-149* (Seville, 1979).

78 Consideration of the relationships between the various editions of the *Postillae* and the *Biblia latina cum postillis Nicolaus de Lyra* with and without woodcuts is beyond the scope of this

paper. Important to note however are the following. The Nicolaus de Lyra, *Postilla super totam Bibliam*. Rome: Conradus Sweynheym & Arnoldus Pannartz, 1471-2, 5 parts, is printed with reserved spaces but no woodcuts (*BMC* IV 14); a copy of this edition containing six 'Mantegnesque' drawings was acquired by Leo S. Olschki from a 'vecchia nobile famiglia del Veneto' but I am unaware of its present whereabouts (R. Artioli, 'La scoperta di sei preziosi disegni in una bibbia del XV', *La Bibliofilia*, 1 (1899), 125-44). The first edition printed in Germany containing woodcuts is: Nicolaus de Lyra, *Postilla super totam Bibliam*. Nuremberg: Anton Koberger, 22 January 1481 (*BMC* II, 419). The 1481 woodcuts were reused in the *Biblia latina cum postillis Nicolai de Lyra*. Nuremberg: Anton Koberger, 1485 (*GW* 4288). The German woodcuts in part inspired the first illustrated Venetian edition, *Biblia latina cum postillis Nicolai de Lyra*. Venice: [Bonetus Locatellus], for Octavianus Scotus, 8 Aug. 1489 (*GW* 4291; Essling 132) but, as will be seen, these woodcuts also draw upon miniatures and diagrams by the Pico Master. On these editions see L. Donati, 'Della prima bibbia italiana illustrata (Venezia 1489)', in *Miscellanea di scritti di bibliografia ed erudizione in memoria di Luigi Ferrari* (Florence, 1952), pp. 252-9; and Armstrong, 'Il Maestro di Pico', as note 2, 27-30 and fig. 42.

79 See note 78.
80 See above and note 65.
81 See note 78 for the 1489 Bible. The so-called *Bible of Jean, Duc de Berry*, a French manuscript of 1388-90, typifies the manuscript tradition; it has two sets of diagrams of the 'Dial of Ahaz' (BAV, MS Vat. Lat. 50-1; *I Vangeli dei Popoli*, as note 19, pp. 356-7, no. 93, entry by Francesca Manzari).
82 *The Painted Page*, as note 13, p. 195.
83 See note 78.
84 For the Creation of Eve see Armstrong, 'Il Maestro di Pico', as note 2, fig. 42; for the Vision of Isaiah see Donati, 'Della prima bibbia italiana illustrata', as note 78, fig. 6. In addition to the comparisons already noted, see also the King Saul in the 1471 *Biblia italica* in Zürich (col. pl. 11) which clearly prefigures the enthroned figure of God in the 1489 Vision of Ezekiel woodcut (fig. 16).

PRINTING THE BIBLE IN THE FIFTEENTH CENTURY

1 *GW* 4236; *ISTC* ib00561000. The verses are printed in *BMC* III 745: 'Fontibus ex Grecis Hebreorum quoque libris | Emendata satis et decorata simul | Biblia sum presens superos ego testor et astra | Est impressa nec in orbe mihi similis | Singula queque loca cum concordantiis extant | Orthographia simul quoque bene pressa manet.'
2 For Kontoblakes in Basel see *Græcogermania: Griechischstudien deutscher Humanisten: Die Editionstätigkeit der Griechen in der italienischen Renaissance (1469-1523)*, ed. by Reinhard Barm & Dieter Harlfinger (Weinheim, 1989), 311. Reuchlin's Latin *Vocabularius* was first published by Amerbach in 1478 (*ISTC* ir00155000); the Greek companion volume was never finished.
3 See p. 125 below.
4 See Alastair Hamilton, 'Humanists and the Bible', in *The Cambridge Companion to Renaissance Humanism*, ed. by Jill Kraye (Cambridge, 1996), pp. 100-17. Though not printed until the sixteenth century, Valla's work was not forgotten in the late 1470s; the two surviving manuscripts of the earlier recension were copied in 1477 and 1478: BNF, ms. Nouv. Acq. Lat. 502; Valencia, Biblioteca de la Catedral, ms. 170; see Lorenzo Valla, *Collatio novi testamenti*, ed. by Alessandro Perosa (Florence, 1970), at pp. xi and xv.
5 For instance, an edition also printed by Amerbach, Cato, *Disticha de moribus*. Basel: [Johann Amerbach], 14 June 1486 (*GW* 6284; *ISTC* ic00297000), sig. c1ʳ: 'Non alta sapere

concupiscas: | Mitte arcana dei celum inquirere quid sit | Cum sis mortalis que sunt mortalia cura'.

6 For instance, Heinrich von Absberg, bishop of Regensburg, who commissioned the *Obsequiale Ratisponense*. Nuremberg: Georg Stuchs, 12 Feb. 1491 (*ISTC* io00004000), and emphasized the desire for uniformity, sig. q7ʳ: 'Pontificum vero qui summam curam fidelium habent, officium est ut fideles ipsos in fidei unitate per debitum ecclesiarum ceremoniarum ritum instruant, edificent et preservent, cui rei Obsequiorum sive Benedictionum liber uniformis maxime conducere facile perpendi poterit'; see also Uwe Neddermeyer, *Von der Handschrift zum gedruckten Buch: Schriftlichkeit und Leseinteresse im Mittelalter und in der frühen Neuzeit. Quantitative und qualitative Aspekte*, Buchwissenschaftliche Beiträge aus dem Deutschen Bucharchiv München, 61 (Wiesbaden, 1998), p. 467. Also M. K. Duggan, pp. 71-81 in this volume.

7 Also Cristina Dondi, pp. 53-70 in this volume.

8 The entries were written by Dr Alan Coates and Dr Bettina Wagner, and were revised by me, in my former role as editor of the Bodleian Incunable Project. Later, in 2000-1, I undertook a second, more comprehensive, revision of the descriptions. 76 of the 81 editions of the Bible in Latin without a commentary listed by *GW* are in the Bodleian Library, making it the largest collection anywhere. The BL, which holds 71 editions, has four editions not present in the Bodleian (*GW* nos 4202, 4217, 4261, and 4266). *ISTC* contains records for two editions not contained in *GW*, a proof sheet from about 1458 (*ISTC* ib00526500), and an edition from Cologne, about 1480, which survives only in a fragment of two conjugate leaves (*ISTC* ib00570500). All 13 recorded editions of the Latin Bible with various commentaries are present in the BL or in the Bodleian. The article is thus based on the examination of all incunable editions of the Bible, except one (*GW* 4251). The Bodleian Incunable Project is described in Kristian Jensen, *Incunabula in the Bodleian Library*, Patrimonia 66 (Berlin, 1992).

9 Written in the 1920s, probably by Kurt Ohly. These entries remain of fundamental importance.

10 Denise Hillard has the main responsibility for Latin bibles in *CIBN*. She has also explored bibles printed in France in an article, 'Les Éditions de la Bible en France au XVᵉ siècle', in *La Bible imprimée dans l'Europe moderne*, ed. by Bertram Eugene Schwarzbach (Paris, 1999), pp. 68-82.

11 'The Text of the Gutenberg Bible', in *Trasmissione dei testi a stampa nel periodo moderno, vol. II: Il seminario internazionale Roma-Viterbo 27-29 giugno 1985*, ed. by Giovanni Crapulli (Rome, 1987), pp. 43-84.

12 'The Changing Shape of the Vulgate Bible in Fifteenth-century Printing Shops', in *The Bible as Book: the First Printed Editions*, ed. by Kimberley van Kampen & Paul Saenger (London, 1999), pp. 53-70; many of Paul Needham's stimulating thoughts will be touched on in this article.

13 Edoardo Barbieri, *Le Bibbie italiane del Quattrocento e del Cinquecento: Storia e bibliografia ragionata delle edizioni in lingua italiana dal 1471 al 1600* (Milan, 1992).

14 Hillard, as note 10.

15 *Mémoire sur l'établissement du texte de la Vulgate: Ière partie, Octateuque*, Collectanea biblica latina, 6 (Rome, 1922). His discussion of the text of early printed editions is found in part 2, tellingly named 'Aperçu sur les progrès de la critique du texte'. Quentin evidently saw fifteenth-century work on the biblical text as part of the same enterprise as his own, that of establishing the 'vulgate' Bible. *Biblia sacra iuxta latinam vulgatam versionem ad codicum fidem*, iussu Pii PP XI, cura et studio monachorum Sancti Benedicti commissionis Pontificiae ... sodalium, praeside Aidano Gasquet (Rome, 1926-).

16 Quentin, *Mémoire*, as note 15, p. 94: 'une conclusion ressort de cette étude des premières

éditions typographiques de la Vulgate: c'est que leur texte ne peut être d'aucune utilité pour le critique …'. He established that the edition from Vicenza (GW 4224) was not dependent on the B42, but, as it was in agreement with a number of Italian manuscripts, it too was of no importance to him. See also H. Schneider, 'Der Text der 36zeiligen Bibel und des Probedruckes von circa 1457', *Gutenberg-Jahrbuch* (1955), 57-61, at pp. 61 and 68, on the Vicenza edition, which he believes to have been printed from an Italian manuscript of the eleventh to the twelfth centuries.

17 F. C. Burkitt, 'The Text of the Vulgate', *Journal of Theological Studies*, 24 (1923), 406-14.

18 Pasquali in his review of P. Collomp, *La Critique des textes* (Paris, 1931) in *Gnomon*, 8 (1932), 127-34. S. Timpanaro, *La genesi del metodo del Lachmann*, 2nd edn (Padua, 1985), in particular at p. 48, note 18. Quentin mainly explains his method in his *Essais de critique textuelle (ecdotique)* (Paris, 1926).

19 Faced with the argument that in a textual tradition like that of the Bible it can be difficult to establish *a priori* what is an error, Pasquali insisted that in establishing a stemma the critic must rely on errors from which a correct text cannot be established by conjecture. Pasquali, as note 18, p. 131, saw Quentin's reluctance to use his own judgement as a result of hierarchically induced timidity, calling his approach 'etwas zu katholisch-mönkisch'.

20 Quentin, *Mémoire*, as note 15, pp. 93-4.

21 A *Leitfehler* in the terminology of Paul Maas, *Textual Criticism* (Oxford, 1958), p. 42.

22 See for instance Paul Needham's list of variant readings in 'The Text', as note 11, at pp. 66-85. Needham, incidentally, at p. 51, criticized Quentin for not including readings from both settings of the B42 in his apparatus. As both the first and the second settings are irrelevant, by Quentin's own criteria it would have more appropriate to exclude both.

23 *Der Text der Gutenbergbibel zu ihrem 500jährigen Jubiläum untersucht*, Bonner biblische Beiträge, 7 (Bonn, 1954), p. 98.

24 In my view the contribution of Heinrich Schneider has been undervalued by Needham, in 'The Text', as note 11, p. 44, who says that Schneider's description of fifteenth-century manuscripts is 'not specifically concerned with Gutenberg's text'.

25 Robert Weber, 'Der Text der Gutenbergbibel und seine Stellung in der Geschichte der Vulgata', in *Johannes Gutenbergs zweiundvierzigzeilige Bibel: Faksimile-Ausgabe nach dem Exemplar der Staatsbibliothek Preußischer Kulturbesitz Berlin, Komentarband*, ed. by Wieland Schmidt & Friedrich Adolf Schmidt-Künsemüller (Munich, 1979), pp. 11-31, at pp. 28-9.

26 Hillard, as note 10, at p. 69.

27 Weber, as note 25, at p. 27 was as explicit as Quentin in his approach to the B42: 'Leider hat dieser Text viele Mängel.' This is a relevant observation for a textual critic, but one which is of limited use for a scholar interested in the Bible in the fifteenth century.

28 On the improving intervention of editors in vernacular texts see Brian Richardson, *Printing, Writers and Readers in Renaissance Italy* (Cambridge, 1999), especially at pp. 150-5.

29 The five groups outlined by GW are invaluable for the purpose of the catalogue, but they constitute a static model, which makes it difficult to see the increasingly active exchange of texts between editions.

30 A good introduction to the 'Paris Bible' and its formation is Laura Light, 'French Bibles *c.* 1200-30: a New Look at the Origin of the Paris Bible', in *The Early Medieval Bible: Its Production, Decoration and Use*, ed. by Richard Gameson (Cambridge, 1994), pp. 155-76. Laura Light, 'Versions et révisions du texte biblique', in *Le Moyen Age et la Bible*, ed. by Pierre Riché & Guy Lobrichon (Paris, 1984), pp. 55-93, especially at p. 92, points out that an often assumed relation between the university and 'Paris Bible' must be treated with caution: few Bible manuscripts seem to be produced using the pecia method, and few can be shown to have a direct link to university teaching. Similarly Richard Rouse & Mary

Rouse, *Illiterati et uxorati: Manuscripts and Their Makers, Commercial Book Producers in Medieval Paris 1200-1500* (London, 2000), pp. 31-2, use the rapid diffusion of the 'Paris Bible' as evidence for a commercial Parisian book trade already in the thirteenth century, independent of the university.

31 Schneider, as note 23, at p. 21 suggested that variant readings found in later editions of the Bible might derive from compilations of variants, the so-called *correctoria*, and this suggestion has been taken up by later writers; e.g. Needham, 'The Text', as note 11, p. 49; also Henri-Jean Martin, *Mise en page et mise en texte du livre français: La naissance du livre moderne (xive-xviie siècles)* (Paris, 2000), p. 283. There is, however, little evidence for *correctoria* having had an impact on the texts or on marginal variants in manuscript Bibles, cf. Laura Light, 'Versions', as note 30, at p. 90. See also the excellent survey of the Paris Bible and the correctoria by Raphael Loewe, 'The Medieval History of the Latin Vulgate', in *The Cambridge History of the Bible: 2, The West from the Fathers to the Reformation*, ed. by G. W. H. Lampe (Cambridge, 1969), pp. 102-54, who at pp. 145-52 refers to J. Wordsworth, *Old-Latin Biblical Texts: No. I, The Gospel According to St Matthew* (Oxford, 1883), Appendix 1, pp. 49 and 50 for the suggestion that Stephanus used the *Correctoria* of William le Breton in his Bible from 1538-40.

32 N. R. Ker, *Medieval Manuscripts in British Libraries*, 4 vols (Oxford, 1969-72), vol. 1: *London*, pp. 96-7. Light, 'Versions', as note 30, at p. 92, emphasizes the continued diversity of Bibles, and the need for studying the non-Parisian biblical tradition, in particular from the point of view of the divergent textual material which is included.

33 Friedrich Stegmüller, *Repertorium biblicum medii aevi*, 11 vols (Madrid, 1950-80), nos 327, 468, 507, 511, 510, 515, 512, 513, 519+517, 524, 521, 526, 528, 531, 534, 538, 539, 543, 547, 553, 589, 640, and 839.

34 Stegmüller, as note 33, nos 430, 674, 677, 633, 636, 637, 806, 812, 818, 822, 823, 824, 825, and a prologue to Ecclesiasticus ('Multum nobis ...') and Jerome's letter to Damasus, on the New Testament ('Nouum opus ...').

35 The issue of IV Ezra in B42 has been examined by Paul Needham in 'The Compositor's Hand in the Gutenberg Bible: a Review of the Todd Thesis', *Papers of the Bibliographical Society of America*, 77 (1983), 341-71, at 348-51, and further in his 'Division of Copy in the Gutenberg Bible: Three Glosses on the Ink Evidence', *Papers of the Bibliographical Society of America* 79 (1985), 411-26, at 413-14. In these two exemplary passages of analytical bibliography Needham concludes that IV Ezra was not part of the main manuscript used in Gutenberg's workshop. More work on Rhenish fifteenth-century manuscript bibles might help us further with understanding the environment where IV Ezra would be an expected part of the biblical corpus and thus the intellectual background for the Bible as produced by Gutenberg.

36 GW 4202 (a good assessment of the research on the 36-line Bible is Felix de Marez Oyens, *The Würzburg Schottenkloster–Spencer–Liverpool Copy of the 36-line Bible* (London: Christies, 27 November 1991); *GW* nos 4203, 4204, 4205, 4206, 4207, 4208, 4209, 4211, 4213, 4214, 4218, 4226, 4244, 4229, 4235, and 4230. In many cases *GW*, supplemented by *CIBN*, establishes which edition served as copy text for later editions. On the relation between the first eight, see in particular the analysis in Paul Needham, 'The Text', as note 11; on *GW* 4204 see also *CIBN* B-364. In *CIBN* Denise Hillard has established the relative order of the editions produced in Cologne by Götz, and re-dated several; *CIBN*'s chronological order is *GW* 4235 (about 1478); *GW* 4230 (after 1478); *GW* 4244 (9 May 1480); *GW* 4229 (after 1480 and ascribed by *CIBN* B-400 to Götz's successors). Hillard's argument seems unassailable although contradicted by a purchase note of 1478 attached to the Bodleian copy of *GW* 4229 (*Bod-inc* B-264; shelfmark Auct. 2Z 1.1,2).

37 Needham, 'The Text', as note 11, p. 56.

38 *GW* 4212.

39 Quentin, *Mémoire*, as note 15, p. 78.

40 *Incipit*: 'Qui memor esse cupit librorum bibliothecae ...'. Exactly the same texts are found in Richel's edition from 1475 (*GW* 4215), whereas Koberger's edition from 1477 (*GW* 4227) omits the verses from Guido Vicentinus's *Margarita bibliae*. According to *GW*, no. 4227 is set from no. 4212, excepting the last gathering.

41 *GW* 4232.

42 Psalm 105 and following. This same model was followed by Koberger in his next three editions (*GW* 4234, 4239, and 4243), the last one being from 14 April 1480. The same corpus was published in Cologne by Conrad Winters in 1479 (*GW* 4240).

43 *GW* 4210.

44 Edited in Giovanni Andrea Bussi, *Prefazioni alle edizioni di Sweynheym e Pannarz proto-tipografi romani*, ed. by Massimo Miglio, Documenti sulle arti del libro, 12 (Milan, 1978), 56-7.

45 See H. T. Andrews in R. H. Charles, *Apocrypha and Pseudepigrapha of the Old Testament*, vol. 2 (Oxford, 1913), pp. 83-122, with this edition noted on p. 90.

46 On the importance of this text in Humanist Rome see Luciano Canfora, *Il viaggio di Aristea* (Rome, 1996), pp. 61-70 ('Niccolò V come Tolomeo II'), and Concietta Bianca, 'Il soggiorno romano di Aristea', *Roma nel Rinascimento: Bibliografia e note*, 1996, 36-41.

47 [Rome: Sixtus Riessinger, not after 1467] (*ISTC* ih00160800; for Aristeas see *GW* 2330).

48 Needham, 'The Text', as note 11, at p. 57, describes pseudo-Aristeas as 'a piece of writing that contributes nothing to a Vulgate Bible'. Also Martin, as note 31, p. 284, and Edwin Hall, *Sweynheym and Pannartz and the Origins of Printing in Italy; German Technology and Italian Humanism in Renaissance Rome* (McMinnville, 1991), p. 51, here in relation to Riesinger's edition of Jerome, although the theme of translating from the Greek must be said to be central for understanding Jerome and his activity. On Jerome's use of the Septuagint, see H. F. D. Sparks, 'Jerome as Biblical scholar', in *The Cambridge History of the Bible, I: From the Beginnings to Jerome*, ed. by P. R. Ackroyd & C. F. Evans (Cambridge, 1970), pp. 510-41.

49 On Traversari and the Septuagint, see Hamilton, as note 4, at p. 101. Also Edoardo Barbieri, *Il libro nella storia: Tre percorsi* (Milano, 2000), the chapter 'Morfologie del libro in un monastero camaldolese del quattrocento: il caso S. Mattia di Murano', pp. 1-115, especially at pp. 3-5.

50 Bussi, *Prefazioni*, as note 44, p. 56.

51 Alberto Vaccari, *Scritti di erudizione e di filologia, I* (Rome, 1952), pp. 1-23, the section entitled 'La fortuna della lettera d'Aristea in Italia'. Squarzafico's praise of Aristeas is quoted in Barbieri, as note 13, pp. 202-3.

52 Needham, 'The Text', as note 11, at p. 57 describes the edition as 'bizarre-looking', but see Lilian Armstrong, p. 83 in this volume.

53 See A. d'Esneval, 'Le Perfectionnement d'un instrument de travail au début du XIIIᵉ siècle: les trois glossaires bibliques d'Etienne Langton', in *Culture et travail intellectuel dans l'occident médiéval*, ed. by G. Hasenohr & J. Longère (Paris, 1981), pp. 163-75.

54 Prefaces: to Chronicles (Stegmüller, as note 33, no. 327); to Wisdom (no. 468); to Baruch (no. 491); to Hosea (no. 507); to Joel (no. 511); three to Amos (nos 515, 512, and 513); to Abdias (nos 519, 517); two to Jonah (nos 524 and 521); to Micha (no. 526); to Nahum (no. 528); to Habakkuk (no. 531); to Zephaniah (Sophonias) (no. 534); to Haggai (no. 538); three to Matthew (cf. nos 590, 591, and 589); Acts (no. 633); to Apocalypse (no. 839). Of these nos 591 and 633 seem not to be part of the prefaces which occur as standard with

the 'Paris Bible', cf. the list of the standard 64 prefaces in Ker, *Medieval Manuscripts*, as note 32.

55 *GW* 4219: as it includes the dedication to the pope, we can be sure that it depends on the Roman edition. There is a manuscript bible copied from the Roman edition dated 1507 (Milan, Archivio capitolare della Basilica Ambrosiana, M 44).

56 *GW* 4221.

57 *GW* 4212. See note 38.

58 Gathering [q6^v] ends with the rubric for IV Ezra, but the two following leaves [q7-8] have been cancelled.

59 See Marie-Louis Polain, *Catalogue des livres imprimés au quinzième siècle des bibliothèques de Belgique*, 4 vols (Brussels, 1932), no. 647a and *CIBN* B-384 (*GW* 4227; see note 40).

60 *GW* 4228, but wanting the Eusebian Tables and the verses from Guido Vicentinus.

61 *GW* 4225.

62 It also included a poem of 15 hexameters, preceding the colophon, likewise in hexameters. Its relation to the intellectual environment of the University of Paris has been studied by Denise Hillard, as note 10, and I shall revert to it later.

63 *GW* 4242.

64 *GW* 4217.

65 *GW* 4224.

66 *CIBN* B-376; *GW* 4217.

67 *GW* 4216.

68 Needham, 'The Text', as note 11, at p. 70. As against the numerous recorded shared variant readings, this is a textbook example of an *error significativus*. The passage in the 1462 edition is not only erroneous; we can show that it must be specific to the 1462 edition by explaining how it came about. It is furthermore improbable that it would have been interpolated into another textual tradition, as it is obviously wrong. Any text with this reading must therefore depend directly or indirectly on the 1462 edition.

69 Quentin, *Mémoire*, as note 15, p. 94; also e.g. Needham in *The George Abrams Collection* (London: Sotheby's, 16-17 Nov. 1989), lot 27.

70 Prefaces: to Proverbs (Stegmüller, as note 33, no. 455); two to Jeremiah (nos 485, and 490); to the twelve Prophets (no. 501); two to Joel (nos 510 and 508), to Maccabees (no. 552); to the four Gospels (no. 596); to 1 Corinthians (no. 690); to 2 Corinthians (no. 697); two to Acts (nos 637 and 640). Of these only nos 508 and 640 are among the standard 64 prefaces which go with the 'Paris Bible', as listed by Ker, *Medieval Manuscripts*, as note 32.

71 *GW* 4216, 4220, 4222, 4223, 4231, 4233, 4237, 4238, 4241, 4245, 4247, 4253, and 4256.

72 *GW* 4220, containing an exchange of two letters between Blasius Romerus, who was financially involved in the edition, and the nobleman Thomas Taquius, whose support was sought.

73 *GW* 4237. See Hillard, as note 10, at pp. 72-3.

74 *GW* 4236. Maurice E. Schild, *Abendländische Bibelvorreden bis zur Lutherbibel*, Quellen und Forschungen zur Reformationsgeschichte, 39 (Gütersloh, 1970), p. 108, is wrong to claim that the inclusion of numerous new prefaces first appeared in this edition: they all derive from the Venice tradition.

75 *GW* 4212. See p. 121.

76 This is thus not an innovation introduced by Froben in his 1491 edition (*GW* 4269; cf. note 101 below), as suggested by Paul Needham, *The Estelle Doheny Collection Part I: the Fifteenth-Century Books including the Gutenberg Bible* (New York: Christie, Manson & Woods, 22 Oct. 1987), lot 64. The relation of the *registra*, or *capitulationes* and of the *casus summarii*, to *capitula* lists which occurred in the pre-Parisian Bibles is a vast topic to be explored; on the *capitula* see Otto Schmid, *Über verschiedene Eintheilungen der Heiligen*

Schrift insbesondere über die Capitel-Eintheilung Stephan Langtons im XIII. Jahrhunderte (Graz, 1892), pp. 25-55; Donatien de Bruyne, *Sommaires, divisions et rubriques de la Bible latine* (Namur, 1914); and A. d'Esneval, 'La division de la Vulgate latine en chapitres dans l'édition parisienne du xiiiᵉ siècle', *Revue des sciences philosophiques et theologiques*, 62 (1978), 559-68.

77 *Incipit*: 'Dominica prima in adventu Domini ...'. See *Patrologia Latina*, vol. 78, col. 1367 and vol. 151, col. 949. See also Theodor Klauser, *Das römische Capitulare evangeliorum: Texte und Untersuchungen zu seiner ältesten Geschichte: I. Typen*, 2nd rev. edn (Münster, 1972), especially p. xvii, where the ninth century is described as the period when this text was most widely copied. In the later Middle Ages it is occasionally found in complete bibles or in manuscripts of the New Testament.

78 *Incipit*: 'Gignit et Exit. Leuiticus. Numeri quoque Deut; Ios ...', partly edited in Quentin, *Mémoire*, as note 15, p. 81; cf. Hans Walther, *Initia carminum ac versuum medii aevi posterioris latinorum: Alphabetisches Verzeichnis der Versanfänge mittellateinischer Dichtungen*, Carmina medii aevi posterioris latina, 1 (Göttingen, 1959), nos 7141 and 7146; 12 lines of near hexameter verse.

79 *Incipit*: 'Marcus romanis, sed Johannes asianis, | Lucas achaiis, Matheus scripsit hebreis | Matheus scripsit euangelium anno domini 39. | Marcus 43, Lucas 53, Johannes 83.' Cf. Quentin, *Mémoire*, as note 15, p. 81.

80 On the use of *capitula*, *summaria*, and mnemonic verses in biblical studies, see for instance Karl Stackmann 'Die Bedeutung des Beiwerks für die Bestimmung der Gebrauchssituation vorlutherischer deutscher Bibeln', in *De captu lectoris: Wirkungen des Buches im 15. und 16. Jahrhundert dargestellt an ausgewählten Handschriften und Drucken*, ed. by Wolfgang Milde & Werner Schuder (Berlin, 1988), pp. 273-88, who at p. 280 quotes Luther for having known by heart all *capitula*. Opinions were divided as to their usefulness; they were said to be a waste of time in an entry on a Bible with mnemonic verses in the library catalogue of the Carthusians of Salvatorberg: 'Verum videtur quod huiusmodi versus plus curiositatis et occupationis habeant quam utilitatis, presertim quoad tardos in memoria et in ingenio'; see *Mittelalterliche Bibliothekskataloge Deutschlands und der Schweiz, II: Bistum Mainz, Erfurt*, ed. by Paul Lehmann (Munich, 1928), pp. 239-593, at p. 273.

81 GW 4257 ascribed to Strasbourg, the 'Printer of the 1483 Vitas patrum', but on this printer in general see Victor Scholderer, 'Michael Wenssler and His Press at Basel', in *Fifty Essays in Fifteenth- and Sixteenth-Century Bibliography*, ed. by Dennis E. Rhodes (Amsterdam, 1966), pp. 46-60, at p. 52.

82 GW 4246, giving another, longer, version of the mnemonic verses on the order of the books of the Bible, making improvements to the metre. *Incipit*: 'Generat., Exodus, Levi., Numeri, quoque Deutro. ...', 14 lines of near hexameters. He also included Stephen Langton's *Interpretationes nominum hebraeorum*.

83 Amerbach's next edition, from 1482 (GW 4248); Grüninger's edition from Strasbourg 1483 (GW 4252); Amerbach's edition from 1486 (GW 4258), Drach's edition from Speyer 1486 (GW 4259); and Prüss's edition from 1486 which however does not include Langton's *Interpretationes nominum hebraeorum* (GW 4260, according to GW reset gathering by gathering from GW 4248). Also Hochfeder's Nuremberg edition 'not after 1493' (GW 4272) followed this pattern, but excluded everything after the verses 'Fontibus e graecis hebraeorum quoque libris ...', thus being the only German edition of this group not to include the *Capitulare lectionum et evangeliorum*.

84 GW 4249, omitting, however, the verses on the recipients of letters from the Evangelists, and the dates of writing of the Gospels.

85 GW 4254.

86 Franciscus Moneliensis was associated first with Jenson, from the late 1470s, and later with

Herbort, mainly in editing legal texts; ISTC lists 15 editions with contributions by him. See also Martin Lowry, *Nicholas Jenson and the Rise of Venetian Publishing in Renaissance Europe* (Oxford, 1991), especially pp. 162-3. Cimbriacus is mentioned in Alessandro Benedetti, *Diaria de bello Carolino*, ed. by Dorothy M. Schullian, Renaissance Society of America Text Series, 1 (New York, 1967), p. 17.

87 *GW* 4255.

88 *GW* 4263.

89 *GW* 4264.

90 A further indication is a shared variation in the text: where the earlier editions had read '*Biblia quem retinent sequitur nunc metricus ordo*', Herbort's second edition and Drach's both read '*sic*' for '*nunc*'.

91 *GW* 4262.

92 In some copies we find a sheet inserted after leaf 1, containing a preface to the whole Bible and a list of the books of the Bible with summaries, for instance the BL copy, as described in *BMC* III 765 (IB.37595). This edition also contains a fourth preface to the book of Joel.

93 'Translatores seu interpretes Biblie', *incipit*: 'Notandum quod translatores et interpretes Biblie multi fuerunt …' *Patrologia Latina*, vol. 113, cols 23-6; Quentin, *Memoire*, as note 15, p. 84. And 'Quatuor sunt modi seu regule exponendi Sacram Scripturam', *Incipit*: 'Notandum quod omnis sacra scriptura quadriformi ratione distinguitur siue exponitur …'. Quentin, *Memoire*, as note 15, p. 84.

94 Kesler followed Amerbach in including the *Capitulare lectionum et evangeliorum*, the passage on the translators of the Bible, and the note on the four ways of interpreting the Bible.

95 It begins with Herbort's version of the mnemonic verses on the order of the books of the Old Testament, and omits the verses 'Fontibus ex Grecis Hebreorum quoque libris …'.

96 *GW* 4265.

97 It contains the *capitulationes*, the note on the translators and, indeed, the fourth preface to Joel; cf. note 92.

98 *GW* 4268.

99 *GW* 4262, but now omitting the verses on the order of the books of the Bible although the verses are added by hand in the Bodleian Library copy (*Bod-inc* B-299; Bib. Lat. 1491 c.3).

100 Sheet a2.7. See *GW* 4268, Anmerkung.

101 *GW* 4269.

102 It is shorter than the two earlier versions 'Genesis, Exo., Leui., Numerorum, Deuteronomi., | Post Josue, Judicum, Ruth, Regum, Paralip …', 11 near heaxameters. However, it has an introductory distich: 'Perspice nunc, lector, quis debitus ordo librorum | Biblia quos sociat, ordinat atque probat.' It ends with two hexameters: 'Sit benedictus Deus et homo de virgine natus | Credentes verbis sacris saluare paratus.'

103 In his 'Ad diuinarum litterarum verarumque diuitiarum amatores exhortatio'. It contains also the first lines of the extract from Guido Vicentinus's *Margarita* which were first included in Richel's edition of the Bible [Basel: Bernhard Richel, not after 1474] (*GW* 4212; see note 38) and which last had made an occurrence in a printed edition form in 1476 (*GW* 4221; cf. note 56). Measurements of the Bodleian Library copy: *Bod-inc* B-300; shelfmark: Auct. M inf. 1.13.

104 *GW* 4271.

105 *DBI*, vol. 14, cols 651-2. But for his various editorial activities see in particular Brian Richardson, *Print Culture in Renaissance Italy: the Editor and the Vernacular Text 1470-1600* (Cambridge, 1994), pp. 29-30.

106 As note 93.

107 This Venice edition was followed by Angelus and Jacobus Britannicus in 1496, now

also naming Georgius Britannicus as an editor (*GW* 4276), and again by Hieronymus de Paganinis in Venice in 1497 (*GW* 4278).

108 *GW* 4275. This edition also contains a woodcut of Jerome, with four elegiac distichs, new to the biblical corpus, *incipit*: 'Simachus atque Theodotion vel septuaginta | Addo aquilam et quorum nomina lata paten t …'.

109 *GW* 4274.

110 See Stegmüller, as note 33, 1175-85; Quentin, *Mémoire*, as note 15, p. 85; edited in Alexander de Villa Dei, *Das Doctrinale*, ed. by Dietrich Reichling & Theodor Reichling, Monumenta Germaniae Paedagogica, 12 (Berlin, 1893), at pp. xlii-xliii.

111 *GW* 4255; cf. note 87. Bevilaqua repeated this edition in 1498 (*GW* 4280). Thus not all editions classified by *GW* as belonging to the 'Fontibus e grecis …' group contain these verses.

112 *GW* 4267. Proctor and *GW* assigned to Amerbach, while *BMC*'s ascription to Piscator has been reinforced by Vera Sack, *Die Inkunabeln der Universitätsbibliothek und anderer öffentlicher Sammlungen in Freiburg im Breisgau und Umgebung* (Wiesbaden, 1985), no. 648. It has not been possible to relate it chronologically to the two other editions of 1491.

113 It does not contain the mnemonic verses nor Froben's other introductory matter.

114 See note 63.

115 Piscator reproduced this version of the biblical corpus in his edition from about 1493-4 (*GW* 4270), and it was copied by Mathias Huss in Lyon in 1494 (*GW* 4273).

116 *GW* 4277.

117 Grüninger's edition contains Gabriel Brunus's table in Froben's revised version; it also includes the woodcut image of Jerome and the associated verses which we found in Froben's second edition.

118 *GW* 4279. Perhaps spurred on by Pivard's 1497 edition, Bevilaqua updated his editions also to include the *casus summarii*, but he did not follow Pivard's example of numbering the introductory tables of contents (*GW* 4280).

119 *GW* 4281.

120 Margaret T. Gibson, 'The Glossed Bible', in Karlfried Froehlich & Margaret T. Gibson, *Biblia latina cum glossa ordinaria: Introduction to the Facsimile Reprint of the Editio Princeps, Adolph Rusch of Strassburg 1480/81* (Turnhout, 1992), pp. vii-xi.

121 Margaret Gibson, *The Bible in the Latin West* (London, 1993), p. 9.

122 *GW* 4286. On the consortium see Martin Lowry, *Nicholas Jenson*, as note 86, especially pp. 163-8.

123 The two bible editions produced by Herbort (*GW* 4254 and 4255) after he stopped working for the Consortium naturally enough had a commentary, but they also showed awareness of textual developments emanating from Germany, as shown above.

124 *Postilla super totam Bibliam*. Rome: Conradus Sweynheym & Arnoldus Pannartz, 1471-2 (*ISTC* in00131000). This edition contains the *Postillae litterales*, not both the *Postillae morales* and *litterales*, as stated by A. Gosselin, 'A Listing of the Printed Editions of Nicolaus de Lyra', *Traditio*, 26 (1970), 399-426, at p. 406.

125 Cyprianus, *Opera*. Rome: Conradus Sweynheym & Arnoldus Pannartz, [Jan. or Feb.] 1471 (*GW* 7883; *ISTC* ic01010000); see Bussi, *Prefazioni*, as note 44, at p. 53.

126 *ISTC* in00133000.

127 *GW* 4209. This lends further support to Needham, *Doheny Collection*, as note 76, lot 16, and Needham, *Incunables from the Schøyen Collection* (New York, Sotheby's, 12 Dec. 1991), lot 6, who sees Mentelin in association with Rusch as responsible for the work of the R-printer and dates this Bible 'about 1473'.

128 It may be that the production of the *Postillae* provides part of the explanation for Koberger's last uncommented edition of the Bible of 1482 (*GW* 4250), which surprisingly represents

something of a throwback to the B42 text group, and, except for Stephen Langton's *Interpretationes nominum hebraeorum*, lacks all the accretions to the text which were present in his earlier editions.

129 An example is Paulus Butzbach of Mantua who printed four part-editions of the *Postillae litterales*, on the Gospels, on the Psalter, on the letters of Paul, and on the Acts of the Apostles (*ISTC* in00130000, in00124000, in00122000, and in00115000).

130 Gratianus, *Decretum (cum apparatu Bartholomaei Brixiensis)*. Venice: Nicolaus Jenson, 28 June 1474 (*GW* 11354).

131 See Karl Stehlin, 'Regesten zur Geschichte des Buchdrucks bis zum Jahre 1500: Aus den Büchern des Staatsarchivs, der Zunftarchive und des Universitätsarchivs in Basel, II', *Archiv für Geschichte des deutschen Buchhandels*, 12 (1889), 6-70, at p. 61, a donation from Johann Amerbach, probably in 1485 or 1486: 'Item procuravit nobis a Magistro Johanne Petri socio eius Bibliam cum Lira more librorum iuris in margine coniunctam valoris 6 flor. In 4 voluminibus.' The monks confirm what J. P. Gumbert has noted, in 'The Layout of the Bible Gloss in Manuscript and Early Print', in *The Bible as Book*, as note 12, pp. 7-13, at p. 10, that the printed Bible with the *Glossa ordinaria* used a layout known from legal rather than biblical texts.

132 In the case of Aulus Gellius they considered publishing a separate commentary, but printed instead 28 pages of rubrics, to make up for the absence of marginal notes, exhorting the reader to write ample notes for himself. See the letter to Paulus II, in Aulus Gellius, *Noctes Atticae*. Rome: In domo Petri de Maximis [Conradus Sweynheym & Arnoldus Pannartz], 11 Apr. 1469 (*GW* 10593; *ISTC* ig00118000), edited in Bussi, *Prefazioni*, as note 44, at p. 25.

133 *GW* 4288; 4289; 4293; 4294.

134 The three subsequent not-Koberger editions being: Venice: Franciscus Renner, de Heilbronn, 1482-83 (*GW* 4287); [Lyon]: Johannes Siber, [after 7 May 1485, about 1488] (*GW* 4290); Venice: [Bonetus Locatellus], for Octavianus Scotus, 8 Aug. 1489 (*GW* 4291).

135 See Gosselin, as note 124, at pp. 399-400 on Lyra's study of Hebrew, and for the fifteenth-century controversy between Paul of Burgos and Matthias Döring, with an extensive list of literature on Lyra. See also Katharina Colberg, 'Döring, Matthias', in *VL*, II, 207-10.

136 Venice: Paganinus de Paganinis, 18 Apr. 1495 (*GW* 4283). Bernardinus Gadolus, Eusebius Hispanus, and Secundus Contarenus were editors involved in the project; see *Documenti per servire alla storia della tipografia veneziana*, ed. by R. Fulin, Estratto dall'Archivio Veneto, 32, parte 1 (Venice, 1882), pp. 24-5.

137 Basel: Johann Froben & Johann Petri de Langendorff, 1 Dec. 1498 (*GW* 4284).

138 [Basel]: Johann Amerbach, for Anton Koberger, [1498-1502] (*GW* 4285).

139 In 1481 Rudolph von Scherenberg, the prince-bishop of Würzburg, had a missal printed by Reyser, reinforcing his attempt to impose uniformity by requiring all clerics in his diocese to buy the work, fixing the price at four Rhenish guilders, granting 40 days of indulgence to all who were involved in the production of the book, who bought it, or who read or heard Mass from it. *Missale Herbipolense*. [Würzburg: Georg Reyser, 1481] *ISTC* im00663900, Scherenberg's letter sig. [b1] recto. See also M. K. Duggan, p. 74 in this volume.

140 See R. Fulin, as note 136, at pp. 20-1, for 14 March 1478, a contract between Leonardus Wild of Regensburg and Nicolaus de Frankfordia, stipulating a run of 930 copies (*GW* 4233), for which Leonardus was to be paid 240 gold ducats. He was to be provided with the paper, the payment to be received in rates as gatherings were delivered. Among Latin Bibles only the Naples edition is known with certainty to have been sponsored, as appears from the correspondence printed in it. A successful attempt was made after publication to get papal support for the printers of the Roman edition, but not specifically for the Bible. It has been suggested that the Bishop of Strasbourg financed *GW* 4203, see John Flood,

'Johann Mentelin und Ruprecht von Pfalz-Simmern: Zur Entstehung der Straßburger 'Parzival'-Ausgabe vom Jahre 1477', in *Studien zu Wolfram von Eschenbach: Festschrift für Werner Schröder zum 75. Geburtstag*, ed. by Kurt Gärtner & Joachim Heinzle (Tübingen, 1989), pp. 197-209, at pp. 197-8; and that Georg von Schaumberg, bishop of Bamberg, may have had some involvement in the production of *GW* 4202; see Felix de Marez Oyens, as note 36, at p. 58. Bibles produced in the earliest years of printing may have been sponsored, as may editions from non-commercial centres, Vicenza and Piacenza, but so far there is no evidence for this. It would also be interesting to know the arrangements financial or practical between Gabriel Brunus, guardian of the Franciscan Convent of Venice, who provided a table of contents for Hieronymus de Paganinis' edition from 1492. The first Italian translation was sponsored by the Camaldolese house of S. Mattia di Murano. See Edoardo Barbieri, as note 49, at pp. 27-8.

141 Margaret Gibson, *The Bible in the Latin West* (London, 1993), p. 9, note 40.

142 Looking at Koberger's uncommented editions 7 copies are recorded in Italy of *GW* 4218; 3 of *GW* 4277, one being in a Tyrol collection; 9 of *GW* 4232; 5 of *GW* 4234; 3 of *GW* 4239; 2 of *GW* 4243; 5 of *GW* 4288. These figures do not necessarily all represent books which actually were in Italy in the fifteenth century, rather they indicate that there is no evidence for a massive impact of these editions, when compared with the overwhelming presence in Italian libraries of contemporary Venetian editions of the Bible. See for instance note 158.

143 *GW* 4269. *ISTC* records 25 copies in Italian locations.

144 *GW* 4286. *ISTC* records 39 copies in German libraries.

145 *GW* 4287. *ISTC* records 41 copies in German libraries.

146 *GW* 4288; *GW* 4289; *GW* 4293; *GW* 4294.

147 *GW* 4291. 11 copies are recorded in German locations by *ISTC*. This is in part a raw figure, but the great difference between this and the 39 and 41 copies of the previous editions is some indication of the relative impact of the editions on Germany.

148 *GW* 4282; *GW* 4284. Of the former there are 24 copies with Italian locations recorded in *ISTC*, one of them at least grandly decorated in Venice; see Armstrong, 'Il Maestro di Pico: Un miniatore veneziano del tardo Quattrocento', *Saggi e memorie di storia dell'arte*, 17 (1990), 9-39, no. 46. Although this figure is in part raw and an early Italian provenance has not always been verified, their occurrence is signifcantly at variance with other bible editions and probably reflects a different pattern of distribution. One of the two BL copies is from St Benedetto, the Benedictine monastery of the congregation of St Justina in Mantua; *BMC* I 92 (IC. 813). Of the latter edition 16 copies are represented in Italian collections.

149 *GW* 4283. There are 252 copies of this edition recorded in Italian locations.

150 *ISTC* records 38 copies.

151 Oscar Hase, *Die Koberger: Eine Darstellung des Buchhändlerischen Geschäftsbetriebes in der Zeit des Überganges vom Mittelalter zur Neuzeit* (Leipzig, 1885), p. 292; see also Karlfried Froehlich, 'The Printed Gloss', in *Biblia latina cum glossa ordinaria*, as note 120, pp. xii-xxvi, at pp. xviii-xix.

152 See Hase, *Die Koberger*, as note 151, p. 294.

153 See on this topic also Lotte Hellinga, 'Peter Schoeffer and the Book Trade in Mainz: Evidence for the Organisation', in *Bookbindings and Other Bibliophily: Essays in Honour of Anthony Hobson*, ed. by Dennis Rhodes (Verona, 1994), pp. 131-84, especially at pp. 136-7. See also *The Library of Abel E. Berland: Part II English Literature and Fine Incunabula* (New York, Christie's 9 Oct. 2001), lot 381, a copy of Renner's edition from 1480, *GW* 4241, which was bound for Johannes de Westphalia, the printer, who evidently sold Venetian Bibles as part of his activity as a book dealer. On Westphalia as a dealer see now especially Paul Needham, 'Continental Printed Books Sold in Oxford, *c.*1480-3:

Two Trade Records', in *Incunabula: Studies in Fifteenth-Century Printed Books Presented to Lotte Hellinga*, ed. by Martin Davies (London, 1999), 243-70; also Rudolf Juchhof, 'Johannes de Westfalia als Buchhändler', *Gutenberg Jahrbuch* (1954), 133-6.

154 For an overview of the export book trade to Germany see Neddermeyer, as note 6, especially pp. 395-403, 'Internationaler Buchmarkt', pp. 420-22, 'Reich und Italien'; on the commercial connections between Venice and Germany see for instance Gerhard Rösch, 'Il Fondaco dei Tedeschi', in *Venezia e la Germania: arte, politica, commercio i due civiltà a confronto* (Milan, 1986), pp. 51-72.

155 *GW* 4241. *ISTC* records 55 copies in Italian libraries.

156 *GW* 4253. *ISTC* records 30 copies in Italian libraries.

157 *GW* 4254. *ISTC* records 29 copies in Italian libraries.

158 *GW* 4255, an edition particularly frequently found in Italian collections, 56 copies being recorded by *ISTC* in Italian collections.

159 *GW* 4245, likewise frequent in Italian libraries, with 53 copies recorded in *ISTC*.

160 *GW* 4256.

161 *GW* 4247. *ISTC* records 20 copies in Italian libraries.

162 On some of the Italian business relations of Venetian exporters see Angela Nuovo, *Il commercio librario nell'Italia del Rinascimento* (Milan, 1998), pp. 68-86. On the importation of books into Rome see Paolo Cherubini, Anna Esposito, Anna Modigliani, and Paola Piacentini, 'Il costo del libro', in *Scrittura, biblioteche e stampa a Roma nel Quattrocento: Atti del 2° seminario 6-8 maggio 1982*, ed. by Massimo Miglio and others, Littera antiqua, 3 (Vatican City, 1983), pp. 323-553, at pp. 429-31, with the customs records on pp. 538-53.

163 Rudolf Hirsch, *Printing, Selling and Reading 1450-1550* (Wiesbaden, 1967), p. 44, suggests that an over-production of bibles in the late 1470s could be part of the explanation for the crisis which affected the Italian production of printed books in the early 1480s.

164 For instance the BL copy acquired by a Jean Chardalle, a cantor of Metz, and decorated for him in Rome (*BMC* IV 12; IC.17163); Chardalle was probably in Rome in the early 1470s and while there also bought his copy of Johannes Lapus de Castellione, *Allegationes*. [Rome]: Sixtus Riessinger, [1470], decorated for him in Rome, now in the Bodleian Library (*Bod-inc* C-109; shelfmark: Douce 303).

165 Lotte Hellinga, 'Importation of Books Printed on the Continent into England and Scotland before *c.*1520', in *Printing the Written Word: the Social History of Books, circa 1450-1520*, ed. by Sandra L. Hindman (Ithaca, NY, 1999), pp. 205-24, at p. 215.

166 Hillard, as note 10, here at pp. 71-2.

167 This point was also made by L. D. Sheppard and George Painter in their introduction to *BMC* vol. X, p. xi, where they discussed the absence of classical texts printed in Spain.

168 Examples of bibles bought in Paris are the Cambridge University Library copy of *GW* 4241 (J. C. T. Oates, *A Catalogue of the Fifteenth-Century Printed Books in the University Library Cambridge* (Cambridge, 1954), no. 1674); and the Modena, Biblioteca Estense copy of *GW* 4277; see Domenico Fava, *Catalogo degli incunaboli della r. Biblioteca Estense di Modena* (Florence, 1928), no. 309. See Rouse, *Illiterati*, as note 30, at pp. 320-3, on Hermann of Statboen's Parisian trade in printed books in years before 1474, and more generally on the availability of printed books in Paris, whether imported or not.

169 [Cologne: Heinrich Quentell, about 1480] (*ISTC* ib00570500), consisting of imperfect conjugate leaves, in Haarlem Stadsbibliotheek.

170 *GW* 4243, see Paul Needham, *Incunabula from the Court Library at Donaueschingen* (London: Sotheby's, 1 July 1994, lot 52).

171 *GW* 4216; the Bodleian Library copy measures some 280 mm high (*Bod-inc* B-251; shelfmark: Auct. M 2.1).

172 For instance the Bodleian Library copy of *GW* 4253, Renner's edition from 1483 (*Bod-inc*

B-286; shelfmark: Auct. M inf. 1.12).

173 See e.g. Margaret Gibson, *The Bible in the Latin West* (London, 1993), no. 19.

174 See also M. H. Black, 'The Evolution of a Book-Form: the Octavo Bible from Manuscript to the Geneva Version', *The Library*, 5th series, 16 (1961), 15-28.

175 See Richard A. Goldthwaite, *Wealth and the Demand for Art in Italy 1300-1600* (Baltimore, 1993), pp. 19-20.

176 Twelve of the fifteen Venetian Latin Bible editions from before 1486 were printed by German printers, whereas none of the seven Venetian editions printed after 1485 had any German involvement. Marino Zorzi, 'Stampatori tedeschi a Venezia', in *Venezia e la Germania* (Milan, 1986), pp. 115-40, especially at p. 132-3, explains the decline in German involvement with the outbreak of the plague from 1484-6 and with increased hostility against German traders after the war with Sigismund of Austria from 1487. More generally see Victor Scholderer, 'Printing at Venice to the End of 1481', *The Library*, 4th series, 5 (1925), 129-52.

177 This point is made in a general way by Brian Richardson, *Print Culture*, as note 105, p. 2: 'Secondly the printer or publisher would want the edition to be as complete as possible, especially if there were rival editions competing for the market.' On p. 35 Richardson points out that in the field of Italian literature Venetian printers were keenly aware of the production of Italian competitors in the publishing of Italian texts, and copied their additional material to remain competitive.

178 Goldthwaite, *Wealth*, as note 175, at pp. 27-9.

179 See Pierre Petitmengin, 'La Bible à travers les inventaires de bibliothèques médiévales', in *Le Moyen Age et la Bible*, ed. by Pierre Riché & Guy Lobrichon (Paris, 1984), pp. 31-53, at pp. 36-7 on the bibles in the six convents of Regensburg, and pp. 37-8 on the Europe-wide nature of biblical collections in religious houses of the late Middle Ages.

180 See for instance N. R. Ker, 'The Provision of Books', in *The History of the University of Oxford, volume III: The Collegiate University*, ed. by James McConica (Oxford, 1986), pp. 441-519, at p. 447.

181 The substance of the catalogue of of B.V.M. de Pratis, Leicester, must be dated to before 1463: published in *The Libraries of the Augustinian Canons*, ed. by T. Webber & A. G. Watson, Corpus of British Medieval Library Catalogues, 6 (London, 1998), pp. 104-399, nos 1–17. See also T. Webber, 'Latin Devotional Texts and the Books of the Augustinian Canons of Thurgarton Priory and Leicester Abbey in the Late Middle Ages', in *Books and Collectors 1200-1700: Essays Presented to Andrew Watson*, ed. by J. P. Carley & C. G. C. Tite (London, 1997), pp. 27-41.

182 Needham, 'The Text', as note 11, at p. 53 assumes that it was true of almost all copies of B42 owned by religious houses.

183 The copies in Göttingen and at Eton College were evidently used in a refectory, but we do not know when: see Paul Schwenke, 'Die Gutenbergbibel', in *Johannes Gutenbergs zweiundvierzigzeilige Bibel: Ergänzungsband zur Faksimile-Ausgabe*, ed. by Paul Schwenke (Leipzig, 1923), no. 5, p. 8, and no. 28 p. 14. The two copies in the BL both have careful pronunciation marks, of a very banal nature indicating the appropriate stress. This is perhaps an indication that they were used in a refectory, but possibly not. In any case we cannot date the pronunciation marks with any certainty. Also private readings left marks in bibles, showing where the reader had got to at specific times, for instance the copy now in Cracow of *GW* 4275 (Froben's edition of 1495 in 8°): 'Hec Biblia est Ioannis Zarnovite, lectaque per eundem manuque est ipsius in marginibus consignata, cum lectione complementum factum est, Cracouie in ecclesia Nor.(berti?) xviij Maij siue feria tercia Rogacionum a, mdxij'; see Wladislaus Wisłocki, *Incunabula typographica Bibliothecae Universitatis Jagellonicae Cracoviensis inde ab inventa arte imprimendi us ad a. 1500*

(Cracow, 1900), pp. 71-2. Christopher De Hamel, *The Book: a History of the Bible* (London, 2001), pp. 194-5, has suggested that there was a revived interest in large-format bibles in the mid-fifteenth century, but also warns, pp. 214 and 215, against assuming that all copies of the B42 were produced for use in religious houses.

184 I can quote only three uncommented printed bibles definitely bought by institutions: the Premonstratensians in Windberg, who purchased extensively, bought a bound bible in 1481, presumably printed, for 6 Rhenish guilder: see *Mittelalterliche Bibliothekskataloge Deutschlands und der Schweiz, vol. IV/1, Bistümer Passau und Regensburg*, ed. by Christine Elisabeth Ineichen-Eder (Munich, 1977), p. 584. The Carthusians in Constanz bought a copy of GW 4248 in 1487: see P. L. Van der Haegen, *Basler Wiegendrucke: Verzeichnis der in Basel gedruckten Inkunabeln mit ausführlicher Beschreibung der in der Universitätsbibliothek Basel vorhandenen Exemplare* (Basel, 1998), no. 16,12. In 1482 the Dominican nuns of Unterlinden bought a bible for the use of their confessors: *Les dominicaines d'Unterlinden, II: Catalogue des Œuvres* (Paris, 2001), n. 162: 'Sororibus subtiliensibus in columbaria pertinet iste liber emptus pro confessoribus anno domini 1482, rubricata est'; the catalogue does not give a proper description but mentions that the edition has 47 lines, which makes it likely that it is either GW 4236 or GW 4246. I have no doubt that more such examples can be found, but they will remain relatively rare.

185 For instance the numerous bibles owned by lay Sicilians in the late fifteenth century, with collections ranging from over a hundred items to just a single book: see Henri Bresc, *Livre et société en Sicile (1299-1499)* (Palermo, 1971), *ad indicem*, the owners being mainly nobles and lawyers. Widespread private ownership of printed bibles in late fifteenth-century Verona is confirmed by work in progress on private libraries by Caterina Crestani; see also her 'La biblioteca di Giacomo Conte Giuliani (1480)', *Bollettino della Biblioteca Civica di Verona*, 3 (1997), 13-41.

186 For instance the Windesheimer Augustinian canons in Aachen sold a bible donated by the dean of St Servatius in Utrecht because it did not conform with their own bible type; the money was used to buy a more suitable version, see Thomas Kock, *Die Buchkultur der Devotio moderna: Handschriftenproduktion, Literaturversorgung und Bibliotheksaufbau im Zeitalter des Medienwechsels* (Frankfurt am Main, 1999), pp. 63-4.

187 Kock, *Die Buchkultur*, as note 186, at p. 66 with note 55, mentions that during the fifteenth century most donations to the houses of the Windesheimer reform movement were of money and that most of those who gave books were clerics. Books were given by outsiders either to found chantries or because they were useful to the friars. Nigel Palmer, *Zisterzienser und ihre Bücher: die mittelalterliche Bibliotheksgeschichte von Kloster Eberbach im Rheingau unter besonderer Berücksichtigung der in Oxford und London aufbewahrten Handschriften* (Regensburg, 1998), p. 185, comments on the need for liturgical books for the numerous private masses which were said at Eberbach.

188 For a good account see Auguste Molinier, *Les Obituaires français au moyen âge* (Paris, 1890), especially pp. 24-46, who outlines the connection of anniversary prayers and masses with letters of confraternity.

189 Martin Mergetheimer bequeathed to the Benedictines of Ebersberg a copy of GW 4209 (*BSB-Ink* B-414) 'ob suffragia anime communicanda ne tartareis absorpta suppliciis dei (quam aequanimiter corporeis alligata uinculis expectabat) visione non donaretur'.

190 Examples of bibles containing a request for Masses are: the copy of GW 4206 (*Bod-inc*: 241(1); shelfmark: Auct. M 1.9) given by Ulrich Zell, the printer, to the Augustinian nuns, St Maria Rosa in Ahlen 'ut suas annuatim Deo omnipotenti fundant preces pro eius anima et suorum parentum'; on Zell's donation see see L. A. Sheppard, 'Two Benefactions of Ulrich Zell', *The Library*, 5th Series, 12 (1957), 271-3. Zell's benefaction is recorded in the list of benefactors of the house: see Wilhelm Kohl, *Das Bistum Münster, 1: die Schwesternhäuser*

nach der Augustinerregel, Germania Sacra, Neue Folge, 3 (Berlin, 1968), 349: 'Meister Ulricus Zeel von Hanno, de uns gaff 5 gebunden boke'; prayers were due on 23 January. The copy of *GW* 4208 (*BSB-Ink* B-413(2)) given to the Augustinian canons in Weyarn in 1476 by Ludwig Wüst 'pro anniuersario habendo per conuentum prefati monasterii'. Wüst is duly listed in the list of anniversaries of Weyarn: cf. *Mittelalterliche Bibliothekskataloge Deutschlands und der Schweiz, IV/2: Bistum Freising Bistum Würzburg*, ed. by Günter Glauche & Hermann Knaus (Munich, 1979), p. 864. Examples of bibles given in return for prayers or for the salvation of the soul are: the copy of *GW* 4214 (*Bod-inc* B-249; shelfmark: Auct. V 3.2,3) bequeathed by Hermann Proninck, master of the fabric of the cathedral of Münster to a convent, probably the Carthusian house Castrimaria in Weddern near Dülmen, with the injunction 'Orate fideliter pro anima eiusdem et omnium suorum'; a copy of *GW* 4247 (*Bod-inc* B-281; shelfmark: Bibl. Lat. 1481 d.1) containing the note 'A uso di suora Maria. Perpetua fate orazione per me'; a copy of *GW* 4294 (*Bod-inc* B-324; shelfmark: Auct. 6Q 3.30,31), given by Michael Münichofer, plebanus in Seebach to the Benedictines at St Michael in Metten in 1503, with other books 'in remedium anime sue et in usum fratrum reseruandum'; a copy of one volume of *GW* 4282 (the glossa ordinaria edition from *c.*1480) given by Sebald Schreyer to the church library of St Sebald in 1486 'pro saulte anime mee ac conthoralis Margarethe kamermaisterin progenitorumque' (Barbara Hellwig, *Inkunabelkatalog des germanischen Nationalmuseums Nürnberg* (Wiesbaden, 1970), no. 191). Schreyer gave all four volumes to St Sebald: see *Mittelalterliche Bibliothekskataloge Deutschlands und der Schweiz, III: Bistum Augsburg, Eichstätt, Bamberg*, ed. by Paul Ruf (Munich, 1932), at p. 693, although this book does not feature in the extensive list of his donations at pp. 685-90; a copy of *GW* 4282 (*BSB-Ink* B-442) given to Altötting in 1515 by Udalricus Obermaier, a canon et plebanus, 'ut orent deum per me'; a copy of *GW* 4219 was bequeathed to Tegernsee by Georg Arbaitter plebanus in Ried 'pro salute anime sue' in 1490 (now in Worcester College, Oxford, see Dennis E. Rhodes, *A Catalogue of Incunabula in All the Libraries of Oxford University outside the Bodleian* (Oxford, 1982), no. 347).

191 Bibles presented by lay people to institutions without inscriptions requesting prayers or masses are numerous. One example will suffice, the copy of B42 now in the Bodleian Library, presented by Erhard Neninger (*c.*1420-75), mayor of Heilbronn, to the Carmelites of Heilbronn not later than 1474 (*Bod-inc* B-237; shelfmark: Arch. B b.10,11).

192 See for instance J. T. Rosenthal, *The Purchase of Paradise: Gift Giving and the Aristocracy, 1307-1485* (London, 1972), p. 86: English wills record books given by lay people as part of payment for prayers 'in fair numbers ... if not in great variety'.

193 Except the copy of his edition from 1479 (*GW* 4236) which ends in 'oretur pro eo' possibly in a later hand; Van der Haegen, as note184, no. 16,3.

194 See Stehlin, as note 131, no. 1623 at pp. 61-3: 'Oretur pro venerabili magistro Johanne de Amerbach, cive et impressore Basiliensi, magno benefactore nostro qui consuevit de omni opere suo dare primicias domui nostre ....'

195 See Stehlin, as note 131, nos 1624-9.

196 Also Ulrich Zell's benefaction to the nuns at Ahlen. See note 190.

197 The 6th Bavarian State Library copy (*BSB-Ink* B-442) of *GW* 4282 was presented to an institution in 1487 'mero pietatis zelo'.

198 On this see Goldthwaite, *Wealth*, as note 175, especially pp. 129-48, the chapter entitled 'The Material Culture of the Church and Incipient Consumerism'.

199 Goldthwaite, *Wealth*, as note 175, p. 125 and *passim* talks about the 'appropriation of liturgical space by private interests'; in the case of the Bible it is more a question of the appropriation of liturgical time, and of space in religious libraries. E. König, 'The History of Art and the History of the Book at the Time of the Transition from Manuscript to Print',

in *Bibliography and the Study of Fifteenth-Century Civilisation* (London, 1987), pp. 154-84, suggested that the proliferation of bibles could be associated with the Windesheim reform movement; this view has been criticized and the connection may be too narrowly conceived, but there obviously is a wider connection with the increasing lay devotional involvement with the Church and thus at least indirectly with the various reform movements.

200 See for instance Rouse, *Illiterati*, as note 30, at pp. 321-2 on the donation of the Mainz 1470 edition of Jerome's letters (*ISTC* ih00165000) to St Victor in Paris by Peter Schoeffer and Conrad Henkis, endowing masses for the soul of Johann Fust themselves and their relatives, friends and benefactors. The value of the book exceeded the value of the Masses for they also got 12 écus d'or in return.

201 The question why the books of the Carthusians in Buxheim show so little sign of use is posed by Volker Honemann, 'The Buxheim Collection and its Dispersal', *Renaissance Studies*, 9 (1995), 160-88, at 175-6.

202 In the words of Jonathan Alexander, 'Patrons, Libraries and Illuminators in the Italian Renaissance', in *The Painted Page: Italian Renaissance Book Illumination 1450-1550*, exhibition catalogue ed. by Jonathan J. G. Alexander (Munich, 1994), pp. 11-20, at p. 11; see Lilian Armstrong in this volume, note 18, at p. 89.

203 See *The Painted Page*, as note 202, catalogue no. 1.

204 Armstrong's study 'Il Maestro di Pico', as note 148, shows how the master moved from illumination of manuscript to illumination of printed books, to the production of woodcuts. See also for instance Mirella Levi d'Ancona, *Miniatura e miniatori a Firenze dal XIV al XVI secolo* (Florence, 1962), p. 137, in the ledgers of St Maria Nova, June 1486: Spese straordinarie: payment to 'Gherardo e Monte fratelgi e filiuoli di Giovanni di Miniato miniatori L sei piccoli...' for decoration and binding of a printed bible (in forma).

205 See Eberhard König, 'Die Illuminierung der Gutenbergbibel', in *Johannes Gutenbergs zweiundvierzigzeiligen Bibel*, as note 25, pp. 70-125, with further observations and corrections in his *Gutenberg-Bibel: Handbuch zur B42: Zur Situation der Gutenberg-Forschung, Ein Supplement* (Münster, 1995).

206 For the Vienna copy of B42 see Ilona Hubay, 'Die bekannten Exemplare der zweiund-vierzigzeiligen Bibel und ihre Besitzer', in *Johannes Gutenbergs zweiundvierzigzeiligen Bibel*, as note 25, pp. 127-55, no. 27, p. 145.

207 For instance two copies of *GW* 4286, Herbort's edition with Lyra's *Postillae* from 1481, one now in BNF, according to Lilian Armstrong illuminated in part by Benedetto Bordon (*CIBN* B-428); the Vatican copy, a dedication copy to Sixtus IV, Francesco della Rovere (1414-84). Armstrong, 'Il Maestro di Pico', as note 148, lists four copies of commented bibles all decorated by one workshop, no. 56 (a copy of *GW* 4282 the Strasbourg edition with the Glossa Ordinaria, now in Padua, Biblioteca Capitolare del Duomo); nos 60, 61, and 70.

208 According to *ISTC* vellum copies are known to survive of 14 editions: *GW* 4201; 4202; 4204; 4206; 4208; 4216; 4220; 4222; 4223; 4238; 4241; 4263; 4286; 4287.

209 *CIBN* B-382 2nd copy (*GW* 4222), owned by Juan de Zuniga (fifteenth century); Francisco Alvarez de Toledo (*c.* 1510); Philip V, king of Spain. For a full description of the decoration see F. Avril, *Bibliothèque nationale: Manuscrits enluminées de la péninsule iberique* (Paris, 1983), no. 154, pp. 138-41; and *Des livres rares depuis l'invention de l'imprimerie*, ed. by Antoine Coron (Paris, 1998), no. 15.

210 *CIBN* B-382 3rd copy; decorated for S. Giorgio Maggiore; a further example of an elegantly decorated copy of Jenson's 1476 edition is Modena, Biblioteca Estense, α.B.1.15: see Giordana Mariani Canova, *La miniatura veneta del rinascimento* (Venice, 1969), catalogue no. 104, p. 160. Armstrong, 'Il Maestro di Pico', as note 148, nos 48-50 at pp. 33-4 lists three copies of Jenson's 1479 edition illuminated by one miniaturist or his workshop alone.

Notes

211 Armstrong, 'Il Maestro di Pico', as note 148, nos 42-3, 48-50, 60-1, and 70.

212 Lilian Armstrong, 'The Impact of Printing on Miniaturists in Venice after 1469', in *Printing the Written Word*, as note 165, pp. 174-202. See also Lilian Armstrong, 'The Hand-Illumination of Printed Books in Italy 1465-1515', in *The Painted Page*, as note 202, pp. 35-47, in particular at pp. 38-41.

213 Armstrong, 'Il Maestro di Pico', as note 148, at p. 14 on a financially determined grading of decorations.

214 See again Armstrong, 'Il Maestro di Pico', as note 148, at p. 16 on how in the earliest years customers for Venetian decorated incunables were Venetian nobles, whereas later in the 1480s non-noble buyers became an important group of buyers.

215 See the suggestions regarding Jensons's breviary of 1478 in Lilian Armstrong, 'Nicolaus Jenson's *Breviarium Romanum*, Venice, 1478: Decoration and Distribution', in *Incunabula: Studies in Fifteenth-Century Printed Books Presented to Lotte Hellinga*, ed. by M. Davies (London, 1999), pp. 421-67, at p. 451. On the role of decorated books in the 'complex web of Italian patronage and politics' see also Lilian Armstrong, 'Opus Petri', *Viator*, 21 (1990), 385-412, at 409. Natalie Z. Davies, 'Beyond the Market: Books as Gifts in Sixteenth-Century France', *Transactions of the Royal Historical Society*, 5th ser. 3 (1983), 69-88, discussed the book as a gift within the sixteenth-century system of patronage.

216 For instance two bibles used in the refectory of St Thomas and St Apollinaris, Pavia, *GW* 4263 and *GW* 4271 the former being in 4° measuring some 200 mm high, the latter being in 8° measuring 170-180 mm; see Fridericus Ageno, *Librorum saec. XV impressorum qui in publica ticinensi bibliotheca adservantur catalogus* (Florence, 1954), nos 126 and 127; and the copy of *GW* 4222, a small folio, with the inscription: 'A.P.A. Kalend. Nouembris ... ad aduentum domini Ezechielem prophetam: Librumque duodecim prophetarum tam in ecclesia quam in refectorio legimus': see M. Pellechet, *Bibliothèque publique de Versailles: Catalogue des incunables et des livres imprimés de MD. à MDXX* (Paris, 1889), no. 35. It is worth remembering what was said by Luigi Balsamo in 'La Bibbia in tipografia', in *La Bibbia a stampa da Gutenberg a Bodoni*, Firenze, Biblioteca Medicea Laurenziana Biblioteca Nazionale Centrale 8 ottobre – 23 november 1991, ed. by Ida Zatelli (Florence, 1991), 13-51, at p. 19: 'Occorre quindi una certa cautela nell'attribuire valenze funzionali decisive a tali scelte tipografiche relative al supporto materiale del testo, che certo erano meno importanti del fattore linguistico.'

217 See also Mary Kay Duggan on the 'triumph of private reading and meditation among clerics', in this volume at p. 72.

218 Brian Richardson, *Printing, Writers and Readers in Renaissance Italy* (Cambridge, 1999), p. 149.

219 *Die Frankfurter Gutenberg-Bible: Ein Beitrag zum Buchwesen des 15. Jahrhunderts* (Frankfurt am Main, 1990), pp. 76-91 on corrections derived from a manuscript source; on pp. 91-4 on manuscript concordances in the margins, apparently not derived from a printed source. The Bodleian Library's copy of the B42, for instance, has in its margins numerous careful corrections to the text, mostly, perhaps, of an insignificant kind, but showing a careful approach to the text.

220 See Paul Needham, 'The Text', as note 11, at p. 56.

221 In the Bodleian Library's copy of *GW* 4213 (*Bod-inc* B-248; shelfmark: Auct. 1Z 2.3,4).

222 In the BL's copy of *GW* 4218 (*BMC* II 413, IC 7131).

223 The copy of *GW* 4222 sold as part of *The Estelle Doheny Collection*, as note 76, lot 89.

224 Added by hand in the Bodleian copy of *GW* 4268 (*Bod-inc* 299; shelfmark: Bib. Lat. 1491 c.3).

225 The copy of *GW* 4221 now in Corpus Christi College, Cambridge (Epm 6) has a German manuscript table of contents at the end.

226 *GW* 4235; *BMC* III 239, IB 3837, dated in *CIBN*.

227 [Deventer: Richardus Pafraet, between 1477 and Nov. 1479] (*BMC* IX 41, IB.47537).

228 *GW* 1575 (*Bod-inc* B-252(2); shelfmark: Auct. Y 3.7,8).

229 To mention only a few: Jerome's *Commentaria in Bibliam*. Venice: Johannes & Gregorius de Gregoriis, de Forlivio, 1497-8 (*ISTC* ih00160000), ed. by Bernardinus Gadolus, who worked also on Paganinus's amalgamation of the *glossa ordinaria* and Lyra's *Postillae*. Alexander de Ales, *Summa universae theologiae* (Partes I-IV). Nuremberg: Anton Koberger, 1481-2 (*GW* 871). Three editions of Petus Lombardus's glosses on the psalter, two of which (*ISTC* ip00476000 and ip00477000) were printed by Sensenschmidt and Frisner in 1475 or 1476 and in 1478, evidently to be seen in conjunction with their bible editions from 1475-6. The nineteen recorded editions of the sentences of Petrus Lombardus, all but three of which were produced by or for printers who were also responsible for bible editions.

230 Jacques Verger, 'L'Exégèse de l'université', in *Le Moyen Age et la Bible*, ed. by Pierre Riché & Guy Lobrichon (Paris, 1984), pp. 199-232, at p. 228 refers to the various evangelical movements which tended to lead to a return to the text itself.

231 The purchases of the commented editions are clearly an important phenomenon. We are confronted by conscious choices of texts. See *Mittelalterliche Bibliothekskataloge, vol. IV/1*, as note 184, p. 584: *GW* 4282, the first edition of the Bible with the *Glossa ordinaria*, bought by the Premonstratensians in Windberg in 1480 for 23 Rhenish guilder, the copy of *GW* 4282, bought by the Carthusians in Legnicz in 1481 (Bronisław Kocowski, *Katalog inkunabułow Biblioteki Uniwersyteckiej we Wrocławiu* (Wrocław, 1959), no. 528); the copy of *GW* 4282, bought in London for the Cistercians at Stratford Lanthorne (J. C. T. Oates, *A Catalogue of the Fifteenth-Century Printed Books in the University Library Cambridge* (Cambridge, 1954), no. 124); the copy now in the Biblioteca Estense in Modena of Renner's 1482 edition of the Bible with the commentary of Lyra was bought in 1506, 24 years after its publication by a religious house (Domenico Fava, *Biblioteca estense di Modena* as note 168, no. 313). The copy of Froben's edition of 1498 with Lyra's *Postillae* was bought in 1500 by Vitus, the abbot of Žd'ár na Sázavou in Moravia (Isak Collijn, *Katalog der Inkunabeln der Kgl. Bibliothek in Stockholm* (Stockholm, 1914), no. 212). There is no plain Bible but a 'biblia cum Nicolao de Lira in 3 voluminibus 8 floreni' in the 1497 list of books bought for the Carmelites in Augsburg during Matthias Fabri's tenure as prior, see *Mittelalterliche Bibliothekskataloge Deutschlands und der Schweiz, III: Bistum Augsburg, Eichstätt, Bamberg* ed. by Paul Ruf (Munich, 1932), pp. 27-30, at p. 28. This was among the thirteen books bought by Fabri for the convent from his own money, 'de patrimonio meo'. The Augsburg Carmelites also got a three-volume bible with Lyra as a donation from the printer Erhard Ratdolt; see p. 31.

232 See note 131.

233 Honemann, 'The Buxheim Collection' as note 201, at pp. 175-6, notes that many Buxheim books which have signs of use can be shown to have acquired their manuscript additions before they came to Buxheim.

234 *GW* 4233.

235 Fulin, as note 136, at pp. 24-5: In the privilege granted to Paganinus de Paganinis for the printing of the Bible with both the *Glossa ordinaria* and the *Postillae* of Lyra. It is stated that a copy of the *glossa ordinaria* would cost 12 Ducats (=15 Rhenish guilder). This must refer to the Strasbourg edition (*GW* 4282).

236 See note 231.

237 A. Lőkkös, *Catalogue des incunables imprimés à Genève 1478-1500* (Geneva, 1978), no. 90, *GW* 4264, Drach's edition from 1489, was bought in 1491 for two florins by Johannes Ruch, sacerdos.

238 Leonhard Hoffmann, 'Gutenberg und die Folgen: Zur Entwicklung des Bücherpreises

im 15. und 16. Jahrhundert', *Bibliothek und Wissenschaft*, 29 (1996), 5-23, at p. 9. On the point at which printed books began to fall in price see also Leonhard Hoffmann, 'Buchmarkt und Bücherpreise im Frühdruckzeitalter', *Gutenberg-Jahrbuch*, 75 (2000), 73–81, Neddermeyer, as note 6, II, pp. 831–62; and the section 'Buying printed books' in Brian Richardson, *Printing, Writers and Readers in Renaissance Italy* (Cambridge, 1999), 112-18.

239 Hillard, as note 10, at p. 73.

240 The copy of *GW* 4247 which belonged to Mathurin Brouard, priest of Notre-Dame de Fontenay-le-Comte, 12 July 1498, and later of his successor Thibault Thore (Hélène Richard & Pierre Campagne, *Catalogues régionaux des incunables des bibliothèques publiques de France, XIV, Région Poitou-Charente – Région Limousin* (Paris, 1996), no. 110). The Modena, Biblioteca Estense copy of *GW* 4277 mentioned above, Fava, *Biblioteca Estense di Modena*, as note 168, no. 309. The Basel Universitätsbibliothek copy of *GW* 4228 has two inscriptions which indicate that it belonged to a parish church, one reading 'Hic liber pertinet ecclesie de Saxlen', but the inscription is not dated (P. L. Van der Haegen, as note 184, no. 9,11). A copy of *GW* 4210 which in 1520 belonged to Francisicus Ferrabolus, a priest in Volungo, in the diocese of Brescia (Ugo Baroncelli, *Gli incunaboli della biblioteca queriniana di Brescia* (Catalogo) (Brescia, 1970), no. 174). A copy of *GW* 4223 owned by a 'presbyter' in Empoli in 1478 (Viktor Madsen, *Katalog over det Kongelige Biblioteks inkunabler* (Copenhagen, 1935-63), no. 670); a copy of *GW* 4263 was owned, probably in the fifteenth century, first by J. Charmot, 'plebanus' in Damvant, and then by Jacobus Rozel 'curatus' in Courfaivre; see Romain Jurot, *Catalogue des incunables du Fonds ancien de la Bibliothèque cantonale jurasienne à Porrentruy* (Zurich, 2000), no. 38.

241 A copy of Koberger's edition with Lyra's *Postillae* from 1487 (*GW* 4289) belonged to Konrad Greve who signs himself pastor in Grefrath (Heinz Finger, *Universitäts- und Landesbibliothek Düsseldorf Inkunabelkatalog* (Wiesbaden, 1994), no. 194). He was one of the major benefactors of the Augustinian canons in Neuss (Oberkloster), and since 1492 pastor of St Stephan in Grefrath.

242 A few examples: all six volumes of *GW* 4284 were bequeathed to the Convent of the Franciscans in Greifswald around 1500 by Martin Barow vicar in St Maria, Lübeck (*Inkunabeln in Greifswalder Bibliotheken*, ed. by Thomas Wilhelmi and others (Wiesbaden, 1997), no. 147). A copy of the four-volume *GW* 4293 belonged to J. Polz, a priest in the diocese of Bamberg 1495 (*BSB-Ink* B-469). A copy of the four-volume *GW* 4289 was bought by a Magister Stephanus Lindenberger 'presbyterum ratisponensem – tunc temporis plebanum aput sanctum Petrum Tridenti 1503' (*BSB-Ink* B-459). In 1493 a 'plebanus' in Emmen, in the canton of Lucerne, owned a copy of *GW* 4288, Koberger's edition with Lyra's Postillae from 1485 (Inge Dahm, *Aargauer Inkunabel-Katalog* (Aarau, 1985), at p. 62).

243 See for instance the library of St Mang in Kempten, edited in *Mittelalterliche Bibliothekskataloge Deutschlands und der Schweiz, III: Bistum Augsburg, Eichstätt, Bamberg*, ed. by Paul Ruf (Munich, 1932), pp. 136-43.

244 *ISTC* ib00650500 (*BMC* IX 158). On Johannes de Westphalia's publishing programme see Wytze Hellinga & Lotte Hellinga, *The Fifteenth-century Printing Types of the Low Countries*, 2 vols (Amsterdam, 1966), vol. 1, p. 60. His New Testament fits their view of Johannes de Westphalia as an innovative printer in tune with his cultural environment. Perhaps we also should see in this context the edition of Nicolaus de Lyra, *Postilla super Novum Testamentum cum additionibus Pauli Burgensis et replicationibus Matthiae Doering* [Strasbourg: Printer of Henricus Ariminensis (Georg Reyser?), about 1474-7] (*ISTC* in00122500). Also the three editions of the New Testament in Czech confirm the link with reforming movements (*ISTC* ib00650600; ib00650650; ib00650700); and the two New Testaments in French (*ISTC* ib00651000 and ib00652000); on these see Hillard,

as note 10, at p. 79.

245 On this shift from Hebrew to Greek biblical scholarship as reflected in Erasmus, see Louis Bouyer, 'Erasmus in Relation to the Medieval Biblical Tradition', in *The Cambridge History of the Bible: 2, The West from the Fathers to the Reformation*, ed. by G. W. H. Lampe (Cambridge, 1969), pp. 492-505.

246 On sig. [a]2ʳ: 'Conclamant omnes quemlibet fidelem qui se litteras nosse profitetur sacre scripture noticiam presertim quantum ad illam biblie partem quam nouum testamentum uocant habere teneri, sed maxime eos quibus aut subditorum cura aut uerbi dei predicatio commissa est. Re etiam compertum est paucis ad integram bibliam comparandam suppetere copias, complures etiam opulentiores gestabilibus delectari libris. His ergo motus maiorumque meorum sacre theologie professorum autoritate persuasus, nonnullorum etiam religiosorum secularumque clericorum zelo deuictus, presens manuale uolumen quod totum nouum testamentum continet ad laudem dei imprimere utinam omine bono temptaui. Factum qui in eo fructum inuenerit probet.'

247 See the general remark on the importance of Lyra for preachers, 'both mendicant and seculars' by Karlfried Froehlich, 'An Extraordinary Achievement: the *Glossa Ordinaria* in Print', in *The Bible as Book*, as note 12, pp. 15-21, at p. 19.

248 See Klauser as note 77, p. xxii.

249 The copy GW 4222 now in the Bibliothèque publique de Versailles has a note stating that it was used for reading both in the refectory and in church. See note 216. At a much higher level, the prefatory letter to the edition of the bible with the gloss of Hugo of St Victor (GW 4285) states that the glosses are useful for preaching: see *Die Amerbachkorrespondenz: I, Die Briefe aus der Zeit Johann Amerbachs 1481-1513*, ed. by Alfred Hartmann (Basel, 1942), letter no. 83, dated 29 Oct. 1498, from Amerbach (although the authorship is doubtful) to Anton Koberger: 'Extant multifaria etiam quae ad concionandam atque exhortandum populum christianum accommodatissima sunt illic adiecta.' See also the copy now in Cracow of GW 4275, as note 183.

PRINTED BOOKS AS A COMMERCIAL COMMODITY

1 This is a revised version of a paper first published under the title 'The Printed Book as a Commercial Commodity in the Fifteenth and Early Sixteenth Centuries', in *Gutenberg-Jahrbuch*, 76 (2001), 172-82.

2 Uwe Neddermeyer, *Von der Handschrift zum gedruckten Buch: Schriftlichkeit und Leseinteresse im Mittelalter und in der frühen Neuzeit. Quantitative und qualitative Aspekte*, Buchwissenschaftliche Beiträge aus dem Deutschen Bucharchiv München, 61 (Wiesbaden, 1998), I, pp. 319-20. For a critique of Neddermeyer's study see Helmut Zedelmaier, 'Das Buch als Recheneinheit: Überlegungen zur Erforschung der Buchkultur', *Historisches Jahrbuch*, 120 (2000), 291-300.

3 Marshall McLuhan, *The Gutenberg Galaxy: the Making of Typographic Man* (London, 1962), p. 125. On the impact of printing on the modern age see Elizabeth Eisenstein, *The Printing Press as Agent of Change: Communications and Cultural Transformations in Early Modern Europe* (Cambridge, 1979); and Michael Giesecke, *Der Buchdruck in der frühen Neuzeit: Eine historische Fallstudie über die Durchsetzung neuer Informations- und Kommunikationstechnologien* (Frankfurt am Main, 1991).

4 See F. Geldner, 'Zum ältesten Missaldruck', *Gutenberg-Jahrbuch*, 36 (1961), 101-6.

5 The term mass production arose only in the early twentieth century – the earliest occurrence noted in the Oxford English Dictionary dates from 1920.

6 The encounter is related in a letter dated 12 March 1455 to Cardinal Juan de Carvajal. See Erich Meuthen, 'Ein frühes Quellenzeugnis (zu Oktober 1454?) für den ältesten Buchdruck',

Gutenberg-Jahrbuch, 57 (1982), 108-18; Ferdinand Geldner, 'Enea Silvio de' Piccolomini und Dr. Paulus Paulirinus aus Prag als Zeugen für die beiden ältesten Bibeldrucke', *Gutenberg-Jahrbuch*, 59 (1984), 133-9; Leonhard Hoffmann, 'Die Gutenberg-Bibel: eine Kosten- und Gewinnschätzung auf der Grundlage zeitgenössischer Quellen', *Archiv für Geschichte des Buchwesens*, 39 (1993), 255-319, at 255-9; and Martin Davies, 'Juan de Carvajal and Early Printing: the 42-line Bible and the Sweynheim and Pannartz Aquinas', *The Library*, 6th ser., 18 (1996), 193-215. Whereas Meuthen thought the 'vir mirabilis' was Gutenberg himself, the consensus appears to be that this is improbable and that it is more likely to have been Fust or Schöffer. On the problem of the number of copies that could be supplied see Davies, p. 199, note 14.

7 Kai-Michael Sprenger, '"volumus tamen, quod expressio fiat ante finem mensis Maii presentis". Sollte Gutenberg 1452 im Auftrag Nikolaus von Kues' Ablaßbriefe drucken?', *Gutenberg-Jahrbuch*, 74 (1999), 42-57. That no copy of this indulgence is known perhaps simply reflects the vicissitudes of survival, but it may well also have been a task that Gutenberg, for some reason, was not yet able to realize technically (though theoretically two thousand copies within the time available should have been feasible; see Hoffmann, as note 6, p. 282). Sprenger observes (p. 56, note 74) that of the indulgences of 1454/55 only 50 survive out of an estimated print run of ten thousand. For a full survey of available information about the print-runs of broadsides see Falk Eisermann, 'Auflagenhöhen von Einblattdrucken im 15. und frühen 16. Jahrhundert', in *Einblattdrucke des 15. und frühen 16. Jahrhunderts: Probleme, Perspektiven, Fallstudien*, ed. by Volker Honemann, Sabine Griese, Falk Eisermann, & Marcus Ostermann (Tübingen, 2000), pp. 143-77.

8 Hoffmann, as note 6, p. 304. On indulgences generally see Nikolaus Paulus, *Geschichte des Ablasses im Mittelalter*, 2nd enlarged edn (Darmstadt, 2000).

9 See John L. Flood, 'Ein Almanach auf das Jahr 1492 mit einer Übersicht über die Augsburger Kalenderproduktion des 15. Jahrhunderts', *Gutenberg-Jahrbuch*, 87 (1992), 62-71.

10 On the latter see Nine Robijntje Miedema, *Die 'Mirabilia Romae': Untersuchungen zu ihrer Überlieferung mit Edition der deutschen und niederländischen Texte*, Münchener Texte und Untersuchungen zur deutschen Literatur des Mittelalters, 108 (Tübingen, 1996). Miedema's provisional count of printed editions of all periods of the *Mirabilia* and related texts (the *Historia et descriptio*, the *Indulgentiae*, and the *Stationes*) records 150 in Latin, 54 in German, 13 in Dutch, 112 in Italian, 29 in French, 17 in Spanish, and one in English.

11 The dates on which the Latin editions were issued are instructive: 24 January, 23 February, 7 March, 30 April, 12 July, 22 July, 16 August, 7 September, and 21 December 1500. There was clearly a steady demand throughout the year.

12 Neddermeyer, as note 2, II, p. 794.

13 Personalized prefaces and dedications are another aspect of this. Davies, as note 6, p. 205, in discussing a preface to Aquinas, *Catena aurea*. Rome: Conradus Sweynheym & Arnoldus Pannartz, 1470 (*ISTC* it00225000), remarks: 'This is the only example known to me from the fifteenth century of a book being addressed to a dead patron. It might be seen as another step towards marking off printed books as a mass commodity – the success of the product is not dependent on its being well received by its first recipient.'

14 On monastery presses see Neddermeyer, as note 2, I, pp. 351-5, and further literature cited there.

15 Eisenstein, as note 3, p. 15. On Trithemius, who is interesting for his contemporary views on scribes and printing, see Michael Embach, 'Skriptographie versus Typographie: Johannes Trithemius' Schrift "De laude scriptorum"', *Gutenberg-Jahrbuch*, 75 (2000), 132-44.

16 On scribes and the pecia system of copying (which was practised in Italy, France, Spain and England, but not in Germany) see Karl Christ, 'Petia: ein Stück mittelalterlicher Buchgeschichte', *Zentralblatt für Bibliothekswesen*, 55 (1938), 1-44; *La Production du livre*

universitaire au Moyen Age, ed. by Louis J. Bataillon, Bertrand G. Guyot, & Richard H. Rouse (Paris, 1988); and Hermann Baumeister, 'Der Pariser Universitätsbuchhandel im Mittelalter (1250-1350): das Pecia-System als vor-typographische Buchmanufaktur', *Buchhandelsgeschichte* (2000), no. 2, pp. B68-B75. See also Gerhardt Powitz, 'Pecienhand-schriften in deutschen Bibliotheken', *Bibliothek und Wissenschaft*, 31 (1998), 211-31.

17 Eisenstein, as note 3, p. 46.

18 Thus we hear of one notary receiving payment for preparing 200 copies of Pope Eugene IV's indulgence for the church of St Lambert at Liège in 1443 and five further scribes being paid for making 40, 42, 43, 49, and 30 copies respectively. See Volker Honemann, 'Vorformen des Einblattdruckes', in *Einblattdrucke des 15. und frühen 16. Jahrhunderts*, as note 7, pp. 1-43, here pp. 8-9.

19 Lauber supplied customers as far afield as Zurich, Constance, Nuremberg, Würzburg, and the lower Rhine. For the most recent study of his business see Andrea Rapp, *'bücher gar hübsch gemolt': Studien zur Werkstatt Diebold Laubers am Beispiel der Prosabearbeitung von Bruder Philipps 'Marienleben' in den Historienbibeln IIa und Ib*, Vestigia Bibliae: Jahrbuch des Deutschen Bibel-Archivs Hamburg, 18 (Berne etc., 1998). Aspects of the commercial operation of a scriptorium are also discussed in: Wolfgang Oeser, 'Die Brüder des gemeinsamen Lebens in Münster als Bücherschreiber', *Archiv für Geschichte des Buchwesens*, 5 (1963/64), cols 197-398.

20 Otto W. Fuhrmann, *Über die Auflagenhöhe der ersten Drucke*, Kleiner Druck der Gutenberg-Gesellschaft, 61 (Mainz, 1956), p. 16.

21 '... dardurch viel zeit mag ersparet werden / und in einem tag mehr durch zwo Personen gesetzt unnd getrucket wurde / dann zuvor zwentzig oder mehr inn etlich Jaren erschreiben könden ...' (Bernhart Hertzog, *Chronicon Alsatiae: Edelsasser Chronick*, Strasbourg: B. Jobin 1592; cited after: *L'Alsace au siècle de la Réforme (1482-1621): Textes et documents*, ed. by Jean Lebeau & Jean-Marie Valentin (Nancy, 1985), p. 219).

22 Hoffmann, as note 6, p. 288. Later (p. 291) he adds four other ancillary workers to the tally. Hoffmann's calculations represent an interesting exercise, but how far they correspond to reality is debatable. Eva-Maria Hanebutt-Benz, in *Gutenberg aventur und kunst: Vom Geheimunternehmen zur ersten Medienrevolution. Katalog zur Ausstellung der Stadt Mainz anlässlich des 600. Geburtstages von Johannes Gutenberg* (Mainz, 2000), p. 170, calculates that setting B42 would have taken four compositors 325 10-hour working days, and she passes other critical comments on Hoffmann's calculations on pp. 186 and 189, note 41.

23 Neddermeyer, as note 2, I, p. 342. We cannot consider the impact of printing on scribes in detail here, but recent studies of this question include: Hans-Jörg Künast, 'Die Augsburger Frühdrucker und ihre Textauswahl: oder: Machten die Drucker die Schreiber arbeitslos?', in *Literarisches Leben in Augsburg während des 15. Jahrhunderts*, ed. by Johannes Janota & Werner Williams-Krapp, Studia Augustana, 7 (Tübingen, 1995), pp. 47-57; and Tilo Brandis, 'Die Handschrift zwischen Mittelalter und Neuzeit: Versuch einer Typologie', *Gutenberg-Jahrbuch*, 72 (1997), 28-57.

24 Whereas the paper used for manuscripts had to be sized and dried twice to ensure that the ink did not spread, paper intended for use with viscous printing ink needed to be sized and dried only once, making the manufacturing process quicker and cheaper. See Gerhard Piccard, 'Papiererzeugung und Buchdruck in Basel bis zum Beginn des 16. Jahrhunderts', *Archiv für Geschichte des Buchwesens*, 8 (1967/68), cols 25-322, here cols 273 and 279.

25 See Elly Cockx-Indestege, 'Das 'Gepeet puechl extraordinarij' oder das Stundenbuch des Kaisers Maximilian I.', in *Ars impressoria: Entstehung und Entwicklung des Buchdrucks. Eine internationale Festgabe für Severin Corsten zum 65. Geburtstag*, ed. by Hans Limburg, Hartwig Lohse, & Wolfgang Schmitz (Munich, New York, London, Paris, 1986), pp. 231-50.

26 On this see Peter M. H. Cuijpers, *Teksten als koopwaar*, Bibliotheca bibliographica

neerlandica, 35 (Nieuwkoop, 1998), pp. 50-3.

27 As Rudolf Hirsch, *Printing, Selling and Reading 1450-1550*, 2nd edn (Wiesbaden, 1974), pp. 44-5, observes, until the early 1480s we find too many printers publishing the same texts, with the result that the market soon became saturated. Fortunately, this was balanced by a growing demand at this time for smaller, more portable books. The same decade saw an increase, perhaps of the order of 60 per cent, in the size of print-runs, and a fall in the price per printed sheet. See Willem Heijting, 'Success in Numbers', *Quærendo*, 29 (1999), 275-96, at 295. Heijting's study, a bibliometric analysis of the output of Gheraert Leeu at Gouda and Antwerp between 1477 and 1492, shows how Leeu's production declined in line with a general economic crisis around 1482 and how, as printer and publisher, he responded to changed circumstances.

28 Edwin S. Hunt & James M. Murray, *A History of Business in Medieval Europe, 1200-1550* (Cambridge, 1999), p. 201. It was around 1480 that the printed book finally emancipated itself from the model of the handwritten book. See Carl Wehmer, 'Inkunabelkunde', *Zentralblatt für Bibliothekswesen*, 57 (1940), 214-32, at 226.

29 For examples see Wolfgang Reuter, 'Zur Wirtschafts- und Sozialgeschichte des Buchdruckgewerbes im Rheinland bis 1800 (Köln–Bonn–Düsseldorf)', *Archiv für Geschichte des Buchwesens*, 1 (1958), 642-736, at p. 665.

30 Nicolaus Cusanus's wish to see 'haec sancta ars', which had developed in Germany, brought to Rome is expressly mentioned in Sweynheim and Pannartz's 1470 Rome edition of Jerome. See Giovanni Andrea Bussi, *Prefazioni alle edizioni di Sweynheym e Pannarz prototipografi romani*, ed. by Massimo Miglio, Documenti sulle arti del libro, 12 (Milan, 1978), p. 4. In the preface to William of Ockham's *Dialogorum libri septem adversus haereticos*. [Lyon]: Johannes Trechsel, 1494 (*ISTC* io00009000), Jodocus Badius Ascensius similarly celebrates the art as 'divina imprimendi facultas'. The sixteenth-century Reformers likewise considered it a divine gift.

31 In Mainz finance was, in theory, readily accessible: it was close to Frankfurt with its wealthy patriciate, its fair and its international trading connections, and through the archbishop of Mainz, one of the greatest princes of the Holy Roman Empire, it had access to the emperor himself. Access to capital and markets also explains why printing established itself predominantly in commercial centres such as Augsburg (1468), Nuremberg (1468/70), Strasbourg (1458/59?), Ulm (1473), Basel (1468?), Cologne (1464/65), Leipzig (1481), and Lübeck (1473) and, in view of the importance of liturgical works, in ecclesiastical centres such as Bamberg (1458/59), Breslau (1475), Würzburg (1479), etc. The availability of potential customers, rather than capital, explains why university towns like Ingolstadt (1484), Heidelberg (1485), Freiburg im Breisgau (1490?), and Tübingen (1498) in due course had presses, too. Towns notable only for the fact that the aristocracy resided there, on the other hand, scarcely figured (though Konrad Fyner set up a printing business at Urach in 1478/79 at the instance of Count Eberhard of Württemberg).

32 Piccard, as note 24, col. 278, reckons the price of manuscript paper in chancery size at 1-1.5 guilders a ream *c.*1480. What determined the prices scribes charged is not clear: obviously the cost of materials was a factor, but what price do you put on labour, especially when you have to consider competition (there were some forty professional scribes working in Milan around 1440, while it is claimed that a little later at Paris there were six thousand copyists, scriveners, and illustrators at work) and the current prices for new or second-hand books? Pascale Bourgain, 'L'Édition des manuscrits', in *L'Histoire de l'édition française*, ed. by Henri-Jean Martin & Roger Chartier (Paris, 1982-6), I, p. 66, speaks of people paying anything between 1.6 to 5.6 times the cost of the parchment for a scribe's labour.

33 See Reuter, as note 29, p. 664.

34 At Basel Pamphilus Gengenbach seems to have been able to establish himself as a printer

through a timely, lucrative marriage. See Kerstin Prietzel, 'Pamphilus Gengenbach, Drucker zu Basel (um 1480-1525)', *Archiv für Geschichte des Buchwesens*, 52 (1999), 229-461, here 242, 245.

35 The *Independent on Sunday*, 11 June 2000 (Travel section).

36 E. P. Goldschmidt, *Medieval Texts and Their First Appearance in Print*, Supplement to the Bibliographical Society's Transactions, 16 (London, 1943), p. 13.

37 One example is Michael Furter of Basel who, despite a wide-ranging publishing programme and although diversifying into bookbinding and bookselling, was declared bankrupt at his death (in 1516/17). See Ferdinand Geldner, *Die deutschen Inkunabeldrucker* (Stuttgart, 1968-70), I, p. 126. Others who got into difficulties included Jakob Wolff (Pforzheim), Kilian Fischer (Basel), Lienhart Holle (Ulm), and Moritz Brandis whose debts forced him to flee from Leipzig to Magdeburg.

38 On Drach see Ferdinand Geldner, 'Das Rechnungsbuch des Speyrer Druckherrn, Verlegers und Grossbuchhändlers Peter Drach', *Archiv für Geschichte des Buchwesens*, 5 (1964), cols 1-196, here col. 24.

39 See Rudolf Juchhoff, 'Johannes de Westfalia als Buchhändler', *Gutenberg-Jahrbuch*, 29 (1954), 133-6.

40 Geldner, as note 38, col. 12.

41 See Reuter, as note 29, p. 668; Claudia Schnurmann, *Kommerz und Klüngel: der England-handel Kölner Kaufleute im 16. Jahrhundert*, Veröffentlichungen des Deutschen Historischen Instituts London, 27 (Göttingen and Zurich, 1991), p. 50. Formally censorship may be said to have begun under Innocent VIII in 1487 (see *Bullarum diplomatum et privilegiorum sanctorum Romanorum Pontificum Taurinensis editio*, t. V (Turin, 1860), p. 327, no. XIII). On censorship: Ulrich Eisenhardt, *Die kaiserliche Aufsicht über Buchdruck, Buchhandel und Presse im Heiligen Römischen Reich Deutscher Nation 1496-1806* (Karlsruhe, 1970). On printing in university towns see Severin Corsten, 'Universities and Early Printing', in *Bibliography and the Study of Fifteenth-Century Civilisation*, ed. by Lotte Hellinga & John Goldfinch, British Library Occasional Papers, 5 (London, 1987), pp. 83-123.

42 A little later, Luther too complained about the profusion of books, some written because their authors were driven by ambition, others by a desire for profit. See Johannes Aurifaber, *Tischreden oder Colloquia Doct. Mart. Luthers* (Eisleben, 1566), fol. 22^r. See also the complaints gathered together in John L. Flood, 'The Book in Reformation Germany', in *The Reformation and the Book*, ed. by Jean-François Gilmont, English edition and translation by Karin Maag, St Andrews Studies in Reformation History (Aldershot, 1998), pp. 21-103, here pp. 52-3.

43 See Lotte Hellinga, *Caxton in Focus* (London, 1982), pp. 101-2; also Gabriele Müller-Oberhäuser, 'Buchmarkt und Laienlektüre im englischen Frühdruck: William Caxton und die Tradierung der mittelenglischen courtesy books', in *Laienlektüre und Buchmarkt im späten Mittelalter*, ed. by Thomas Kock & Rita Schlusemann, Gesellschaft, Kultur und Schrift. Mediävistische Beiträge, 5 (Frankfurt am Main, 1997), pp. 61-107, at p. 81.

44 See Frieder Schanze, 'Wieder einmal das 'Fragment vom Weltgericht' – Bemerkungen und Materialien zur 'Sibyllenweissagung', *Gutenberg-Jahrbuch*, 75 (2000), 42-63. As for the Mainz Donatus editions, *ISTC* records 24 in the B36 type (*ISTC* id00314625-id003164), 22 in the B42 type (*ISTC* id0031 6450-id00318400), and a further five apparently printed by Peter Schöffer after 1466 (id00318500-id0038900).

45 Hoffmann, as note 6, p. 318.

46 Hoffmann, as note 6, p. 303. He calculates Gutenberg's own share of the net profit as 2721.5 guilders (p. 305). He cites another instance of a mark-up of about 400 per cent for an edition of 1000 copies of a book of hours in Catalan, printed by Johann Gherlinc in 1489. For recent work on prices of early printed books see also Leonhard Hoffmann, 'Gutenberg und die

Folgen: Zur Entwicklung des Bücherpreises im 15. und 16. Jahrhundert', *Bibliothek und Wissenschaft*, 29 (1996), 5-23; Martin Davies, 'Two Book-Lists of Sweynheim and Pannartz', in *Libri, tipografi, biblioteche: Richerche storiche dedicate a Luigi Balsamo*, ed. by A. Ganda & E. Grignani (Florence, 1997), pp. 25-53; Cuijpers, as note 26, pp. 33-50; Neddermeyer, as note 2, II, pp. 831-62; and Leonhard Hoffmann, 'Buchmarkt und Bücherpreise im Frühdruckzeitalter', *Gutenberg-Jahrbuch*, 75 (2000), 73-81.

47 Thus Fuhrmann, as note 20, p. 37.

48 Müller-Oberhäuser, as note 43, p. 92.

49 The list is found in vol. V of Nicolas of Lyra's Bible commentary, Rome: Konrad Sweynheym & Arnold Pannartz 1472 (British Library: IC.17184). The titles in question are detailed in BMC IV, p. 15; see also the introduction to that volume.

50 See BMC IV, p. viii. See Neddermeyer, as note 2, I, pp. 311-12. He is doubtless right in saying (I, p. 326,) that, generally, the problem for the early printers was less that of selling their product to a sceptical public than that of having overstretched themselves financially. As small publishers find today, no matter how good the product, one must invest money and effort in distribution, too, if a business is to be a success.

51 Hoffmann, as note 6, p. 307. On the sales and distribution of the Nuremberg Chronicle see Peter Zahn, 'Die Endabrechnung über den Druck der Schedelschen Weltchronik (1493) vom 22. Juni 1509: Text und Analyse', *Gutenberg-Jahrbuch*, 66 (1991), 177-213.

52 *Die Amerbachkorrespondenz*, 10 vols, ed. by Alfred Hartmann & Beat Rudolf Jenny (Basel, 1942-95), and the selection in *The Correspondence of Johann Amerbach: Early Printing in its Social Context*, selected, translated, edited, with commentary by Barbara C. Halporn (Ann Arbor, 2000).

53 Letter of 11 April 1503; Halporn, p. 251.

54 For example, the letters from Jakob Wimpheling to Amerbach of 28 January and 31 May 1505; Halporn, pp. 123 and 125-6.

55 Hoffmann, as note 6, p. 311, refers to Bruno Kuske, 'Die Entstehung der Kreditwirtschaft und des Kapitalverkehrs', in Bruno Kuske, *Köln, der Rhein und das Reich: Beiträge aus fünf Jahrzehnten wirtschaftsgeschichtlicher Forschung* (Cologne, 1956), pp. 48-138.

56 Letter of 15 May [1484?]; Halporn, p. 18.

57 Letter of 1 March 1500; Halporn, p. 230. See also the letter of 19 May 1500; Halporn, p. 231.

58 Letter of 24 May 1503; Halporn, p. 252.

59 Halporn, p. 224.

60 This is the conclusion of Cuijpers, as note 26, pp. 246-57, based on his study of Dutch printers before about 1560. There is no reason to suspect things were any different elsewhere.

61 If the calculations presented by Ursula Rautenberg, 'Das Werk als Ware: der Nürnberger Kleindrucker Hans Folz', *Internationales Archiv für Sozialgeschichte der deutschen Literatur*, 24 (1999), 1-40, are reasonably accurate, Folz's press would seem to have been in use for barely more than about nine days a year between 1483 and 1488.

62 Herbert G. Göpfert, 'Zur Geschichte des Autorenhonorars', in Herbert G. Göpfert, *Vom Autor zum Leser: Beiträge zur Geschichte des Buchwesens* (Munich, 1977), pp. 155-64, at p. 158.

63 Embach, as note 15, p. 141 and note 46, and particularly Dieter Kartschoke, 'Nihil sub sole novum?', in *Geschichtsbewußtsein in der deutschen Literatur des Mittelalters*, ed. by Christoph Gerhardt, Nigel F. Palmer, & Burghart Wachinger (Tübingen, 1985), pp. 175-88, here pp. 186-8. By 1488, when Folz seems to have stopped printing, there were already eleven High German and two Low German printed Bibles circulating (GW 4295-4305 and GW 4307-8).

64 For early booksellers' posters see the reproductions in Konrad Burger, *Buchhändleranzeigen*

des 15. Jahrhunderts (Leipzig, 1907). Albert Ehrman & Graham Pollard, *The Distribution of Books by Catalogue* (Cambridge, 1965), pp. 32-9, listed 47 such advertisements dating from before 1500; for addenda see Sylvia Kohushölter, 'Lateinisch-deutsche Bücheranzeigen der Inkunabelzeit', in *Einblattdrucke des 15. und frühen 16. Jahrhunderts*, as note 7, pp. 445-66. Of the 33 examples known from Germany, 23 were in Latin, 4 were bilingual, and 6 were in German. The title of the present paper is adapted from one of the earliest such advertisements, by Peter Schöffer of Mainz in 1469/70, reproduced as no. 3 in Burger's selection.

65 Equally poorly appointed was the short-lived business of Marx Ayrer who also printed a few short pieces at Bamberg around 1492/93 with the financial support of the vellum dealer Hans Bernecker. One of the items printed was the *Sibyllenweissagung* (dated 8 June 1492; *ISTC* is00492620), the vernacular text with which Gutenberg himself had experimented.

66 Holger Nickel, 'Inkunabeln als Überlieferungsträger – besonders zeitgenössicher Texte', in *Einblattdrucke des 15. und frühen 16. Jahrhunderts*, as note 7, p. 124, makes the interesting observation that whereas one might imagine that it was the publishers of monumental tomes who ran the risks, it appears to have been generally the case that it was the publishers of smaller, shorter books, living a hand-to-mouth existence and dependent on immediately finding customers, who went to the wall.

67 Several of the items he printed may be construed as being critical of political and social conditions, which is not uninteresting given that this was only a few years before the outbreak of the Reformation and the Peasants' War. Tellingly, he was later forced to leave Bamberg after publishing a lampoon on Duke Albrecht of Saxony whose son had failed to be elected as bishop of Würzburg.

68 Examples by Sporer include: *Hertzog Ernsts ausfart*. Bamberg 1493 (*ISTC* ie00104900) and Erfurt 1500 (*ISTC* ie00105000). For further examples see Hans Widmann, *Der deutsche Buchhandel in Urkunden und Quellen* (Hamburg, 1965), vol. II, pp. 108-11. The increasingly effective use of the title-page for advertising purposes went hand in hand with commercially more efficient book production. It was obviously a waste of paper to leave the front page, let alone the whole of the first leaf, blank (a practice which may well be associated with the fact that books produced in multiple copies had to be stored before they found customers). By using the outside front cover for the title and starting the text on the inside of the same leaf economies could be made, and the use of smaller type meant that more lines could be accommodated on a page, resulting in fewer pages and fewer pulls of the press being needed.

69 See Josef Benzing, *Jakob Kobel zu Oppenheim 1494 1533: Bibliographie seiner Drucke und Schriften* (Wiesbaden, 1962), nos 6, 18, 20, 37. For the acrostics see John L. Flood, 'Offene Geheimnisse: Versteckte und verdeckte Autorschaft im Mittelalter', in *Autor und Autorschaft im Mittelalter: Kolloquium Meißen 1995*, ed. by Elizabeth Andersen, Jens Haustein, Anne Simon, & Peter Strohschneider (Tübingen, 1998), pp. 370-96; also Cynthia J. Brown, *Poets, Patrons and Printers: Crisis of Authority in Late Medieval France* (Ithaca & London, 1995), ch. 4: 'Changing authorial signatures in late medieval books'.

70 See John L. Flood, 'Lucas Cranach as Publisher', *German Life and Letters*, n.s. 48 (1995), 241-63.

71 See Margaret M. Smith, *The Title-Page: its Early Development 1460-1510* (London & New Castle, DE, 2000). A more extensive investigation of early title pages is being undertaken under the direction of Professor Ursula Rautenberg at Erlangen.

72 I have previously written at some length about this in relation to sixteenth-century songbooks; see John L. Flood, 'Das Lied im Verlagsprogramm deutscher Drucker des 16. Jahrhunderts', in *Lied im deutschen Mittelalter: Überlieferung, Typen, Gebrauch. Chiemsee-Colloquium 1991*, ed. by Cyril Edwards, Ernst Hellgardt, & Norbert H. Ott (Tübingen, 1996), pp. 335-50.

73 On early colophons generally see Alfred W. Pollard, *An Essay on Colophons* (Chicago, 1905).

74 For example, *Hie hebt sich an das aller nüczlichest bůch genant die vierundzweinczig guldin harpfen*. Augsburg: Johann Bämler, [before 22.4.1472] (*ISTC* in00222000); *Hienach volget ein gar schöne Chronick vnd hÿstori* [of the Seven Wise Masters of Rome]. Augsburg: Johann Bämler 1473 (*ISTC* is00451000); *Hie hebt sich an ein schöne Hÿstori wie Troÿa die kostliche Stat erstöret ward*. Augsburg: Johann Bämler 1474 (*ISTC* ic00775900); *Das abenteürlich bůch beweyset vns von einer frawen genandt Melusina*. Augsburg: Johann Bämler 1474 (*ISTC* im00475600); *Hienach volgt ain hüpsche liepliche historie ains edeln fürsten herczog Ernst von bairn*. Augsburg: Anton Sorg, *c.*1475 (*ISTC* ie00102900).

75 Privileges might grant a printer an effective monopoly in a particular place for a specified period (e.g. the privilege granted by Venice to Johannes de Spira for five years in 1469) or the exclusive right to print a particular work. The use of acrostics, too, may in some cases have served to preserve the integrity of a work and protect the author's or publisher's intellectual property; see Flood, as note 69.

76 This figure from my own database is considerably higher than that given in Charles Schmidt, *Jean Grüninger 1483-1531*, Répertoire bibliographique strasbourgeois jusque vers 1530, I (Strasbourg, 1893) or even Miriam Usher Chrisman, *Bibliography of Strasbourg Imprints, 1480-1599* (New Haven & London, 1982).

77 See Walter Baumann, 'Die Druckerei Stuchs in Nürnberg (1484-1537)', *Gutenberg-Jahrbuch*, 29 (1954), 122-32.

78 The most recent study of Grüninger, although focusing on a small segment of his output, is: Jürgen Schulz-Grobert, *Das Straßburger Eulenspiegelbuch: Studien zu entstehungsgeschichtlichen Voraussetzungen der ältesten ältesten Drucküberlieferung*, Hermaea. Germanistische Forschungen, n.F. 83 (Tübingen, 1999), especially ch. 2.

79 Hunt & Murray, as note 28, p. 202.

ORATIONS CROSSING THE ALPS

1 For the purpose of my discussion of the transmission of this genre it seems unnecessary to consider the discussion of the late medieval use of antique rhetorical principles. As an introductory orientation should be mentioned: John W. O'Malley, *Praise and Blame in Renaissance Rome: Rhetoric, Doctrine, and Reform in the Sacred Orators of the Papal Court, c.1450-1521*, Duke monographs in medieval and Renaissance studies, 3 (Durham, NC, 1979), and John M. McManamon, *Funeral Oratory and the Cultural Ideals of Italian Humanism* (Chapel Hill & London, 1989). On earlier terminology see Thomas Haye, *Oratio: mittelalterliche Redekunst in lateinischer Sprache*, Mittellateinische Studien und Texte; 27 (Leiden, etc., 1999), p. 6 ff. Haye also mentions legal pleading (pp. 7 and 323), but I have not identified any legal texts among the orations.

2 *Sermo habitus in die Annuntiationis, 1484*. [Rome: Bartholomaeus Guldinbeck, after 12 Aug. 1484]. *GW* 4503. *ISTC* ib00763000. *Sermo habitus in die Trinitatis, 1485*. [Rome: Bartholomaeus Guldinbeck, after 29 May 1485]. *GW* 4504. *ISTC* ib00764000.

3 *Sermo in commemoratione victoriae Bacensis*. [Rome: Stephan Plannck, about 1495]. *GW* 6153. *ISTC* ic00229000.

4 *Sermo in publicatione confoederationis inter Innocentium VIII et Venetos*. [Rome: Eucharius Silber, after 2 Feb. 1487]. *GW* 6618. *ISTC* ic00462000.

5 *Sermo de passione habitus in dominica quinta quadragesimae*. Rome: Printer of Sixtus IV 'Bulla' (H 14811), *c.*1480]. H 7599. *ISTC* is00139000.

6 *Sermo contra Turcorum persecutionem*. Rome: Eucharius Silber, after 27 Dec. '1481' [i.e. 1480]. H 15460. *ISTC* it00126000.

7 Hermann Knaus, 'Amicus', *Beiträge zur Inkunabelkunde*, 3, 3rd series (1967), 184-6.

8 Lucien Febvre, *Pour une Histoire à part entière* (Paris, 1962), p. 552.

9 Peter Burke, *Culture and Society in Renaissance Italy 1420-1540* (London, 1972), pp. 209-10.

10 Burke, p. 209.

11 *Oratio coram Calixto III de oboedientia Friderici III.* [Rome: Stephan Plannck, 1488-90]. H 208. *ISTC* ip00731000.

12 Ladislaus Vetesius, *Oratio ad Sixtum IV pro praestanda oboedientia Mathiae Hungarorum Regis.* [Rome: Johannes Schurener, de Bopardia, after 2 Feb. 1475]. H 16079. *ISTC* iv00266300.

13 Bernardinus Carvajal, *Oratio ad Alexandrum VI nomine Ferdinandi et Isabellae.* [Rome: Stephan Plannck, after 19 June 1493]. *GW* 6145. *ISTC* ic00221000.

14 Nicolaus Capranica, *Oratio in funere Bessarionis Cardinalis habita* [Rome: Stephan Plannck, *c.*1480]. *GW* 6029. *ISTC* ic00125000.

15 [Paris]: Guy Marchant, 21 Oct. 1500. *GW* 4185. *ISTC* ib00520000.

16 Petrus Ransanus, *Oratio in funere Francisci de Toleto, Cauriensis episcopi, habita 1479.* [Rome: Johannes Bulle, after 15 Mar. 1479]. H 13692. *ISTC* ir00028450.

17 *Oratio in funere Leonardi de Robore.* [Rome: Bartholomaeus Guldinbeck, after 11 Nov. 1475]. *GW* 10276. *ISTC* if00300500. [Rome]: Ulrich Han (Udalricus Gallus), [after 11 Nov. 1475]. *GW* 10277. *ISTC* if00301000. [Rome: Stephan Plannck, 1481-7]. *GW* 10278. *ISTC* if00302000. [Rome: Eucharius Silber, *c.*1483-93]. *GW* 10279. *ISTC* if00303000. [Rome: Johannes Schoemberger, *c.*1483-4]. *GW* 10280. *ISTC* if00304000.

18 *Oratio parentalis de obitu Guillermi Perreri.* [Rome: Eucharius Silber, after 17 Dec. 1500]. *GW* 5018. *ISTC* ib01076000.

19 *Oratio super electione Innocentii VIII, habita 26 Aug. 1484.* [Leipzig: Marcus Brandis, after 26 Aug. 1484]. *ISTC* ip00270000. [Rome: Eucharius Silber, after 26 Aug. 1484]. *ISTC* ip00270500. [Rome: Stephan Plannck, after 26 Aug. 1484]. *ISTC* ip00271000. [Rome: Stephan Plannck, after 26 Aug. 1484]. *ISTC* ip00271500. [Rome: Bartholomaeus Guldinbeck, after 26 Aug. 1484]. *ISTC* ip00272000. [Rome: Stephan Plannck, after 26 Aug. 1484]. *ISTC* ip00273000.

20 O'Malley, as note 1 above, p. 22 and elsewhere.

21 *Oratio pro Bertucio Lamberto; Epistola ad Ludovicum Scledeum.* Ludovicus Scledeus: *Epistola ad Cassandram.* Angelus Tancredus: *Epistola ad Cassandram.* Franciscus Niger: *Carmen in Cassandram.* Venice: Johannes Lucilius Santritter & Hieronymus de Sanctis, 19 Jan. 1488. *GW* 9888. *ISTC* if00163000. *Oratio pro Bertucio Lamberto; Epistola ad Ludovicum Scledeum.* Ludovicus Scledeus: *Epistola ad Cassandram.* Angelus Tancredus: *Epistola ad Cassandram.* Franciscus Niger: *Carmen in Cassandram.* Modena: Dominicus Rocociolus, 1494. *GW* 9890. *ISTC* if00165000. *Oratio pro Bertucio Lamberto. Epistola ad Ludovicum Scledeum.* Ludovicus Scledeus: *Epistola ad Cassandram.* Angelus Tancredus: *Epistola ad Cassandram.* Franciscus Niger: *Carmen in Cassandram.* Petrus Danhauser (Abietiscola): *Epistola ad Cassandram.* Conradus Celtis: *Ode ad Apollinem.* [Nuremberg: Peter Wagner, after 22 Nov. 1489]. *GW* 9889. *ISTC* if00164000. See Cassandra Fedele, *Letters and Orations*, ed. & transl. by Diana Robin (Chicago, 2000). I thank Falk Eisermann for this reference.

22 O'Malley, as note 1 above, p. 26.

23 *Oratio habita in principio studii Bononiensis.* [Bologna: Bazalerius or Caligula de Bazaleriis, *c.*1495]. *GW* 3855. *ISTC* ib00332600.

24 *Oratio coram gymnasio Bononiensi pronunciata.* Bologna: Franciscus (Plato) de Benedictis, 19 Oct. 1495. *GW* 9717. *ISTC* if00050000.

25 *Oratio pro principio Studii Bononiensis.* Bologna: Hieronymus de Pullis & Johannes de Mazochis, 1492. H 6412. *ISTC* id00366800.

26 *Oratio ad Taurinatem Academiam.* [Turin: Nicolaus de Benedictis & Jacobinus Suigus de

Suico, *c.* 1495]. IGI 2221-A. *ISTC* ib01276500.

27 *Oratio pronuntiata in senatu Venetiarum*. Rome: Georgius Teutonicus (Herolt or Lauer), for Johannes Philippus de Lignamine, 24 July 1481. H 9411. *ISTC* ij00377000.

28 *Oratio pro morte Mantaninae uxoris Hieronymi Petrucci Senensis*. Siena: [Henricus de Colonia], 1498. GW 513. *ISTC* ia00185000.

29 *Oratio in exsequiis Leonorae ducissae Ferrariae*. [Cremona: Carolus de Darleriis, not before 22 Oct. 1493]. GW 3274. *ISTC* ib00055500.

30 *In Ludovici Mariae Sfortiae laudes oratio*. [Milan: Leonardus Pachel, after 28 Nov. 1490]. GW 3809. *ISTC* ib00303800.

31 *Oratio in nuptiis Marchionis Mantuani*. [Brescia: Boninus de Boninis, de Ragusia, after 12 Feb. 1490]. GW 9805. *ISTC* if00107000.

32 *Oratio de eligendo summo pontifice die 6 m. Augusti a. 1492 habita*. Leipzig: Gregorius Böttiger [*c.* 1493]. GW 6151. *ISTC* ic00227000.

33 *Oratio in funere Innocentii VIII*. Add: Sebastianus Baduarius: *Oratio ad Alexandrum VI in praestanda Venetorum oboedientia*. Ed. by Johannes de Velmede. Leipzig: Martin Landsberg [*c.* 1495]. GW 6625. *ISTC* ic00453500.

34 *Oratio apud Alexandrum VI habita pro Mediolanensium principe*. Leipzig: [Gregorius Böttiger, after 13 Dec. 1492]. H 10977. *ISTC* im00409000.

35 *Oratio super electione Innocentii VIII, habita 26 Aug. 1484*. [Leipzig: Marcus Brandis, after 26 Aug. 1484]. GW, *Nachträge*. 273. *ISTC* ip00270000.

36 *Oratio metrica in principio studii Bononiensis habita*. [Printer of Capotius (Martin Landsberg?), 1486-9]. H 14330. *ISTC* is00165000. This text is not preserved in an Italian imprint.

37 *Oratio ad Fridericum III Imperatorem et Maximilianum I Regem Romanorum*. Ed. by Petrus Danhauser. [Nuremberg: Peter Wagner, after 2 Apr. 1490]. GW 3346. *ISTC* ib00106000.

38 *Oratio pro Bertucio Lamberto. Epistola ad Ludovicum Scledeum*. Ludovicus Scledeus: *Epistola ad Cassandram*. Angelus Tancredus: *Epistola ad Cassandram*. Franciscus Niger: *Carmen in Cassandram*. Petrus Danhauser (Abietiscola): *Epistola ad Cassandram*. Conradus Celtis: *Ode ad Apollinem*. [Nuremberg: Peter Wagner, after 22 Nov. 1489]. GW 9889. *ISTC* if00164000. See note 2 above.

39 Johannes Franciscus de Pavinis, *Oratio in laudem Leopoldi Marchionis Austriae*. [Passau: Johann Petri, 1485-93?]. H 12533. *ISTC* ip00244000.

40 Nicolaus, Episcopus Modrusiensis, *Oratio in funere Petri Cardinalis S. Sixti*. [Rostock: Fratres Domus Horti Viridis ad S. Michaelem, 1476]. H 11772. *ISTC* in00049500.

41 *Orationes tres contra Turcos*.[Franciscus Philelphus: *Ad Carolum VIII regem Francorum*. Philelphus: *Ad Pium II papam*. Pius II: *Oratio habita in conventu Mantuano*, 26 Sept. 1459. [Strasbourg: Johann (Reinhard) Grüninger, *c.* 1497]. Polain, Belgique 2918. *ISTC* i000069700.

42 Octavianus de Martinis, *Oratio in vitam et merita S. Bonaventurae*. [Ulm: Johann Zainer, after 14 Apr. 1482]. Schreiber 4592. *ISTC* im00317050.

43 Dominicus Picolomineus, *Oratio de laudibus liberalium disciplinarum*. [Erfurt: Wolfgang Schenck, *c.* 1505]. HC 12989. *ISTC* ip00631100.

44 See Kristian Jensen, 'The Humanist Reform of Latin and Latin teaching', in *The Cambridge Companion to Renaissance Humanism*, ed. by Jill Kraye (Cambridge, 1996), pp. 63-81, at p. 66.

45 Jacobus Wimpheling, *Pro concordia dialecticorum et oratorum oratio habita ad gymnosophistas Heidelbergenses anno 1499 pridie Id. Aug.* [Mainz: Peter von Friedberg, after 13 Aug. 1499]. R, Supplement 222. *ISTC* iw00022500.

46 *Oratio quaerulosa contra invasores sacerdotum*. [Cologne: Heinrich Quentell, *c.* 1495]. E. Voulliéme, *Der Buchdruck Kölns bis zum Ende des fünfzehnten Jahrhunderts* (Bonn,

1903), 1270 *ISTC* iw00042000.

47 *Oratio quaerulosa contra invasores sacerdotum.* Delft: [Christiaen Snellaert, between 14 Feb. 1494 and 1495]. *ISTC* iw00043000. Delft: [Christiaen Snellaert, between 14 Feb. 1494 and 1495]. HC 16195. *ISTC* iw00043500.

48 *Oratio quaerulosa contra invasores sacerdotum.* [Speyer: Conrad Hist, *c.* 1496]. H 16193* = 12027. *ISTC* iw00044000.

49 *Oratio quaerulosa contra invasores sacerdotum.* [Augsburg: Johann Froschauer, *c.* 1496-1500]. H 16194*. *ISTC* iw00045000.

50 *Oratio quaerulosa contra invasores sacerdotum.* [Basel?: n. pr., after 1500?] Also recorded as: [Johann Bergmann, de Olpe, *c.* 1495]. H 16192*. *ISTC* iw00046000.

51 Hervicus de Amsterdamis, *Oratio funebris in Fridericum Bavariae Ducem.* Strasbourg: Johann (Reinhard) Grüninger, [after 19 May 1498]. *GW* 12393. *ISTC* ia00567000.

52 *Oratio invocatoria in missa quodlibet Lipsiensi.* [Leipzig: Martin Landsberg, not before 1497]. H 16197*. *ISTC* iw00055000. *Oratio habita ad Raimundum Peraudi, episcopum Gurcensem.* [Leipzig: Jacobus Thanner, 1503]. *IBP* Postinc 87. *ISTC* iw00054300.

53 *Oratio de duodecim excidiis observantiae regularis.* [Mainz: Peter von Friedberg, after 28 Aug. 1496]. H 15637. *ISTC* it00449000. *Oratio de vera conversione mentis ad deum.* [Mainz: Peter von Friedberg, after 20 Nov. 1500]. H 15638. *ISTC* it00450000.

54 *Oratio in synodo Argentinensi habita a. 1482.* [Strasbourg: Heinrich Eggestein, after 18 Apr. 1482]. *GW* 10585. *ISTC* ig00116500. *Oratio in synodo Argentinensi habita a. 1482.* [Strasbourg: Heinrich Knoblochtzer, not before 1482]. *GW* 10586. *ISTC* ig00116000.

55 Jacobus Locher, *Oratio de studio humanarum disciplinarum et laude poetarum.* H 10166. *ISTC* il00263000.

56 Henricus de Horst, *Oratio habita in receptione Romanorum regis Maximiliani.* [Cologne: Johann Guldenschaff, after 2 Apr. 1486]. *GW* 12230. *ISTC* ih00041500.

57 Priamus Capotius, *Oratio metrica in universitate Lipsiensi habita.* [Leipzig: Printer of Capotius (Martin Landsberg?), 1487-8]. *GW* 6025. *ISTC* ic00123000. Embaldus Kleve, *Oratio in laudem Vincentii de Thomais Ravennatis 1497.* With additions by Martinus Polichius de Mellerstadt and Nicolaus Thurius. [Leipzig: Conrad Kachelofen, not before 1503]. H 9783. *ISTC* ik00026300.

58 Petrus Antonius de Clapis, *Oratio in laudem civitatis universitatisque Heidelbergensis.* With additions by Robertus Gaguinus and Johannes Gallinarius. Ed. by Valentinus Celido. [Mainz: Peter von Friedberg, after 4 Oct. 1499]. *GW* 7057. *ISTC* ic00700000. Jacobus Han, *Oratio pulchra et elegans de statu clericali.* [Mainz: Peter von Friedberg, after 30 Apr. 1493]. *GW* 12118. *ISTC* ih00004500.

59 Theodoricus Gresemundus, *Oratio ad synodum Moguntinam.* [Strasbourg: Martin Flach (printer of Strasbourg), not before 1499]. *GW* 11512. *ISTC* ig00486000. Urbanus Prebusinus, de Brünn, *Oratio mordacissima.* [Strasbourg: Johann (Reinhard) Grüninger, *c.* 1500]. H 4006. *ISTC* ip00958000.

60 Conradus Summenhart, *Oratio funebris in officio exsequiarum Eberhardi ducis in Württemberg.* Tübingen: Johann Otmar, 1498. H 15182. *ISTC* is00864000.

61 Hermolaus Barbarus, *Oratio ad Fridericum III Imperatorem et Maximilianum I Regem Romanorum.* [Alost: Thierry Martens, shortly after 13 Aug. 1486]. *GW* 3343. *ISTC* ib00103000.

62 *Oratio ad Fridericum III Imperatorem et Maximilianum I Regem Romanorum.* [Rome: Stephan Plannck, after 13 Aug. 1486]. *GW* 3345. *ISTC* ib00105000.

63 *Oratio ad Fridericum III Imperatorem et Maximilianum I Regem Romanorum.* [Venice: Antonius de Strata, de Cremona, after 13 Aug. 1486]. *GW* 3344. *ISTC* ib00104000.

64 *Oratio de laudibus gymnasii Parisiorum.* [Paris: Ulrich Gering, *c.* 1478]. *GW* 4141. *ISTC* ib00488800.

65 *Oratio ad studiosos artium humanitatis.* [Paris: André Bocard?, after 12 Oct. 1493]. *GW* 10467. *ISTC* ig00021000.

66 *Oratio ad Philippum II Sabaudiae ducem.* Lyon: [Nicolaus de Benedictis & Jacobinus Suigus, after 11 June 1496]. *GW* 6036. *ISTC* ic00130400. *Oratio ad Maximilianum Caesarem.* Lyon: Nicolaus de Benedictis & Jacobinus Suigus, [after 13 Sept. 1496]. *GW* 6037. *ISTC* ic00130600.

67 Ernst Schulz, *Aufgaben und Ziele der Inkunabelforschung: Jacques Rosenthal zum 70. Geburtstag* (Munich, 1924), 16: '... auf etwa ein Dutzend italienischer Ausgaben kommt eine einzige nichtitalienische. Außerhalb Italiens werden nur in Paris, in den Niederlanden und in Leipzig antike Texte in nennenswertem Umfang gedruckt; in Deutschland wäre daneben noch (mit Abstand) Straßburg zu nennen'.

68 Rudolf Hirsch, *Printing, Reading, and Selling,* 2nd edn (Wiesbaden, 1967), p. 140.

69 *Oratio in conventu Ratisponensi anno 1471 habita.* [Rome: Stephan Plannck, c.1487]. *GW* 5940. *ISTC* ic00075000. *Oratio in conventu Ratisponensi anno 1471 habita.* [Rome: Stephan Plannck, c.1488-90]. *GW* 5940. *ISTC* ic00076000.

70 *Oratio in funere Friderici III imperatoris Viennae habita.* Vienna: [Johann Winterburg, after 8 Dec. 1493]. H 12621. *ISTC* ip00284000.

71 *Oratio in funere Friderici III imperatoris Viennae habita.* [Rome: Stephan Plannck, after 8 Dec. 1493]. H 12620. *ISTC* ip00283000. *Oratio in funere Friderici III imperatoris Viennae habita, repetita per Jacobum Barinum.* [Leipzig: Martin Landsberg, c.1494]. *GW* (Nachtr) 274. *ISTC* ip00284100.

72 *Oratio ad Alexandrum VI pro Philippo Bavariae Duce.* Venice: Aldus Manutius, Romanus, 1 Sept. 1498. H 13883. *ISTC* ir00153500.

73 'Ursprünglich Beiband eines Sammelbandes', the phrase used by *BSB-Ink*.

MIXING POP AND POLITICS

1 For general overviews, see Michael Schilling, *Bildpublizistik der frühen Neuzeit: Aufgaben und Leistungen des illustrierten Flugblatts in Deutschland bis um 1700* (Tübingen, 1990); *Das illustrierte Flugblatt in der Kultur der Frühen Neuzeit: Wolfenbütteler Arbeitsgespräch 1997,* ed. by Wolfgang Harms & Michael Schilling (Frankfurt/M. etc., 1998). Many early modern broadsides are published in the facsimile edition *Deutsche illustrierte Flugblätter des 16. und 17. Jahrhunderts,* vols 1-, ed. by Wolfgang Harms & others (Tübingen, 1985- [in progress]); useful introduction by Harms in vol. 1, pp. vii-xxx. For fifteenth-century broadsides, see the collection of essays *Einblattdrucke des 15. und frühen 16. Jahrhunderts. Probleme, Perspektiven, Fallstudien,* ed. by Volker Honemann, Sabine Griese, Falk Eisermann, & Marcus Ostermann (Tübingen, 2000). Special thanks to Christine Magin in Münster and Arjo Vanderjagt and Jan R. Veenstra in Groningen for their help.

2 Elizabeth L. Eisenstein, *The Printing Press as an Agent of Change: Communications and Cultural Transformation in Early-Modern Europe,* 2nd edn (Cambridge, 1980). The book on Gutenberg in question is Stephan Füssel, *Johannes Gutenberg* (Reinbek, 1999), p. 152, which is partly identical with his *Gutenberg und seine Wirkung* (Frankfurt/M., 1999). The latter was also reprinted in the exhibition catalogue *Gutenberg und seine Wirkung,* Staats- und Universitätsbibliothek Göttingen, 23 June – 29 October 2000, ed. by Elmar Mittler & Helmut Rohlfing (Frankfurt/M. and Göttingen, 2000).

3 Falk Eisermann, *Verzeichnis der typographischen Einblattdrucke des 15. Jahrhunderts im Heiligen Römischen Reich Deutscher Nation* (Wiesbaden, 2002 [forthcoming]).

4 Dieter Wuttke, 'Sebastian Brant und Maximilian I: eine Studie zu Brants Donnerstein-Flugblatt des Jahres 1492', in *Die Humanisten in ihrer politischen und sozialen Umwelt,* ed. by Otto Herding & Robert Stupperich (Boppard, 1976), pp. 141-76, at pp. 142-6;

Notes

Pia Reimen, '"Der Donnerstein zu Ensisheim": zu einem Flugblatt Sebastian Brants', *Germanistik Luxemburg*, 5 (1993), 1-13.

5 Wuttke, 'Sebastian Brant und Maximilian', as note 4, pp. 143-5.

6 Humanist broadsides by Brant and others are listed in Appendix A, which henceforth is referred to as 'A' plus number, here: A.1. It is also no. 1 in the facsimile edition *Flugblätter des Sebastian Brant*, ed. by Paul Heitz, epilogue by Franz Schultz (Strasbourg, 1915), through which most of Brant's broadsides are accessible. See also the edition Sebastian Brant, *Kleine Texte*, ed. by Thomas Wilhelmi, 2 vols (Stuttgart-Bad Cannstatt, 1998); bibliographies: Thomas Wilhelmi, *Sebastian Brant. Bibliographie* (Bern etc., 1990); *Sebastian-Brant-Bibliographie: Forschungsliteratur von 1800 bis 1985*, ed. by Joachim Knape & Dieter Wuttke (Tübingen, 1990).

7 Dieter Wuttke, 'Erzaugur des Heiligen Römischen Reiches Deutscher Nation: Sebastian Brant deutet siamesische Tiergeburten', *Humanistica Lovaniensia*, 43 (1994), 106-31.

8 A.2 = *Flugblätter des Sebastian Brant*, no. 5.

9 A.3 through A.5 = *Flugblätter des Sebastian Brant*, nos 6 and 19; Wolfgang D. Wackernagel, Vera Sack, & Hanspeter Landolt, 'Sebastian Brants Gedicht an den heiligen Sebastian: ein neuentdecktes Basler Flugblatt', *Basler Zeitschrift für Geschichte und Altertumskunde*, 75 (1975), pp. 9-50.

10 A.6 = *Flugblätter des Sebastian Brant*, no. 8.

11 Broadsides: A.7 = *Flugblätter des Sebastian Brant*, no. 7; for the other edition see Wilhelmi, *Bibliography*, no. 91; text in Brant, *Kleine Texte*, as note 6, vol. 1.1, pp. 236-41 nos 153-4 and vol. 2, pp. 68-9.

12 Edwin H. Zeydel, *Sebastian Brant* (New York, 1967), pp. 51-2.

13 A.13 = *Flugblätter des Sebastian Brant*, no. 20, and two other editions: a Strasbourg edition of the Latin text, extant in two fragmentary copies in the University Library at Erlangen, and a German translation published by Bergmann. These two are recorded neither in *GW* nor in the Brant bibliographies and have preliminarily been given *GW* supplement nos. 5040/5 and 5040/10 (with thanks to Dr Holger Nickel for the information); for the German text in Staatsbibliothek zu Berlin – Preußischer Kulturbesitz, preserved in two fragments, see Anneliese Schmitt, *Die Inkunabeln der Deutschen Staatsbibliothek zu Berlin: Im Anschluß an Ernst Voulliéme* (Berlin, 1966), nos 617,10 and 617,10a. The Latin text (with German translation) is also available online: http://www.phil.uni-freiburg.de/SFB541/B5/schwabenkrieg/brant.html As far as we know, Brant published only two more broadsides after 1500: 'Von der vereyn der kunigen und anschlag an die turchen', referring to the Habsburg-Valois treaty of October 1501, and 'Von der wunderlichen zamefugung der obersten planeten' in 1504, a somewhat gloomy prognostication; see *Flugblätter des Sebastian Brant*, nos 21-2.

14 Still indispensible is Wilhelm Ludwig Schreiber, *Handbuch der Holz- und Metallschnitte des XV. Jahrhunderts*, 8 vols (Leipzig, 1926-30); Hans Körner, *Der früheste deutsche Einblattholzschnitt* (Mittenwald, 1979). For recent research, see the studies in *Einblattdrucke des 15. und frühen 16. Jahrhunderts*, as note 1, by Ursula Rautenberg, 'Warum Einblattdrucke einseitig bedruckt sind: zum Zusammenhang von Druckverfahren und medialem Typus', pp. 129-42, Sabine Griese, 'Gebrauchsformen und Gebrauchsräume von Einblattdrucken des 15. und frühen 16. Jahrhunderts', pp. 179-208, Nikolaus Henkel, 'Schauen und Erinnern: Überlegungen zu Intentionalität und Appellstruktur illustrierter Einblattdrucke', pp. 209-43, and Peter Schmidt, 'Beschrieben, bemalt, zerschnitten: Tegernseer Mönche interpretieren einen Holzschnitt', pp. 245-76.

15 Christiane Andersson, 'Polemical Prints in Reformation Nuremberg', in *New Perspectives on the Art of Renaissance Nuremberg. Five Essays*, ed. by Jeffrey Chipps Smith (Austin, TX, 1985), pp. 40-62.

16 For example the prayer *Ave sanctissima Maria* combined with an indulgence, attributed to pope Sixtus IV. It was published as an illustrated typograph by printers all over Germany: the Latin text by Friedrich Riederer in Freiburg (not in *Einbl.*; *c.*1493-9) and Conrad Hist in Speyer (*Einbl.* 1327; *c.*1495); in Basel, Nikolaus Kessler (*Einbl.* 388; *c.*1485) and Johannes Amerbach (*Einbl.* 1328; *c.*1495) printed German translations, and various Low German and Latin editions came from an unknown printing house in Lübeck after 1493 (*Einbl.* 389, 1327a, and others which are not recorded in *Einbl.*). Woodcuts are documented in Schreiber (as note 14), nos 1031, 1047, 1053, 1088a, 1107, and 1878m. For further transmission see *VL*, 3 cols 80-4, esp. 81-2. Broadside no. 14 in Appendix B, *Temptationes daemonis temptantis hominem de septem peccatis mortalibus* [Strasbourg: Printer of the Breviarium Ratisponense, *c.*1482], is also preserved in a woodcut version (Schreiber 1863). For the phenomenon in general, see Falk Eisermann, 'Medienwechsel – Medienwandel. Geistliche Texte auf Einblattdrucken und anderen Überlieferungsträgern des 15. Jahrhunderts', in *Das illustrierte Flugblatt,* as note 1, pp. 35-58.

17 Falk Eisermann & Volker Honemann, 'Die ersten typographischen Einblattdrucke', *Gutenberg-Jahrbuch* (2000), 88-131 at pp. 128-9.

18 B.2.

19 B.3, B.4.

20 A.4.

21 B.12; see *VL* 10, cols 1520-2.

22 A.19. The author is probably identical with the Augsburg priest and schoolmaster Johannes Pinicianus who became 'poeta laureatus' in 1518; see Jan-Dirk Müller, *Gedechtnus: Literatur und Hofgesellschaft um Maximilian I* (Munich, 1982), pp. 63, 74, 339.

23 A.16, one edition printed by Matthias Hüpfuff and a reprint by Grüninger, the only copy of which is in Stuttgart, Württembergische Landesbibliothek; see Frieder Schanze, 'Inkunabeln oder Postinkunabeln? zur Problematik der "Inkunabelgrenze" am Beispiel von 5 Druckern und 111 Einblattdrucken' in *Einblattdrucke des 15. und frühen 16. Jahrhunderts,* as note 1, pp. 45-122, at p. 84.

24 *Einbl.* 1538. See article in *VL* 10, cols 1418-20; for a plate of *Einbl.* 1538 see Schanze, 'Inkunabeln', as note 23, p. 122.

25 *GW* 5021 and 5022 = *Flugblätter des Sebastian Brant,* nos 3 and 4.

26 Overview: *VL* 11 (Supplement), cols 65-72; *Hundert Kalender-Inkunabeln,* ed. by Paul Heitz, accompanying text by Konrad Haebler (Strasbourg, 1895); Leonhard Hoffmann, 'Almanache des 15. und 16. Jahrhunderts und ihre Käufer', *Beiträge zur Inkunabelkunde,* 3rd ser., 8 (1983), 130-43; John L. Flood, 'Ein Almanach auf das Jahr 1492 mit einer Übersicht über die Augsburger Kalenderproduktion des 15. Jahrhunderts', *Gutenberg-Jahrbuch* (1992), 62-71.

27 Zeydel, *Brant,* as note 12, p. 39.

28 Eckehard Simon, *The Türkenkalender (1454) Attributed to Gutenberg and the Strasbourg Lunation Tracts* (Cambridge, Mass., 1988), p. 1. See also article in *VL* 9, cols 1161-2; Ferdinand Geldner, 'Der Heiliggrabkalender für 1478 (Kreuzfahrtlied), sein Drucker Heinrich Eggestein und der Türkenkalender für 1455', in *Scritti in onore di Giuseppe Turrini* (Verona, 1973), pp. 241-59.

29 Pierre L. Van der Haegen, 'Ein Kalendergedicht auf das Jahr 1471: ein Beitrag zur frühesten Basler Buchdruckergeschichte', *Basler Zeitschrift für Geschichte und Altertumskunde,* 83 (1983), 183-91.

30 Neumondkalender for 1478: *GW* 1330 (Heinrich Eggestein); Tüsch: *ISTC* ito0495200 (Printer of the Breviarium Ratisponense); Neumondkalender for 1500: *Einbl.* 1499 (Bartholomäus Kistler).

31 A.17.

32 A.18. About Locher see Günter Heidloff, *Untersuchungen zu Leben und Werk des Humanisten Jakob Locher Philomusus (1471-1528)*, Ph.D. thesis Freiburg (publ. Münster, 1975), about this print pp. 334-6. 'De monstroso puero' was also printed as a booklet by Johannes Kachelofen in Ingolstadt (Munich, Bayerische Staatsbibliothek, 4° Inc. c.a. 660); see Heidloff, pp. 55-6 no. XVIa, and Irene Ewinkel, *De monstris: Deutung und Funktion von Wundergeburten auf Flugblättern im Deutschland des 16. Jahrhunderts* (Tübingen, 1995), pl. 27, at p. 317.

33 A.14, A.15, A.19, A.20 (Celtis et al.), A.21, A.22 (Ulsenius); on the latter see Catrien G. Santing, *Geneeskunde en Humanisme: een intellectuele biografie van Theodericus Ulsenius (c. 1460-1508)* (Rotterdam, 1992), and her 'Medizin und Humanismus: die Einsichten des Nürnbergischen Stadtarztes Theodericus Ulsenius über *Morbus Gallicus*', *Archiv für Geschichte der Medizin (Sudhoffs Archiv)*, 79 (1995), 138-49.

34 Sow of Landser: A.9 = *Flugblätter des Sebastian Brant*, nos. 10 and 11; Foxhunt: A.12 = *Flugblätter des Sebastian Brant*, no. 18. For both see the comprehensive study by Vera Sack, *Sebastian Brant als politischer Publizist: Zwei Flugblatt-Satiren aus den Folgejahren des sogenannten Reformreichstags von 1495* (Freiburg, 1997).

35 But see Sabine Griese, 'Sammler und Abschreiber von Einblattdrucken. Überlegungen zu einer Rezeptionsform am Ende des 15. und Anfang des 16. Jahrhunderts', in *Humanismus und früher Buchdruck: Akten des interdisziplinären Symposions vom 5./6. Mai 1995 in Mainz*, ed. by Stephan Füssel & Volker Honemann (Nuremberg, 1997), pp. 43-69.

36 Wuttke, 'Sebastian Brant und Maximilian', as note 4, p. 153.

37 See in general Falk Eisermann, 'Auflagenhöhen von Einblattdrucken im 15. und frühen 16. Jahrhundert', in *Einblattdrucke des 15. und frühen 16. Jahrhunderts*, as note 1, pp. 143-77.

38 See Jan-Dirk Müller, 'Poet, Prophet, Politiker: Sebastian Brant als Publizist und die Rolle der laikalen Intelligenz um 1500', *LiLi: Zeitschrift für Literaturwissenschaft und Linguistik*, 10 (1980), 102-27, at pp. 104-5.

39 See Eisermann, 'Auflagenhöhen', as note 37, pp. 151-5 for details; and Eisermann, 'Der Ablaß als Medienereignis. Kommunikationswandel durch Einblattdrucke im 15. Jahrhundert. Mit einer Auswahlbibliographie', in *Tradition and Innovation in an Era of Change – Tradition und Innovation im Übergang zur Frühen Neuzeit*, ed. by Rudolf Suntrup & Jan R. Veenstra (Frankfurt/M. etc., 2001), pp. 99-128.

40 A.6.

41 A.7; Wimpfeling's letter in *Der Briefwechsel des Konrad Celtis*, ed. by Hans Rupprich (Munich, 1934), pp. 168-71, and in Jakob Wimpfeling, *Briefwechsel*, ed. by Otto Herding & Dieter Mertens, 2 vols (Munich, 1990), vol. 1, p. 246. Both editions contain numerous other details concerning the humanist exchange of manuscripts, prints, maps, pictures, handwritten poems, and the like.

42 Ms C 687 (fol. 222), written *c.* 1500 (Margarete Andersson-Schmitt, Håkan Hallberg, & Monica Hedlund, *Mittelalterliche Handschriften der Universitätsbibliothek Uppsala. Katalog über die C-Sammlung*, vol. 6: Handschriften C 551-935 (Stockholm, 1993), pp. 279-96).

43 GW 5032.

44 Munich, Bayerische Staatsbibliothek, Clm 24523, fols 1^r-4^r; Augsburg, Staats- und Stadtbibliothek, 4° Cod. 11, fols 2^r-5^r; Strasbourg, Bibliothèque Nationale et Universitaire, Hs. 137, fols 58^r-60^r; Dieter Wuttke, 'Wunderdeutung und Politik: zu den Auslegungen der sogenannten Wormser Zwillinge des Jahres 1495', in *Landesgeschichte und Geistesgeschichte: Festschrift für Otto Herding zum 65. Geburtstag*, ed. by Kaspar Elm, Eberhard Gönner, & Eugen Hillenbrand (Stuttgart, 1977), pp. 217-44, at p. 221 n. 10.

45 A.5.

46 Hamburg, Staats- und Universitätsbibliothek, Cod. hist. 31e, fol. 213^v and fols 413^v-414^r.

47 Munich, Clm 14053, fols 112ᵛ-113ᵛ; for details and illustrations, see Griese, 'Sammler', as note 35, pp. 57-68.

48 *Die Graphiksammlung des Humanisten Hartmann Schedel: Ausstellung Bayerische Staats-bibliothek 20. Juni – 15. September 1990*, ed. by Béatrice Hernad (Munich, 1990). For the interesting printing history of the latter print (*GW 6464*), see Christine Bachmann, *Wahre vnd eygentliche Bildnus: Situationsbezogene Stilisierungen historischer Personen auf illustrierten Flugblättern zwischen dem Ende des 15. und der Mitte des 17. Jahrhunderts* (Frankfurt/M. etc., 2001), pp. 27-41.

49 *Congratulatio* (A.6) in Antonius de Prato Veteri, *Repertorium iuris super Bartoli*. Milan: [Johannes Antonius de Honate], 13 January 1486 (*GW 2250*); another flyleaf in one of the four volumes bound with the *Repertorium* is a broadside by Johannes Stabius of 1502, see Ilona Hubay, *Incunabula der Staats- und Stadtbibliothek Augsburg* (Wiesbaden, 1974), no. 154. *De pestilentiali scorra* (A.11) in Andreas Barbatia, *Repetitio et Lectura super titulo: de testamentis et ultimis voluntatibus*. Bologna: Ugo Rugerius, 15 Juli 1490 (*GW 3373*). *Carmen theologicum* (A.20) in Odofredus Bononiensis, *Lecturae super Codice*, Trino, 1514; for the latter see Paul Geissler, 'Ein unbekannter Reuchlin-Wiegendruck', in *Festschrift für Josef Benzing zum sechzigsten Geburtstag*, ed. by Elisabeth Geck (Wiesbaden, 1964), pp. 120-6. Peutinger also had a copy of the aforementioned *Zeichen der falschen Gulden* broadsides (*Einbl. 1564*) and a huge collection of similar matter, see Hans-Jörg Künast, 'Die Graphiksammlung des Augsburger Stadtschreibers Konrad Peutinger', in *Augsburg, die Bilderfabrik Europas: Essays zur Augsburger Druckgraphik der Frühen Neuzeit*, ed. by John Roger Paas (Augsburg, 2001), pp. 11-19.

50 As pointed out recently by Sack, *Sebastian Brant*, as note 34, pp. 11, 25, 38.

51 Parallel findings in the political communication of early-fifteenth-century Poland are reported by Edward Potkowski, 'Schrift und Politik im 15. Jahrhundert: Die Anfänge politischer Publizistik in Polen', *Frühmittelalterliche Studien*, 28 (1994), 355-73. Potkowski uses the term 'representative audience': courts, ecclesiastical dignitaries, politicians, intellectuals, 'homines litterati' (pp. 372-3).

52 Peter Burke in the revised reprint of his *Popular Culture in Early Modern Europe* (Aldershot etc., 1999), pp. xvi-xxii, discusses 'The problem of the "popular"', pointing out that 'the borderline between the different cultures of the people and the culture of the elites … is a fuzzy one', and refers to Michael Bakhtin's concept of the 'transgression of boundaries' (p. xvi) as a key to the understanding of cultural interaction. As far as I know, incunabulists and historians of literature have not yet discussed the relation between 'elite' and 'popular' cultures with regard to fifteenth-century printing; thus the following paragraph can only try to present some data which may be considered relevant for future studies.

53 *GW 5709* (Printer of Hundorn), 10578 (Sporer), 10579 (Prüss). The texts of *GW 5709* and 10578 are printed in *Flugblätter des Sebastian Brant*, pp. VI-VII.

54 See Wuttke, 'Wunderdeutung', as note 44, pp. 234-5 and plate 4; Eugen Holländer, *Wunder, Wundergeburt und Wundergestalt in Einblattdrucken des fünfzehnten bis achtzehnten Jahrhunderts. Kulturhistorische Studie* (Stuttgart, 1921), p. 73 and plate 22.

55 Falk Eisermann, 'Erfurter Ephemeriden. Perspektiven eines vielseitigen Mediums', in *Bücher und Bibliotheken in Erfurt*, ed. by Michael Ludscheidt & Kathrin Paasch (Erfurt, 2000), pp. 29-46 at pp. 38-40.

56 See Wuttke, 'Wunderdeutung', as note 44, pp. 233-4; Holländer, *Wunder*, as note 54, pp. 338, 340-1.

57 Eichstätt, Universitätsbibliothek, Cod. st. 346, fols 266ʳ and 283ʳ; see Karl Heinz Keller, *Mittelalterliche Handschriften der Universitätsbibliothek Eichstatt*, vol. 2 (Wiesbaden, 1999), 57-61, at p. 59.

58 The various implications of the problem are discussed by Schanze, 'Inkunabeln', as note 23,

pp. 45-58.

59 Frieder Schanze, 'Der Buchdruck eine Medienrevolution?', in *Mittelalter und frühe Neuzeit: Übergänge, Umbrüche und Neuansätze*, ed. by Walter Haug (Tübingen, 1999), pp. 286-311.

60 See Wackernagel et al., 'Sebastian Brants Gedicht', as note 9.

61 All texts in Latin; listed are prints with full-scale illustrations only.

62 Excluding almanacs, calendars, and non-figural, decorative woodcuts.

63 There are also two reprints from Augsburg and Basel (*GW* 9893 and 9894). For these in some respect peculiar prints see Rudolf Suntrup, '*Misterium eukaristie*: zum Text-Bild-Programm eines allegorisch-dogmatischen Einblattdrucks des ausgehenden 15. Jahrhunderts', in *Einblattdrucke des 15. und frühen 16. Jahrhunderts*, as note 1, pp. 349-69.

64 About this workshop Frieder Schanze, 'Zu Erhard Etzlaubs Romweg-Karte, dem Drucker Kaspar Hochfeder in Nürnberg und einem unbekannten Nürnberger Drucker in der Nachfolge Hochfeders', *Gutenberg-Jahrbuch* (1996), 126-40.

THE INCUNABLE COLLECTION OF ST EMMERAM

1 'You will hardly find a town in Bavaria whose beauty one can admire more than that of Salzburg. ... Yet even larger is Regensburg, memorable for the cathedral of St Peter and the stone bridge across the Danube and several churches of saints: but even more so for the monastery of St Emmeram, in which according to pope Leo lies the body of St Denis which was furtively removed from Paris.' Pope Pius II (formerly Aeneas Silvius Piccolomini), *De ritu, situ, moribus et conditione Teutoniae, sive Germania*. Leipzig: Wolfgang Stöckel, 9 Apr. 1496, fol. C6ᵛ (*BSB-Ink* P-100: 4° Inc.c.a. 1338 m); for a modern edition, see Aeneas Silvius, *Germania*, with Jakob Wimpfeling, *Responsa et replicae ad Eneam Silvium*, ed. by Adolf Schmidt (Cologne, 1962), at p. 52. The description dates back to 1457/8, see ibid. p. 3.

2 The origins of the cathedral date back to the eighth century; the Gothic building was begun in the thirteenth century. For a reconstruction of its appearance in 1442, see Achim Hubel & Manfred Schuller, *Der Dom zu Regensburg: Vom Bauen und Gestalten einer gotischen Kathedrale* (Regensburg, 1995), p. 125 pl. 116. The first German manuals on architecture were published by a member of the Roritzer family who were responsible for the running of the cathedral masons' guild during the largest part of the fifteenth century: Matthaeus Roritzer, *Büchlein von der Fialen Gerechtigkeit*. [Regensburg]: M[atthaeus] R[oritzer], 28 June 1486 (Ilona Hubay, *Incunabula der Universitätsbibliothek Würzburg* (Wiesbaden, 1966), 1862) and *Geometria* [German]. [Regensburg: Matthaeus Roritzer, about 1487-8] (*BSB-Ink* R-266).

3 See Eberhard Dünninger, *Weltwunder Steinerne Brücke: Texte und Ansichten aus 850 Jahren* (Amberg, 1996).

4 See Andreas Kraus, *Civitas regia: das Bild Regensburgs in der deutschen Geschichtsschreibung des Mittelalters*, Regensburger historische Forschungen, 3 (Kallmünz, 1972), pp. 38 sqq.

5 See *Mittelalterliche Bibliothekskataloge Deutschlands und der Schweiz*, vol. IV/1: *Bistümer Passau und Regensburg*, ed. by Christine Elisabeth Ineichen-Eder (Munich, 1977) [abbreviated as *MBK*], p. 135.

6 The following summary is based on *Lexikon des Mittelalters*, 10 vols (Munich, 1980-99), here vol. 7 (1995), cols 563-9.

7 Walter Ziegler, 'Regensburg am Ende des Mittelalters', in *Albrecht Altdorfer und seine Zeit: Vortragsreihe der Universität Regensburg*, ed. by Dieter Henrich, Schriftenreihe der Universität Regensburg, 5, 2nd edn (Regensburg, 1992), pp. 61-82, at p. 64.

8 See e.g. Alois Schmid, 'Ratisbona Benedictina: die Regensburger Benediktinerklöster St. Emmeram, Prüll und Prüfening während des Mittelalters', in *Regensburg im Mittelalter:*

Beiträge zur Stadtgeschichte vom frühen Mittelalter bis zum Beginn der Neuzeit, ed. by Martin Angerer & Heinrich Wanderwitz in co-operation with von Eugen Trapp (Regensburg, 1995), vol. 1, pp. 177-86. The fundamental studies of the history of St Emmeram are still: Bernhard Bischoff, *Literarisches und künstlerisches Leben in St. Emmeram (Regensburg) während des frühen und hohen Mittelalters*. Munich, Univ., Diss., 1933. Bischoff, 'Studien zur Geschichte des Klosters St. Emmeram im Spätmittelalter (1324-1525)', *Studien und Mitteilungen zur Geschichte des Benediktiner-Ordens und seiner Zweige*, 65 (1953/54), 152-98. Both articles have been republished in Bischoff, *Mittelalterliche Studien: Ausgewählte Aufsätze zur Schriftkunde und Literaturgeschichte* (Stuttgart, 1967), vol. 2, pp. 77-155. Walter Ziegler, *Das Benediktinerkloster St. Emmeram zu Regensburg in der Reformationszeit*, Thurn-und-Taxis-Studien, 6 (Kallmünz, 1970).

9 See Karl Langosch, 'Arnold von St. Emmeram', in *VL* 1 (1978), cols 464-70.

10 See Franz Josef Worstbrock, 'Wilhelm von Hirsau OSB', in *VL* 10 (1999), cols 1100-10, and Joachim Wiesenbach, 'Wilhelm von Hirsau und die Sphaera: Zum sogenannten Astrolabium von St. Emmeram', in *Romanik in Regensburg: Kunst, Geschichte, Denkmalpflege. Beiträge des Regensburger Herbstsymposions zur Kunstgeschichte und Denkmalpflege vom 18. bis 20. November 1994*, Regensburger Herbstsymposion zur Kunstgeschichte und Denkmalpflege, 2 (Regensburg, 1996), pp. 108-14.

11 Sabine Gäbe, *Otloh von St. Emmeram, 'Liber de temptatione cuiusdam monachi': Untersuchung, kritische Edition und Übersetzung*, Lateinische Sprache und Literatur des Mittelalters, 29 (Bern, 1999).

12 On the history of the library of St Emmeram and other libraries in Regensburg, see Ziegler, *Das Benediktinerkloster*, as note 8, pp. 190-6; *Bibliotheken zu St. Emmeram in Regensburg*, ed. by Max Piendl, Thurn-und Taxis-Studien, 7 (Kallmünz, 1971); Bernhard Bischoff, 'Die mittelalterlichen Bibliotheken Regensburgs', *Verhandlungen des Historischen Vereins für Oberpfalz und Regensburg*, 113 (1973), 49-58; Joseph D. Kyle, 'The Monastery Library at St. Emmeram (Regensburg)', *Journal of Library History*, 15 (1980), 1-21; *Wissenschaftliche Bibliotheken in Regensburg: Geschichte und Gegenwart*, ed. by Hans-Joachim Genge & Max Pauer, Beiträge zum Buch- und Bibliothekswesen, 18 (Wiesbaden, 1981); Eberhard Dünninger, 'Die Bibliothek von St. Emmeram als Spiegel von Literatur und Wissenschaft', in *St. Emmeram in Regensburg: Geschichte – Kunst – Denkmalpflege. Beiträge des Regensburger Herbstsymposiums vom 15. – 24. November 1991*, Thurn-und-Taxis-Studien, 18 (Kallmünz, 1992), pp. 235-43.

13 Max Piendl, 'St. Emmeram in Regensburg: Die Baugeschichte seiner Klostergebäude', in *Beiträge zur Baugeschichte des Reichsstiftes St. Emmeram und des Fürstlichen Hauses in Regensburg*, ed. by Max Piendl, Thurn-und-Taxis-Studien, 15 (Kallmünz, 1986), pp. 133-364, esp. at pp. 262-9.

14 The gospel-book was given to St Emmeram by Arnulf of Carinthia not before 893. Now Munich, Bayerische Staatsbibliothek, Clm 14000, see Elisabeth Wunderle, *Die Handschriften aus St. Emmeram in Regensburg. Vol. 1: Clm 14000-14130*, Katalog der lateinischen Handschriften der Bayerischen Staatsbibliothek München = Catalogus codicum manu scriptorum Bibliothecae Monacensis. Tomus IV. Series nova 2,1 (Wiesbaden, 1995), pp. 3-7.

15 Munich, Bayerische Staatsbibliothek, Clm 14485. The manuscript was in St Emmeram by 993, see *MBK* p. 144, and was borrowed in 1493 by the humanist Conrad Celtis, who published the editio princeps of the plays, with wood-cuts by Albrecht Dürer, in 1501, see *VD16: Verzeichnis der im deutschen Sprachbereich erschienenen Drucke des XVI. Jahrhunderts* (Stuttgart, 1983-95), H 5278.

16 The catalogues are edited in *MBK* pp. 99-388. For illustrations, see Nikolaus Henkel, 'Buchbesitz und Wissensorganisation', in *Gelehrtes Regensburg, Stadt der Wissenschaft: Stätten der Forschung im Wandel der Zeit* (Regensburg, 1995), pp. 28-32.

17 *Adbreviatio librorum* (*MBK* pp. 143-6, no. 25).

18 'Zuwachsverzeichnis' (*MBK* pp. 146-9, no. 26).

19 Cf. *MBK* pp. 146 and 148.

20 *MBK* pp. 152-61 no. 30.

21 *MBK* p. 154.

22 See Piendl, 'St. Emmeram in Regensburg', as note 13.

23 Munich, BSB, Clm 14397, fols 14^r-19^v.

24 The Registrum covers 185 libraries in England, Scotland and Wales and lists about 1400 titles, see *Registrum Anglie de libris doctorum et auctorum veterum*, ed. by Richard H. Rouse & Mary A. Rouse, Corpus of British Medieval Library Catalogues, 2 (London, 1991), p. xiii.

25 See *MBK* p. 116.

26 See ibid. and Bischoff, *Mittelalterliche Studien*, as note 8, pp. 139-40.

27 St Emmeram was the only Regensburg institution apart from the cathedral and the Alte Kapelle to run a public school before the foundation of the city school in the early sixteenth century, see Ziegler, *Das Benediktinerkloster*, as note 8, p. 172.

28 By the end of the fifteenth century, university attendance declined drastically: not a single monk can be found in any matriculation list after 1493, see Ziegler, *Das Benediktinerkloster*, as note 8, p. 173.

29 *MBK* pp. 119-20 and pp. 179-84 no. 34b. The list was drawn up by Menger about 30 years after Poetzlinger's death. See also Bischoff, *Mittelalterliche Studien*, as note 8, p. 130, and Ian F. Rumbold, 'The Library of Hermann Pötzlinger (ca. 1415-1469), Rector Scolarium at the Monastery of St Emmeram, Regensburg', *Gutenberg-Jahrbuch*, 60 (1985), 329-40. According to Rumbold (p. 331), Pötzlinger had already obtained a BA from the University of Vienna in 1439.

30 See Wunderle, *Die Handschriften*, as note 14, pp. XIII-XIV.

31 See *MBK* pp. 121 sqq., Bischoff, *Mittelalterliche Studien*, as note 8, pp. 129-34 and Ziegler, *Das Benediktinerkloster*, as note 8, pp. 29-35.

32 See *MBK* pp. 123-4, Bischoff, *Mittelalterliche Studien*, as note 8, pp. 134-7 and Wunderle, *Die Handschriften*, as note 14, pp. XV-XVI.

33 *MBK* pp. 164-76 no. 32. The catalogue was later bound together with Menger's (see below note 41) in Munich, BSB, Clm 14675, fols 132-41.

34 *MBK* pp. 184-5 no. 35.

35 See *MBK* pp. 129 sqq.

36 See *VD16*, as note 15, G 4135 and Gunther der Dichter, *Ligurinus*, ed. by Erwin Assmann, Monumenta Germaniae Historica 1 / 7, 63 (Hannover, 1987), p. 32.

37 See Ernst Kyriss, *Verzierte gotische Einbände im alten deutschen Sprachgebiet* (Stuttgart, 1951), workshop no. 29 (pls 65 and 66), listing two manuscripts and 129 printed books from 1474 to 1516. See also Wunderle, *Die Handschriften*, as note 14, p. 376, s.v. Gotische Einbände mit Einzelstempeln (St. Emmeram).

38 See D15 and *MBK* p. 376, 7572-4 in the list below.

39 On him, see Bischoff, *Mittelalterliche Studien*, as note 8, pp. 138-9 and Ziegler, *Das Benediktinerkloster*, as note 8, pp. 36-42.

40 Menger was the son of a Regensburg stone mason; he had joined the monastery in 1482, see Ziegler, *Das Benediktinerkloster*, as note 8, pp. 171 and 208.

41 *MBK* pp. 185-385 no. 36 (Clm 14675, fols 1^r-131^v). On Menger's catalogue, see Karl Schottenloher, 'Ein handschriftlicher Inkunabelkatalog aus dem Jahre 1500', in *Zeitschrift für Bücherfreunde*, Neue Folge 23 (1931), cols 92-4; Bischoff, *Mittelalterliche Studien*, as note 8, pp. 143-6 and Ziegler, *Das Benediktinerkloster*, as note 8, pp. 190-3.

42 The list at the end of this article contains short descriptions of 47 incunable volumes (containing 52 editions) which can be identified with a high degree of certainty with entries

in Menger's catalogue. As a number of texts occur several times in the catalogue (see e.g. B18 and L8, G4 and [M11], M15 and *MBK* p. 373, 7440-3), the identity with a surviving copy of the edition can only be assumed if Menger's textual and codicological description matches the evidence. Therefore, incunables which differ substantially from Menger's description have been excluded even if they have a St Emmeram provenance. Occasionally, books which were in the library when the catalogue was compiled cannot be matched with a catalogue description, see e.g. Munich, BSB, 4° Inc.c.a. 1190 which was bought by Münzer in 1497 (*BSB-Ink* B-759) and Munich, BSB, 4° Inc.s.a. 801 e which was bought by Münzer in 1501 (*BSB-Ink* F-117, P-570, D-100, C-151).

43 The only exception is the first item, a vellum copy of the Fust & Schöffer edition of Cicero's *De officiis* printed in 1465 (*GW* 6921), probably the earliest printed book in the library: 'Primo liber officiorum Marci Tulii Ciceronis Arpinatis consulisque Romani ac oratoris maximi ad Marcum Tulium Ciceronem filium suum, et incipit: "Quamquam te, Marce fili, annum iam audientem" etc. Item paradoxa eiusdem Tullii, et incipit: "Animadverti, Brute, sepe Catonem avunculum tuum, cum in senatu sentenciam diceret" etc. Item versus XII sapientum scilicet Baxilii, Asmenii etc. Item Manlio Torquato Flaccus de vite huius humane brevitate per comparacionem temporis metra sequencia: "Diffugere nives" etc. Hec omnia in uno parvo volumine, id est textpleter. Et tantum de libris inpressis in pergameno, et est anno Domini M. CCCC. LV. In civitate Moguntinensi impressum' (*MBK* p. 335 with the shelfmark A1. In this article, Menger's catalogue numbers will be used for identification of individual volumes; page and line references to *MBK* will only be given in cases where no numbers appear in the catalogue).

44 Ziegler, *Das Benediktinerkloster*, as note 8, p. 191, gives a figure of 350 manuscripts on vellum and 180 on paper plus about 200 incunables, Rumbold, 'The Library of Hermann Pötzlinger', as note 29, p. 330, claims that 'the library contained nearly 900 manuscripts and more than 300 printed books'.

45 Numbers I4-I7 are missing; an unnumbered volume was entered in the empty space later in slightly darker ink. The volume with the number L6 was also added after 1501, as it was found in the cell of father Leonhard Gruber after his death in 1503; see also Ziegler, *Das Benediktinerkloster*, as note 8, p. 208.

46 The only shelf-mark inscriptions which match Menger's catalogue numbers can be found in items N3 and N7-9, which entered the library after the catalogue had been completed. Some shelf-mark inscriptions do not match Menger's catalogue and may be evidence of later reshelving.

47 In group A, only eight editions are listed including two Bible editions in four (A3-6) and two (A8-9) volumes respectively, a six-volume edition of Nicolaus de Lyra (A10-15), a four-volume edition of Alexander de Ales (A16-19) and two volumes of Duns Scotus, *Quaestiones* (A20-B1).

48 F14, for similar phrases see E4 and F12-H1.

49 The volume in possession of frater Kilian (*MBK* p. 373, 7433-9) combines three medical works printed in Venice between 1497 and 1501.

50 See e.g. E4, which contains two editions produced by Albrecht Kunne in Memmingen in 1483, and *MBK* p. 373, 7433-9 (see the preceding note). *MBK* pp. 376-7, 7574-80 contains three editions printed in Leipzig between 1493 and 1499 as well as two Strasbourg editions dated 1496-8.

51 *MBK* pp. 383-5.

52 Ziegler, *Das Benediktinerkloster*, as note 8, p. 191. See also Andreas Kraus, 'Die Bibliothek von St. Emmeram: Spiegelbild der geistigen Bewegungen der frühen Neuzeit', in *Bibliotheken zu St. Emmeram*, as note 12, pp. 1-42, here pp. 7-11.

53 See Ziegler, *Das Benediktinerkloster*, as note 8, p. 193.

54 See I16: *tabulam invenies B1*; I17: *theologia Platonica folio 338*; K15: *circa litteram L1 cum reliquis*; A16, D15 and I12: *habens tabulam in principio*; B18: *in fine libri registrum bonum secundum ordinem alphabeti habens* (cf. also B8, D5, E4).

55 Menger describes the quires of a handwritten *libellus* as *primus est octernus, secundus sexternus, tertius octernus, quartus novenernus, quintus triternus*, see *MBK* p. 187.

56 A manuscript in eighth-century insular script (Clm 14080) is described as *[scriptura] antiqua minus legibilis*, see *MBK* ibid.

57 C13, see also E4, G6, K10, and N7.

58 See Albrecht Dürer, *Woodcuts and Wood Blocks*, ed. by Walter L. Strauss (New York, 1980), no. 8.

59 *MBK* p. 376, 7572-4 shows that *Ytalica impressio* really refers to the country of origin rather than roman type: the edition was printed in Gothic type.

60 Among the few exceptions is A1, possibly the oldest and most precious printed book in the library which takes a prominent position as A1 at the very beginning of the catalogue, see above note 43. Other exceptions occur in the section of schoolbooks, see *MBK* pp. 380-1.

61 It is interesting to compare this evidence with that from the few catalogue numbers which contain texts only printed in this combination in one edition. B16, E19, K2, and K14 were printed in Venice; B17, F11, H4 in Lyon; K3 in Basel, F20 in Heidelberg, A1 in Mainz; E14 in Louvain, F17 in Rome, D8 in Vicenza. Other editions from Venice are contained in F18, Strasbourg in F12 and I19, Basel in G10, Cologne in G6, Hagenau in G7, Mainz in G8, Nuremberg in G19, Strasbourg in I19, Urach in G15, from Memmingen, Erfurt, Esslingen, and Augsburg in F14-F16, from Paris, Nuremberg, Ingolstadt, and Mainz in G9, from Augsburg and Esslingen in H1.

62 See also *MBK* pp. 187-8.

63 D5 and G15 were bound in Kyriss, *Verzierte gotische Einbände*, as note 37, workshop 138, M15 in Kyriss, workshop 44.

64 K7 and *MBK* pp. 376-7, 7574-80 were bound in Kyriss, *Verzierte gotische Einbände*, as note 37, workshop 81.

65 K15 was bound in Kyriss, *Verzierte gotische Einbände*, as note 37, workshop 103.

66 See *MBK* p. 377, 7579-80.

67 See *MBK* p. 380, 7724-5.

68 *MBK* p. 376, 7572-4.

69 See also Peter Schmid, 'Der Personenstand des Klosters St. Emmeram in Regensburg im Jahr 1497', *Verhandlungen des Historischen Vereins für Oberpfalz und Regensburg*, 127 (1987), 149-151, where a list of the names of 27 monks and 5 lay brothers is given.

70 On the fluctuating membership of the convent during the fifteenth and sixteenth centuries, see Ziegler, *Das Benediktinerkloster*, as note 8, p. 168.

71 *Scholasticalia impressa* (*MBK* pp. 380-1).

72 *MBK* pp. 381-5.

73 On his biography, see *MBK* pp. 125-6. His printed books are listed under the numbers L7-N5, see pp. 365-72, but also on pp. 376-7. M17 (*MBK* p. 368) is Celtis's 1501 edition of Hrotsvith's works. On his collecting interests see Ziegler, *Das Benediktinerkloster*, as note 8, p. 193.

74 See Ziegler, *Das Benediktinerkloster*, as note 8, p. 209.

75 According to Ziegler, *Das Benediktinerkloster*, as note 8, p. 208, Kilian died before 1515. As his books (*MBK* p. 373, 7433-9) were entered into the library catalogue after the one owned by frater Marcus and before Vischpach's donation, it seems likely that he died between 1505 and 1508.

76 *MBK* p. 374, 7452-9; the donation was recorded both in the book and the catalogue entry.

77 *MBK* p. 374, 7462.

78 *MBK* p. 374, 7474.

79 *MBK* p. 378, 7639.

80 On Hoffmann, also known as Ostrofrancus, see *MBK* p. 126, Bischoff, *Mittelalterliche Studien*, as note 8, pp. 146-8, Ziegler, *Das Benediktinerkloster*, as note 8, pp. 178-90 and Günter Glauche, 'Die Regensburger Sodalitas litteraria um Christophorus Hoffmann und seine Emmeramer Gebäude-Inschriften', in *Scire litteras. Forschungen zum mittelalterlichen Geistesleben*, ed. by Sigrid Krämer & Michael Bernhard, *Bayerische Akademie der Wissenschaften, Philosophisch-Historische Klasse: Abhandlungen*, Neue Folge, 99 (Munich, 1988), pp. 187-200. Hoffmann's nephew Örtlein died in 1498; he is described as Hoffmann's *avunculus* in Menger's catalogue, see *MBK* p. 376, 7558. See however the inscriptions in K7 and in the incunable Johannes Greusser (Tuberinus), *Passio Christi cum expositionibus.* Nuremberg: Peter Wagner, 1495 (BMC II 465: London BL, IA.8003).

81 *MBK* p. 376, 7535.

82 *MBK* p. 378, 7642-6.

83 *MBK* p. 379, 7669-70.

84 *MBK* pp. 383-5. Some doubt has been shed on Menger's statement by Christian Bauer, *Geistliche Prosa im Kloster Tegernsee: Untersuchungen zu Gebrauch und Überlieferung deutschsprachiger Literatur im 15. Jahrhundert*, Münchener Texte und Untersuchungen zur deutschen Literatur des Mittelalters, 107 (Tübingen, 1996), pp. 250-1. Bauer claims that Menger indiscriminately listed all books in German as intended for the lay brothers, irrespective of their contents.

85 *MBK* p. 255.

86 The Bible is mentioned twice in the catalogue: *MBK* p. 336 (fol. 84va) with the shelf-marks A8 and A9, and pp. 383-4 (fol. 129^v).

87 *MBK* p. 384, 7863.

88 *Omnia prememorata Lactancii scripta in uno alio volumine mediocri, parum differens a primo quoad impressionem, in aliis vero nihil nisi duplicem tabulam habet … Illum librum emit abbas Erasmus, precedentem vero antecessor suus Johannes abbas. K 5.* A copy of the Venetian edition of 1478 from St Emmeram is in the BSB (*BSB-Ink* L-7,3: 2° Inc.c.a. 751).

89 Munich, BSB, 2° Inc.c.a. 1740 (*BSB-Ink* B-722,4 and C-455,3); an inscription reads: 'hoc egregium volumen comparauit Reverendus Jn christo pater et dominus dominus Johannes Tegernpeck Abbas huius Cenobii Anno etc. octogesimooctauo. Praesentem Librum Emit magister petrus ab eximio viro doctore Nicolao Bernawer ratisbonae in monasterio sancti emmerami praesente müscateller [the bookseller Johannes Muscatel] sabato ante misericordiam domini [9. 4.] Anno domini M° quingentesimosecundo quem ad dies vite sue retinere vult propter praefatum dominum doctorem.'

90 Johann Baptist Kraus (abbot 1742-62): *Bibliotheca Principalis Ecclesiae et Monasterii Ord. S. Benedicti ad S. Emmeramum Ratisbonae*, 4 vols ([Regensburg], 1748), see Stephan Kellner & Annemarie Spethmann, *Historische Kataloge der Bayerischen Staatsbibliothek München: Münchner Hofbibliothek und andere Provenienzen*, Catalogus codicum manu scriptorum Bibliothecae Monacensis 11 (Wiesbaden, 1996), p. 384.

91 For the history and contents of the Fürst Thurn und Taxis-Hofbibliothek, see *Handbuch der Historischen Buchbestände in Deutschland*, ed. by Bernhard Fabian. Vol. 12: *Bayern I – R*, ed. by Eberhard Dünninger (Hildesheim, 1996), pp. 247-59.

92 A new catalogue is in process; the first volume was edited by Elisabeth Wunderle, *Die Handschriften*, as note 14. The second volume is in preparation by Ingeborg Neske.

93 See *Handbuch der Historischen Buchbestände*, vol. 12 (1996), pp. 222-9 and Michael Drucker, 'Die Inkunabeln der Staatlichen Bibliothek: Herkunft, Bestandsentwicklung, Erschließung', in *Bücherschätze in Regensburg: Frühe Drucke aus den Beständen der Staatlichen Bibliothek*, ed. by Nikolaus Henkel (Regensburg, 1996), pp. 11-14. The *c.* 1100

incunables kept there come from a whole range of Regensburg libraries: apart from St Emmeram, former owners were the Dominicans, Carmelites, Franciscans, Capuchins, and Regular Canons, as well as the episcopal libraries and the library of the Kurmainzische Gesandtschaft; unfortunately, no provenance index exists for the incunables.

94 I am grateful to Alan Coates and Kristian Jensen for providing me with information about the collections in their charge.

95 Incunable bibliographies and catalogues often provide insufficient information on these points. On the textual side, it is necessary to provide a complete list of contents as they occur in an edition; for the copy-specific description, even the minutest provenance information ought to be recorded in modern incunable catalogues in addition to the more generally accepted details like bindings and ownership inscriptions: more elusive features like sale-catalogue numbers or duplicate numbers and old shelf-marks should be recorded as well as information on source and date of acquisition by the present owner; not just the items bound together today should be listed, but also those bound together originally (as recorded in old lists of contents and evident from an old foliation or matching decoration). See also Paul Needham, 'Copy Description in Incunable Catalogues', in *PBSA* 95:2 (2001), pp. 173-239.

96 I am grateful to Armin Schlechter for providing me with information about this copy from his unpublished Heidelberg incunable catalogue.

97 I am grateful to Nicholas Pickwood for providing me with information about this copy.

98 I am grateful to Angelika Pabel for providing me with information about this copy.

INDEX

Index

Index